Mali

WORLD BIBLIOGRAPHICAL SERIES

General Editors:
Robert G. Neville (Executive Editor)
John J. Horton

Robert A. Myers   Hans H. Wellisch
Ian Wallace   Ralph Lee Woodward, Jr.

John J. Horton is Deputy Librarian of the University of Bradford and was formerly Chairman of its Academic Board of Studies in Social Sciences. He has maintained a longstanding interest in the discipline of area studies and its associated bibliographical problems, with special reference to European Studies. In particular he has published in the field of Icelandic and of Yugoslav studies, including the two relevant volumes in the World Bibliographical Series.

Robert A. Myers is Associate Professor of Anthropology in the Division of Social Sciences and Director of Study Abroad Programs at Alfred University, Alfred, New York. He has studied post-colonial island nations of the Caribbean and has spent two years in Nigeria on a Fulbright Lectureship. His interests include international public health, historical anthropology and developing societies. In addition to *Amerindians of the Lesser Antilles: a bibliography* (1981), *A Resource Guide to Dominica, 1493-1986* (1987) and numerous articles, he has compiled the World Bibliographical Series volumes on *Dominica* (1987), *Nigeria* (1989) and *Ghana* (1991).

Ian Wallace is Professor of German at the University of Bath. A graduate of Oxford in French and German, he also studied in Tübingen, Heidelberg and Lausanne before taking teaching posts at universities in the USA, Scotland and England. He specializes in contemporary German affairs, especially literature and culture, on which he has published numerous articles and books. In 1979 he founded the journal *GDR Monitor*, which he continues to edit under its new title *German Monitor*.

Hans H. Wellisch is Professor emeritus at the College of Library and Information Services, University of Maryland. He was President of the American Society of Indexers and was a member of the International Federation for Documentation. He is the author of numerous articles and several books on indexing and abstracting, and has published *The Conversion of Scripts and Indexing and Abstracting: an International Bibliography*, and *Indexing from A to Z*. He also contributes frequently to *Journal of the American Society for Information Science*, *The Indexer* and other professional journals.

Ralph Lee Woodward, Jr. is Professor of History at Tulane University, New Orleans. He is the author of *Central America, a Nation Divided*, 2nd ed. (1985), as well as several monographs and more than seventy scholarly articles on modern Latin America. He has also compiled volumes in the World Bibliographical Series on *Belize* (1980), *El Salvador* (1988), *Guatemala* (Rev. Ed.) (1992) and *Nicaragua* (Rev. Ed.) (1994). Dr. Woodward edited the Central American section of the *Research Guide to Central America and the Caribbean* (1985) and is currently associate editor of Scribner's *Encyclopedia of Latin American History*.

VOLUME 207

Mali

Andrea L. Stamm, Dawn E. Bastian,
Robert A. Myers

Compilers

CLIO PRESS
OXFORD, ENGLAND · SANTA BARBARA, CALIFORNIA
DENVER, COLORADO

British Library Cataloguing in Publication Data

Stamm, Andrea L.
Mali. – (World bibliographical series; v. 207)
1. Mali – Bibliography
I. Title   II. Bastian, Dawn E.   III. Myers, Robert A.
016.9′6623

ISBN 1–85109–166–1

ABC-CLIO Ltd.,
Old Clarendon Ironworks,
35A Great Clarendon Street,
Oxford OX2 6AT, England.

ABC-CLIO Inc.,
130 Cremona Drive,
Santa Barbara,
CA 93117, USA.

Designed by Bernard Crossland.
Typeset by Columns Design Ltd., Reading, England.
Printed in Great Britain by The Looseleaf Company, Midsomer Norton.

THE WORLD BIBLIOGRAPHICAL SERIES

This series, which is principally designed for the English speaker, will eventually cover every country (and some of the world's principal regions and cities), each in a separate volume comprising annotated entries on works dealing with its history, geography, economy and politics; and with its people, their culture, customs, religion and social organization. Attention will also be paid to current living conditions – housing, education, newspapers, clothing, etc. – that are all too often ignored in standard bibliographies; and to those particular aspects relevant to individual countries. Each volume seeks to achieve, by use of careful selectivity and critical assessment of the literature, an expression of the country and an appreciation of its nature and national aspirations, to guide the reader towards an understanding of its importance. The keynote of the series is to provide, in a uniform format, an interpretation of each country that will express its culture, its place in the world, and the qualities and background that make it unique. The views expressed in individual volumes, however, are not necessarily those of the publisher.

VOLUMES IN THE SERIES

1 *Yugoslavia*, Rev. Ed., John J. Horton
2 *Lebanon*, Rev. Ed., C. H. Bleaney
3 *Lesotho*, Rev. Ed., Deborah Johnston
4 *Zimbabwe*, Rev. Ed., Deborah Potts
5 *Saudi Arabia*, Rev. Ed., Frank A. Clements
6 *Russia/USSR*, Second Ed., Lesley Pitman
7 *South Africa*, Rev. Ed., Geoffrey V. Davis
8 *Malawi*, Rev. Ed., Samuel Decalo
9 *Guatemala*, Rev. Ed., Ralph Lee Woodward, Jr.
10 *Pakistan*, David Taylor
11 *Uganda*, Rev. Ed., Balam Nyeko
12 *Malaysia*, Ian Brown and Rajeswary Ampalavanar
13 *France*, Rev. Ed., Frances Chambers
14 *Panama*, Eleanor DeSelms Langstaff
15 *Hungary*, Thomas Kabdebo
16 *USA*, Sheila R. Herstein and Naomi Robbins
17 *Greece*, Richard Clogg and Mary Jo Clogg
18 *New Zealand*, R. F. Grover
19 *Algeria*, Rev. Ed., Richard I. Lawless
20 *Sri Lanka*, Vijaya Samaraweera
21 *Belize*, Second Ed., Peggy Wright and Brian E. Coutts
23 *Luxembourg*, Rev. Ed., Jul Christophory and Emile Thoma
24 *Swaziland*, Rev. Ed., Balam Nyeko
25 *Kenya*, Rev. Ed., Dalvan Coger
26 *India*, Rev. Ed., Ian Derbyshire
27 *Turkey*, Merel Güçlü
28 *Cyprus*, Rev. Ed., P. M. Kitromilides and M. L. Evriviades
29 *Oman*, Rev. Ed., Frank A. Clements
30 *Italy*, Lucio Sponza and Diego Zancani
31 *Finland*, Rev. Ed., J. E. O. Screen
32 *Poland*, Rev. Ed., George Sanford and Adriana Gozdecka-Sanford
33 *Tunisia*, Allan M. Findlay, Anne M. Findlay and Richard I. Lawless
34 *Scotland*, Eric G. Grant
35 *China*, New Ed., Charles W. Hayford
36 *Qatar*, P. T. H. Unwin

37 *Iceland*, Rev. Ed., Francis R. McBride
38 *Nepal*, John Whelpton
39 *Haiti*, Rev. Ed., Frances Chambers
40 *Sudan*, Rev. Ed., M. W. Daly
41 *Vatican City State*, Michael J. Walsh
42 *Iraq*, Second Ed., C. H. Bleaney
43 *United Arab Emirates*, Frank A. Clements
44 *Nicaragua*, Rev. Ed., Ralph Lee Woodward, Jr.
45 *Jamaica*, Rev. Ed., K. E. Ingram
46 *Australia*, Second Ed., I. Kepars
47 *Morocco*, Rev. Ed., Anne M. Findlay and Allan M. Findlay
48 *Mexico*, Rev. Ed., George Philip
49 *Bahrain*, P. T. H. Unwin
50 *Yemen*, Rev. Ed., Paul Auchterlonie
51 *Zambia*, Anne M. Bliss and J. A. Rigg
52 *Puerto Rico*, Elena E. Cevallos
53 *Namibia*, Rev. Ed., Stanley Schoeman and Elna Schoeman
54 *Tanzania*, Rev. Ed., Colin Darch
55 *Jordan*, Ian J. Seccombe
56 *Kuwait*, Rev. Ed., Frank A. Clements
57 *Brazil*, Rev. Ed., John Dickenson
58 *Israel*, Second Ed., C. H. Bleaney
59 *Romania*, Andrea Deletant and Dennis Deletant
60 *Spain*, Second Ed., Graham Shields
61 *Atlantic Ocean*, H. G. R. King
62 *Canada*, Ernest Ingles
63 *Cameroon*, Mark W. DeLancey and Peter J. Schraeder
64 *Malta*, Rev. Ed., David Boswell and Brian Beeley
65 *Thailand*, Michael Watts
66 *Austria*, Denys Salt with the assistance of Arthur Farrand Radley
67 *Norway*, Leland B. Sather
68 *Czechoslovakia*, David Short
69 *Irish Republic*, Michael Owen Shannon
70 *Pacific Basin and Oceania*, Gerald W. Fry and Rufino Mauricio
71 *Portugal*, P. T. H. Unwin
72 *West Germany*, Donald S. Detwiler and Ilse E. Detwiler
73 *Syria*, Ian J. Seccombe
74 *Trinidad and Tobago*, Frances Chambers
75 *Cuba*, Jean Stubbs, Lila Haines and Meic F. Haines
76 *Barbados*, Robert B. Potter and Graham M. S. Dann
77 *East Germany*, Ian Wallace
78 *Mozambique*, Colin Darch
79 *Libya*, Richard I. Lawless
80 *Sweden*, Leland B. Sather and Alan Swanson
81 *Iran*, Reza Navabpour
82 *Dominica*, Robert A. Myers
83 *Denmark*, Kenneth E. Miller
84 *Paraguay*, R. Andrew Nickson
85 *Indian Ocean*, Julia J. Gotthold with the assistance of Donald W. Gotthold
86 *Egypt*, Ragai N. Makar
87 *Gibraltar*, Graham J. Shields
88 *The Netherlands*, Peter King and Michael Wintle
89 *Bolivia*, Gertrude M. Yeager
90 *Papua New Guinea*, Fraiser McConnell
91 *The Gambia*, David P. Gamble
92 *Somalia*, Mark W. DeLancey, Sheila L. Elliott, December Green, Kenneth J. Menkhaus, Mohammad Haji Moqtar, Peter J. Schraeder
93 *Brunei*, Sylvia C. Engelen Krausse and Gerald H. Krausse
94 *Albania*, Rev. Ed., Antonia Young
95 *Singapore*, Stella R. Quah and Jon S. T. Quah
96 *Guyana*, Frances Chambers
97 *Chile*, Harold Blakemore
98 *El Salvador*, Ralph Lee Woodward, Jr.
99 *The Arctic*, H. G. R. King
100 *Nigeria*, Robert A. Myers
101 *Ecuador*, David Corkhill
102 *Uruguay*, Henry Finch with the assistance of Alicia Casas de Barrán
103 *Japan*, Frank Joseph Shulman
104 *Belgium*, R. C. Riley
105 *Macau*, Richard Louis Edmonds
106 *Philippines*, Jim Richardson
107 *Bulgaria*, Richard J. Crampton
108 *The Bahamas*, Paul G. Boultbee
109 *Peru*, John Robert Fisher
110 *Venezuela*, D. A. G. Waddell

111 *Dominican Republic*, Kai Schoenhals
112 *Colombia*, Robert H. Davis
113 *Taiwan*, Wei-chin Lee
114 *Switzerland*, Heinz K. Meier and Regula A. Meier
115 *Hong Kong*, Ian Scott
116 *Bhutan*, Ramesh C. Dogra
117 *Suriname*, Rosemarijn Hoefte
118 *Djibouti*, Peter J. Schraeder
119 *Grenada*, Kai Schoenhals
120 *Monaco*, Grace L. Hudson
121 *Guinea-Bissau*, Rosemary Galli
122 *Wales*, Gwilym Huws and D. Hywel E. Roberts
123 *Cape Verde*, Caroline S. Shaw
124 *Ghana*, Robert A. Myers
125 *Greenland*, Kenneth E. Miller
126 *Costa Rica*, Charles L. Stansifer
127 *Siberia*, David N. Collins
128 *Tibet*, John Pinfold
129 *Northern Ireland*, Michael Owen Shannon
130 *Argentina*, Alan Biggins
131 *Côte d'Ivoire*, Morna Daniels
132 *Burma*, Patricia M. Herbert
133 *Laos*, Helen Cordell
134 *Montserrat*, Riva Berleant-Schiller
135 *Afghanistan*, Schuyler Jones
136 *Equatorial Guinea*, Randall Fegley
137 *Turks and Caicos Islands*, Paul G. Boultbee
138 *Virgin Islands*, Verna Penn Moll
139 *Honduras*, Pamela F. Howard-Reguindin
140 *Mauritius*, Pramila Ramgulam Bennett
141 *Mauritania*, Simonetta Calderini, Delia Cortese, James L. A. Webb, Jr.
142 *Timor*, Ian Rowland
143 *St. Vincent and the Grenadines*, Robert B. Potter
144 *Texas*, James Marten
145 *Burundi*, Morna Daniels
146 *Hawai'i*, Nancy J. Morris and Love Dean
147 *Vietnam*, David Marr and Kristine Alilunas-Rodgers
148 *Sierra Leone*, Margaret Binns and Tony Binns
149 *Gabon*, David Gardinier
150 *Botswana*, John A. Wiseman
151 *Angola*, Richard Black
152 *Central African Republic*, Pierre Kalck
153 *Seychelles*, George Bennett, with the collaboration of Pramila Ramgulam Bennett
154 *Rwanda*, Randall Fegley
155 *Berlin*, Ian Wallace
156 *Mongolia*, Judith Nordby
157 *Liberia*, D. Elwood Dunn
158 *Maldives*, Christopher H. B. Reynolds
159 *Liechtenstein*, Regula A. Meier
160 *England*, Alan Day
161 *The Baltic States*, Inese A. Smith and Marita V. Grunts
162 *Congo*, Randall Fegley
163 *Armenia*, Vrej Nersessian
164 *Niger*, Lynda F. Zamponi
165 *Madagascar*, Hilary Bradt
166 *Senegal*, Roy Dilley and Jerry Eades
167 *Andorra*, Barry Taylor
168 *Netherlands Antilles and Aruba*, Kai Schoenhals
169 *Burkina Faso*, Samuel Decalo
170 *Indonesia*, Sylvia C. Engelen Krausse and Gerald H. Krausse
171 *The Antarctic*, Janice Meadows, William Mills and H. G. R. King
172 *São Tomé and Príncipe*, Caroline S. Shaw
173 *Fiji*, G. E. Gorman and J. J. Mills
174 *St. Kitts-Nevis*, Verna Penn Moll
175 *Martinique*, Janet Crane
176 *Zaire*, Dawn Bastian Williams, Robert W. Lesh and Andrea L. Stamm
177 *Chad*, George Joffé and Valérie Day-Viaud
178 *Togo*, Samuel Decalo
179 *Ethiopia*, Stuart Munro-Hay and Richard Pankhurst
180 *Punjab*, Darshan Singh Tatla and Ian Talbot
181 *Eritrea*, Randall Fegley
182 *Antigua and Barbuda*, Riva Berleant-Schiller and Susan Lowes with Milton Benjamin
183 *Alaska*, Marvin W. Falk
184 *The Falkland Islands*, Alan Day
185 *St Lucia*, Janet Henshall Momsen

186 *Slovenia*, Cathie Carmichael
187 *Cayman Islands*, Paul G. Boultbee
188 *San Marino*, Adrian Edwards and
    Chris Michaelides
189 *London*, Heather Creaton
190 *Western Sahara*, Anthony G.
    Pazzanita
191 *Guinea*, Margaret Binns
192 *Benin*, J. S. Eades and Chris Allen
193 *Madrid*, Graham Shields
194 *Tasmania*, I. Kepars
195 *Prague*, Susie Lunt
196 *Samoa*, H. G. A. Hughes
197 *St. Helena, Ascension and Tristan
    da Cunha*, Alan Day

198 *Budapest*, Mátyás Sárközi
199 *Lisbon*, John Laidlar
200 *Cambodia*, Helen Jarvis
201 *Vienna*, C. M. Peniston-Bird
202 *Corsica*, Grace L. Hudson
203 *Amsterdam*, André van Os
204 *Korea*, J. E. Hoare
205 *Bermuda*, Paul G. Boultbee and
    David F. Raine
206 *Paris*, Frances Chambers
207 *Mali*, Andrea L. Stamm, Dawn E.
    Bastian, Robert A. Myers

Contents

PREFACE xiii

INTRODUCTION xvii

THE COUNTRY AND ITS PEOPLE 1

EXPLORERS' AND TRAVELLERS' ACCOUNTS (TO THE EARLY 20TH
   CENTURY) 8

RECENT TRAVEL AND GUIDEBOOKS 18

GEOGRAPHY AND GEOLOGY 27
   Geography   27
   Geology   29
   Maps and atlases   31

FLORA AND FAUNA 34

PREHISTORY AND ARCHAEOLOGY 42

HISTORY 56
   General and regional   56
   Precolonial (to 1883)   60
   French colonial (1883-1960)   73
   Timbuktu   77

POPULATION 81
   Population and demography   81
   Migration (internal and external)   82
   Censuses   85

ETHNIC GROUPS 89

Contents

LANGUAGES AND DIALECTS 100
   General   100
   French, the official language   101
   National languages   102

RELIGION 113

SOCIETY AND SOCIAL CONDITIONS 120

MEDICINE, HEALTH AND NUTRITION 124

POLITICS 131
   General and regional   131
   Independence, Modibo Keita and Malian socialism (1960-68)   134
   Dictatorship of Moussa Traoré (1968-91)   136
   Democratization and the presidency of Alpha Oumar Konaré (1991-)   137

LAW 141

INTERNATIONAL RELATIONS 144
   General and regional   144
   Mali Federation   146
   ECOWAS (Economic Community of West African States)   147
   Relations with developed countries   148

THE ECONOMY AND ECONOMIC DEVELOPMENT 149

FINANCE AND BANKING 158

TRADE AND COMMERCE 160

AGRICULTURE 164

TRANSPORT 173

LABOUR, THE LABOUR MOVEMENT AND TRADE UNIONS 175

ENVIRONMENT, ECOLOGY AND URBAN STUDIES 178
   Environment and ecology   178
   Urban studies   186

EDUCATION 189

LITERATURE 195

THE ARTS 205
   Visual arts 205
      General 205
      Metalwork 209
      Bogolanfini, or painted mud cloth 211
      Architecture 211
   Performance, theatre and dance 213
   Music 217
   Film 223

ORAL LITERATURE AND FOLKLORE 229
   Epic of Soundiata 229
   Other epics 232
   Tales, fables and legends 236
   Proverbs and riddles 240
   Other folklore and oral traditions 241

SPORTS AND LEISURE ACTIVITIES 244

LIBRARIES, ARCHIVES, MUSEUMS AND RESEARCH 246
   Libraries 246
   Archives 247
   Museums 249
   Research 251

BOOKS AND PUBLISHING 253

MASS MEDIA 256

STATISTICS 260

ENCYCLOPAEDIAS, DIRECTORIES AND YEARBOOKS 263

NEWSPAPERS AND PERIODICALS 269
   Newspapers 269
   Periodicals 270

BIBLIOGRAPHIES 274
   General 274
   Regional 280
   Mali 281

INDEX OF AUTHORS 287

Contents

INDEX OF TITLES 299

INDEX OF SUBJECTS 321

MAP OF MALI 329

Preface

This work was prepared at Alfred University in Alfred, New York, and Northwestern University Library in Evanston, Illinois, the location of the largest separate collection of Africana materials in the world, the Melville J. Herskovits Library of African Studies. Since this collection is particularly strong in materials either about or from countries of Sub-Saharan Africa, including Mali, this was an ideal location at which to carry out the bulk of this project. Approximately ninety-five per cent of items listed in this bibliography are held by the Library, and may be requested through normal interlibrary loan channels. To our knowledge, no other current general annotated bibliography about Mali in English presently exists.

Needless to say, when compiling a bibliography of this size, it is impossible to be comprehensive or exhaustive. Our goal was to create a work that would cover many facets of Mali's culture, its place in Africa and the world, past and present, and the features and qualities that make it unique. In each subject-based chapter, we have provided a representative sample of the available literature in English and French. Annotations vary in length but are generally substantive and will give readers a good impression of what each title concerns. The chapters also vary in length, as it was difficult to locate materials on certain subjects. For example, much has been published about Mali's oral tradition and history; in comparison, little has been written about science and technology or education. To find relevant titles, we have had to search through general reference tools and specialist journals, and have found it necessary to cite some books, journals, and other materials that are not widely available. Works cited only within annotations are not necessarily of lesser importance; placement was governed by space limitations.

Special mention must be made of the valuable electronic, multimedia, and other non-print resources which are now available, the titles of which were omitted from this bibliography because they are beyond its scope. These include such items as *Living in the Sahel*, an interactive videodisc about Mali containing twenty-five thousand photographs, seventy minutes of live recordings, and twenty minutes of documentary film; *MaliNet*, a French-language Internet resource on which a wide range of information about Mali is available, including, for example, a general country profile, facts about personalities such as Cheick Modibo Diarra, adviser on NASA's Mars Pathfinder Project, plus current election and tourist information; and the video recording *Beyond Timbuktu* (executive producer Avie Littler; 50 minutes, colour, 1988), a segment of the television series *Nature* (co-produced by WNET/ Thirteen, BBC-TV and MPC Television), a beautifully filmed look at birdlife in the Inland Niger River Delta including the area's human ecology, notably the roles of irrigated rice agriculture, the Peul herders and Bozo fishermen.

Since the Clio World Bibliographical Series is primarily aimed at the English-speaker, titles selected for inclusion in this volume are typically in that language. Apart from scholarly works on historical, social and environmental topics, few sources about Mali have been published in English, though in recent years the amount of English-language materials has grown steadily. Anyone engaged in a study of Mali that is less in-depth should find enough literature in English on most subjects; it is impossible, however, to undertake extensive academic research on Mali without consulting the numerous works published in French, many of which were included here because of their special importance, or because few or no English sources on a specific topic could be located. A small number of titles in other Western European languages is also included.

The entries in each chapter of this bibliography are arranged in alphabetical order by title.

About 'Sudan'

Attempts to locate publications on the present-day Republic of Mali may be complicated or less successful if one is unaware of the distinctions between *Sudan*, *Sudan Region*, *Western Sudan* and *French Sudan*.

The word *Sudan*, spelled *Soudan* in French, comes from the Arabic phrase *bilād es Sūdān*, meaning 'land of the black people'. As a geographical term, it is used to describe the part of Africa immediately south of the Sahara. *Sudan Region* refers to an area of north central Africa south of the Sahara and Libyan deserts and north of the rainy tropics, extending more than 3,500 miles across the African continent from the west coast to the mountains of Ethiopia. *Western Sudan* is the term applied to the area just south of the Sahara in West Africa, including the countries of Burkina Faso, Mali, Mauritania, Niger, parts of northern Nigeria, and Senegal.

The French and British both applied the name *Sudan* to colonial political jurisdictions under their control. To the French, what is now Mali was known as *French Sudan* (French Soudan or Soudan Français) from 1890 to 1899 and again from 1920 to 1958. For a brief period, from October 1958 to September 1960, Mali was officially the *Sudanese Republic*.

The British referred to the territory around the Nile River stretching from southern Egypt into equatorial Africa as *the Sudan*. This territory became the Anglo-Egyptian Sudan in 1899 and adopted the name *Republic of the Sudan* when independence was gained in 1956. This region should not be confused with the areas mentioned in the previous two paragraphs and is not covered by the present bibliography.

A note on orthography

There is considerable variation in orthography of Malian place-names, ethnic groups, and languages, depending primarily on the language of the text. Regarding place-names, for example, the fabled city of Timbuktu has numerous variants which appear throughout this work and others. The German spelling 'Timbuktu,' and its variant 'Timbucktu' have passed into English and the former has become widely used in recent years. Major English-language works have employed the spelling 'Timbuctoo', and this is considered the correct English form by scholars; 'Timbuctou' and 'Timbuctu' are sometimes used as well. The French continue to use the spelling 'Tombouctou', as they have for over a century; variants include 'Temboctou' (used by explorer René Caillié) and 'Tombouktou', but they are seldom seen. Variant spellings exist for other places as well, such as Jenne (Djenné) and Segu (Ségou).

Concerning the form of name for ethnic groups and languages, we have tried in our annotations to retain the form used by the author while also supplying alternative spellings in parentheses. Because we thought the subject index should collocate materials on the same subject, we decided to choose a preferred subject term. For ethnic groups, we used the preferred term found in entries of P. J. Imperato's *Historical Dictionary of Mali* (e.g., Peul and Sarakolé, not Fula and Soninké). For languages, since Imperato did not always cite the specific language spoken by an ethnic group in its entry in his dictionary, we used the preferred term found in the Internet version of *Ethnologue: Languages of the World* (e.g., Fulfulde and Bambara, not Peul and Bamana). Similar variations exist in the names of historical kingdoms/empires (e.g., Peul Empire of Macina, or Macina), personal names such as Soundiata (Sunjata, Sunjara, etc.) and names of Arabic origin such as Umar Tal (or Al-Hadj Omar) which we have also collocated in the subject index under one form.

Preface

The Western reader may be surprised to learn that there are more letters in the Malian alphabet than in the roman alphabet. For the few instances where these special letters must be cited, such as where they appear in the titles of works we included, we have retained the appropriate non-roman character. They appear in the International Phonetic Alphabet as the consonants 'ɲ' and 'ŋ' and vowels 'ɛ' and 'ɔ'. Examples include 'Daɲɛgafe kɛrɛnkɛrɛnnen' and 'Lexique soŋay-français'.

Acknowledgements

Andrea Stamm and Dawn Bastian would like to express their profound gratitude for the invaluable assistance given to them at Northwestern University Library during the course of compiling this bibliography. Mette Shayne and the staff of the Melville J. Herskovits Library of African Studies offered advice and helped locate materials. Without the expert assistance and patience of Gary Strawn, Melissa Jacobi, and Robert Trautvetter, we would never have been able to master the intricacies of data manipulation and our indexing software. Finally, the staff of the Interlibrary Loan Department assisted greatly in obtaining materials not held by the Library.

Robert Myers is indebted to many individuals for their contributions of time, recommendations, lists of publications, accession lists, and support in its many forms. The Alfred University Herrick Memorial Library staff has provided incomparable assistance. He is especially grateful to Linda Hardy and the late Trevor Jones for their skill and persistence in interlibrary loan acquisitions, and to reference librarian Frank McBride who located articles on Mali. An Alfred University Faculty Development Grant made possible visits to the National Museum of African Art Library and the Library of Congress in Washington, Cornell University in Ithaca, New York, and the Melville J. Herskovits Library of African Studies at Northwestern University. In particular, thanks are extended to Martha Anderson, John Butsch, David Conrad, Katherine Dettwyler, Kate Ezra, Barbara Frank, Judy Goff, Marilyn Hurlbert, David McGuire, Susan McIntosh, Mette Shayne, Janet Stanley, and Virginia and Vic Yurkewich. WBS Executive Editor Robert G. Neville's patience and confidence in this effort have been boundless. Scholar-physician Pascal James Imperato set a standard of generosity and collegiality which shall remain a model. Cathie Chester, and Robert, Cary and Piper Chester have been inspirational throughout the long process of this compilation.

Introduction

The country and its peoples

Mali, officially known as the Republic of Mali (République du Mali, in French), is a landlocked country in the heart of West Africa. With an area of approximately 482,000 square miles (1,248,000 square kilometres), it is slightly smaller than the region's largest state of Niger and slightly less than twice the size of Texas. Its name derives from the great Malinké kingdom of Mali which flourished from the 13th to the 16th century on the upper and middle Niger River. Bridging the Sahel from north to south, Mali is bordered by Mauritania to the west, Algeria to the north, Niger and Burkina Faso to the east, and Côte d'Ivoire, Guinea and Senegal to the south. Mali has long functioned, because of its physical location, as a commercial and cultural crossroads between Islamic North Africa and the black African nations to the south.

Mali's terrain is largely flat, consisting of plains and plateaux. In the north, rolling sand-covered plains known as the Tanezrouft and Taoudenni lie within the Sahara Desert. Flood plains of the Inland Niger River Delta, comprising a total surface area of over 40,000 square miles, cover central Mali. Sandstone elevations are found in the south, the Futa Jallon mountain range near Guinea, and the Adrar des Iforas, an eroded sandstone plateau, in the northeast, which is part of the Sahara's Hoggar mountain system. The eastern part of Mali, most of which is quite flat, contains one of the most spectacular land formations in West Africa, the Bandiagara plateau and cliffs, which rise to a height of 1,200 feet and run from southwest to northeast for about 150 miles.

Traversing the country for 1,010 miles is the Niger River and its tributaries, which form the life-blood of and main link between the far-flung Malian people. A vital source of irrigation water and fish, nearly one-third of its total length flows through Mali, entering the country from Guinea in the southwest, flowing in a northeasterly direction for about 600 miles to Timbuktu, through the most densely populated parts of the country, then turning due east for about 200 miles, at which point it veers southeast and enters Niger. The Niger Valley is an important agricultural region, as receding floodwaters leave behind cultivatable land with rich alluvial soils and pasture for thousands of livestock.

The great Senegal River also flows through Mali, but for a shorter distance. In extreme western Mali, it forms where the Bafing and Bakoye rivers converge and flows in a northwesterly direction to Kayes and then into Senegal and Mauritania, veering westwards before emptying into the Atlantic Ocean.

Malian territory lies north of the tropical-forest zones of Africa where humidity and rainfall are high, and all three of its climatic zones (Sudanic, Sahelian, and Saharan) are characterized as hot and dry. Annual rainfall is heaviest in the Sudanic zone, varying from twenty to fifty-five inches (500 to 1,400 mm) per year. Average temperatures here, in the southern part of Mali, vary from 75° to 86°F (24° to 30°C). Above the Sudanic zone is the Sahelian, where rainfall varies from twenty inches (500 mm) of rain per year in the southern areas to approximately eight inches (200 mm) in the northern section. Average temperatures here range from 73° to 97°F (23° to 36°C). The Saharan zone is in the north of Mali, where temperatures exceed 117°F (47°C) during the day and plummet to 39°F (4°C) at night; rainfall here is negligible. Water shortages are a major problem throughout Mali and drought is a constant threat, particularly in the north.

Despite the apparent uniformity of Mali's climate, two major seasons exist. The dry season extends from November to June; during the first part of the season, from November to January, temperatures are cooler, dropping to 70°F (21°C) as the *alize* wind blows cool air out of the northeast. Starting in February, the dry season is marked by progressively rising temperatures as the *harmattan* wind sweeps hot, dry air from the Sahara, causing temperatures to rise to a daily average of 105°F (41°C).

The cool rainy season, during which severe thunderstorms accompanied by gusty winds are common, is marked by a distinct beginning and end. It begins in mid-June and ends in October, at which time temperatures again rise and the humidity remains high, until the *alize* winds return. Most rain falls during July and August.

Mali can also be divided into three vegetation zones. The southern Sudanic zone, characterized by wooded savannahs and riverine forests, is dominated by herbaceous vegetation. Trees which grow here include bastard mahogany, kapok, shea butter, silk cotton, and mango, the last of which was introduced by the French. The Sahelian zone is characterized by steppe vegetation; plant growth is sparse and the incidence of trees is less than in the Sudanic zone. Here can be found cram-cram grass and trees resistant to drought, such as the baobab, palmyra, doum palm, acacia thorn tree and a number of mimosa species. Plant life gradually diminishes as one heads northwards and disappears upon entering the Saharan zone.

Mali's animal life, like its plant life, is limited. Wildlife was once abundant in the Sudanic and Sahelian zones, but the numbers of most large herbivores and carnivores have been significantly reduced, and in some areas they have disappeared. Droughts, environmental degradation, and expanding human populations, combined with poaching and lax enforcement of game protection laws, have taken their toll. Lions, panthers, hyenas, gazelles, giraffes, elephants, and several types of antelope can be found, as well as a wide variety of birds, monkeys, and snakes. Crocodiles and hippopotami, Mali's national symbol, inhabit the rivers. Mali has two national game reserves: the Menaka Reserve in the east and the Parc National de la Boucle de Baoulé in the west; conservation efforts, focusing on environmental degradation in the Inland Niger Delta, have been considerable.

Generally speaking, Mali's soils are of poor quality. Shallow soils containing iron are found in the south; large areas of rock and gravel interrupt the desert sands in the north. Rich alluvial soils in the central delta are important to the agriculture of the Niger Valley, while the inland delta contains grey-coloured clay soil – the quality of which, unfortunately, is not much improved by seasonal flooding of the Niger River.

Mali is blessed with some mineral reserves, but they are smaller than those of other African countries and are largely untapped. They include iron ore, bauxite, petroleum, gold, silver, tin, copper, lead, tungsten, zinc, nickel, manganese, lithium, marble, limestone, uranium, salt, and phosphate. Some deposits are found in such remote areas that it is uneconomic to exploit them at present.

Mali's administrative and commercial capital is Bamako, its largest city. Situated along both sides of the upper Niger, it was a village settlement consisting of a few hundred inhabitants when occupied by the French in 1883. Its estimated population at independence in 1960 was 120,000; by 1994 it had increased considerably to approximately 800,000. 'Bamako' is derived from the Bambara words *bama* (crocodile) and *ka* (rivulet). Despite the fact it is a large, bustling city, and Mali's major trading centre and entrepôt, Bamako has retained, in marked contrast to other African capitals, a traditional character and lifestyle.

According to 1996 estimates, Mali's population is just over 9.5 million; about three million Malian nationals live outside the country, with sizeable communities in neighbouring African countries, France, and elsewhere in Europe. Mali is sparsely inhabited, with over 80 per cent of its population residing in small villages in rural areas; about one-tenth of the population is nomadic. The population is unevenly distributed, its density varying from seventy persons per square mile in the south-central part of the country, in the Niger corridor between Timbuktu and Bamako, to near zero in the northern desert.

Apart from Bamako, only a few other Malian cities have sizeable populations: Kayes and Mopti (both 70,000); Segou (90,000); San (45,000); and Sikasso (75,000). The creation of new local industries has inspired population growth in a number of towns, including Bla, Fana, and Koutiala.

In 1996, females accounted for a slight majority of the population at 51.13 per cent, versus 48.87 per cent for males. This difference is explained in part by the emigration of young men to labour markets in Ghana, Côte d'Ivoire and Liberia as well as France and, more recently, the United States. The annual population growth rate has remained stable at 2.5 per cent for the past twenty years. Almost half the Malian population is less than fifteen years of age. Mali's relatively high birth and death rates (49.0 and 20 per 1,000, respectively) are roughly equivalent to those of West Africa as a whole; most deaths occur in children under the age of two. Average life expectancy is a short forty-four years.

Despite the fact that Mali possesses a relatively well-developed health-care system, there is a shortage of trained medical personnel, which hinders delivery of adequate health care to the nation as a whole. Malnutrition is one of the nation's biggest health concerns; periodic cholera outbreaks have occurred and leprosy is a problem, as well as the health effects associated with female genital mutilation, which is widely practised in Mali. As we write, the number of documented cases of AIDS in Mali remains low. Increased migration to urban areas, fuelled by drought, has created its own health problems as well as intensifying the conditions of unemployment and homelessness.

Mali's population comprises several major ethnic groups, as well as a number of smaller ones. The Bambara (Bamana) are the most numerous, a sedentary agricultural people constituting about one-third of the total population. The second-largest group is the Peul (Fula), traditional nomadic pastoralists of Mali and the western Sahel in general, though many have embraced farming, politics, and other professions. This group is concentrated in the Inland Niger Delta, around the city of Mopti, but is found elsewhere in Mali as well. The Sarakolé (Soninke), descendants of the founders of the Ghana Empire, inhabit the Sahel in northwestern Mali; they are farmers and merchants.

The Malinké (Maninka), descendants of the great Mali Empire, share cultural and linguistic characteristics with the Bambara. The Songhay, an important ethnic group with a rich history, live along the Niger River from Djenné to Asongo. The Dogon, whose art and culture have become known throughout the world, inhabit the plateau region around Bandiagara. The Senufo and a related group, the Minianka, are farmers living in southeastern Mali. Other Malian ethnic groups include the Bozo and Somono, who are fishermen, the Tuareg of the northeast and the Maure (Moors) of the Sahel, both primarily nomadic pastoralists, and the Diawara, Khassonké, Tukulor, and Dioula.

Mali's official language is French; in addition, a number of indigenous languages and dialects are spoken. Bambara is spoken by two-thirds of the population and is the lingua franca in western, central, and southern Mali. Fulfulde – the Peul language – is the lingua franca of the Inland Delta. Songhay (Songai) is widely spoken in eastern and northeastern Mali; Arabic is spoken by the Maure, and the Tuareg continue to speak their ancient Berber language, Tamasheq.

French is also the language of educational instruction in Mali, and was adopted in an attempt to resolve the problems associated with promoting literacy among a linguistically diverse population. Literacy in French is low and is concentrated in urban areas; according to 1990 estimates, adult literacy is only 17 per cent. Education is free and officially compulsory for those between the ages of seven and sixteen; attendance is not enforced, however, and only about one-fifth of children of primary school age actually attend school. In fact, Mali has one of the lowest rates of school enrolment in the world.

Primary education begins at the age of six, secondary education at the age of twelve. Secondary education is carried out within two different programmes – one academic, one technical. There is no university in Mali, but seven institutions provide higher education in the fields of agriculture, administration, business studies, education, engineering, medicine, and management. Many students attend colleges and universities abroad, especially in Senegal, France, and Eastern Europe.

There are three main religions in Mali. Islam dates from the 11th century and is practised by a majority of the population; figures in reliable published sources vary from 65 to 90 per cent. However, elements of indigenous religious beliefs and practices are often retained. Most of the rest of the people are animists, and a small number (about 1 per cent) are Christian.

Mali possesses a developing, rural economy based primarily on subsistence and commercial agriculture, livestock herding, and fishing. Agriculture accounts for approximately half of the gross domestic product (GDP) and employs over 80 per cent of the workforce. Industry holds only a minor position in the economy, accounting for about seven per cent of the GDP and employing less than two per cent of the workforce. As most parts of the country are desert or semi-desert, economic activity is largely confined to the Sudanic-Sahelian regions irrigated by the Niger River. Severe drought, fluctuations and changes in international trade, inflation, rising oil prices and political upheaval have all had an impact on Mali's rate of economic growth in recent decades. Growth trends of the overall GDP have been particularly erratic in the 1990s, but steady growth has been predicted for the remainder of the decade with expansion of the market for cotton exports and an increase in gold production. Although small gains have been realized in both agriculture and industry, Mali today remains one of the poorest countries in the world, with an average annual per capita income of US$260.

Although agricultural production is basically at subsistence level, with minimal mechanization, Mali is generally self-sufficient in food production. Major food crops include millet, sorghum, rice, corn (maize), yams, and cassava; the main commercial crops are cotton, peanuts, rice, and tobacco. Fish are caught for both domestic consumption and export to other African countries. A fishery industry was developed with foreign aid starting in the 1960s; today Mali produces 100,000 metric tons of dried and cured fish annually. Livestock (including cattle, sheep, and goats) are numerous and Mali is one of West Africa's major producers and exporters, though herds were significantly impacted by drought in the 1970s and 1980s. Raising livestock is the principal economic activity of the arid north; overall production accounts for approximately 50 per cent of agriculture's contribution to the GDP.

Mali's industrial sector, which is primarily state-owned, contributes only 15 per cent to the GDP, concentrating mainly on small-scale processing of agricultural products and manufacturing of consumer goods to meet local needs. Most manufactured items are imported, primarily from France. Established factories include producers of such goods as textiles, ceramics, furniture, cement, peanut oil, soap, canned goods, sugar, ginned cotton, cigarettes, and matches.

Mali has suffered a chronic trade deficit ever since independence was achieved in 1960; this deficit remains a primary obstacle to economic growth. Mali's chief trading partner is France, a main source of foreign aid together with the Soviet Union, China and the United States, as well as other countries in Europe. Mali is heavily dependent on both foreign aid and cash remittances from emigrants to help offset the trade deficit. Other principal trading partners include

Western Europe and countries of the franc zone, which Mali re-entered in 1968 after a brief withdrawal. Chief exports include raw cotton and cotton products, gold, dried and smoked fish, and livestock; major imports are machinery, appliances and transport equipment, foodstuffs, chemical and petroleum products, textiles, and construction materials.

Mali's inadequate surface transportation infrastructure, coupled with its landlocked position, further handicap its economy. Despite substantial investment in road-building in the early 1960s and 1970s, the road system remains underdeveloped; few paved roads or adequately maintained dirt roads exist outside the Niger Valley. Mali's only railroad is the dilapidated 600-mile (960-km) line that runs between Bamako and Dakar, the Atlantic port capital of neighbouring Senegal. Mali's other link with the sea, Côte d'Ivoire's capital of Abidjan, is over 800 miles (1280 km) from the populous Niger corridor. Dependence on these two shipping routes greatly increases Mali's import and export costs. Because Mali's road and rail facilities are in such poor condition, its inland waterways are of great importance to its transportation system. The mid-1990s saw implementation of a major modernization and restoration programme for road facilities and part of the Bamako–Dakar railway.

Domestic and international air transport was at one time provided by Air Mali. This national airline, mismanaged and saddled with large debts, ceased operation following an accident in 1986. In 1988, Air Mali was re-started under a new name, Tombouctou Air Service; internal air service is now provided by Société des Transports Aériens (STA). Mali's main airport is at Bamako, which is linked by air to France, Morocco, and other countries in West Africa.

Early history

Despite the fact that Mali is today one of the world's poorest nations, lacking resources and influence, it can boast of a rich and glorious history. The territory covered by its modern borders contains what was once some of the earliest and most powerful African empires and kingdoms, which flourished between the ninth and nineteenth centuries.

Evidence of life in the Malian Sahara previous to that prestigious period is provided by Palaeolithic and Neolithic remains, as well as rock paintings and carvings. Numerous traces of late prehistoric civilizations have been found in other parts of Mali. A series of important excavations has revealed evidence of an unbroken period of life in Djenné, a culturally and commercially important city-state in the Inland Delta, from about 300 BC to 1400.

Introduction

Trans-Saharan caravan routes linking the Niger Valley to North Africa moved gold, slaves, salt, ivory, civet, gum arabic, and ostrich feathers for almost a thousand years, starting in approximately 300 AD. These trade routes were controlled by the great West African empires that were founded at their origins and are known primarily through Arabic writings and oral tradition. First was the Sarakole Empire of Ghana, a federation of kingdoms which originated as early as the 4th century, reached its height about 1000 AD, and declined after the 11th century. Situated between the Niger and Senegal rivers and known as 'the land of gold' to the Muslim world, the Ghana Empire covered primarily what is now northwestern Mali and parts of Mauritania. The Malinké Empire of Mali, on the Upper and Middle Niger, began in the 12th century, reached its zenith in the middle of the 14th century, and declined in the 15th century. Following the Ghana Empire's loss of control of the trade routes to the militant Almoravids, members of an Islamic reform movement, the Mali Empire ultimately assumed the Ghana Empire's hegemony in the region. Under Malian control the trans-Saharan trade reached its peak and the caravan routes moved east through Djenné and Timbuktu, which became major centres of finance and culture. Founded by the legendary Soundiata Keita, the 'lion prince' who ruled from ca. 1230 to 1260, the empire's borders eventually stretched to encompass much of present-day Mali, Senegal, Gambia, and parts of Mauritania. By the 13th century it had become one of the world's largest suppliers of gold. The Mali Empire's most famous king was the devout and wise Kankan Moussa, also known as Mansa Moussa (or Musa), who ruled from 1307 to 1337. Making a splendorous pilgrimage to Mecca in 1324-25, with five hundred slaves and much gold to spend and distribute as gifts, he returned with Muslim scholars and architects to enhance the reputations of cities like Timbuktu and Gao as important places of culture and learning.

Following the Mali Empire's decline, due more to pressures on its frontiers by the Tuareg, Mossi, Wolof, and Tukulor peoples than internal instability, the Songhay Empire of the Gao-Timbuktu region (1335-1591) slowly expanded its rule and eventually controlled much of present-day Mali and parts of Niger and Burkina Faso. The Songhay Empire originated as a small chiefdom established on the banks of the Niger in 670 AD. The Empire expanded its hegemony and reached its peak under Sonni Ali Ber, who ruled from 1465 to 1492, and Askia Mohammed, who ruled from 1492 to 1529. Under Songhay control, Djenné and Timbuktu flourished as centres of commerce and Islamic scholarship. Ahmed el Mansur, who became Sultan of Morocco in 1578, acquired an interest in securing Songhay's land and gold wealth. In 1591, a Moroccan army of 4,000 men, equipped with firearms, crossed the Sahara and routed the Songhay, who wielded only spears and bows and arrows. With the disintegration of Songhay administration, political chaos and instability ensued, and trade and commerce were disrupted. Timbuktu's scholars, viewed as a threat by the Moroccans, were imprisoned, exiled or killed, and the city's prosperity, intellectual life, and reputation as an international Islamic centre of learning were lost. Moroccan political and military domination over the sprawling Songhay Empire was never complete, however, and did not last for more than a century, with parts of it eventually breaking into unstable states and chiefdoms. New trade routes in gold and slaves began to emerge closer to coastal areas, where Europeans were busy establishing trading posts. The Muslim monopoly on trade in West Africa was broken, and the base of the Sahel's wealth destroyed.

A number of other strong kingdoms also rose in Mali, including the Peul kingdom of Macina (1400-1862), a vassal of the Mali Empire until 1494, the Bambara kingdom of Segou (1600-1862), whose economy was based on slave-trading and grain production, and the animist Bambara kingdom of Kaarta (1633-1854), all in the central part of the country. The Kénédougou kingdom of the Senufo people developed in southern Mali in the 17th century and fell in 1898 when its capital of Sikasso was seized by the French, who gradually started to penetrate the present-day Malian region, from Senegal in the west, in the latter half of the 19th century.

The French conquest

Nineteenth-century Malian history and politics were chiefly characterized by Islamic *jihads* (religious wars), development and extension of the Tukulor Empire, and French colonial expansion and conquest. In 1810, Cheikou Amadou Bari, a Muslim cleric, overthrew the ruling dynasty of the Peul kingdom and established the Peul Empire of Macina, a theocratic Islamic state. Seeking to convert the peoples of the western Sudan to a more pure form of Islam, Muslim cleric Umar Tal founded the Tukulor Empire after launching the first of a series of *jihads* in 1852, conquering Kaarta in 1854, Segou in 1862, and Macina, also in 1862. In 1864 Umar was killed in a skirmish with the Peul and his eldest son Amadou succeeded him, ruling from Segou and attempting to exert control, through civil war, over the entire Tukulor Empire, which had been divided among Amadou, his brothers Abibu, Moktar and Muntaga, and cousin Tijani. Amadou, however, proved to be a less effective ruler than his father, he never secured allegiance from his brothers and other powerful Tukulor leaders, and the Bambara inhabitants of his domains led constant revolts against his rule. Thus, the vast empire left behind by Umar Tal was reduced to many small states whose loyalty to Amadou was tenuous at best.

In 1855, the French established a presence in western Mali when General Louis Faidherbe installed the fortified village of Medine on the Senegal River near the town of Kayes. Eager to facilitate trade through control of the Niger River Valley, and wary of British designs on that region, the French regarded the Ségou Tukulor Empire as the main obstacle to its acquisition. Engaging in a series of military campaigns and diplomatic manoeuvres, the French succeeded in steadily advancing eastwards, building forts on the western frontier of Tukulor territory and gaining control of lands extending to Kita. The latter was due primarily to the efforts of Captain Joseph-Simon Gallieni, whose mission was to court indigenous powers and cement relations with those who opposed the Tukulor. Between 1880 and 1881 he signed protectorate treaties with chiefs at Bafoulabé and Kita.

In 1883, General Gustave Borgnis-Descordes advanced French control to the Niger, capturing Bamako, by means of a series of military campaigns against the Tukulor and Moslem *imam* warrior Samory Touré, who founded an empire to the south. Colonel Louis Archinard, Borgnis-Descordes's protégé, successfully led military operations against Samory and gradually destroyed the Tukulor Empire, capturing Koundian in 1889, Ségou and Ouossebougou in 1890, Kaarta in 1891, and Macina and Bandiagara in 1893. Amadou Tall retreated to Kaarta after Ségou's fall, but was driven out when the French seized it. He then went to Macina but the French drove him out again and he and his followers fled to the Sokoto caliphate in northern Nigeria. Samory Touré was driven into the Ivory Coast (Côte d'Ivoire), captured in 1898, and exiled to Gabon. That same year, French forces led by Colonel H. M. Audeod attacked and conquered Sikasso, capital of Kénédougou. Timbuktu fell under French control in 1894 when it was conquered by Joseph-Jacques Joffre.

The French ruled the territory that became the Republic of Mali in 1960 for a period of 68 years, during which time both its name and borders were modified upon several occasions and it was administered under different governance. From 1880 to 1890 it was called Upper Senegal (Haut-Fleuve); between 1890 and 1899, Mali was known as the French Sudan (Soudan Français). In 1899 the French Sudan was broken up and some of its parts were incorporated into the colony of French Guinea (now Guinea), Dahomey (currently Benin) and the Ivory Coast; other parts were administratively merged with what is now Senegal and sections of present-day Burkina Faso, Mauritania, and Niger. This large territory was called Upper Senegal and Middle Niger

(Haut-Sénégal et Moyen-Niger) until 1902 and Senegambia and the Niger (Sénégambie et Niger) from 1902 to 1904. In 1904 France's West African colonies became the federation of French West Africa (Afrique Occidentale Française or AOF, based in Dakar), at which time Senegambia and the Niger was renamed Upper Senegal and Niger (Haut Sénégal et Niger). The name French Sudan was restored in 1920 and retained until 1958, when the territory became the Sudanese Republic. Mali's borders were again altered in 1947, when some of its territory was transferred to Mauritania and the newly re-created colony of Upper Volta. Between 1880 and 1892, and again from 1899 to 1904, the colony was subordinate to Senegal. It was administered by military officers, *commandants-supérieurs*, from 1880 to 1892, and thereafter by lieutenant governors and governors.

Decolonization, independence, and the rise of Malian socialism

After the Second World War, a strong nationalist movement developed in the French Sudan and other African colonies which forced France to gradually relinquish control. In 1946, the first political parties rose in the French Sudan: the Sudanese Union (Union Soudanaise or US), founded by Mamadou Konaté and Modobo Keita, and its main rival, the Sudanese Progressive Party (Parti Progressiste Soudanais). That same year, at a congress held in Bamako, African political parties struggling against French colonialism founded an interterritorial party called the Democratic African Assembly (Rassemblement Démo-cratique Africain or RDA), with the Sudanese Union, later the Union Soudanaise-RDA, as its local branch. Winning its first seats in the French National Assembly, also in 1946, the RDA was established throughout French West Africa and French Equatorial Africa (Afrique Equatoriale Française or AEF). In 1956, the French government introduced sweeping governmental reforms in French West Africa with passage of the *loi cadre* (reorganizing law), which significantly increased the powers of elected territorial assemblies and allowed them to form their own cabinets. As a result, both the power of the governor-general of French West Africa and unity within the federation was weakened. The new reforms also led to the US-RDA's sweeping victories over the Sudanese Progressive Party in the 1956 elections for the French National Assembly. The two parties eventually merged and the US-RDA, headed by its charismatic leader, Keita, was the only political party left in the French Sudan by 1959.

On 28 September 1958, a referendum was held in French West Africa on the future status of its territories. The French Sudan and all others, with the exception of Guinea, voted to approve the Constitution of the Fifth French Republic, which dissolved the federation and allowed voters in French West Africa the opportunity to choose immediate independence or autonomy within the French Union. The French Sudan reluctantly voted to remain a part of the French community and became the Sudanese Republic (République Soudanaise), which then sought to unite with other French-speaking West African states to form a new political federation. French and African support for this idea was lacking, however, and only Senegal joined with the new Sudanese Republic to form the Mali Federation in January 1959, with Modibo Keita as its elected president. In June 1960 the federation successfully pressed for independence from France, but Senegal chose to secede in August, as the Senegalese disagreed with Keita and his followers on a number of key policy issues, including relations with France, distribution of offices and power, and command of the armed forces. Senegal voted for its own independence from France, which was recognized, and the Sudanese followed suit. On 22 September 1960, the Republic of Mali was proclaimed in Bamako by a congress of the US-RDA, with Modibo Keita as its first president.

Keita rapidly distanced the newly independent Mali from France, Africanized the civil service, and embarked on a programme of radical socialism, establishing diplomatic and economic ties to the Eastern bloc, employing hundreds of Soviet advisers, and building a state-run economy. In 1962 Mali established its own currency, the Mali franc, outside of the franc zone. The socialist political and economic courses charted by Keita severely weakened an economy already in dire straits at independence, and became vastly unpopular with large segments of the Malian population. At the beginning of 1967, Keita entered into negotiations with France and secured its support of the failing Malian economy. As part of their agreement, Mali re-entered the French franc zone and consented to reduce government expenditures and devalue the Malian franc by 50 per cent.

By this time, Keita's days in power were numbered. French supervision of the Malian economy was viewed by the Marxist radicals who surrounded Keita as a violation of ideology and basic party principles. In an attempt to pacify them, Keita launched a 'cultural revolution' in August 1967, the goal of which was to purify ideologically the party's structure. From that point on, until his overthrow in 1968, Keita controlled both the party and the country. He dissolved the National Political Bureau and gave total power over the party and government to the newly revived National Committee for the Defence of the Revolution (Comité National de Défense de la Révolution), originally created in 1966. Party moderates were excluded from its membership. Changes in the party's structure occurred at all levels, except in villages and subsections. The Popular Militia, the party's armed segment, was granted extensive powers which it greatly abused. Dissent was widely suppressed by its members through unsubstantiated arrests, detention without trial and torture, and harassment of army officers, all of which greatly alienated the masses. On 18 January 1968, the National Assembly, created at Mali's independence in 1960, dissolved itself and granted Keita the authorization to appoint a legislative delegation.

The 1968 coup and dictatorship of Moussa Traoré

The Popular Militia became increasingly visible throughout Mali in 1968, and more daring in its treatment of the army. On 19 November 1968, a group of fourteen young officers led by Moussa Traoré launched a nearly bloodless *coup d'état* which overthrew the Keita regime. They established the Military Committee of National Liberation (Comité Militaire de Libération Nationale or CMLN), with Traoré as its president and Yoro Diakité as vice-president; on 22 November, a provisional government was established with Diakité as president, a position he held until Traoré replaced him in September 1969. The Committee announced that its top priorities were to improve the country's economic and financial situations and promised a return to civilian rule by the following year. Personal rivalries and policy differences made this promise difficult to fulfil, however, and led to the removal of two committee members, Diakité and Malik Diallo, in 1971. The CMLN did not greatly modify Keita's socialist policies, and in fact retained a state-controlled economy which eventually caused serious problems. In the short term, some modifications to domestic policy did introduce some economic changes and personal liberties which were refreshing to a people weary of the oppression and deprivation that marked Keita's dictatorship. The Committee's foreign affairs policy closely mirrored that of Keita, which was to profess non-alignment while maintaining a close relationship with the Communist bloc; relations with France and other Western countries did warm, however.

In June 1974, Malians overwhelmingly voted to approve a new constitution which the CMLN presented to the electorate. Parts of it were similar or identical to those of the constitution adopted at independence in 1960, but there were some differences as well. The new constitution provided for universal suffrage, a secret ballot, a popularly elected assembly, a single political party, and the election of a president for a five-year term. It also required a transition to civilian rule by 1979, during which time the CMLN would continue to control the country. Traoré announced the formation of the new party, the

Democratic Union of the Malian People (Union Démocratique du Peuple Malien or UDPM), in 1976; its implementation was delayed, however, until 1979 because of differences among members of the CMLN concerning the sharing of power with civilians. In June 1979, general elections were held, with Traoré the overwhelming choice of voters for president. Shortly afterwards, the CMLN dissolved itself. Although a popularly elected assembly and predominantly civilian cabinet now existed, Traoré and the military continued in essence to control the country's affairs. He was re-elected president in June 1985.

Traoré's military dictatorship lasted for a total of twenty-three years, ending in 1991. A pragmatic and highly skilled politician, Traoré managed to survive a total of five coup attempts as well as purges within the CMLN. His power was also sustained, however, with flagrant corruption which was rife at virtually all levels of government. During his rule, Traoré was beset by a number of overwhelming problems: searing droughts in 1970-74, 1978 and the early 1980s; chronic food shortages; growing unrest among students, unemployed graduates and union workers; plus severe economic hardships which left the Malian people among the poorest in the world. Mali was the recipient of much international and bilateral aid, but donors such as the International Monetary Fund eventually pressured Traoré to shift to a free-enterprise economic system after attempts at better management and improved efficiency were exhausted. In 1984, Mali was admitted to the French-allied West African Monetary Union (Union Monétaire Ouest-Africaine), and the Malian franc was replaced by the CFA franc. A number of state-owned enterprises were sold or dismantled, and the government severed its control of the grain market.

Traoré also had to contend with two armed conflicts with Burkina Faso, one in 1974-75 (when it was called Upper Volta) and a more serious one in 1985, both involving a long-standing dispute over an economically desirable piece of territory known as the Agacher Strip. Fortunately, these conflicts were very brief and the dispute was resolved to the satisfaction of both sides by the International Court of Justice in The Hague in 1986.

In 1990, Traoré was confronted with a serious rebellion by the Tuareg minority in the north and, closer to home, a growing pro-democracy movement. Severely mistreated and oppressed by successive Malian governments, the Tuareg had taken refuge in neighbouring Niger, Algeria and Libya during the drought of 1970-74; the latter two countries repatriated the Tuareg in the late 1980s because deteriorating economic conditions made it difficult to remain their hosts. Militarily trained during their years of exile, the Tuareg sought to reclaim what was theirs and to avenge their past treatment at the hands of the Malian government and army. Armed and encouraged by Libya, the Tuareg rebels launched attacks against army posts and administrative centres, later demanding total independence of the Azawad, a large area of Sahel and desert in northern Mali. Heavy-handed army reprisals against Tuareg civilians not involved in military actions followed. Plagued by regular military setbacks and casualties, and realizing the threat to the security of his regime, Traoré entered into negotiations with the Tuareg, with Algeria in the role of mediator, in early 1991. A fragile peace agreement was reached and the Malian government agreed to a majority of Tuareg demands, including the creation of an autonomous Tuareg region. Traoré was praised for his rationality by Tuareg leader Iyad Ag Ghali.

Traoré could ill afford to be uncompromising, however, as unrest had been building in Bamako. Angered by government corruption, limited employment opportunities, and a dictatorship masquerading as democratic civilian rule, students, trade unionists and the unemployed joined forces with pro-democracy groups and pushed for a change in government. In late 1990, 30,000 people took to the streets of Bamako and peacefully demonstrated in support of multi-party democracy. In January 1991, the National Union of Malian Workers (Union Nationale des Travailleurs du Mali, or UNTM) organized a general strike, demanding a 50 per cent pay raise; the city was paralysed for two days. Massive strikes, demonstrations and riots, some violent, continued throughout February and early March, with protesters reiterating their demands for an end to one-party rule and freedom of the press. Demonstrations turned especially violent when protesters were met by security forces wielding machine-guns, touching off rioting and looting that lasted from 22 to 24 March; during this time some 106 people were killed and 708 injured. Traoré finally announced he was willing to discuss democratization, but protesters were now demanding that he resign. Provoked by the three-day slaughter, the army reacted during the night of 25-26 March 1991 and Traoré was overthrown in a coup led by a former military ally, Lieutenant Colonel Amadou Toumani Touré.

Democratization and beyond

Touré and twenty-four other military officers immediately announced the creation of a National Reconciliation Council (Conseil de Réconciliation Nationale or CRN) and the dissolution of Traoré's government, the legislature, and the 1974 constitution; the UDPM was disbanded. Following negotiations with pro-democracy groups, during which Touré was warned by both their members and Western donors that another military regime would not be tolerated, the CRN was dissolved on 31 March 1991 and a Committee of Transition for the Welfare of the People (Comité de Transition Pour le Salut du Peuple or CTSP) was established with fifteen civilian and ten military members, including Touré as chairman. This group's purpose was to direct Mali's transition to a democratically elected government.

On 2 April, President Touré asked Soumana Sacko, a former Minister of Finance who had resigned from Traoré's corrupt government and possessed a reputation for honesty and integrity, to be prime minister of the transitional government.

Touré organized a National Conference to consider Mali's political future, which was held from 29 July to 12 August 1991. A new constitution was approved by a majority of voters on 12 January 1992; municipal elections took place a week later. On 24 February and 8 March, legislative elections were held, and presidential elections on 12 and 26 April. Alpha Oumar Konaré, a prominent historian, archaeologist, and head of Mali's most important pro-democracy group, the Alliance for Democracy in Mali (Alliance Pour la Démocratie au Mali or ADEMA), became Mali's first democratically elected president in over 30 years.

Touré's brief presidency lasted just fifteen months, during which time he admirably fulfilled his goal to move the country towards democratic governance – a gesture that has been voluntarily made by only one other military ruler in Sub-Saharan Africa. Touré also immediately confronted the issues surrounding the continuing hostilities between the government and Tuaregs, as the peace negotiated in January 1991 was not a lasting one. The cycle of Tuareg rebel attacks and military reprisals continued throughout 1991, and Touré steadily moved negotiations forward, resulting in a National Pact between the Malian government and rebel Tuareg groups, signed on 12 April 1992. This agreement provided for more Tuareg representation in the army, civil service and government, and peace returned to most areas where rebels had been operating. These achievements assured Touré's popularity with the Malian people, but his tenure was so short he had no time to confront other serious challenges on the domestic front, all of which were inherited by Konaré when he assumed office in June 1992: state-owned enterprises that remained unprofitable, weak industrial and private sectors unable to absorb school graduates, an enormous civil service consisting of people demanding higher wages and further entitlements, student demands for higher stipends and guaranteed state employment upon graduation, a burgeoning foreign debt, continued reliance on foreign aid, and a critical lack of natural resources.

As provided by the new constitution, Konaré was elected to serve a five-year term. A widely respected man of vision, possessing political and leadership skills and integrity, Konaré's first months in office were nevertheless quite difficult. Students and trade unionists continued their respective demands for better entitlements and pay raises, and members of the UNTM called for another general strike just a month after Konaré's inauguration. Rebellious airforce troops displayed their unhappiness over wages and benefits, and sporadic armed conflicts with the Tuaregs continued in the north. In addition, while Konaré's party, ADEMA, controlled the National Assembly, other parties held power at the local level.

The November 1992 trial of ex-president Traoré and sixteen former ministers of his regime for 'blood crimes' and the deaths of civilians in the March 1991 riots cast a shadow over Konaré's early presidency. Traoré and three of his senior aides were sentenced to death in February 1993, but their executions were commuted by Konaré in December 1997. Attention also focused on an embezzlement scandal involving Abdoulaye Camara, the Minister of Mines, Industry, and Energy.

In April 1993, violent student protests broke out. Triggered by a belief that moves were afoot by the government to change the leadership of the unofficial students' union, the Association of Students and Pupils of Mali (Association des Elèves et Etudiants du Mali or AEEM), these protests brought down the government of prime minister Younoussi Touré on 9 April. Additionally, students were angered by the government's failure to follow through on its campaign promise to increase student grants and other entitlements. Konaré now recognized the need to broaden his political base and build working coalitions with other parties. He therefore appointed as prime minister Abdoulaye Sékou Sow, former director of the National School of Administration (Ecole National d'Administration), a centre of student revolt. Konaré also brought the National Committee of the Democratic Initiative (Comité National d'Initiative Démocratique or CNID) into the government, a party that, together with some others that were now allowed to exist under the new constitution, had been excluded.

A number of events occurred which tarnished Konaré's reputation as guardian of Malian democracy. In January 1993, opposition parties characterized Mali's new press law, adopted in November 1992, as 'antidemocratic'. These parties also levelled accusations that ADEMA was limiting their access to state-owned radio and television. In April, Reporters Sans Frontières, a French organization dedicated to defending freedom of the press, publicly condemned a two-year prison sentence given to two journalists of *Les Echos*, an independent newspaper founded by Konaré (he severed ties when elected), for violation of the new press laws. Following more student riots in February 1994, the government closed down Radio Kaira, one of Mali's independent radio stations which maintained close ties to certain opposition groups. In November, Sambi Touré, editor of the independent weekly *Nouvel Horizon*, was arrested for defaming Konaré and publishing false information about him, charges of which he was acquitted early the following year.

Konaré's image further deteriorated with the bungling of the electoral process in 1997. Widely praised for its smooth 1992 democratic transition, Mali's second attempt to hold multi-party elections was marked by widespread organizational problems and led to a political crisis which, at the time of writing, continues to rock the country. On 4 March 1997, Konaré dissolved the National Assembly in an attempt to accelerate the electoral process, which had been delayed for technical reasons. Although this act was in conformity with the constitution, members of the opposition criticized it vehemently, stating that it did not resolve the situation and that the government was responsible for the problems which caused the delay. The first round of legislative elections went forward on 13 April; serious irregularities and confusion led international observers to question the validity of the polls. These included disputes over details on voter cards and voting lists and a lack of voting materials altogether. In addition, many polling stations failed to open on time, both in Bamako and outlying areas. The results of the flawed polls showed that ADEMA had swept the board and would probably have won anyway; it was a clear signal that Konaré's party had consolidated its power base since the 1992 elections.

Konaré and his supporters opened talks with opposition parties on 18 April 1997, proposing the legislative elections be annulled in accordance with opposition demands. Opposition parties also pressed for the resignation of the government, the dissolution of the Commission Electorale Nationale Indépendente (CENI), the independent national electoral commission, and a restructuring of the electoral timetable. ADEMA insisted, however, that the presidential election go forward as planned in May and the local elections in June (the latter were postponed indefinitely). On 11 May, Konaré was re-elected with a comfortable 85 per cent of the vote. A new round of legislative elections took place on 20 July and 3 August. Angered by the government's refusal to accede to their demands, radical opposition parties boycotted both sets of elections, which were marked by violent demonstrations and political disturbances designed to disrupt the vote.

Konaré's democratic credentials were further eroded by Amnesty International in its damning 1997 report *Mali: Basic Liberties at Risk.* Its contents include allegations of police torture of opposition supporters jailed during the violence associated with the election controversies. The report also condemns the detention of opposition leaders, declaring there were no grounds upon which they could be held, although it does concede that some oppositionists were probably responsible for the initial violence which broke out after the April legislative election.

While Konaré can be credited with several main achievements during his first five years in office – including increases in the rate of economic growth, a reduction in the budget deficit, and improved prospects for a lasting peace with the Tuaregs – his position remains tenuous. The political situation remains deadlocked, both ADEMA and the opposition are divided, and tensions are still high in Bamako. Even the efforts of the popular former president Touré, now respected as a leader and mediator of regional and international conflicts, have been unsuccessful in bringing the two sides together. The opposition continues to insist that negotiations can go forward only after an audit of CENI and the resignation of the government. Ominously, two coup attempts have been reported in the last eighteen months, and officers in the armed forces are reportedly unhappy with the political standoff and Konaré himself. It remains to be seen if Konaré's second presidency will be a success and whether democracy will continue to survive in Mali.

The Country and Its People

1 **Africa on file.**
Facts on File. New York: Facts On File, 1995. 2 vols. (loose-leaf).
In this current reference source which permits reproduction for 'non-profit educational use', Mali is covered in volume 2 (p. 4.56-65). There are 5 maps (major cities and transport routes, administrative boundaries, physical features, industry and natural resources, and agricultural areas), a fact sheet (covering geography, ethnic groups, languages, government, etc.), a timeline, demographic statistics, economic statistics, and a brief summary of culture and everyday life. It also includes a separate section of twenty-two maps of Africa, showing data on Mali such as boundary disputes (with Burkina Faso), civil wars, daily calorie intake, desertification, environmental problems, famine, labour migration, population density, etc. See also *African history on file* (New York: Facts on File, 1994. 1 vol. loose-leaf).

2 **L'Afrique du Sahel: le Sénégal, la Gambie, la Mauritanie, le Mali, le Niger, le Tchad, le Soudan.** (Sahelian Africa: Senegal, Gambia, Mauritania, Mali, Niger, Chad, Sudan.)
Edited by Suzanne Agnely, Jean Barraud, Jacques Chevrier. Paris: Larousse, 1980. 81p. in various pagings. maps. (Beautés du Monde).
Each segment of this book is a self-contained, unsequentially numbered introduction to a Sahelian country. Thirteen striking photographs accompany the chapter on Mali by Jacques Chevrier (12p.) describing the country, its history, the Dogon area and 'Timbuktu the mysterious'.

3 **Background notes: Mali.**
Edited by Anita Stockman. Washington, DC: Government Printing Office, April 1993. 6p. map. bibliog. (Department of State Publication, no. 8056. Background Notes Series).
This useful publication, updated at irregular intervals, offers a succinct profile of the country, its geography, peoples, history, government and political conditions,

1

economy, foreign relations, defence and US–Malian relations. It includes 'Travel notes', a brief reading list and a full-page map. Similar versions appeared in December 1989 (8p.) and April 1986 (8p.), both edited by Juanita Adams, and in February 1984 (8p.) and August 1981 (4p.), edited by Joanne R. Reams. The US State Department Bureau of Consular Affairs also published a 'Mali – consular information sheet' (2p.) on 24 December 1992.

4   **Bamako, capitale du Mali.** (Bamako, capital of Mali.)
    Marie-Louise Villien-Rossi. *Bulletin de l'IFAN,* vol. 28, series B,
    no. 1-2 (1966), p. 249-380. maps. bibliog.

In this essential source on Bamako, the author provides a thorough account of the city's origins, climate, growth, economy, population structure, social organization, modern infrastructure and health conditions. The study contains four maps of Bamako, historical drawings, eight photographs and an excellent bibliography (p. 373-78) listing archival sources, maps, periodicals, bibliographies and 99 books and articles. Villien-Rossi also authored 'Bamako, capitale du Mali' (Bamako, capital of Mali) in *Cahiers d'Outre-Mer,* vol. 16 (1963), p. 379-83.

5   **Djenné, sur le Nil-des-Noires.** (Jenne, on the Black Nile.)
    Pierre Alexandre. *L'Histoire,* no. 92 (Sept. 1986), p. 58-88. maps.
    bibliog.

For those who read French, this is a lively sketch of the city, its people and history, generously illustrated with photographs.

6   **Haut-Sénégal-Niger.** (Upper Senegal-Niger.)
    Maurice Delafosse, prefaces by Robert Cornevin, Gov. M. Clozel.
    Paris: Larose, 1912. Reprinted, Paris: G. P. Maisonneuve et Larose,
    1972. new ed. 3 vols. maps. bibliog.

This remains one of the most important encyclopaedic works on the large region of Francophone West Africa of which present-day Mali was an administrative part. Volume one (428p. 7 maps. 28 photographs) covers the land, the peoples and their languages. Volume two (428p. 13 maps, including a fold-out map of the conquest of the French Soudan. 30 photographs) covers history. Volume three (316p. 2 maps, including a separate map of 'Haut-Sénégal et Niger', scale 1:5,000,000. 21 photographs) concerns empires, a chronological bibliography (p. 219-30) and an extensive index (p. 231-307). R. Cornevin contributes 'Maurice Delafosse et le Haut Sénégal-Niger' to the new edition (p. v-xxviii) with a bibliography of Delafosse's works (p. xxvi-xxviii). M. Clozel, Governor of Haut-Sénégal-Niger (1916-17), authored a 'Préface de l'édition de 1912' (p. 1-12). Louise Delafosse offers a biography of her father (1870-1926) in *Maurice Delafosse* (Paris: Société Française d'Histoire d'Outre-Mer, 1976. 428p. map. 68 illustrations).

7   **Historical dictionary of Mali.**
    Pascal James Imperato. Lanham, Maryland; London: Scarecrow Press,
    1996. 3rd ed. 363p. maps. bibliog. (African Historical Dictionaries,
    no. 11).

This indispensable compendium is essential for the study of Mali. Imperato, the respected scholar of Mali, presents a note on the spellings of 'Sudan' and

'Timbuktoo', a superb chronology of Mali history from 5000 BC to June 1995, twelve tables of rulers of ancient kingdoms, administration, military leaders, economic and population data, six maps (p. lxxx-lxxxv) including one showing movements of Peul nomads, and an excellent wide-ranging introduction to the country. The dictionary itself (p. 23-253) offers lucid, cross-referenced biographical sketches of people and descriptions of places, administrative bodies, kingdoms, and terms, from 'Abibu Tall' to 'Zahan, Dominique'. The bibliography (p. 255-362) contains an excellent bibliographical introduction (p. 255-76), the best of its type in English, and over 1,600 entries (upon occcasion marred by typographical errors) of books, journals, journal articles, films and videos, published primarily in French and English and occasionally in German. The unannotated and unindexed bibliography is divided into the following categories: 'General works', 'Cultural works', 'Economic works', 'Historical works', 'Political and judicial works and current events', 'Scientific works', 'Women's issues', 'Social works', 'Education', and 'Religion'.

8   **Let's visit Mali.**
Kim Naylor.   Basingstoke, England: Macmillan, 1987. 96p. map. (Let's Visit Places & Peoples of the World Series).

This fine introduction for children of elementary school age offers a survey of Malian history and peoples, an account of a journey down the River Niger, descriptions of agriculture, the economy and prospects for the future. A map and numerous colour photographs complement the text. Thomas O'Toole's *Mali – in pictures* (Minneapolis, Minnesota: Lerner Publications, 1990. 64p.) is a prolifically illustrated introduction for children and includes chapters on the topography, history, society, economy, and governmental structure of Mali.

9   **Mali.**
Peterborough, New Hampshire: Cobblestone Publishing Co., 1997. 40p. map. bibliog. (Faces, vol. 13, no. 6).

A delightful look at Mali, aimed at the junior high school student. Topics range from a trip down the Niger River; a look at 'magical, mystical Timbuktu'; the salt trade; a story about Ananse, the trickster; a look at the Dogon; 'the baobab tree: life source of the Dogon'; two crossword puzzles, one about the Niger and the other about Timbuktu; easy instructions on how to make your own *bogolanfini*, or painted mud cloth; a bibliography of books for young readers; American museums that have West African collections; and a list of Internet sites related to Mali (Republic of Mali, tips for the traveller, art of Africa, playing with time, music of Africa), complete with electronic addresses, some of which are already out of date. All of the numerous illustrations are in black and white except for those on the cover.

10   **Le Mali.** (Mali.)
Joseph Roger de Benoist.   Paris: L'Harmattan, 1989. 265p. maps. bibliog. (Collection A la Rencontre de . . .).

This volume contains a sustained overview of the country, its geography, history, ancient empires, peoples, colonial and post-colonial development and contemporary nature, by region. The indexes (p. 223-44) have information on political organization, economic data for 1982-86, education, the army, cultural life, transport and tourism. It has thirteen photographs, eight maps, a bibliography (p. 245-47) and general index (p. 249-61). The author, a member of the Société des Missionnaires d'Afrique (Pères

Blancs), also authored *L'Afrique occidentale française de 1944 à 1960* (French West Africa from 1944 to 1960) (Dakar: Nouvelles Editions Africaines, 1983. 620p.) and *Eglise et pouvoir colonial au Soudan français: les relations entre administrateurs et missionnaires dans la Boucle du Niger (1885-1945)* (see item no. 361).

11 **Mali.**
Eno Beuchelt. Bonn, Germany: K. Schroeder, 1966. 153p. maps. bibliog. (Die Länder Afrikas, Band 34).
This is an interesting survey, in German, of the geography, history, population, culture, politics and economy of Mali. The chapter on the economy (p. 97-142) is the longest by far. In the text there are seven maps, and a small fold-out map appears at the end. The author studied the Bambara in 1957 and 1958 and wrote *Kulturwandel bei den Bambara von Ségou* (Cultural change in the Bambara of Segou) (Bonn, Germany: K. Schroeder, 1962).

12 **Mali.**
Alan Carpenter, Thomas O'Toole, Mark La Pointe. Chicago, Illinois: Children's Press, 1975. 94p. maps. (The Enchantment of Africa).
This well-illustrated book offers an excellent introduction to Mali for late primary school children. It provides an introduction to Mali's geography, ethnic groups, history, government, natural resources, and major cities.

13 **Mali.**
Series coordinator, Patricia S. Kuntz, consultant for Mali, Gerald Cashion. Gainesville, Florida: University of Florida, Center for African Studies, 1984. 1 vol. (loose-leaf). bibliog. (Country Orientation Notebooks for Africa, no. 8).
Although this loose-leaf publication was designed for consultants working on agriculture-related projects, it is actually of interest to a much broader audience. It contains a compilation of previously published articles, reports and essays by many authors and on most aspects of Mali: history; society; politics; current events; agriculture; development; economy. The last section is a slide-tape module with thirty-nine slides. Chiefly in English, although some sections are in French. In some libraries it may be catalogued under the series title: Country Orientation Notebooks for Africa.

14 **Mali: 1995 post report.**
United States. Department of State. Washington, DC: US Dept. of State, 1995. 24p. maps. bibliog. (Department of State Publication, no. 9212).
'Directed to official U.S. Government employees and their families' (Preface), this concise publication packs a lot of practical information into a few pages. The first section describes the host country, the second gives details about the American Embassy in Bamako (emphasizing living conditions for Americans), and the last part covers travel information. The brief bibliography (p. 23-24) is excellent. It is updated every three to four years.

15 **Mali, a country profile.**
Washington, DC: Office of US Foreign Disaster Assistance, Agency for
International Development, Department of State, 1988. 77p. maps.
bibliog.

This study is an excellent source of basic data on the country as well as on disaster-related issues. The report consists of chapters on 'General information' (p. 1-21), 'Disaster vulnerability' (p. 22-34), 'Disaster preparedness and assistance' (p. 35-61), 'Appendices' (p. 62-74) covering the 1984-85 drought and the 1987 yellow fever epidemic, and a useful bibliography (p. 75-77). It also includes addresses and descriptions of international relief agencies and organizations working in Mali, and a colour map (scale 1:11,000,000, CIA map no. 5027289-77(542164)). Cecily Mango authored a similar study for the same agency, *Mali: a country profile* (Jan. 1980. 2nd ed. 47p.) with the same map and a bibliography (p. 45-47). See also the US Agency for International Development's *Country development strategy statement FY1985: Mali* (Washington, DC: USAID, Jan. 1983. 63p.) which describes Mali's needs and economic performance and the objectives and strategy of US assistance efforts, especially in the agricultural sector. Hella Pick's 'Mali, a country profile', *Africa Report*, vol. 7, no. 1 (Jan. 1962), p. 7-8, 23, provides a clear snapshot of the country at that time.

16 **Mali: a prospect of peace?**
Rhéal Drisdelle. Oxford, England: Oxfam (UK and Ireland), 1997.
64p. map. bibliog. (Oxfam Country Profile).

This slim volume is an excellent overview of the current situation in Mali. While it briefly covers some history and civilization, it focuses on recent economic, social and political conditions.

17 **Mali: a search for direction.**
Pascal James Imperato. Boulder, Colorado: Westview Press; London:
Dartmouth, 1989. 170p. maps. bibliog. (Profiles: Nations of
Contemporary Africa).

This study, with its four maps, five tables, twenty photographs, excellent chapter notes (p. 149-58) and valuable bibliography (p. 159-62), provides the best introduction in English to Mali, its peoples and their history and politics. Chapters are: 'Introduction' (p. 1-13); 'Early history' (p. 15-37); 'Conquest, colonial rule, and independence' (p. 39-55); Malian politics since independence (p. 57-79); 'Culture and society' (p. 81-105); 'The economy' (p. 107-28); and 'Mali's international relations' (p. 129-48). The work is based on the author's twenty-three years of residence in and study of Mali.

18 **Le Mali, carrefour des civilisations – Mali, cradle of civilisations.**
Paris: Editions Delroisse, 1971. 160p. maps.

This volume 'produced for and on behalf of the Government of Mali' is in French, with an English translation by A. North Coombes. It contains a collection of colourful photographs with bilingual captions, organized around six regions *(cercles)* of Mali, following brief introductory remarks (p. 4-9). It also includes numerous photographs of Bamako, the Dogon country and 'Tombouctou, the mysterious' (p. 112-18).

19 **Mali: guide d'information, décembre 1992.** (Mali: information guide, December 1992.)
Ambassade de France à Bamako. Mission de Coopération et d'Action Culturelle. Paris: Ministère de la Coopération et du Développement, 1993. 66p. map. bibliog.

An excellent beginning source for the French-speaker. It includes chapters on generalities (physical and human geography, history, political and administrative organization, economy, infrastructure); cooperation with France; international relations; and conditions of life (getting settled, diplomatic addresses, health, schooling, leisure).

20 **Mali – potential and problems.**
Christoph Güdel. *Swiss Review of World Affairs,* vol. 31 (Sept. 1981), p. 9-14. map.

The author gives an informative overview of 'Aid from East and West'; 'Swiss development aid', especially well-drilling in southern Mali, an agricultural training centre and the Niarela Craft Training Centre in Bamako; and 'Natural and man-made problems' (agriculture, deforestation and politics). The article includes three photographs.

21 **The road to Timbuktu.**
E. J. Kahn, Jr. *The New Yorker* (4 Nov. 1985), p. 82, 87-88, 90, 92, 94-99, 101, 103-4.

The author describes his trip to Mali and sketches the country's economic plight.

22 **Le Soudan français.** (French Soudan.)
Georges Spitz, preface by Governor Edmond Louveau. Paris: Editions Maritimes et Coloniales, 1955. 111p. maps. bibliog. (Pays Africains, no. 5).

Although the numerical information is dated, students of Mali who read French will find here useful chapters on the country, the people, history, political and administrative structure, social works, the economy and tourism. A bibliography (p. 106-9), five maps and eight photographs enhance the volume. E. Louveau was governor of the French Soudan from 1946 to 1952. *Connaissance de la République du Mali: un peuple, un but, une foi* (Becoming acquainted with the Republic of Mali: one people, one goal, one faith) by Bakari Kamian and edited by the Secretary of State for Information and Tourism (Bamako: The Editor, 1960. 119p.) is a fine survey of the country at the time of independence and provides information on geography, population, ethnic groups, cities, history, politics, economics and transportation. It includes an administrative map (p. 47) and black-and-white photographs. A more recent publication is Philippe Decraene's *Le Mali* (Paris: Presses Universitaires de France, 1980. 125p.) which sketches the country and its peoples, precolonial and colonial and independent history. It has a bibliography of thirty-six references (p. 123-25), but neither map, pictures nor index.

23 **Teaching about Francophone Africa.**
Mary Merryfield, Adama Timbo. Bloomington, Indiana: Indiana
University, African Studies Program, 1983. 115p. map.
This useful guide for teachers, available in either English or French, covers general
subjects for the large Francophone region and is divided into four parts: 'Background
on the history and geography . . .'; 'French influences in Africa'; 'Cross-cultural
understanding'; and 'Resource materials in French'. It includes brief sections on Mali:
'Scenarios for cross-cultural understanding – U.S. and Malian perceptions' (p. 66-67,
69-70) and 'Bargaining in Mali' (p. 83-85, 101-2).

Le Mali. (Mali.)
See item no. 174.

Pays du Sahel: du Tchad au Sénégal, du Mali au Niger. (Countries of the
Sahel: from Chad to Senegal, from Mali to Niger.)
See item no. 178.

Explorers' and
Travellers' Accounts
(to the early
20th century)

24 **An account of Timbuctoo and Housa, territories in the interior of Africa, by El Hage Salam Shabeeny; with notes, critical and explanatory. To which is added, letters descriptive of travels through west and south Barbary, and across the mountains of Atlas; also, fragments, notes, and anecdotes; specimens of the Arabic epistolary style, &c, &c.**
James Grey Jackson. London: Longman, Hurst, Rees, Orme, Brown, 1820. Reprinted, London: Frank Cass, 1967. 547p. maps. (Cass Library of African Studies. Travels and Narratives, no. 25).
Most of this interesting work concerns travels and observations relevant to Morocco and northwest Africa. Nevertheless, it contains 'An account of a journey from Fas to Timbuctoo, performed in or about the year 1787, A.C.' by El Hage Abd Salam Shabeeny (p. 1-36) who stayed in Timbuctoo three years; a fold-out map of caravan routes from Fas and Arguin to Timbuctoo; a wordlist of English, Mandinga and Arabic (p. 373-77); Jackson's translation of Shereef Ibrahim's account of Mungo Park's death (p. 406-18); miscellaneous other letters on Park's death (p. 424-25); the supposed linkage of the Niger River with the Nile; health and 'historical fragments' on the capture of Timbuctoo by Muley Hamed about 1580; and expeditions to Timbuctoo by Muley El Arsheed in 1670 (p. 521-23) and by Muley Hamed Dehebby (p. 523-24). The volume is well indexed (p. 525-47).

25 **Berbers and blacks; impressions of Morocco, Timbuktu and the Western Sudan.**
David Prescott Barrows. New York and London: Century Company, 1927. Reprinted, Westport, Connecticut: Negro Universities Press, 1970. 251p. maps.
'This narrative comprises the record of a holiday trip to Timbuktu, and a part of the world little known and under-appreciated' (p. 11). Among the fourteen chapters are: 'The railroad' (p. 118-30), 'The Niger' (p. 131-41), 'Timbuktu' (p. 142-57) and 'The

bush' describing his travel from Mopti to Ouagadougou by horseback. In addition to well-integrated historical descriptions, he offers observations on African veterans, colonial exploitation, government and 'The black' (p. 233-45). The reprint lacks the sketch map of West Africa and routes across the Sahara, but includes two diagrams and forty-four period photographs by the author.

26 **De Saint-Louis à Tripoli par le lac Tchad: voyage au travers du Soudan et du Sahara accompli pendant les années, 1890-91-92.**
(From Saint-Louis to Tripoli by way of Lake Chad; voyage through Sudan and the Sahara accomplished during the years 1890, 1891, 1892.) Lieut. Colonel P. L. Monteil. Paris: F. Alcan, 1895. 462p. maps.

Monteil was charged with exploring this region of West Africa in order to try to improve the lines of demarcation (drawn to France's disadvantage in 1890) between the English and French territories. He travelled 7,800 kilometres in two years, from Saint-Louis (in Senegal) to Tripoli, passing through modern-day Mali, Burkina Faso, Niger, Nigeria, and Libya. Within Mali, he explored Segou, signed a treaty in San, and continued to Koutiala and Sikasso. The work includes sixteen maps and sixty-five engravings. In 1885 and 1886, he published two maps of Sudan, one at a scale of 1:100,000 and another at 1:750,000.

27 **De Saint-Louis au port de Tombouktou: voyage d'une canonnière française, suivi d'un vocabulaire sonraï.** (From Saint-Louis to the port of Timbuktu: journey of a French gunboat, followed by a Songhay vocabulary.)
Edmond Caron. Paris: A. Challamel, 1891. 376p. maps.

Caron describes his voyage down the Niger River on the gunboat *Niger* to Timbuktu in 1887 in a futile effort to obtain treaties from local groups. Jean Gilbert Nivomé de Jaime also provides an account in *De Koulikoro à Tombouctou à bord du 'Mage', 1889-1890* (From Koulikoro to Timbuktu on the 'Mage', 1889-90) (Paris: Dentu, 1892. 436p.) which appeared in a new edition two years later as *De Koulikoro à Tombouctou sur la canonnière 'Le Mage'* (Paris: Les Librairies Associés, 1894. 456p. maps).

28 **Du Niger au Golfe de Guinée par le pays de Kong et le Mossi.** (From the Niger to the Gulf of Guinea by Kong and Mossi country.)
Le Capitaine Binger. Paris: Hachette, 1892. Reprinted, Paris: Musée de l'Homme, 1980. 2 vols. maps. bibliog. (Mémoires de la Société des Africanistes).

In volume one (513p., nine chapters, 119 illustrations), Capt. Binger (1856-1936) provides a masterful account of his mission to what is now southern Mali, including visits to Keyes, Bamako, and Sikasso, Burkina Faso, and Côte d'Ivoire. His primary description is of Kong and the Mossi. Volume two (411p., seven chapters, 89 illustrations) describes the part of the journey in today's northern Ghana, the Gourounsi, Gondja, Bondoukou, Djimi and his joining the mission of Marcel Treich-Laplene and final journey to the coast. The appendices (p. 349-411) contain reports on the costs of the mission, meteorology, geography, flora and fauna, the history of the Sonr'ay, Mandé, Bamana dynasties (p. 366-91) with 39 linguistic references (p. 378-79); a plan of Waghadougou, regional maps of population density, religion,

Peul and Mande distribution, culture locations and trade (p. 397-402); diagrams of facial markings for the Mossi, Bobo, Gourounga, Hausa, Songho and others. A large (scale 1:900,000), detailed fold-out map of the upper Niger to the Gulf of Guinea, showing the route taken by Binger in 1887-89, is attached.

29 **French enterprise in Africa: the personal narrative of Lieut. Hourst of his exploration of the Niger.**
Lieutenant Hourst, translated by Mrs Arthur Bell.   London: Chapman & Hall, 1898. 520p. map.

In 1896, Lt Hourst led an expedition down the Niger River beginning in Timbuktu and ending in the sea near Bussa, in present-day Nigeria. By signing several treaties with the Tuaregs, he helped lay claim to Eastern Mali and Western Niger for the French. Chapter V (p. 199-249) is a description of the Tuareg people, 'an interesting race, which has perhaps been unjustly calumniated' (p. 198). In Chapter VIII (p. 356-402), Hourst describes the threat of attack by the Toucouleurs, 'the hereditary enemies of French influence in Africa' (p. 383). The work includes a fold-out map (scale 1:1,000,000) of the Niger River from Timbuktu to Bussa.

30 **Les grandes missions françaises en Afrique occidentale.** (The great French missions to West Africa.)
Le Ct Chailley.   Dakar: IFAN, 1953. 145p. maps. bibliog. (Initiations Africaines, no. 10).

In this useful summary of French exploration of West Africa, the reader will find chapters on René Caillié (p. 35-40), Commandant Faidherbe (p. 41-45), 'Le bond décisif du Sénégal du Niger' (p. 47-52), 'Les navigations sur le Niger: occupation de Tombouctou' (p. 53-60), Monteil (p. 63-67), 'Le fruit mûr: dans la boucle du Niger' (p. 101-2). It includes six maps and a handy chronology of the principal missions (p. 133-34) divided by region such as 'La boucle du Niger', 'Le cours du Niger', etc.

31 **The history and description of Africa, and of the notable things therein contained.**
Leo Africanus, translated by John Pory, edited with introduction and notes by Robert Brown.   London: Printed for the Hakluyt Society, 1896. 3 vols. maps. bibliog. (Works Issued by the Hakluyt Society, no. 92-94).

This famous account by the great traveller Leo Africanus (1493-1552 or 1560), originally in Arabic and published in Italian in 1526, contains a lengthy introduction and account of the author's life by Brown (p. i-cxi), Africanus's nine books (pages consecutively numbered) relating his travels, with notes to each by Brown. Africanus visited Genni (Djenné), Araoan (Arawan), Gualata (Walata), Gago (Gao), Cabra (Kabara), Tombuto (Timbuktu) and sailed along the Niger, perhaps in 1510. In Book Seven, he offers 'A description of the kingdome of Ghinea,' 'Of the kingdome of Melli,' 'Of the kingdome of Tombuto' and 'Of the towne and kingdome of Gago' (p. 822-27). Four small maps show his travels, northwest Africa, and the continent as understood in 1600.

32 Ibn Battúta: travels in Asia and Africa: 1325-1354.

Translated and selected by H. A. R. Gibb. London: G. Routledge, 1929. Reprinted, London: Darf, 1983. 398p. maps. (The Broadway Travellers).

Gibb provides an introduction (p. 1-40) to one of the world's greatest travellers, notes (p. 341-83) and indexes of geographical and personal names (p. 385-98). In chapter fourteen (p. 317-39), Ibn Battuta describes his journey in 1352-53, from Fès (Fez) to the salt mines of Taguázá and on to Timbuktu and Gao. Several notable publications of and on Ibn Battuta are: his own *Voyage dans le Soudan* (Voyage in the Sudan. Translated by MacGuckin de Slane. Paris: Imprimerie Royale, 1843. 62p.); *Voyages d'Ibn Batouta* (Paris: Imprimerie Impériale, 1853-58. 4 vols) contains the Arabic text, edited and translated by C. Defrémery and B. R. Sanguinetti; Battuta's *Textes et documents relatifs à l'histoire de l'Afrique*, extracts translated and annotated by R. Mauny, V. Monteil, A. Djenidi, S. Robert and J. Devisse (Dakar: Université de Dakar, 1966. 87p.); and Ross E. Dunn's *The adventures of Ibn Battuta: a Muslim traveler of the fourteenth century* (Beckenham, England: C. Helm, 1986. 357p.). See also Thomas J. Abercrombie's 'Ibn Battuta, Prince of Travelers', *National Geographic*, vol. 180, no. 6 (Dec. 1991), p. 2-49, which includes photographs of the mosque at Djenné and other scenes in Mali.

33 The journal of a mission to the interior of Africa, in the year 1805. Together with other documents, official and private, relating to the same mission. To which is prefixed an account of the life of Mr. Park.

Mungo Park. London: J. Murray; Philadelphia, Pennsylvania: Edward Earle, 1815. Reprinted, Saint Clair Shores, Minnesota: Scholarly Press, 1973. 302p. map.

This fascinating volume contains an 'Account of the life of Mungo Park' (1771-1805, p. 1-94) 'by the editor' which includes several of Park's letters and a 1804 memoir on planning an expedition to Africa, appendices (p. 97-126), a list of eleven 'African words' (p. 126), the journal from 27 April 1805 to 15 November 1805 (p. 127-259) which ends with his departure from 'Sego' (Segou) and 'Isaaco's journal' (p. 261-302) translated from the Arabic of his 1810 journey to determine the fate of Park. The journal of Amadi Fatouma, Park's last guide, is contained in Isaaco's account (p. 294-99). A large fold-out map (scale 1 inch to 60 miles) showing Park's two expeditions (1795-96, 1805) is included. T. Coraghessan Boyle's *Water music* (Boston: Little, Brown; New York: Penguin, 1981. 437p.) is a remarkable imaginative account of Park's final expedition for which Boyle, whose impetus is 'principally aesthetic rather than scholarly' reshapes historical facts 'with full knowledge and clear conscience' (Apologia, p. x).

34 Missions to the Niger.

Edited by E. W. Bovill. Cambridge, England: Cambridge University Press for the Hakluyt Society, 1964-66. 4 vols. maps. bibliog. (The Hakluyt Society, Second Series, nos. 123, 128-30).

Volume one (no. 123, 1964. 406p.) contains 'The journal of Friedrich Hornemann's travels, from Cairo to Mourzouk, the Kingdom of Fezzan, in Africa in the years 1797-8' (London: Nicol, 1802, p. 43-122) introduced by Bovill (p. 3-41). More important for Mali studies is 'The letters of Major Alexander Gordon Laing, 1824-1826' (p. 185-341), Bovill's important introduction (p. 125-84, including 'The story of Timbuktu', p. 168-73), appendices (p. 342-90) with bibliography (p. 391-94) and index. Laing was in Timbuktu from 13 August till 22 September 1826 and died thirty miles away in Sahab (or Es Seheb) on 24 September 1826. Bovill reconstructs his visit and demise from R. Caillié, Laing himself, a letter from Sheikh el Muktar to the Bashaw of Tripoli, and from later investigations, in the chapters entitled 'Timbuktu' (p. 308-18) and 'The search for Laing' (p. 319-29). The other volumes are on the Bornu mission, 1822-25 (nos. 128-30) and mention Timbuktu, Kabara, Mungo Park and the Niger River only briefly. In *The Niger explored* (London: Oxford University Press, 1968. 263p.) Bovill vividly recounts the explorations of Mungo Park (second journey, 1805-6, p. 1-31), the expedition of Capt. William Gray and Staff-Surgeon Dochard to Bamako in 1821 (p. 33-35) and the travels of Capt. Alexander Gordon Laing to Timbuktu in 1826 (p. 149-87). Ten maps, fifteen illustrations and a 'Select bibliography' (p. 249-50) fill out this volume which was completed shortly before the author's death in December 1966.

35 My march to Timbuctoo.

Joseph-Jacques-Césaire Joffre, introduction by Ernest Dimnet.

New York: Duffield & Company, 1915. 169p. maps.

During his three years' stay in the region, General Joffre (1852-1931) superintended the construction of the Kayes to Bafoulabé railway and as a major led the famous expedition to secure Timbuctoo for the French. Joffre describes in clear direct prose his march from Ségou to Timbuctoo, 27 December 1893 to 12 February 1894. E. Dimnet provides an informative introduction (p. 1-48), presenting 'Joffre as soldier' and 'Joffre as writer.' The main text is Joffre's fleshed-out diary and commentary, 'Operations of the Joffre column before and after the occupation of Timbuctoo' originally published in 1895. In it he describes the march, the occupation, geography and ethnography of the region, 'operations against the Touareg' and communications and situation on 10 July 1894. The volume has a small map of Timbuctoo and a 'Map of the expedition to Timbuctoo' (scale 1 inch to 26 miles).

36 Nouveau voyage dans le pays des nègres, suivi d'études sur la colonie du Sénégal, et de documents historiques, géographiques et scientifiques. (New voyage to the country of the negroes, followed by studies on the colony of Senegal, and historical, geographical and scientific documents.)

Anne Raffenel. Paris: Imprimerie de N. Chaix, 1856. 2 vols.

As an officer in the French navy, Raffenel led an expedition into West Africa in 1846, where he travelled from Saint-Louis on the Senegalese coast, to Bakel and Galam, and then into Mali. In volume 1 – 'c'est la partie anecdotique, littéraire et amusante' (p. i) – he recounts the details of the expedition. In volume 2, he describes the colony of Senegal, its history and commercial exploitation, the ethnic groups and political states encountered (e.g., the Peuls of Macina, the states of Timbuktu, Djenne and Segu, Fulahs, etc.), meteorological and scientific observations. The book includes a folded map of the region covering as far east as Timbuktu. Raffenel was imprisoned by the Bambara in Kaarta for eight months.

37   **The road to Timbuktu.**
Lady Dorothy Mills.   London: Duckworth, 1924. 262p. map.

Despite the author's disclaimers, she provides an interesting account of experiences in
Bamako, Ségou, Sansanding, Mopti, Dienné, Timbuktu (where she spent a fortnight,
'more or less invalide . . .') and along the Niger River. 'I spent just three months in the
A. O. F., travelling as fast as local conditions would permit. Except at Dakar, the
landing place, Bamako, the jumping-off place, and Timbuktu itself, which in all
account for three weeks, much of that time spent ill in bed, I never passed more than
forty-eight hours in the same place. Obviously my knowledge cannot be profound!'
(Preface, p. 7). She includes fourteen photographs of the trip.

38   **The search for the Niger.**
Christopher Lloyd.   London: Collins, 1973. 220p. maps. bibliog.

Following the initial chapter 'The mystery of the Niger' (p. 13-26), Lloyd describes
the efforts of explorers Mungo Park, William Gray, Gordon Laing, René Caillié and
Henry Barth, 'perhaps the greatest traveller there has ever been in Africa,' (p. 161).
He includes eighteen illustrations and a bibliography (p. 210-13).

39   **The strong brown god: the story of the Niger River.**
Sanche de Gramont [Ted Morgan].   Boston, Massachusetts: Houghton
Mifflin, 1976, ©1975. 1st American ed. 350p. maps. bibliog.

To research this book the author and his wife followed the river's entire 2,600-mile
course over three months in 1972, a journey which included taking the paddlewheel
Liberté from Mopti to Gao, being arrested in Mopti and laid low by a mysterious fever
in Timbuctu. He recounts the riveting story of Europeans' search for and exploration
of West Africa's greatest river. Among those explorers in this dramatic tale are
Mungo Park, Réné Caillié, Gordon Laing, Richard Lander, Heinrich Barth, William
Balfour Baikie, Frederick Lugard and Sir George Goldie. The Pulitzer Prize-winning
author changed his name to Ted Morgan when he became an American citizen.

40   **Through Timbuctu and across the great Sahara; an account of an**
      adventurous journey of exploration from Sierra Leone to the source
      of the Niger, following its course to the bend at Gao and thence
      across the great Sahara to Algiers.
Captain A. H. W. Haywood.   London: Seeley, Service & Co., 1912.
349p. map.

Captain Haywood of the Royal Artillery, quartered at Sierra Leone and due six
months' leave, set out on 6 January 1910 for the headwaters of the Niger, the French
Soudan, Bamako, Koulikoro, Mopti, Lake Dhebo, Timbuktu (7-12 April), Gao and
then travelled north 1,560 miles across the Sahara arriving in Marseilles on 11 June.
His account is notable for its descriptions of people, geography, and of birds and
mammals he observed. The appendix (p. 341) lists 'Principal game shot during the
expedition showing the measurement of best heads obtained' including elephant tusks
weighing 52 pounds each. A fold-out map shows his route (scale 1 inch to 300 miles)
and there are forty-five photographs taken on the journey. This work was also
published in Philadelphia, Pennsylvania by Lippincott in 1912.

41 **Timbuctoo.**
Leland Hall. New York and London: Harper & Brothers, 1927. 278p.

In this first-person account, the author describes his nearly three-month-long stay in Timbuctoo. The story is interesting, but the book provides little historical depth or social description. The author includes seventeen photographs. 'What is Timbuctoo like? . . . Timbuctoo is light; it is silence; it is the faint smell of the desert dust; . . . and the people are movement; they are laughter; . . . they are scorn, affection, fear, trust . . .' (p. 259-60). Captain Cecil D. Priest describes 'Timbuktu, in the sands of the Sahara' in *National Geographic Magazine*, vol. 45, no. 1 (Jan. 1924), p. 73-85. His account is interesting and he provides sixteen photographs of the city, its people and environs.

42 **Timbuctoo the mysterious.**
Félix Dubois, translated into English by Diana White. New York: Longmans, Green and Co., 1896. Reprinted, New York: Negro Universities Press, 1969. 377p.

In this famous travelogue, the author (b. 1862) uses vivid prose to convey readers from Paris to the Niger River, through the towns along the river and finally to Timbuctoo. Extensive description of Jenne (p. 80-88, 143-88), the Songhois (p. 89-121), Moors in the Sudan (p. 122-42) and of Timbuctoo (p. 208-371) are included. 'Truly she is enthroned upon the horizon with the majesty of a queen. She is indeed the city of imagination, the Timbuctoo of European legend' (p. 209). Dubois includes 153 illustrations 'from photographs and drawings made on the spot' and an index (p. 372-77). Among the eleven maps and plans are maps of the Songhoi Empire, Jenneri (Jenne) region, and Jenne, Timbuctoo and Kabara and of Timbuctoo itself. Dubois also wrote *La vie au continent noir* (Life in the Black continent) (Paris: J. Hetze, 1893. 301p.), about an expedition to French Sudan between December 1892 and February 1893; and *Notre beau Niger* (Our beautiful Niger) (Paris: Flammarion, 1911. 299p.).

43 **Timbuktu, Reise durch Marokko, die Sahara und den Sudan ausgeführt im Auftrage der Afrikanischen Gesellschaft in Deutschland in den Jahren 1879 und 1880.** (Timbuktu: voyage through Morocco, the Sahara and the Sudan which was commissioned by the African Society in Germany in the years 1879 and 1880.)
Dr. Oskar Lenz. Leipzig, Germany: F. A. Brockhaus, 1884. 2 vols. maps.

In 1879-80, Lenz travelled from Tangiers, Morocco, across the Atlas Mountains to Tindouf, Algeria, then headed south through the Sahara Desert into present-day Mali exploring Arouane, Timbuktu (1-19 July 1880), Bassikunnu (southeastern Mauritania), where he turned west to Sokolo, and Medina, and terminating in Saint-Louis, Senegal. The portion of greatest interest here is on Timbuktu, covered in volume 2, chapters 3 to 5 (p. 86-169). Volume 1 (430p.) contains one map and twenty-nine illustrations. Volume 2 (408p.) contains eight maps (in greater detail) and twenty-eight illustrations. Also available in microfilm in German, and in French translation as: *Timbouctou: voyage au Maroc, au Sahara et au Soudan* (Paris: Hachette, 1886-87. 2 vols).

44 **Travels and discoveries in North and Central Africa: being a journal of an expedition undertaken under the auspices of H. B. M.'s government in the years, 1849-1855.**
Heinrich Barth. New York: Harper, 1857-59. Reprinted, London: F. Cass, 1965. 3 vols. maps.

Barth's (1821-65) classic account of his travels is reprinted in a centenary edition containing fifteen fold-out route maps, dozens of illustrations, a chronology of his travels, invaluable appendices and a brief biographical sketch by A. H. M. Kirk-Greene (vol. 1, p. ix-xvii). Volume three (800p.) contains the brilliant record of his travel from Kukuwa, Bornu (19 November 1852) through Zinder, Sokoto, Katsena, along the Niger River, across the Hombori region, Tawárek (Tuareg) encampments, to Kábara and into Timbuktu (arrived 7 September 1853, departed 17 May 1854; p. 269-431). He describes Gógó (Gao, 19 June 1854; p. 479-93), his return to Sokoto, Kano and the journey from Kukuwa to Europe. He provides four route maps and sixty-seven illustrations, including a 'Ground plan of Timbuktu'. Among numerous appendices (p. 633-783) are a 'Chronological table of the history of Songhay and the neighboring kingdoms' (AD 300-1855; p. 657-83), itineraries in the western Sahara (p. 683-70), a list of Arab or Moorish tribes (p. 711-18), a vocabulary of the Temáshight or Tárkiye (p. 724-63), chief towns and residences of the independent Songhay (p. 768) and 'Fragments of a meteorological register' (p. 769-83). Maps include a 'Map of the route between Say and Timbúktu, including the survey of the Niger' (scale 1:1,000,000).

45 **Travels in the interior districts of Africa.**
Mungo Park. New York: Arno Press, 1971. 372p. (Physician Travelers).

In this account (p. 1-363), one of the most famous in the annals of African exploration, Park, a surgeon, describes his exploration 'to ascertain the course, and if possible, the rise and termination' of the River Niger. The journal was 'drawn up from original minutes and notices made at the proper moment and preserved with great difficulty' (Preface, p. vii). Park includes 'A vocabulary of the Mandingo language' (p. 365-72). Major James Rennell authored the Appendix, 'Geographical illustrations of Mr. Park's journey' (p. iii-xcii), a discussion of Park's observations. The volume contains six plates, large fold-out maps of Park's route, northern Africa and a 'Chart of the lines of magnetic variation in the seas around Africa' and 'A Negro song from Mr. Park's travels set to music by the Duchess of Devonshire and a list of African words' (p. xix-xx). *Travels into the interior of Africa* (London: J. M. Dent, 1954; London: Eland; New York: Hippocrene Books, 1983. 388p. map) contains both of Park's accounts of his trips (Book One: The first journey, p. 1-277; Book Two: The second journey, p. 279-388), indexed and with a map and five plates. The 1983 paperback edition has a new Preface (p. v-x) by Jeremy Swift.

46 **Travels in Western Africa, in the years 1818, 19, 20, and 21: from the River Gambia, through Woolli, Bondoo, Galam, Kasson, Kaarta, and Foolidoo, to the River Niger.**
Major William Gray, Staff Surgeon Dochard. London: J. Murray, 1825. 413p. map.

The British expedition travelled from the western coast of Senegal to the Niger River over the course of four years. From the Gambia River, they traversed central and western Mali. In his conclusion (p. 337-64), Gray summarizes his experience 'not only upon the habits and manners of the people of Western Africa, but also as to the progress they have made towards civilization, as to their political institutions and religious improvement' (p. 337). He also laments the active slave trade (in Kaarta and Galam) and states that 'native princes and traders have a strong and direct interest to oppose the abolition of slavery' (p. 349). 'Description and sketches on botanical subjects' (p. 384-96 plus plates A to D) is a portion of the appendix.

47   **Travels through central Africa to Timbuctoo and across the great desert, to Morocco, performed in the years 1824-1828.**

René Caillié.   London: Colburn & Bentley, 1830. Reprinted, London: Darf, 1992-1994. 2 vols. maps.

René Auguste Caillié (1799-1838) was the first European to visit Timbuktu and write an account of his travels: *Journal d'un voyage à Temboctou et à Djenné, dans l'Afrique centrale, précédé d'observations faites chez les Maures Braknas, les Nalous et d'autres peuples pendant les années 1824, 1825, 1826, 1827, 1829* (Paris: Imprimerie Royale, 1830. 3 vols). In volume one (475p. two plates but no maps), he describes his background and effort to learn Arabic and Islam and details his journey from Saint-Louis (present-day Senegal) on 3 August 1824. Ultimately, he spent thirteen days in Djenné (March 1828), fourteen days in Timbuktu (20 April to 4 May 1828) and nine days in Araouane (May 1828). Descriptions based on his 'fugitive and very laconic notes, written in haste and trepidation' (Preface, vol. 2, p. v) are remarkably fleshed out through the 'scrupulous fidelity' of his memory on a journey of 4,500 miles. Volume two (501p.) includes six plates and two maps (one folds out) of his travels to Jenne and Timbuctoo, an English–Mandingo vocabulary (p. 375-91), English–Kissour vocabulary (spoken at Timbuctoo, p. 392-400), Caillié's itinerary (p. 403-26), notes on the plates (p. 427-30), notes on plants (p. 431-33), miscellaneous notes (p. 434-44), miscellaneous papers and documents (p. 445-62) and correspondence (p. 463-501).

48   **The unveiling of Timbuctoo: the astounding adventures of Caillié.**

Galbraith Welch.   New York: W. Morrow, 1939. Reprinted, New York: Carroll & Graf, 1991. 351p. map.

The author relates in detailed adulatory prose the biography of René Caillié (1799-1838) and especially his exploration from Kakandé at the mouth of the Rio Nuñez near the coast. He began on 19 April 1827, stayed in Timbuctoo from 20 April to 4 May 1828, and then travelled across the Sahara to Tangier where he arrived on 7 September 1828, a distance of about 3,150 miles. 'Caillié was probably the oddest of adventurers in all history, and Caillié's journey was probably the hardest piece of exploration ever performed' (p. 12). Katherine Woods in the *New York Times Book Review* (12 Feb. 1939), p. 9, praises the story's 'ripe flavor' and calls this 'one of the most amazing and exciting of all true adventure stories, and one of the best'. Ralph Thompson in the *New York Times* (8 Feb. 1939), p. 21, calls it 'A trifle too enthusiastic' but writes that it 'reads well and briskly'.

49 **Voyage au Soudan français (Haut-Niger et pays de Ségou)**
1879-1881. (Voyage to French Sudan: Upper Niger and the country of
Segou, 1879-81.)
Le Commandant Gallieni.   Paris: Hachette, 1885. 632p. maps.
In this military expedition from Senegal through Niger River country, central and
western Mali figure prominently. The expedition travelled as far as Segou. Chapters
XXV to XXX interestingly summarize the mission's results; these include hydrography, climatology and meteorology, the Malinkes and Bambaras, and the progress
of Islam. The book includes 2 fold-out maps of the expedition, 15 plans, and 140
wood engravings.

50 **Voyage au Soudan occidental (1863-1866).** (Travels to western Sudan,
1863-66.)
Eugène Mage, introduction by Yves Person.   Paris: Hachette, 1872.
Reprinted, Paris: Karthala, 1980. 308p. map. (Collection Relire).
Mage (1837-69) describes his remarkable journey to Segou where he and his
companion Dr Quintin lived as ambassadors to the Segou-Tukulor empire for two
years and oversaw the signing of a commercial treaty. Mage offers detailed views of
this turbulent period of the Segou-Tukulor empire. This reprint edition includes the
annotations by J. Berlin de Launay. In his introduction Person provides a biography of
Mage and explains his role in the opening of the Soudan to the French. Another
valuable nineteenth-century account is Paul Soleillet's *Voyage à Ségou, 1878-1879;
rédigé d'après les notes et journaux de voyage de Soleillet par Gabriel Gravier*
(Voyage to Segou, 1878-79; edited from the notes and travel journals of Soleillet by
Gabriel Gravier) (Paris: Challamel, 1887. 515p. maps).

Les pionniers du Soudan, avant, avec et après Archinard, 1879-1894.
(The pioneers of Sudan, before, with and after Archinard, 1879-94.)
See item no. 231.

Recent Travel and Guidebooks

51 **Afrique occidentale française. Togo.** (French West Africa. Togo.)
    Gilbert Houlet.   Paris: Hachette, 1958. 542p. maps. bibliog. (Les
    Guides Bleus).

Indexed and unsurpassed in its coverage, this guide includes geography, economy, prehistory and history, religious history, population, the arts, and flora and fauna. The section 'Soudan français – Haute-Volta' (French Sudan and Upper Volta; p. 183-287) provides a map of Bamako and detailed accounts of the major routes and cities throughout the country. The bibliography (p. ccxxiv-ccxxxi) is subdivided into geography, history, ethnography, linguistics, art, flora and fauna and maps. *Le guide du Mali* (Guide to Mali) by Mamadou Doumbia and Mamadou Sy with preface by Modibo Keita (Bamako: Office Malien de Tourisme, 1969. 147p. maps) includes a tour of Mali's (then) six regions and a word list in French, Bambara and English (p. 144) as well as more usual information. Older, yet highly interesting guides include: *Guide de tourisme au Soudan Français* (Guide to tourism in French Sudan), with a preface by Governeur Louveau (Koulouba, Mali: Service de l'Information du Soudan, 1952. 102p.); *Guide du tourisme en Afrique Occidentale Française et au Togo* (Guide to tourism in French West Africa and Togo) (Paris: L'Agence des Colonies and Touring-Club de France, 1947. 6th ed. 155p. bibliog.) by the Ministère de la France d'Outre-Mer; *Guide du tourisme au Soudan français* (Guide to tourism in French Sudan) (Dakar and Casablanca: A. O. F. Magazine, 1938. 74p.), with a preface by Gouverneur F. Rougier.

52 **Au Mali et au Niger.** (To Mali and Niger.)
    Richard Noblet.   Paris: Hachette, 1987. 239p.

Perhaps the best current guide to Mali (p. 10-133) available in French, this guidebook is illustrated with colour photographs and covers geography, Mali today, historical Mali, practical information, Bamako, the Niger River journey, Dogon country, the Inland Delta, Saharan Mali, western Mali, and Sénoufo country. Among the eight maps are maps of Mali, ethnic groups, Bamako and Dogon country. A practical

Bambara lexicon is included (p. 133) along with a brief bibliography (p. 229). This 1987 edition is easier to use than the 1980 edition (236p.) which was arranged differently, grouping the information together on Mali and Niger under each chapter. Arlette Eyraud and Jean Devisse's *Mali, Niger* (Paris: Hatier, 1979. 155p.) describes several tours of Mali (p. 25-80) and Niger (p. 81-144) in detail and includes introductory information (p. 5-24) and practical suggestions (p. 145-55) as well as numerous maps and colourful photographs and paintings.

53 Backpacker's Africa: West and Central.
David Else. Chalfont St. Peter, England: Bradt; Edison, New Jersey: Hunter, 1988. 248p. maps. bibliog.

Mali is covered in Chapter 10 (p. 103-20). It includes a bit of practical information on Mali and descriptions of travel by road, rail and boat. The destinations highlighted are Bandiagara, Bamako, Djenné, Gao, Mopti and Timbuktu. The author then gives a first-hand account of hiking in Dogon country and supplies a map with hiking routes.

54 Beyond the last oasis: a solo walk in the Western Sahara.
Ted Edwards. London: J. Murray, 1985. 209p. maps.

Inspired by Theodore Monod's exploration of the Sahara, in 1983, the author crossed 300 miles of unexplored desert (the 'Saharan Empty Quarter') when he journeyed by camel from Timbuktu, to Araouane, then over into Mauritania where he reached Oualata.

55 Bright continent: a shoestring guide to Sub-Saharan Africa.
Susan Blumenthal. Garden City, New York: Anchor Press, 1974. 545p. maps.

In the informative, interesting chapter on Mali (p. 134-53), Blumenthal introduces the country in general, Bamako with its restaurants and tourist accommodation, Mopti, Sangha, Djenné, Timbuktu, Gao, Kayes and Sikasso, and offers suggestions for 'Getting around Mali' and 'Leaving Mali'. Preliminary chapters of this useful book include 'Preparing for the trip', 'Visas', 'Traveling in Africa (an overview)', and 'Health and the traveler'. Philip M. Allen's chapter 'Mali' (p. 551-64) in Allen and Aaron Segal's *The traveler's Africa: a guide to the entire continent* (New York: Hopkinton & Blake, 1973. 972p.) profiles Mali and includes a brief historical overview and standard sections for tourists. Allen's account, though dated, is refreshingly forthright: 'Of all the places off the West African travel beat, Mali is probably the richest in spirit, but it is hot, remote, uncomfortable, not especially cordial to tourists, and no bargain' (p. 553).

56 Camping with the Prince.
Thomas Bass. *Sierra*, vol. 75, no. 1 (Jan.-Feb. 1990), p. 42-46, 115-17, 145. map.

In this illustrated article, the author describes the $730,000 Inland Niger Delta project of the International Union for the Conservation of Nature and Natural Resources (IUCN) directed by Stephen Cobb to preserve the area's ecology. Bass recounts vividly Prince Philip's visit (as head of the World Wildlife Fund) and reports by Richard Moorehead and Cobb on the political complexities involved. The article is adapted from the first chapter of Bass's book *Camping with the Prince and other tales of science in Africa* (Boston, Massachusetts: Houghton-Mifflin, 1990. 304p.).

57 **Discovery guide to West Africa: the Niger and Gambia River route.**
Kim Naylor. London: Michael Haag, 1989. 2nd ed. 224p. maps.

Most of this fine guide concerns Mali (p. 71-144) although there are shorter sections
on Nigeria, Niger, Senegal and Gambia. Following general information on the country
are useful sections on 'Gao', 'The Songhai empire', 'The Niger River journey',
'Timbuktu', 'Mopti', 'Djenne', 'The Dogon', 'From Mopti to Bandiagara', 'Exploring
the Bandiagara escarpment', 'Continuing upriver to Bamako', 'Bamako to Keyes' and
'Western Mali'. Appendices (p. 172-215) offer historical synopses of the exploits of
Mungo Park, Gordon Laing, René Caillié and Heinrich Barth. The first and second
editions appear identical except for the addition of the word 'Discovery' to the title.
Jay M. Pasachoff's *An exploration near Agades and Timbuktu in advance of the 1973
total solar eclipse* (Pasadena, California: Munger Africana Library, Sept. 1971. 52p.)
describes his trip to Niger and Mali from 24 June to 12 July 1973. He provides
interesting comments on Bamako, where Dr P. J. Imperato escorted him around, as
well as on Tombouctou, Mopti and Dogon country.

58 **Forbidden sands: a search in the Sahara.**
Richard Trench. London: J. Murray, 1978. 197p. map.

In 1974, the adventurous author travelled nearly 1,000 miles by camel caravan from
Chegga, Mauretania, to the infamous salt mines of Taoudenni 'the meanest looking,
most impoverished collection of dwellings that I have ever seen' (p. 120) where 2,000
men produced 3,000 tons of salt each year. 'They were slaves all right – in a system of
debt-bondage' (p. 123). From there he went on to Timbuktu (p. 168-75). Throughout
he offers detailed, personal observations, sprinkled with those of earlier explorers. In
the 'Epilogue: a revolt in the desert' (p. 179-94), Trench describes his visit a year later
to Tindouf, Algeria, and his meeting with Polisario leaders in the Spanish Sahara. He
provides eleven photographs and a map of his journey from Tindouf, Algeria to
Timbuktu. Michael Asher's *Impossible journey: two against the Sahara* (London:
Viking, 1988. 301p.) – published in the US under the title *Two against the Sahara*
(New York: Morrow, 1988. 301p.) – is an account of a 1986 trip by camel and foot
across the Sahara from Nouakchott, Mauritania to Egypt's Nile River. Inspired by
Trench's account, Ernst Aebi describes his life in Araouane in *Seasons of sand* (New
York: Simon & Schuster, 1993. 236p.) where he tried to improve the life of the
villagers by planting trees and vegetables.

59 **Frail dream of Timbuktu.**
Bettina Selby. London: J. Murray, 1991. 230p. map.

The British author travelled through eastern Mali and western Niger on foot or by
canoe, bicycle or car (presumably in the 1980s). 'I was particularly eager to see what I
could of the life of the nomads of the Sahel before they disappeared' (p. 4). Her route
covered Niamey, Niger and into the Aïr Mountains, along the Niger River to Gao and
Timbuktu, through Dogon country, to Djenne, Segou and Bamako. The work includes
eight pages of colour photographs.

60 **Le Mali aujourd'hui.** (Mali today.)
Sennen Andriamirado. Paris: Editions J. A., 1985. 239p. maps.
bibliog.

This excellent guide in French has seventy-two pages of colour photographs by Guy
de Foy and ten maps and plans. The book consists of three parts. Part one (p. 12-97)

surveys geography, flora and fauna, people, the arts, religion and ritual, economy and history. Part two (p. 98-201) describes twenty-two towns, cities, regions and locations, including the Parc National du Baoulé, Dogon country and the Niger Bend. Part three (p. 202-35) offers practical tourist information on reaching Mali, daily life, sports and entertainment, souvenirs, cuisine and tea ('the national drug'). A useful bibliography of French works is included (p. 236) as is an index (p. 237).

61 **Mali, Côte d'Ivoire, Sénégal.**
Mylène Rémy. Paris: Flammarion, 1985. 381p.

This fine guide covers Mali (p. 185-241), Côte d'Ivoire (p. 243-304) and Senegal (p. 305-70) in detail. Preliminary pages (p. 15-183) discuss the region in general, history, religion, social structure, art and literature, practical travel information including crossing the Sahara, and 'Les trois pays de A à Z' (p. 163-83), an alphabetical potpourri of terms. The Mali section describes Bamako and environs, Segou, Djenné, Mopti, Tombouctou, Gao, Sangha and Dogon country and Sikasso and Senoufo country. It includes maps of only Bamako and Mali. Jacqueline Jagu-Roche's *Guide de Bamako: Soudan français, A. O. F.* (Guide to Bamako: French Sudan, French West Africa) published by Service de l'Information, Territoire du Soudan ([n.p.], 1957. 128p.) is of special interest for its photographs, historical information and advertisements. It includes train schedules, lists of officials, telephone numbers and plans of Bamako and Koulouba.

62 **La piste interdite de Tombouctou.** (The forbidden road to Timbuktu.)
Alain Kerjean. Paris: Flammarion, 1984. 288p. (L'Aventure vécue).

Sponsored in part by the Société de Géographie de Paris, the author, Alain Dillon, Emmanuel Guillon and Philippe Barnier retrace René Caillié's 1827-28 travels to Timbuktu through Guinea and northern Côte d'Ivoire during the period from October 1982 to January 1983. He entered Mali on 15 December. Four chapters (p. 191-277) describe their month in Mali, Djenne, the Niger River and Timbuktu. The account of their trip is well integrated with descriptions of Caillié's journey. Throughout the book are dozens of photographs, most in colour, of Guinea and Mali – these were taken by Guillon. The annex (p. 281-85) has a chronology of Caillié's life (1799-1838), a list of European efforts to reach Timbuktu (1670-1893), and a chronology of the French colonization of Guinea. A brief bibliography is included (p. 286-87).

63 **The primitive city of Timbuctoo.**
Horace Miner. Garden City, New York: Anchor Books, 1965. rev. ed. 334p. maps. bibliog.

The author gives us the first full ethnographic account in English of the city, based on his seven months' residence in 1940 to 'provide a picture of primitive urban life' (Introduction, p. xi). He recounts the city's history, but emphasizes the social organization and beliefs of its (then) ethnic groups: Arabs, Tuareg, Bela and Songhoi (Songhay). Miner includes twenty-four photographs, fourteen maps and diagrams, an excellent bibliography, glossary and index. A 'Foreword to the Anchor Edition' (p. vii-viii) and 'Some further consideration' (p. 301-5) have been added to this revised edition, and the bibliography has been updated. Miner also wrote 'Songhoi circumcision', *American Anthropologist*, vol. 44 (1942), p. 625-31, based on this fieldwork.

64 **The Republic of Mali.**
Raymond Brassié.   Paris: Edition La Revue Française, 1969. 24p.
maps.

This well-illustrated booklet provides an informative survey of the country. There are suggested itineraries and short articles including Massa-Makan Diabaté's 'Oral tradition and Mali literature' (p. 2-4), information on the agricultural economy, and a map of Bamako. *Tourist passport, Republic of Mali* by the Commissariat au Tourisme (Paris: Editions Delroisse for the Commissariat, [n.d.]. 46p. map) is in English, shaped like a passport and contains basic 'Practical information for tourists coming to Mali', including a glossary of English and French terms, distances from Bamako to forty-one other cities and towns (p. 42) and a simple tourist map (p. 44-45). A similar guide in French (59p.), *Passeport touristique, République du Mali* (Tourist's passport, Republic of Mali) (Bamako: Office Malien de Tourisme, [n.d.]) has more photographs and a lexicon in French, Bambara and English (p. 55). It describes a route through French Sudan, the Niger River from Gao to Timbuctu and Bamako, the Dogon country and the National Game Preserve of the Baole Loop, and is written by the Inspector General of Water and Forests (Dakar: Office du Tourisme de l'Afrique Occidentale Française, 1958. 4th ed. 54p.).

65 **The road to Timbuctoo.**
John Skolle.   London: V. Gollancz, 1956. 221p. bibliog.

The American author describes two trips across the Sahara in the early 1950s, the first through Algeria to the Hoggar region and Tamanrasset. Two years later (the date is never made clear), he crossed the desert from Algeria to Taoudeni, Mali, by camel caravan and finally on to Timbuctoo itself. Chapters include 'Araouan' (p. 163-91) and 'Timbuctoo' (p. 195-221). Descriptions of the trip are supplemented by relevant historical accounts and information on the Tuareg with whom he travelled. He includes three maps and nineteen photographs, one of which shows 'The author (hands badly swollen from heat and insect bites).'

66 **Sahara handbook.**
Simon Glen.   Brentford, England; New York: R. Lascelles; distributed by Hunter, 1990. 3rd ed. 519p. maps. bibliog.

In this superb practical guide to travelling through the Sahara, the author has written brief but highly useful chapters on many topics: flora and fauna, climate and desertification, history, peoples, explorers and conquerors. He includes maps and an excellent annotated bibliography; details about visas and vaccinations, banks and mail; and information on vehicles, camping equipment, personal health and hygiene, and survival and navigation. Although the reader will not find much in the index on the subject of Mali, it is covered as appropriate (in both the history and peoples chapters, for example) as well as in two north–south (Adrar, Algeria to Gao; Gao to Niamey, Niger) and five east–west (including visiting Gao, Timbuktu, Mopti, Segou, and Bamako) suggested itineraries listed on the map on pages 316-17. There is also detailed information about where petrol (fuel) is available, when to check in with the police, as well as excellent sketch maps which note types of road surfaces and areas which are impassable during the rainy season. Dr K. E. M. Melville's *Stay alive in the desert* (London: R. Lascelles, 1981. 2nd ed. 136p.) although written for Libya in 1970, is an excellent resource for those making a desert crossing. Bénédicte Vaes, Gérard del Marmol and Albert d'Otreppe's *Guide du Sahara* (Sahara guide) (Paris: Librairie Hachette, 1977. 717p.) includes a section 'Sahara et Sahel maliens' (p. 573-621) with first-rate directions for French readers travelling from Niamey, Niger, to Gao, Tombouctou and Mopti, with sketch maps of each route and city and a brief French–Bambara word list (p. 581). *Transafrique: toute l'Afrique en voiture* (Transafrica: all of Africa by car) (Geneva: Editions Olizane, 1995. 8th ed. 687p.) has a chapter on Mali (p. 187-213) containing forty-seven automobile routes and sketch maps of Gao, Mopti, and Timbuktu. It is the continuation of the Swiss Touring Club's *Transafrique: description de routes* (Geneva: Touring Club Suisse, 1983. 6th ed. 425p.) which includes more detailed maps of Malian routes shown on maps F and G.

67 **Sahel, Land der Nomaden.** (The Sahel: land of nomads.)
    Hans Ritter.   Munich, Germany: Trickster, 1986. 270p. bibliog.
The author describes, in German, the peoples and places he encountered during his travels in 1973-74 and 1976-77. In the chapter 'Mali' (p. 127-87) he records observations in and around Bamako, on Islam and on a trip to Timbuktu with Tuaregs. Other chapters describe Morocco, Mauretania and Niger.

68 **Sahel: Senegal, Mauretanien, Mali, Niger: islamische und
    traditionelle schwarzafrikanische Kultur zwischen Atlantik und
    Tschadsee.** (The Sahel: Senegal, Mauretania, Mali, and Niger: Islamic
    and traditional black African culture between the Atlantic and Lake
    Chad.)
    Thomas Krings.   Cologne, Germany: Dumont Buchverlag, 1985. 2nd
    rev. ed. 429p. maps. bibliog. (DuMont Kultur-Reiseführer).
This excellent, well-illustrated (51 colour and 93 black-and-white photographs, 151 drawings, plans and maps) guide in German covers the geography, peoples, culture and history of the Sahel (p. 12-105), Senegal (p. 106-82), Mauretania (p. 183-250), Mali (p. 251-324) and Niger (p. 325-92), and includes a glossary (p. 393-96), a bibliography (p. 397-400, 424) and practical advice for trips (p. 401-24). The Mali section includes useful detail on Bamako, Segu, Djenné, Hamdallaye, Mopti, Dogon country, the Inland Niger Delta, Timbuktu and Gao. The first edition published in 1982 is nearly identical.

69 **Sailing to Timbuctoo.**
    John Marriner.   London: W. Kimber, 1973. 276p. maps.
During the summer and autumn of 1971, the author and his 'faithful seaman-chauffeur' drove a Range Rover from Tlemcen, Algeria, to Mali, Niamey, Agades, Tamanrasset and back across the Sahara. In Mali (p. 146-92), he passed through Amachach, Tessalit, Gao, went by boat to Kabara and on to Timbuctoo, and then drove back along the Niger River to Gao and the border of Niger. Thirteen of the book's fifty-four photographs concern Mali.

70 **The slaves of Timbuktu.**
    Robin Maugham.   London: Longmans, 1961. 234p.
The author integrates extensive excerpts from the accounts of earlier travellers with an expanded diary of his own trip which lasted from 18 December 1958 to 24 February 1959. He travelled by rail, road and steamer to Timbuktu. During his journey he was particularly struck by the presence of slaves among the Tuareg, and he purchased and freed a young male Bela from his Tuareg master for 25,000 francs. The book includes

23

maps of Maugham's route and the routes of G. Laing and R. Caillié, forty-five photographs, chapter notes (p. 221-31) with bibliographical references, and an index.

71 **Timbuctoo, the myth and reality.**
Pascal J. Imperato, Eleanor M. Imperato. *Explorers Journal,* vol. 55, no. 4 (Dec. 1977), p. 146-53.
This article is the best one available describing the past grandeur and present reality of Timbuctoo. E. M. Imperato offers her first impressions during a 1973 trip; P. J. Imperato surveys Timbuctoo's history and describes the city – his observations are based on a month's stay in 1968 and five visits from 1967 to 1975. His account of the city's ethnic groups (Tuareg, Bella, Songhay and Arab) is ethnographically useful, and anyone planning to visit the city will find this article valuable. Elsewhere, P. J. Imperato also provides a popular, illustrated introduction to the fabled city, a social sketch and information on 'getting there' in 'Timbuktu, a city of the past', *Off Hours,* vol. 3, no. 2 (April 1986), p. 17-21. Djibril Diallo enters a plea for international aid to preserve historic Timbuktu in 'City in the sands', *West Africa,* no. 3667 (23 Nov. 1987), p. 2288-89. Klaus-Friedrich Koch explains Timbuktu's mystique and offers an engaging summary of the city's past and present in 'Fabulous Timbuktu', *Natural History,* vol. 86, no. 5 (May 1977), p. 68-75, 77, 96. Eric Fottorino provides a brief recent account of Timbuktu in 'Among the dunes', *World Press Review,* vol. 37, no. 4 (April 1990), p. 77. Tahir Shah's 'The Islamic legacy of Timbuktu', in *Aramco World,* vol. 46, no. 5 (Nov.-Dec. 1995), p. 10-17, is beautifully illustrated with photographs by Stephenie Hollyman.

72 **Timbuktu.**
Remer Tyson. *Chicago Tribune* (12 Jan. 1997, Section 8, p. 19).
This recent article on travelling in Mali gives some brief highlights of the history of Timbuktu in order to encourage tourism in Mali. The cease-fire between the Tuaregs, the 'lords of the desert', and the Mali government means tourism is now safe in Mali. A few places where tourists can find accommodation are recommended, such as the Boucto Hotel (Hôtel Buktu) in Timbuktu and the Grand Hotel in Bamako.

73 **To Timbuktu.**
Mark Jenkins. New York: W. Morrow, 1997. 224p. map. bibliog.
In 1991, Jenkins and three companions took a trip, by kayak, along the Niger River, searching for its source in the mountains of Guinea. After some further harrowing adventures in Algeria and Tunisia, Jenkins motorcycled alone from Bamako to Djenne, then took a ship from Mopti to Timbuktu. His text (which does not follow a typical chronological order) is richly sprinkled throughout with European explorers' accounts.

74 **Tombouctou.** (Timbuktu.)
Edited by Abbas Kader, Michel Baron, preface by Léopold Sédar Senghor. Poitiers-Ligugé, France: Imprimerie Aubin, Editions Comité de Jumelage Saintes–Tombouctou, 1986. 222p. maps. bibliog.
This interesting compendium, profusely illustrated with colour and black-and-white photographs, historical prints and maps, covers the city's geography, history, fauna, daily life, agriculture, architecture, musical instruments, peoples, a description of a

1983 trip to Tombouctou from Tangier, a glossary (p. 221-22), and a brief bibliography (p. 222). René Caillié, who visited Tombouctou in 1828, was from the Saintes region and today the French city of Saintes and Tombouctou are 'twinned' cities.

75 **Traveller's guide to West Africa.**
    Edited by Alan Rake. London: IC Publications; Edison, New Jersey:
    Hunter, 1988. 7th ed. 274p. maps.

The chapter on Mali in this popular guide (p. 188-97) describes the Niger River, culture, history, economy and wildlife, and gives 'general information' with brief notes on Bamako, Djenne, Mopti, Timbuktu and Gao. 'Mali is a country that amply rewards the trouble taken to reach it' (p. 189).

76 **Two rivers: travels in West Africa on the trail of Mungo Park.**
    Peter Hudson. London: Chapmans, 1991. 251p. map.

The author travelled much the same West African route that Mungo Park had described in 1799 in his *Travels into the interior of Africa* (see item no. 45). The map (p. x-xi) graphically shows the reader exactly where Hudson went in his trip through the Gambia, Senegal, Guinea-Bissau, and Mali (completed in March 1991). The focus of the book is on his stay in Mali where he visited Kayes, Nioro, Bamako, Segou and Mopti. See also Hudson's account of his earlier voyage to Africa in *A leaf in the wind* (London: Columbus Books, 1988. 267p.) in which he vividly describes his travels through Africa in the 1980s, focusing on Mali (p. 23-65), Zaïre (p. 67-157) and Somalia (p. 159-267). In Mali he recounts 'Djenne and a walk' (p. 23-46) and 'Matomio' (p. 47-65). He briefly describes Djenne, Segou and a short boat trip on the Niger, but concentrates on his 70-kilometre walk from Djenne to Sai and on the village of Matomio, east of Sai.

77 **West Africa, a Lonely Planet travel survival kit.**
    Alex Newton, David Else. Hawthorn, Australia; Oakland, California:
    Lonely Planet, 1995. 3rd ed. 924p. (Lonely Planet Travel Survival Kit).

The chapter on Mali (p. 519-83) in this excellent guide covers history, peoples, geography, climate, visas, money, language, general information, getting there, Bamako, the Niger River route (Ségou, San, Mopti, Djenné, Timbuktu, Gao), Dogon country, Sikasso and Keyes. It includes simple maps of Bamako, Ségou, Mopti, Djenné, Timbuktu, Gao, trekking routes in the Dogon country, Bandiagara and Kayes. This third edition includes informative chapters on the art and people, as well as the birds of West Africa, and includes many colour photographs of Mali. Geoff Crowther's excellent *Africa: a Lonely Planet shoestring guide* (same publisher, May 1995. 7th ed. 1,100p.) contains similar information on the country (p. 523-43) and sketch maps of Mali, Timbuktu, Bamako, Mopti and Dogon country as well as information on visas, currency, transport and accommodation in the major towns. William Langewiesche describes vividly his 800-mile trip 'Riding the Mali express to Dakar' in the *New York Times* (25 Nov. 1990), sect. 5, p. 14, 16 and includes a map and photograph. In 'The long, long road to Timbuktu', *Travel & Leisure,* vol. 25, no. 2 (Feb. 1995), p. 136-51, 169, Ted Conover describes a tour by twelve Americans to Timbuktu, from Mopti to Konna by boat, and to Tireli village in the Dogon country. The article includes fine photographs by Aldo Rossi as well as paintings and a map by Marc Lacaze and descriptions of four tour 'outfitters'.

78 **West Africa: the rough guide.**
Written and researched by Richard Trillo and Jim Hudgens, additional research on this edition by Emma Gregg, Chris Scott and Jo Winter. London: Rough Guides; distributed by Penguin Books, 1995. 2nd ed. 1,274p. maps. bibliog. (Rough Guides).

Arguably the best source on travel in West Africa. Mali is covered in chapter 4 (p. 291-361) of this excellent, recently updated comprehensive guide. Coverage includes: maps and travel information including transport, hotels, restaurants, nightlife, currency; a brief history; information on Bamako and the regions surrounding Kayes, Ségou, San and Sikasso, Mopti, Djenné, Timbuktu, Dogon country, Bandiagara, Sanga, Koro and Gao; and an index on Mali. Part 3 includes a brief bibliography on Mali (p. 1227-28), and sections on the cinema of Mali (p. 1241-42) as well as Malian and Manding music (p. 1248-50). The compact disc of music created to accompany this book, *The Rough guide to West African music* (London: World Music Network, 1995), contains 5 songs by Malians.

79 **West African travels: a guide to people and places.**
Sylvia Ardyn Boone. New York: Random House, 1974. 1st ed. 430p. maps. bibliog.

The late author includes a useful guide to Mali (p. 97-119) as one of the fourteen countries covered. She focuses on Bamako, its sights, hotels, restaurants and night clubs, but also offers lucid commentary on Mali's history, merchants, legal matters such as visas and photography permits, and suggests other places to visit near the capital.

Geography and Geology

Geography

80 **A comprehensive geography of West Africa.**
Reuben K. Udo. New York: Africana Publishing Co., 1978. 304p.
maps. bibliog.

'The Republic of Mali' (p. 197-208) is one of the very useful geographical studies of the country. In this volume there are also broad regional studies of 'The physical background', 'Resources and economic growth', and 'Regional contrasts'. Mali appears in other standard geographies of the region: 'Mali' (p. 100-3) in H. O. N. Oboli and R. J. Harrison Church's *An outline geography of West Africa* (London: Harrap, 1967. 5th ed. 224p.); 'Countries of the French community', (p. 126-57) in F. G. Higson's *A certificate geography of West Africa* (London: Longman's, Green, 1961. 223p.); 'Soudan (Senegal & Mali)' (p. 223-33) in J. C. Pugh and A. E. Perry's *A short geography of West Africa* (London: University of London, 1960. 288p.); and 'Mali' (p. 685-89) in W. B. Morgan and J. C. Pugh's *West Africa* (London: Methuen, 1969. 788p.).

81 **Le Delta intérieur du Niger: étude de géographie régionale.** (The Inland Niger Delta: a study in regional geography.)
J. Gallais. Dakar: IFAN, 1967. 2 vols. maps. bibliog.

This massive, exceptionally complete study (621 consecutive pages) of the Inland Niger Delta contains an introduction and five parts: geology, geography, flora, early settlements; human populations, including demography; the cultivators of the Delta; pastoralists and fishermen; and commercial and urban life in the Delta. It is especially rich in information on Djenné and Mopti. In addition to forty photographs, forty-seven figures and a lengthy bibliography (p. 613-18), it includes six separate maps (scale 1 cm represents 10 km): ethnic distribution; population density; Peul locations; markets; movements of pastoralists; and morphology and geography). Gallais also wrote a companion volume with the same title but subtitled: *Etude morphologique*

(Morphological study) (Paris: Editions du Centre National de la Recherche Scientifique, 1967. 153p.) which discusses the region's geomorphology, that is, the structure of the earth's features. Gallais takes a fresh look at the same region in his *Hommes du Sahel* (Men of the Sahel) (Paris: Flammarion, 1984. 289p.) where he looks at time and space of the ethnic groups in the region and analyses regional development efforts. See also R. J. McIntosh's 'Floodplain geomorphology and human occupation of the upper Inland Delta of the Niger', *Geographical Journal,* vol. 149, no. 2 (1983), p. 182-201.

82 **Fishing in the Pondo.**
    Pierre Maas, Geert Mommersteeg. *Aramco World,* vol. 41, no. 4
    (1990), p. 22-31. map.

The authors, an architect and an anthropologist respectively, describe the Inner Niger Delta, or Pondo as it is called locally, its geography, history and peoples, especially the Bozo fishermen. Brynn Bruijn contributes numerous photographs. See also Christopher Winters's 1973 doctoral thesis at the University of California, Berkeley, 'Cities of the Pondo: the geography of urbanism in the interior Niger Delta of Mali' (578p.).

83 **Mali: eine geographische Landeskunde.** (Mali: a cultural geography.)
    Hans Karl Barth. Darmstadt, Germany: Wissenschaftliche
    Buchgesellschaft, 1986. 395p. maps. bibliog. (Wissenschaftliche
    Länderkunden, Band 25).

This model study examines the historical, socio-economic and geo-ecological sources of Mali's underdevelopment; the geological, geographical and floral background; the limitations and potentials of the geographical setting; and the social setting, including population structure, migration, cities and towns, traditional industries, fishing and tourism and prospects for development in the future. The information-rich volume contains 57 figures, many of them maps, 71 tables, 26 photographs and an excellent bibliography (p. 353-80), as well as name and subject indexes (p. 381-95).

84 **Mali: official standard names approved by the United States Board
    on Geographic Names.**
    United States, Department of the Interior, Office of Geography.
    Washington, DC: US Government Printing Office, 1965. 263p. map.

This gazetteer has about 17,800 entries for places and features in Mali, including 'standard names approved by the Board on Geographic Names and unapproved variant names, the latter cross-referenced to the standard names' (Foreword, p. i). For example,'Timbuktu' is described as the conventional term, but also included are 'Tombouctou' (French), 'Tombutu', 'Timboctú', and 'Timbuctú'.

Geology

85 **La boucle du Niger (Mali): cartes géomorphologiques et notice projet d'aménagement.** (The Niger Bend (Mali): geomorphological maps and development project notice.)
Jean Pierre Blanck. Strasbourg, France: ULP, Centre de Géographie Appliqué, 1968. 2 vols. map.

This set of materials consists of two booklets and twelve large folding maps of the Niger River basin between Tombouctou and Labbezanga showing geology, hydrology and lithology. The booklets are 'Notice des cartes géomorphologiques de la vallée du Niger entre Tombouctou et Labbezanga (République du Mali)' (Notice of geomorphological maps of the Niger basin between Tombouctou and Labbezanga, Republic of Mali) (31p.), a systematic description and evaluation of the area, with photographs, and 'Projet d'aménagement de la vallée du Niger entre Tombouctou et Labbezanga (Etude géomorphologique)' (Development project of the Niger basin between Tombouctou and Labbezanga, a geomorphological study) (41p.), describing the geomorphological project for the region.

86 **Geology and mineral resources of West Africa.**
J. B. Wright. London; Boston, Massachusetts: Allen & Unwin, 1985. 187p. maps. bibliog.

This regional study is not arranged by country but by geological period and sedimentary basins (e.g., Niger Delta Basin (p. 107-8) and Taoudeni Basin (p. 82-85)). See also Nicolas de Kun's *The mineral resources of Africa* (Amsterdam; London; New York: Elsevier, 1965. 740p. maps. bibliog.) which discusses Mali's bauxite, copper, diamonds, gold, iron ore and zinc deposits in this comprehensive resource for the continent. It offers a history of mining and a country-by-country overview of minerals (Mali, p. 78-79) and describes each mineral, its geology, location and history of extraction. Another source is J. M. Bertrand's *Afrique de l'Ouest: introduction géologique et termes stratigraphiques = West Africa: geological introduction and stratigraphical terms* (Oxford; New York: Pergamon Press, 1983. 396p.). In Chapter 1b (p. 17-26), the general reader will find an introduction to the geology of West Africa, written in English. The other chapters that contain information on Mali are written in French, and would be of interest to the more serious scholar of stratigraphical geology. The 'Lexique stratigraphique' (p. 175-356) defines specific stratigraphical terms and gives the geographical location for each one. The chronological geological index (p. 357-65) also gives the geographical location.

87 **Plan minéral de la République du Mali.** (Mineral plan of the Republic of Mali.)
H. Traoré, J. Méloux, coordinated by J. P. Bassot. Orleans, France: Direction des Recherches et du Développement Minières; Bamako: Direction Nationale de la Géologie et des Mines, 1978. 631p. maps. bibliog.

The development of mineral resources is the goal of this official Malian plan. It includes chapters on historical geological cartography, the geology of Mali, prospecting finds through to 1978, currently known mineral resources, and a proposed plan for future mineral development. This study revealed important findings of phosphates, bauxites, iron, gold, spodumene, manganese and base metals which had not yet been exploited. Many maps are included throughout the text, as well as eleven additional maps (in a pocket) covering various mining and petroleum permits, geological maps, and diamond prospecting. For recent studies on prospecting and the mining of gold in Mali, see Pobanou Hugues Diarra's *L'or, est-il l'une des futures sources de richesses pour le Mali?: résultats du Projet Or Bagoé: document de travail* (Gold, is it one of the future sources of riches for Mali?) (Bamako: Centre Djobila, 1991. 18 leaves); and Philippe Freyssinet's *Géochimie et minéralogie des latérites du Sud-Mali: évolution du paysage et prospection géochimique de l'or* (Geochemistry and mineralogy of the laterites of southern Mali: evolution of the countryside and geochemical prospecting for gold) (Orleans, France: Editions du BRGM, 1991. 277p.) which contains an abstract in English on the back cover.

88 **The Sahara and the Nile: Quaternary environments and prehistoric occupation in northern Africa.**
Edited by Martin A. J. Williams, Hugues Faure. Rotterdam, The Netherlands: Balkema, 1980. 607p. maps. bibliog.

This impressive volume of twenty-two well-illustrated articles covering the huge physical and human terrain of northern Africa includes at least three articles relevant to Malian studies: M. Mainguet, L. Canon, and M. C. Chemin's 'Le Sahara: géomorphologie et paléomorphologie éoliennes' (p. 17-35); M. R. Talbot's 'Environmental responses to climatic change in the West African Sahel over the past 20,000 years' (p. 37-62); and Sharon E. Nicholson's 'Saharan climates in historic times' (p. 173-200). Susan E. Smith's 'The environmental adaptation of nomads in the West African Sahel: a key to understanding prehistoric pastoralists' (p. 467-87) is based on her nine months' fieldwork among Mali's Kel Tamasheq. Notable also is Robert Capot-Rey's *Le Sahara français* (The French Sahara) (Paris: Presses Universitaires de France, 1953. 564p.). Northern Mali is part of the large region whose characteristics, climate, human populations and impact by French development are described in full for the time. The bibliography (p. 494-541) lists 818 works by subject.

89 **Sahara ou Sahel?: quaternaire récent du bassin de Taoudenni (Mali).** (Sahara or Sahel? The Recent Quaternary of the Taoudenni Basin in Mali.)
Edited by N. Petit-Maire, J. Riser, foreword by R. W. Fairbridge.
Paris: Laboratoire de Géologie du Quaternaire du Centre National de la Recherche Scientifique, 1983. 473p. maps. bibliog.

This important book consists of five sections and a general discussion in French although each chapter has an English summary. The sections are: 'L'actuel' (p. 21-44) with articles on geography and climate by J.-C. Celles and J. Riser, 'Vegetation' by J.-C. Celles and R. Manière, 'Fauna' by N. Petit-Maire, and 'Current human problems' by M. Gast; 'Geology and morphology' (p. 45-119) with articles by J. Riser, C. Hillaire-Marcel, P. Rognon, and G. Coudé; 'Palaeobotany' (p. 121-48) with articles by J.-C. Celles and E. Schulz, I. Soulié-Marsche and S. Servant-Vildary; 'Palaeofauna' (p. 149-272) with articles by S. Kelner-Pillault, J.-C. Rosso, P. Carbonel, L. Blanc-Vernet, M. Gayet, F. de Broin, C. Guérin, M. Faure and E. Buffetaut; and 'Palaeoanthropology and prehistory' (p. 273-409) with articles by

O. Dutour and N. Petit-Maire, O. Dutour, M. Raimbault, D. Commelin, and H. Camps-Fabrer. N. Petit-Marie provides a 'general discussion' (p. 411-18). An annex (p. 419-41) by J. Fabre 'Le Sahara Malien septentrional' (The northern Malian Sahara) focuses on Taoudenni and Trhaza, latitude 22-24° north. In addition to 58 tables, 60 plates, 85 figures and extensive chapter bibliographies, there is a map (scale 1:1,000,000) of the Malian Sahara in the Holocene.

Maps and atlases

90 **Atlas du Mali.** (Atlas of Mali.)
Under the direction of Mamadou Traoré, with Yves Monnier, preface by
Amadou Hampâté Bâ.   Paris: Editions J. A., 1980. 64p. bibliog.
(Les Atlas Jeune Afrique).

Eighteen experts, most located in Bamako, collaborated to produce this attractive, useful atlas. The succinct descriptions and colour maps cover topics such as relief, geology, hydrography, climate, biogeography, prehistory and history, population, agriculture, fishing, mining, energy and industry, communication, tourism, commerce, education, health, the Niger Bend, the Inner Niger Delta, the Office du Niger, Bamako and its region, and the Kayes Region. A glossary and nine references (p. 64) are included.

91 **Atlas historique de la boucle du Niger: synthèse des colloques de
Bamako et Niamey, 1975-1976-1977.** (Historical atlas of the Niger
Bend: a synthesis of the symposia of Bamako and Niamey, 1975, 1976,
1977.)
Yveline Poncet, with R. Mauny, J. Rouch, Y. Cissé, C. Meillassoux.
[Paris]: Association SCOA pour la Recherche Scientifique en Afrique
Noire, 1981. 23p. maps. bibliog. (Histoire et Tradition Orale).

This study contains twenty-two separate maps, most at a scale of 1:5,000,000, showing detailed locations of ancient empires, or hypothetical locations; and a booklet (23p.) describing the atlas, the transcriptions of place-names, the efforts at locating the ancient empires of Ghana, Mali and Songhay. The bibliography is on pages 21-23.

92 **The atlas of Africa.**
Regine van Chi-Bonnardel.   New York: Free Press; Paris: Jeune
Afrique, 1973. 335p. maps.

The atlas shows Mali in two useful colour maps (scale 1:8,000,000; p. 122-26). Three folio-sized pages of text describe the country's geography, history, population and economy. The US Army Map Service produced an excellent series of maps covering Mali in nine sheets, scale 1:1,000,000 (Washington, DC: Army Map Service, Corps of Engineers, 1959-64. Series 1301). The maps are updated from older British and French maps compiled in 1951-54. Tombouctou, for example, is on Series 1301, Sheet NE30, Edition 2-GSGS; Bamako is on Sheet ND29, Edition 4-AMS. An older but detailed series is Martonne M. Carde's *Atlas des cercles de l'Afrique Occidentale Française*, Fascicule VIII, *Soudan Français* (Paris: Maison Forest, 1925) showing Mali on maps 95-115, scale 1:500,000.

93 **Bamako et ses environs.** (Bamako and its environs.)
Institut Géographique National. Paris: Institut Géographique National; Bamako: Direction National de Cartographie et de Topographie, 1980. 4 sheets.

This excellent colour map (scale 1:20,000) shows the capital city on four sheets. An inset on the southeast sheet shows 'Communes du District de Bamako'. An earlier version (same title and scale) was published in October 1960 on a single sheet (Dakar: Service Géographique; Paris: Institut Géographique National, Ministère des Travaux Publics et des Transports de la République Française) on the basis of which the US Army Map Service published 'Bamako and its environs' in September 1963 (Series G923, Sheet Bamako, Edition 1-AMS, scale 1:12,500).

94 **Cartes ethno-démographiques de l'Afrique occidentale.**
(Ethno-demographic maps of West Africa.)
J. Richard-Molard, P. Pélissier, G. Brasseur, G. Savonnet, G. Le Moal, P. Mercier. Dakar: Institut Français d'Afrique Noire, nos. 1-5, 1952-63. maps. bibliog.

Sixteen large, separate fold-out maps, scale 1:1,000,000, show in remarkable detail the locations, approximate size and density of the sedentary and nomadic ethnic groups of West Africa up to the 17th parallel North. G. Brasseur charts the distribution of Mali's population in forty-two ethnic groups in the maps and text (1963. 29p.) grouped as 'Feuilles nos. 3 et 4 nord' (Sheets 3 and 4 North).

95 **Mali.**
Central Intelligence Agency. Washington, DC: Central Intelligence Agency, 1977. (no. 502728 9-77(542164)).

This small (22 cm × 17 cm, scale 1:11,000,000) map shows major cities and towns, rivers and three lakes of the Inland Niger Delta. An earlier version (1970; 44 cm × 47 cm, scale 1:4,000,000. no. 77257 4-70) shows relief by shading and spot heights and includes insets showing vegetation, economic activity and population and administrative divisions.

96 **Mali.**
Ministère des Relations Extérieures, Section Géographique.
Paris: Ministère des Relations Extérieures, Section Géographique, 1984.

This small, brightly-coloured map (scale 1:6,200,000) shows ethnic groups, administrative divisions and relief by spot heights. *République du Mali* (Paris; Dakar: Institut Géographique National, July 1971. 2nd ed. scale 1:2,500,000) shows relief, roads, distances, railroads, climatic and vegetation zones, administrative boundaries and populated places. Insets include a location map of West Africa and an indexed map of Mali showing administrative regions and *cercles*. The first edition was published in July 1962. The Office Malien du Tourisme published *République du Mali carte touristique* (Bamako, 1971. scale 1:2,500,000) which shows relief, roads, cities and towns and has an inset map of tourist itineraries. On the reverse side three inset maps show the location of Mali, economic features and tourist attractions, photographs and descriptions of the country, climate, history, and places where accommodation can be found.

97 **République du Mali.** (The Republic of Mali.)
   Issa Baba Traore, Bernard Aubriot.   Paris: F. Nathan, 1970. 17p. maps.
   (Mon Livret de Cartographie).
A small geography textbook with seventeen maps (no scale given) of Mali's relief, climate and vegetation, water resources, population, agriculture, herding and fishing, mines, industry and tourism and of each of six regions. Below each map is a series of study questions.

98 **Ville de Bamako, carte touriste.** (Tourist map of Bamako.)
   Commissariat au Tourisme.   Bamako: Institut National de
   Topographie, Section Cartographie, Commissariat au Tourisme, 1969.
This coloured tourist map (scale 1:10,000) shows streets clearly and is accompanied by a *Guide touriste de Bamako* (Tourist guide of Bamako) (Paris: Editions Delroisse, 1969. 64p.) edited by the Commissariat du Tourisme. The illustrated booklet contains information on ministries, hotels, points of interest, entry requirements, excursions, distances and a 'Petit lexique' of eighty words in French, English and Bambara. A larger map of Bamako (scale 1:5,000) showing streets, ministries, embassies and other features was published as a 'Carte touristique' in July 1966 by the Commissariat au Tourisme, B.P. 191, Bamako.

99 **West African international atlas. Atlas international de l'ouest africain.**
   Organisation of African Unity.   Dakar: Organisation of African Unity, Scientific, Technical and Research Commission, 1968-79. 3 vols. maps. bibliog.
The forty-four large colour maps, most of scale 1:5,000,000, and the gazetteer of the large region contain a wealth of information on Mali. Each map has a separate text in English and French and a bibliography. Maps include: 'Physical map'; 'Relief' (four maps); 'Geology' (two maps); 'Soils'; 'Annual elements of climate' (rainfall, temperature, vapour pressure); 'Zoogeography' (two maps); 'Population density'; 'Industries'; 'Transport routes'; 'Tourism'; 'Sources of energy'; 'Administration and political boundaries' (two maps); 'Schools'; and 'Medical facilities'. High-quality readily available regional maps include Bartholomew's *World Travel Map, Africa North-West* (Edinburgh: J. Bartholomew, 1983. Scale 1:5,000,000); Michelin's *Afrique Nord et Ouest/Africa North and West* (Paris: Michelin, 1983. Scale 1:1,400,000, no. 153); and Shell's *Africa: North and West* (Frankfurt, Germany: VWK, 1983. Scale 1:4,000,000).

The new atlas of African history.
See item no. 176.

Language map of Africa and the adjacent islands.
See item no. 309.

Flora and Fauna

100   **The bats of West Africa.**
D. R. Rosevear.   London: British Museum (Natural History), 1965.
418p. map. bibliog.

This scientific book covers ninety-seven species of bats of West Africa up to the northern limit of the 18th parallel of latitude (most of Sub-Saharan Mali). Illustrations include line-drawings (primarily of skulls) by Joanna Webb and the author. There is a chapter on the preservation of specimens, as well as a helpful gazetteer listing the place-names and countries cited in the literature and an accompanying fold-out map of the region (scale 1:10,000,000).

101   **The birds of tropical West Africa, with special reference to those of the Gambia, Sierra Leone, the Gold Coast and Nigeria.**
David Armitage Bannerman.   London: Crown Agents for the
Colonies, 1930- . 8 vols. maps. bibliog.

Birds found in Mali are among the 1,537 species described in this monumental work which provides the most detailed account of avifauna in the region. Bannerman's more succinct *The birds of West and Equatorial Africa* (Edinburgh: Oliver & Boyd, 1953. 2 vols) omits technical descriptions but still totals 1,526 pages. Other high-quality accounts of Mali's birds are: C. W. Mackworth-Praed and C. H. B. Grant's *Birds of West Central and Western Africa* (London: Longman, 1970, 1973. 2 vols), describing 1,371 birds north to latitude twenty degrees; and William Serle and Gérard J. Morel's *A field guide to the birds of West Africa* (London: Collins, 1977. 351p.), a practical field guide for 1,097 species, of which 726 are covered in detail. For the general reader, John H. Elgood's *Birds of the West African town and garden* (London: Longman, 1960. 66p.) describes and illustrates 100 of the most common birds.

34

102 **Bulletin de l'Association des Naturalistes du Mali.** (Bulletin of the Association of Malian Naturalists.)
Bamako: The Association, 1968- . irregular.

This valuable publication contains a wide range of articles on Mali's flora, fauna, environment and traditional medicine. Examples include: A. Konaré, 'La pêche au Mali' (Fishing in Mali), no. 3 (1972), p. 17-23; M. Koumaré, 'Pharmacopées, médecines traditionnelles africaines & thérapeutique moderne' (Pharmacopoeia, traditional African medicine and modern therapy), no. 3 (1972), p. 52-60; M. Cisse, 'La végétation des environs de Bamako' (Vegetation in the vicinity of Bamako), no. 4 (1973), p. 51-63 and no. 6 (1975), p. 57-73; and N'Golo Diarra, 'Quelques plantes utiles du Mali' (Some useful plants of Mali), no. 5 (1974), p. 31-47.

103 **The carnivores of West Africa.**
D. R. Rosevear. London: Trustees of the British Museum (Natural History), 1974. 548p. map. bibliog. (Publication, no. 723).

The author provides a formal description of carnivores north to the eighteenth parallel of latitude – thus including most of Sub-Saharan Mali – 172 line-drawings by P. Wolseley, M. Shaffer and R. Parsons, and an extensive bibliography (p. 524-37). Rosevear's *The rodents of West Africa* (London: Trustees of the British Museum (Natural History), 1969. 604p.) provides complete descriptions of the most diverse and most numerous mammalian group in the region.

104 **Catalogue des plantes vasculaires du Mali.** (Catalogue of the vascular plants of Mali.)
G. Boudet and-P. Lebrun, with the collaboration of R. Demange.
Maisons Alfort, France: Institut d'Elevage et de Médecine Vétérinaire des Pays Tropicaux, 1986. 480p. bibliog. (Etudes et Synthèses de l'I. E. M.V. T., no. 16).

The classification of Mali's 1,740 vascular plants is divided into pteridophytes, dicotyledons, and monocotyledons. The work includes a history of botanical explorations of Mali (p. 11-14), a bibliography (p. 437-61), an index of family names, and a genus index. Unfortunately, it is not illustrated.

105 **The dangerous snakes of Africa.**
Stephen Spawls, Bill Branch. London: Blandford, 1995. 192p. maps. bibliog.

This readable, recent guide to African venomous snakes covers 93 dangerous species (out of a total of some 400 African species). The description of each species includes its identification, distinguishing characteristics, behaviour, habitat, distribution, snakebite and treatment. On each distribution map, Mali can easily be found. The authors include a chapter as well as a bibliography on African snakebites.

106 **La faune avienne du Mali (Bassin du Niger).** (The avifauna of Mali's
Niger basin.)
P. Malzy. *L'Oiseau et la Revue Française d'Ornithologie* (Paris),
vol. 32 (1962). 81p. map. (Office de la Recherche Scientifique et
Technique Outre-Mer).

This unillustrated special number of the journal details the characteristics of about 220
bird species observed in the late 1950s in the Niger Basin and includes an index of
French and Latin names. *Les passereaux du Mali* (The sparrows of Mali) ([no author
given]. Bamako: Association des Naturalistes du Mali and Les Amis du Parc
Biologique de Bamako, 1970. 53 leaves) describes fifty-one bird species from ten
families. It includes French names, geographical distribution, characteristics, foods
and diagrams of the birds on separate detached pages.

107 **Faune du Sahara.** (Saharan animals.)
Michel Le Berre. Paris: Lechevalier-R. Chabaud, 1989-90. 2 vols.
maps. bibliog. (Terres Africaines).

The author of these attractive and useful volumes describes each animal formally and
locates it in a distribution map which includes Mali. Volume one covers fish,
amphibians and reptiles (332p. bibliog., p. 309-26); volume two covers mammals
(360p. bibliog., p. 329-54); a third volume on birds is in preparation.

108 **Flora of west tropical Africa, the British West African colonies,
British Cameroons, the French and Portuguese colonies south of
the Tropic of Cancer to Lake Chad, and Fernando Po.**
John Hutchinson, John McEwen Dalziel. London: Crown Agents,
1927, 1928, 1931, 1936, 1937. 3 vols. maps. bibliog.

This brilliant study, illustrated with numerous line-drawings, contains a brief account
of 'Botanical exploration in West Africa' for each colony covered and a bibliography
(vol. 1, pt. 1, p. 10-12) in addition to full descriptions of a vast array of vegetation.
J. M. Dalziel's *The useful plants of west tropical Africa* (1937. 612p.) forms a vastly
informative appendix to the first two volumes and has been updated by H. M. Burkill
(see item no. 122). R. W. J. Keay revised and edited volume one, part one in 1954 and
volume two, part two in 1958 for the second edition as did R. N. Hepper for volume
two in 1963, volume three, part one in 1968 and part two in 1972. A. H. G. Alston's
The ferns and fern-allies of west tropical Africa (London: Crown Agents, 1959) is a
supplement to the second edition.

109 **Flore et faune aquatiques de l'Afrique sahelo-soudanienne.**
(Aquatic flora and fauna of the African Sahel and Sudan.)
Edited by J.-R. Durand, C. Lévêque. Paris: ORSTOM, 1980-81.
2 vols. maps. bibliog. (Documentations Techniques, no. 45).

All of Mali falls within the zones covered by the thirty-five well-documented chapters
in these two fact-filled volumes. Volume one (389p.) describes aquatic plants,
protozoans, rotifers, sponges, molluscs and decapods. Volume two (p. 391-873)
includes insects, fish, amphibians, reptiles, birds and mammals. The study is indexed
by scientific name.

110 Flore forestière soudano-guinéenne: A. O. F. – Cameroun –
A. E. F. (Forest flora of the Guinea Sudan: French West Africa,
Cameroon and French Equatorial Africa.)
André Aubréville. Paris: Société d'Editions Géographiques,
Maritimes et Coloniales, 1950. 523p. 40 maps. bibliog.
This is a major work in folio size with 115 figures formally describing West African
flora, with emphasis on the former French colonies. The author (b. 1897) was
Inspector General of the Woods and Forests of the Colonies.

111 Flowering plants in West Africa.
Margaret Steentoft. Cambridge, England; New York: Cambridge
University Press, 1988. 344p. map. bibliog.
This valuable book presents the flowering plants of thirty-eight families found
throughout the broad region including the northern Guinea savannah, the Sudan
savannah and the Sahel of Mali. Introductory chapters discuss species associations
(p. 1-19) and 'Vegetation in West Africa' (p. 20-71). It includes numerous
bibliographical citations and drawings of the flowers and fruits of most plants. M. S.
Nielsen's earlier *Introduction to the flowering plants of West Africa* (London:
University of London, 1965. 246p.) is an excellent introduction to more than 600
species. Botanist Omotoye Olorode's *Taxonomy of West African flowering plants*
(London: Longman, 1984. 158p.) is another useful volume on plants of the region.

112 Guide pour la détermination des arbres et des arbustes dans les
savanes ouest-africaines: (documents pour l'étude de l'écologie des
glossines). (Guide for the determination of trees and shrubs in the West
African savannahs (documents for the study of the ecology of tsetse
flies).)
P. C. Morel. Maisons-Alfort, France: Institut d'Elevage et de
Médecine Vétérinaire des Pays Tropicaux, 1983. 89p. 80 leaves of
plates. maps. bibliog.
Morel lists the most important trees and shrubs for each climatic zone of the West
African savannah. The work includes an index of Latin names as well as their
equivalent in French, Wolof, Foula (Fulfulde), Bambara-Djula, and More (Moore)
(p. 50-78) and there are also clear line-drawings of leaves, flowers and fruits. See also
Ehya Ag Sidiyene's *Des arbres et des arbustes spontanés de l'Adrar des Iforas
(Mali): étude ethnolinguistique et ethnobotanique* (Trees and spontaneous shrubs from
the Adrar of the Iforas (Mali): ethnolinguistic and ethnobotanic study) (Paris:
ORSTOM; CIRAD, 1996. 137p.) for a Tuareg ethnobotanical study of northeastern
Mali.

113 The inundation zone of the Niger as an environment for
Palaearctic migrants.
Peter J. Curry, J. A. Sayer. *Ibis,* vol. 121, no. 1 (Jan. 1979), p. 20-40.
map. bibliog.
The authors describe 108 species of avifauna in Mali's Niger flood plain between
Ségou and Timbuktu in five habitats: wetland; hygrophilous grassland; transition zone;

non-flooded areas; and aerial. They include a detailed description of the climate and geography, a bibliography of twenty-seven key references and a list of common and scientific names for the birds.

114 **Large mammals of West Africa.**
D. C. D. Happold. Harlow, England: Longman, 1973. 105p. map. bibliog. (West African Nature Handbooks).

In this useful book the author discusses the characteristics, distribution, habits and status of seventy species of large mammals from seven orders and fourteen families as well as several species omitted from A. H. Booth's *Small mammals of West Africa* (London: Longman, 1960. 68p. 75 species). Among the national parks and game reserves described are those in Mali: Parc National de la Boucle du Baoulé (established 1952; 5,430 sq. km [2,174 sq. miles]); Réserve des Éléphants (est. 1959; 11,950 sq. km [3,500 sq. miles]); and Réserve de Ansongo-Menaka (date est. unknown; 17,500 sq. km [6,650 sq. miles]). For some animals he includes French, Fulani, Bambara or Songhay names.

115 **The last Sahelian elephants.**
Robert M. Pringle, Noumou Diakite. *Swara*, vol. 15, no. 5 (Sept./Oct. 1992), p. 24-27. map.

In the Gourma region of Mali the 'northernmost viable [elephant] population in Africa' is to be found (p. 24). Poaching is rare in this part of Africa, where the elephants coexist with the Tuareg and Peul populations. However, the nomad pastoralists have settled down and begun to farm, causing competition with the elephants for land and water.

116 **Medicinal plants in tropical West Africa.**
Bep Oliver-Bever, foreword by G. B. Marini Bettolo, preface by T. A. Lambo. Cambridge, England; New York: Cambridge University Press, 1986. 375p. bibliog.

In this remarkable study the author describes plants affecting the cardiovascular system, the nervous system, hormonal secretions, plants with anti-infective activity and those with oral hypoglycaemic action. For each plant, the author describes local uses, plant chemistry and pharmacology. Annik Thoyer-Rozat's *Plantes médicinales du Mali* (Medicinal plants of Mali) (France[?]: [n. p.], 1979. 173p. and also published in a smaller 21 cm. edition in 1981) includes a therapeutic guide organized by illness as well as an alphabetical guide of medicinal plants. The Bambara, Latin and French names are given in addition to the medicinal use and a black-and-white illustration (drawing or photograph). Also of great value is Edward S. Ayensu's *Medicinal plants of West Africa* (Algonac, Michigan: Reference Publications, 1978. 330p.) Ayensu, Director of the Endangered Species Program of the Smithsonian Institution, Washington, DC, illustrates 127 of the 187 medicinal plant species he describes. The useful bibliography (p. 297-300) has sixty-one references and the medicinal index is subdivided by medical problems. Of related interest is *Plantes médicinales contre les hepatites* (Medicinal plants to combat hepatitis) (Ouagadougou: Séminaire de Pabre, Nov. 1982. 62 leaves) by César Fernandez de la Pradilla in which he details the uses of fifty-one species for hepatitis.

117 **La pêche dans le delta central du Niger: approche pluridisciplinaire d'un système de production halieutique.** (Fishing in the central delta of the Niger: pluridisciplinary approach to a halieutic production system.) Jacques Quensière, scientific editor. Paris: ORSTOM : Karthala, 1994. 2 vols. maps. bibliog.

Each year, the Niger River floods the alluvial plain at what is called the Central Delta of the Niger, located entirely within the boundaries of Mali. This scholarly work on fisheries and fishing in Mali reviews the history of fishing in Mali, and considers the natural environment as well as social and technological conditions that impact on fishing in the area. Current problems in Malian fisheries are noted (e.g., overexploitation) and recommendations are made to improve them. The work includes an extensive bibliography (p. 479-95) and eight maps (scale 1:500,000) contained in the second volume.

118 **Les poissons du Niger supérieur.** (Fish of the upper Niger River.) J. Daget. Dakar: IFAN, 1954. 391p. map. bibliog.

The author describes in full species from twenty-six families of fish found in the Niger River from Gao to its headwaters. The work contains 1,412 line-drawings, a bibliography (p. 29, 35-36), vernacular names in Bambara, Bozo, Songhay and Peul (p. 375-81), an index of locality of capture (p. 381-82) and an index of scientific names (p. 382-91). Michael Holden and William Reed focus on eighty of the most common fish of some 200 species found in West Africa in the well-illustrated *West African freshwater fish* (London: Longman, 1972. 68p.). See also Alhassen Konare's *Les poissons du delta central du Niger* (Fish of the central Niger Delta) ([n.p.]: Laboratoire d'Hydrobiologie, 197-[?]. 79p.).

119 **Séminaire National sur le Dromadaire, 2-9 décembre 1985, Gao.** (National Seminar on the Camel, 2-9 December 1985, Gao.) Edited by Gudrun Dahl, for the Séminaire National sur le Dromadaire, 1985, Gao, Mali. Mogadishu: Somali Academy of Sciences and Arts, 1987. 111p. bibliog. (Camel Forum. Working paper, no. 18).

The one-humped camel, an important domestic animal in Mali, is discussed in thirteen papers from the conference. Topics range from herd structure, animal husbandry and parasites, to marketing situation, pastoral nomadism and future research programmes.

120 **Les serpents de l'ouest africain.** (Snakes of West Africa.) André Villiers, preface by J. Guib. Dakar: Université de Dakar, Institut Fondamental d'Afrique Noire, Les Nouvelles Editions Africaines, 1975. 3rd ed. 195p. maps. bibliog. (Initiations et Etudes Africaines, no. 2).

This model study, the best available for West Africa, describes the morphology, distribution, relations with humans, collection and conservation of snakes (p. 15-72) and offers a systematic description of six families (p. 73-171) members of which are identified in 280 figures. A list of West African snakes (p. 173-79), tables of scientific and common names (p. 180-90) and a bibliography (p. 191-95) appear in the Appendices. The author's *Tortues et crocodiles de l'Afrique noire française* (Turtles and crocodiles of Black French Africa) (Dakar: Université de Dakar, IFAN, 1958. 354p.) is also the best work on its subjects in the region. It has an extensive bibliography (p. 341-54) and 290 illustrations. In the popular West African Nature Handbooks series, G. S. Cansdale describes forty-three of the most common snakes in *West African snakes* (London: Longman, 1961. 74p.).

121   **Trees and shrubs of the Sahel: their characteristics and uses.**
       H.-J. von Maydell.   Eschborn, Germany: Deutsche Gesellschaft für
       Technische Zusammenarbeit, 1986. 525p. (Schriftenreihe der GTZ,
       no. 196).

In addition to the botanical characteristics of 114 species in the Sahelian and Sudanian subregion, this excellent useful source contains site requirements and ecology, propagation and conservation, as well as traditional and potential uses. For each plant there are multiple colour photographs. Appendix III contains vernacular names in the following languages: Bambara, Djerma, French, Gourmanche, Haussa, More (Moore), Peulh (Fulfulde), Serer, Tamacheq and Wolof. In *West African trees* (London: Longman, 1972. 72p.), D. Gledhill presents sixty-four of the most common and recognizable West African trees with their common and scientific names. This is a book for laypeople, illustrated with 121 colour and line-drawings by Douglas E. Woodall.

122   **The useful plants of west tropical Africa.**
       H. M. Burkill.   Kew, England: Royal Botanic Gardens, 1985- .
       2nd ed. 5 vols. map.

Most of Mali is in the region (south of 18 degrees N latitude and west of Chad) covered by this remarkable compilation of information on plant life and usage. The only illustration is a colour photograph of the cotton tree, *Ceiba pentandra,* a member of the family *Bombacaceae,* like the baobab tree. This family and its uses are covered thoroughly (p. 270-85) like all of Mali's other trees. The index of 'West African plant names' (p. 777-960) lists every local name the author could locate including many Bambara, Arabic, Tamacheq, Dogon and Songai names as well as a 'List of authorities cited for vernacular names' (p. 687-90); there are also an 'Index of plant species' (p. 691-731) and a list of 'Plant species by usages' (p. 733-76). This is a revision of J. M. Dalziel's 1937 masterpiece of the same title and is a supplement to the second edition of the *Flora of west tropical Africa,* revised and edited by Keay and Hepper (see item no. 108).

123   **A vision in Mali.**
       Ralph Ted Field.   *American Forests,* vol. 97, no. 7-8 (July/Aug.
       1991), p. 28-30, 70. map.

The author, the American Forestry Association's director of education, describes 'revolutionary' efforts by extension agent-farmers to plant a variety of trees (mangoes, *Prosopis, Leucaena* and papaya) on the Dogon plateau eventually to supply local needs for fuel, food, fodder and construction.

124   **West African butterflies and moths.**
       John Boorman.   London: Longman, 1970. 79p. bibliog.

Line-drawings by Richard Bonson, colour photographs by Ben Johnson and a bibliography (p. 77-79) enhance this non-technical description of 225 of the most common butterflies and moths, of which there are some 1,500 and 20,000 species respectively in West Africa. An interestingly detailed ethnozoological account is Marcel Griaule's 'Classification des insectes chez les Dogon' (Classification of insects by the Dogon), *Journal de la Société des Africanistes,* vol. 31 (1961), p. 7-71.

125 **West African lilies and orchids.**
    J. K. Morton.   [London]: Longmans, [1961]. 71p. (West African
    Nature Handbooks).
This slim volume, aimed at the general reader, contains descriptions of forty-eight genera of West African 'true' lilies, the Liliaceae and Amaryllidaceae. Nicely illustrated in colour by Iona Loxton, S. K. Avumatsodo and S. C. Rowles.

Quel usage des plantes médicinales au Mali aujourd'hui? (What use of medicinal plants in Mali today?)
See item no. 406.

Prehistory and
Archaeology

126 **Archaeological investigations of Iron Age sites in the Mema Region, Mali (West Africa).**
Tereba Togola.   PhD thesis, Rice University, Houston, Texas, 1993.
244p. maps. bibliog. (Available from University Microfilms
International, Ann Arbor, Michigan, 1993, order no. AAG9408674).

Based on field research in 1989-90 in a dry alluvial basin northwest of the Inland Niger Delta and south of the lakes region, the author describes iron-using peoples from a millennium ago. His regional site survey identifies 137 archaeological sites, 29 from the Late Stone Age and 108 from the Iron Age, and includes radiocarbon dates from the fourth to the fourteenth century AD. The thesis was directed by Susan Keech McIntosh who, together with her husband Roderick, is one of the pioneers of Malian archaeology.

127 **Archaeological reconnaissance in the region of Timbuktu, Mali.**
Susan Keech McIntosh, Roderick J. McIntosh.   *National Geographic Research*, vol. 2, no. 3 (1986), p. 302-19. maps. bibliog.

The authors report on a survey of 43 sites, adding to 'growing evidence of extensive first-millennium commercial contacts all along the middle Niger. Timbuktu (or an ancestral town) apparently once enjoyed hegemony over a hierarchy of settlements in its hinterland' (p. 302). The article includes several excellent maps and illustrations of sites and artefacts. R. J. and S. K. McIntosh report on an archaeological survey at Dia and link findings there to others at Jenne-jeno and the Timbuktu area in 'Prospection archéologique aux Alentours de Dia, Mali, 1986-1987', *Nyame Akuma* (Calgary), no. 29 (Dec. 1987), p. 42-45. Eric Huysecom contributed 'Preliminary report on excavations at Hamdallahi, Inland Niger Delta of Mali (February/March and October/November 1989)', *Nyame Akuma* (Ames, Iowa), no. 35 (June 1991), p. 24-28. Timothy Insoll authored 'A preliminary reconnaissance and survey at Gao', *Nyame Akuma*, no. 39 (June 1993), p. 40-43.

128 **Die archäologische Forschung in Westafrika.** (Archaeological
research in West Africa.)
Eric Huysecom.   Munich, Germany: C.H. Beck, 1987. 2 vols. maps.
bibliog. (Materialien zur Allgemeinen und Vergleichenden
Archäologie, Band 33).

In this remarkable resource, volume one (p. 1-307) offers an introduction and surveys
of the status of archaeological research in fifteen countries including Mali (p. 46-69);
numerous illustrations, some of Malian sites or artefacts; and a list of carbon-14 site
dates (Mali, p. 296). Volume two (p. 309-851) lists each archaeological site identified
in West Africa, its location, type and bibliographical references. For Mali (p. 417-97),
he lists 874 sites. The bibliography (p. 767-851) is invaluable. There are separate
maps for each country (Mali is map no. 8, but the scale is not shown). See also his
report on the excavation of a Neolithic rock shelter, *Fanfannyégèné I: un abri-sous-
roche à occupation néolithique au Mali: la fouille, le matériel archéologie, l'art
rupestre* (Fanfannyégèné I: a Neolithic rock shelter in Mali: excavation,
archaeological materials, rupestral art) (Stuttgart, Germany: Franz Steiner Verlag,
1990. 79p. + 98p. of plates. maps. bibliog.).

129 **An archeological ethnography of blacksmiths, potters, and masons
in Jenne, Mali (West Africa).**
Adria Jean LaViolette.   PhD thesis, Washington University, 1987.
437p. maps. bibliog. (Available from University Microfilms
International, Ann Arbor, Michigan, order no. 8812760).

Blacksmiths, potters, and masons have been present in the city of Jenné for over two
thousand years. The author presents her research, from an archaeological perspective,
on these particular groups of artisans, who continue to flourish there. She describes
who these artisans are, and how their crafts are organized, controlled and produced. A
final chapter outlines how one can conclude, from archaeological evidence, that these
artisans worked in groups and not just as individuals, in the past as well as now.

130 **Archéologie malienne: collections Desplagnes.** (Malian archaeology:
the Desplagnes collection.)
Annie M. D. Lebeuf, Viviana Pâques.   Paris: Muséum National
d'Histoire Naturelle, 1970. 56p. map. bibliog.

This volume describes formally the objects collected by Lt L. Desplagnes in the
region of Goundam and along the Niger River in 1901 and 1904, and now deposited in
the Musée de l'Homme. The brief bibliography notes five sources (p. 55), and the
objects are depicted in forty-nine figures and photographs.

131 **Bibliographie archéologique du Mali: 1900-1981.** (Archaeological
bibliography of Mali, 1900-81.)
Alpha Oumar Konaré.   Bamako: Editions Imprimeries du Mali, 1983.
77p.

The compiler brings together 542 numbered, unannotated citations, most of them from
French sources. They are indexed by author and region of the country. The most
prominent authors cited include: R. M. A. Bedaux; W. Filipowiak; J. Huizinga; R. J.
and S. K. McIntosh; R. Mauny; Th. Monod; E. Szumowski; and Fr de Zeltner. At the

43

time of publication, the archaeologist compiler, now Mali's president, worked at the Institut Supérieur de Formation et de Recherche Appliquée (ISFRA) in Bamako. Philip L. Ravenhill reviews briefly the exhibit 'Survol de l'archéologie Malienne' at the Musée National, Bamako, from 28 December 1983 to 24 March 1984 in 'Survol de l'archéologie malienne' (Overview of Malian archaeology), *African Arts*, vol. 17, no. 4 (Aug. 1984), p. 76.

132 **Changing paradigms, goals & methods in the archaeology of francophone West Africa.**
Philip de Barros. In: *A history of African archaeology*. Edited by Peter Robertshaw. London: James Currey; Portsmouth, New Hampshire: Heinemann, 1990, p. 155-72. bibliog.

In this excellent survey of evolving research orientations, methods and techniques, the author includes an historical overview of French archaeology, and francophone West African archaeology from the nineteenth century to the mid-1980s. There is also significant discussion of the work of Maurice Delafosse, Raymond Mauny, the Institut Français d'Afrique Noire (est. 1938), Roderick and Susan McIntosh and the emergence of African national priorities. Numerous useful sources appear in the extensive bibliography (p. 320-71). At the time of publication, the author taught ceramic analysis at the University of California at Los Angeles Institute of Archaeology.

133 **Clothing from burial caves in Mali, 11th – 18th century.**
Rita Bolland. In: *History, design, and craft in West Africa strip-woven cloth: papers presented at a symposium organized by the National Museum of African Art, Smithsonian Institution, February 18-19, 1988.* Washington, DC: National Museum of African Art, 1992, p. 53-81. bibliog.

The author reports on the analysis of more than 500 textiles, mostly cotton, some wool, found in nine of twenty-nine caves in the Tellem-Dogon Bandiagara region, and discusses the reconstruction of ancient tunics, caps and blankets. The article is well illustrated, and has useful technical information, a glossary and a bibliography.

134 **Complex societies of West Africa: their archaeology and early history.**
Edited by Roderick J. McIntosh, Susan Keech McIntosh. Houston, Texas: Rice University, Department of Anthropology, 1983. 43p. map. bibliog.

This volume contains five papers presented at a panel organized by the editors at the twenty-fifth annual meeting of the African Studies Association on 4 November 1982. The papers are: R. J. McIntosh, 'Trade and politics at early Jenne-jeno' (p. 1-9); Eugenia Herbert, 'Copper in the Iron Age: the archaeological evidence in a comparative context' (p. 10-16); Merrick Posnansky, 'Some reflections of a comparative nature on first millenium A.D. complex societies in West Africa' (p. 17-22); Timothy F. Garrard, 'Romans, Byzantines and the trans-Saharan gold trade' (p. 23-30); and J. O. Hunwick, 'Gao before 1500: trade and the implantation of Islam' (p. 31-43). R. J. McIntosh also authored *The pulse theory: genesis and accommodation of specialization in the Inland Niger Delta of Mali* (Houston, Texas: Rice University, Center for the Study of Institutions and Values, School of Social Sciences, March 1988. 11p. bibliog. Working paper, no. 4) which became 'The Pulse Theory: genesis and accommodation of specialization in the Middle Niger', *Journal of African History*, vol. 34, no. 2 (1993), p. 181-220, a brilliant discussion of likely patterns of development in the area, illustrated with diagrams and useful bibliographical citations.

135 **Ethnoarchéologie africaine: un programme d'étude de la céramique récente du Delta Intérieur du Niger (Mali, Afrique de l'Ouest).** (African ethnoarchaeology: a study programme of recent ceramics from the Niger Inland Delta.)
Alain Gallay, Eric Huysecom.   Geneva, Switzerland: Université de Genève, 1989. 126 leaves. maps. bibliog.

This preliminary report on work in 1988 and 1989 in an area of the Inland Delta explains in detail the collaborative effort between the University of Geneva and the Institut des Sciences Humaines, Bamako, to link historic and contemporary ceramics with those from archaeological excavations. The authors review other archaeological efforts in the region, make extensive use of historical records and provide many ceramic illustrations, a lengthy bibliography, maps, and a copy of survey protocols. The report was reviewed by S. Bernus in *Journal des Africanistes* (Paris), vol. 59, no. 1-2 (1989), p. 284-86. See also *Hamdallahi, capitale de l'empire peul du Massina, Mali: première fouille archéologique, études historiques et ethnoarchéologiques* by Gallay, Huysecom, M. Honegger and A. Mayor (Stuttgart, Germany: Franz Steiner Verlag, 1990. 58p. + 32p. of plates. maps. bibliog.) reviewed by Peter L. Shinnie in *Nyame Akuma* (Ames, Iowa), no. 36 (Dec. 1991), p. 54-55, and R. McIntosh in *Journal of African History*, vol. 34, no. 2 (1993), p. 325-26.

136 **Excavations at Jenné-Jeno, Hambarketolo, and Kaniana (Inland Niger Delta, Mali), the 1981 season.**
Edited by Susan Keech McIntosh.   Berkeley, California: University of California Press, 1995. 605p. bibliog. (University of California Publications in Anthropology, vol. 20).

Supplemented by many drawings, charts, and plates, the text of this extensive work presents and interprets the results of important excavations that were undertaken in 1981 at three Iron Age settlement mounds in Mali's Inland Niger Delta: Jenné-jeno, Hambarketolo, and Kaniana. Forthcoming (and issued separately) will be a discussion of a regional site survey from the same field season and an interpretive essay that will link the results of both the excavations and the survey.

137 **Finding West Africa's oldest city.**
Susan McIntosh, Roderick McIntosh.   *National Geographic*, vol. 162, no. 3 (Sept. 1982), p. 396-418.

The authors describe the dramatic discoveries of excavations at Jenne-jeno ('ancient Jenne') in 1977 and 1981, which established it as having begun in the third century BC, reached a population of 10,000 by AD 800, and abandoned by 1400. 'It is the oldest known city, and perhaps the most important Iron Age site, in Africa south of the Sahara' (p. 398). Colour photographs by Michael and Aubine Kirtley show excavations, artefacts and aerial views. Other early articles by the McIntoshes include 'Excavation and survey in and near Djenné, Mali', *Nyame Akuma*, no. 10 (1977), p. 36-37; 'Initial perspectives on prehistoric subsistence in the Inland Niger Delta (Mali)', *World Archaeology*, vol. 11, no. 2 (1979), p. 227-43; 'The 1981 season at Jenne-jeno: preliminary results', *Nyame Akuma*, no. 20 (1982), p. 28-32; 'The secrets of ancient Jenne', *Topic*, no. 144 (1983), p. 20-31; 'The early city in West Africa: towards understanding', *African Archaeological Review*, vol. 2 (1984), p. 73-98. Also available is *Excavations at Jenne-jeno, Hambarketolo and Kaniana: the 1981 season* (see above), edited by S. K. McIntosh.

138   **The Inland Niger Delta before the empire of Mali: evidence from Jenne-jeno.**
Roderick J. McIntosh, Susan Keech McIntosh.   *Journal of African History*, vol. 22, no. 1 (1981), p. 1-22. bibliog.

The authors discuss reasons for the absence of references to Jenne-jeno by Arab and European sources prior to the mid-fifteenth century, the chronology of written documentation, and oral traditions and they describe the results and interpretations of their February-April 1977 excavations at Jenne-jeno. 'At her apogee, perhaps A. D. 750 to 1150, Jenne-jeno covered 33 hectares (82 acres) (the present city of 10,000 inhabitants covers 44 hectares)' (p. 16). They mention surveys of nearby sites as well. See also the more popularly written article 'Jenné-jeno: an ancient African city' in *Archaeology*, vol. 33, no. 1 (Jan./Feb. 1980), p. 8-14; and their 'Djenné-jeno – cité sans citadelle,' *La Recherche*, no. 148 (1983), p. 1272-75; 'Forgotten tells of Mali: new evidence of urban beginnings in West Africa', *Expedition*, vol. 25, no. 2 (Winter 1983), p. 35-46; and 'The early city in West Africa: towards an understanding', *African Archaeological Review*, vol. 2 (1984), p. 73-98; R. J. McIntosh's 1979 doctoral thesis at the University of Cambridge was 'The development of urbanism in West Africa: the example of Jenne'.

139   **Islam, archaeology and history: Gao region (Mali) ca. AD 900-1250.**
Timothy Insoll.   Oxford, England: Tempus Reparatum, 1996. 143p. maps. bibliog. (BAR International Series, no. 647).

The author has chosen the important Gao Region for the focus of his archaeological research, and seeks to redress the fact that no systematic study was previously undertaken of the archaeology of Islam in this part of Mali, the Western Sahel, or Sudan. Insoll examines the *Dondon Borey* (traces of past occupation) of the Gao Region between ca. 900 and 1250 AD and documents the introduction, acceptance, and spread of Islam in this part of Mali.

140   **Looting the antiquities of Mali.**
M. Dembélé, J. D. van der Waals.   *Antiquity*, vol. 65, no. 249 (Dec. 1991), p. 904-5.

The authors comment on their joint archaeological project, the archaeological film *African king*, and the widespread destruction of *togue* (dwelling mounds) in the Inner Niger Delta. See also the editorial by Christopher Chippindale in *Antiquity*, vol. 65, no. 246 (March 1991), p. 6-8, also on looting and the *African king*, with excerpts from a letter by R. J. and S. K. McIntosh to Professor M. Tite at the Oxford University Research Laboratory for Archaeology and the History of Art, whose new policy statement by R. R. Inskeep appears as 'Making an honest man of Oxford: good news for Mali' in *Antiquity*, vol. 66, no. 250 (March 1992), p. 114. Mamadi Dembélé and Alain Person earlier reported on dozens of phallic megaliths from a site in the Region of Tombouctou (Timbuktu) in 'Tondiadarou: témoin spectaculaire d'une civilisation protohistorique de l'Afrique de l'ouest' (Tondiadarou: spectacular evidence of a West African protohistoric civilization), *Jamana* (Bamako), vol. 12 (March-April 1987), p. 23-28. See also on this topic, R. J. McIntosh and S. K. McIntosh's 'Dilettantism and plunder: illicit traffic in ancient Malian art', Unesco *Museum* (Paris), vol. 38(1), no. 149 (1986), p. 49-57; and R. J. McIntosh's note 'New Oxford University policy on TL authentication services', *African Arts*, vol. 25, no. 4 (1992), p. 103.

141 **Middle Niger terracottas before the Symplegades Gateway.**
Roderick J. McIntosh. *African Arts*, vol. 22, no. 2 (Feb. 1989), p. 74-83, 103-4. bibliog.

The author vigorously examines theoretical issues in the convergence of art history and prehistory resulting from his work with Middle Niger terracottas from Jenné-jeno, framing the discussion with the metaphor of the Symplegades Gateway from the story of Jason and the Argonauts to represent a pair of barriers to knowledge about past cultures. In an earlier article R. J. McIntosh and Susan K. McIntosh reported on 'Terracotta statuettes from Mali', *African Arts*, vol. 12, no. 2 (Feb. 1979), p. 51-53, 91. Among the works cited in their valuable bibliography (p. 91) is J. Evrard's 'Archéologie ouest-africaine: les figurines en terre cuite du Mali: déscription morphologique et essai de typologie' (West African archaeology: terracotta figurines of Mali: morphological description and typological essay), a three-volume master's thesis at the Université Catholique de Louvain, Belgium. Leon Sironto critiques ideas from their article in 'On the cultural context of terracotta statuettes from Mali', *African Arts*, vol. 13, no. 1 (Nov. 1979), p. 20, 22-23, to which the McIntoshes respond (p. 23-24).

142 **The oldest extant writing of West Africa: medieval epigraphs from Essuk, Saney, and Egef-n-Tawaqqast (Mali).**
Paulo F. de Moraes Farias. *Journal des Africanistes*, tome 60, fasc. 2 (1990), p. 65-113. bibliog.

This paper discusses, in historical context, seven medieval Arabic inscriptions from the sites of Essuk (Aday-n-Ifoyas), Saney (Gao), and Egef-n-Tawaqqast (Bentiya), all located in the Sahara and Niger Valley. Evidence shows that those inscriptions from Essuk and Saney are the oldest known examples of West African writing, dating from the eleventh century. Despite the age of the script found at all three sites, its lettering type still exists within the Arabic calligraphies of West Africa.

143 **Plundering Africa's past.**
Edited by Peter R. Schmidt, Roderick J. McIntosh. Bloomington, Indiana: Indiana University Press, 1996. 280p.

This set of eighteen essays reveals the deep concern and alarm felt by historians, archaeologists, and art historians regarding the mining of ancient sites in Africa to satisfy foreign enthusiasm for exotic antiquities. Samuel Sidibé contributed a chapter entitled 'The fight against the plundering of Malian cultural heritage and illicit exportation'; looting of Malian terracotta statuettes and metal arts is discussed in Michael Brent's 'A view inside the illicit trade in African antiquities'; and McIntosh's 'Just say shame' focuses on recent events in the trade in Malian antiquities. Mali's

1993 bilateral accord with the United States on illicit trade in African antiquities is discussed in various chapters, as are other topics. The volume is well indexed and each chapter is followed by bibliographical references.

144 **La poterie ancienne du Mali: quelques remarques préliminaires = Ancient pottery from Mali: some preliminary remarks.**
Bernard de Grunne.   Munich, Germany: Galerie Biedermann, 1983. 96p. maps. bibliog.

Bernard de Grunne provides a brief introduction in French, German and English to Mali's early pottery from the northern Tumuli Region, the Inland Delta, and to pottery without precise geographical origin. The book also contains plates (p. 31-80) showing eighty-four pots, a list of plates (p. 82-94) and a bibliography (p. 95-96). Roderick J. McIntosh reviews the work in *African Arts*, vol. 17, no. 2 (Feb. 1984), p. 20-22, and discusses the difficulties of dating the artefacts. See also de Grunne's 1987 doctoral thesis at Yale University, 'Divine gestures and earthly gods: a study of the ancient terracotta statuary from the Inland Niger Delta in Mali' (Ann Arbor, Michigan: University Microfilms International, 1987. 266 leaves. maps. bibliog.) and 'Figures equestres du delta intérieur du Niger' (Equestrian figures from the Inland Niger Delta) in *Aethiopia, vestiges de gloire* (Paris: Editions Dapper, 1987, p. 9-13) and his 'Heroic riders and divine horses: an analysis of ancient Soninke and Dogon equestrian figures from the Inland Niger Delta region in Mali', *Minneapolis Institute of Art Bulletin*, vol. 60 (1983-86), p. 78-96.

145 **Pottery variation in present-day Dogon compounds (Mali): preliminary results.**
R. M. A. Bedaux.   In: *Variation, culture and evolution in African populations.* Edited by Ronald Singer, John K. Lundy.   Johannesburg, South Africa: Witwatersrand University Press, 1986, p. 241-48. map. bibliog.

Based on fieldwork carried out primarily in several Dogon villages in 1983-84, this paper examines some of the cultural processes which cause variations in pottery type and use 'and influence the way in which pottery becomes part of the archaeological record'.

146 **Pour une plus grande efficacité de l'inventaire des sites archéologiques du Mali.** (Toward a more effective inventory of the archaeological sites of Mali.)
Michel Raimbault.   In: *Archéologie africaine et sciences de la nature appliquées à l'archéologie, 1er symposium international, Bordeaux 1983.*   Paris: Agence de Coopération Culturelle et Technique; Centre National de la Recherche Scientifique; Talence, France: Centre de Recherche Interdisciplinaire d'Archéologie Analytique de l'Université de Bordeaux-III, 1986, p. 437-48. map. bibliog.

The author, who works at the Institut des Sciences Humaines, Bamako, discusses the necessity, complexities, problems of identification and chronological definition of a systematic inventory of Mali's archaeological sites. He includes a map of principal sites and a copy of the inventory protocol used.

147 **Prehistoric investigations in the region of Jenne, Mali: a study in the development of urbanism in the Sahel.**
Susan Keech McIntosh, Roderick J. McIntosh. Oxford, England: B. A. R., 1980. 2 vols. maps. bibliog. (Cambridge Monographs in African Archaeology, no. 2. BAR International Series, no. 89).

This important monograph reports the results of a 1977 research programme at Jenne-jeno and a regional survey over a 1,100 sq. km. area north and west of the site. Part one, 'Archaeological and historical background and the excavations at Jenne-jeno', describes fieldwork from January to late April 1977, accounts of the site's historical and archaeological background, and essays on Iron Age research in West Africa and Mali. Appendices (p. 194-280) include radiocarbon dates from Jenne-jeno and other sites and specialist reports on faunal remains. Part two, 'The regional survey and conclusions', places Jenne-jeno and its region in perspective. Appendices (p. 466-509) include numerous data, soil analysis and site records. The bibliography is impressive. David A. Aremu reviews the work in *West African Journal of Archaeology* (Ibadan), vol. 19 (1989), p. 164-68, as does J. E. G. Sutton in 'Jenne and its regional roots', *Journal of African History*, vol. 23, no. 3 (1982), p. 413-14.

148 **Preliminary report of excavations at Karkarichinkat Nord and Karkarichinkat Sud, Tilemsi Valley, Republic of Mali, Spring, 1972.**
Andrew B. Smith. *West African Journal of Archaeology*, vol. 4 (1974), p. 33-55. maps. bibliog.

The author reports on the excavation he and M. Yaya Coulibaly, director of the Musée National du Mali, made in January-March 1972. Data from five human burials, stone tools, pottery, beads and faunal remains lead the author to conclude that post-Palaeolithic inhabitants of the Tilemsi Valley were cattle-herding nomads. He suggests that the valley's high water-table made it a corridor for extending the herding complex into West Africa. See Smith's 1974 University of California at Berkeley doctoral thesis, 'Adrar Bous [Niger] and Karkarichinkat [Mali]: examples of post-paleolithic human adaptation in the Saharan and Sahel zones of West Africa' (382p.) and his 'A biogeographical consideration of colonization of the lower Tilemsi Valley in the second millennium B.C.', *Journal of Arid Environments*, vol. 2 (1979), p. 355-61.

149 **Prospections archéologiques dans la zone de la Boucle du Baoulé (Mali).** (Archaeological investigations in the Baoulé Bend (Mali).)
A. C. Heringa, M. Raimbault. *Études Maliennes*, no. 38 (1986), 109p. map.

This is a detailed report on 72 archaeological sites excavated in 1980-81, dating from the twelfth and fourteenth centuries in the region about midway between Bamako and Kayes. It includes seven pages of photographs and a fold-out map (no scale) of the archaeological sites. Early archaeological reports include J. Daget and Z. Ligers, 'Une ancienne industrie Malienne: les pipes en terre' (An ancient Malian industry: clay pipes) *Bulletin IFAN* (Dakar) vol. 24, Series B, 1-2 (1962), p. 12-52, and G. Szumowski 'Fouilles de l'abri sous roche de Kourounkorokale' (Excavations of a rock shelter at Kourounkorokale), *Bulletin IFAN* (Dakar), vol. 18, Series B, 3-4 (1956), p. 462-508.

150 **Protecting Mali's cultural heritage.**
African Arts, vol. 28, no. 4 (Autumn 1995). 112p.

This special issue of the quarterly journal *African Arts* was produced in response to the emergency import restrictions imposed by the United States in September 1993 on archaeological materials from the Inland Niger Delta and the Bandiagara Escarpment. Collectively, its essays provide the reader with various opinions regarding the ban, along with an appreciation of Mali's rich cultural heritage and lamentations concerning its tragic plunder. Guest editor Patrick R. McNaughton's article 'Malian antiquities and contemporary desire' is followed by: 'U.S. efforts to protect cultural property: implementation of the 1970 Unesco Convention' by Maria Papageorge Kouroupas; 'The ban on Mali's antiquities: a matter of law' by Daniel Shapiro; 'The pillage of archaeological sites in Mali' by Samuel Sidibé; 'Beyond reaction and denunciation: appropriate action to the crisis of archaeological pillage' by Philip L. Ravenhill; 'A view from Unesco' by Etienne Clément; 'Africa, the art of a continent: the dilemma of display' by the Royal Academy of Arts, London; 'The good collector and the premise of mutual respect among nations' by Roderick J. McIntosh, Téréba Togola and Susan Keech McIntosh; 'An art historical approach to the terracotta figures of the Inland Niger Delta' by Bernard de Grunne; 'Dogon art at the Musée Dapper: the last reunion?' by Christiane Falgayrettes-Leveau and Michel Leveau; and 'Bring beauty back to Mali' by William Wright.

151 **The rape of Mali.**
Michel Brent. *Archaeology*, vol. 47, no. 3 (May/June 1994), p. 26-31, 34-35, 67. map. bibliog.

Basing his article on lengthy research in Mali, Europe, and the United States, the journalist author describes how 'European dealers and collectors have systematically plundered the heritage of one of the world's poorest countries' (p. 26), ineffective laws, the illicit artefact trade, and the unabated looting throughout Mali. The article is accompanied by Roderick J. McIntosh's 'Plight of ancient Jenne' (p. 32-33) describing his work at Jenne-jeno with Téréba Togola of Bamako's Institute of Human Sciences and the discovery of looters at nearby Mounya. McIntosh writes, 'outside of Egypt, Mali is the African country most richly endowed with archaeological sites' (p. 32). See also R. J. and S. K. McIntosh, 'Dilettantism and plunder: dimensions of the illicit traffic in ancient Malian art', Unesco *Museum* (Paris), vol. 38(1), no. 149 (1986), p. 49-57, and R. J. McIntosh, 'Resolved: to act for Africa's historical and cultural patrimony', *African Arts*, vol. 24, no. 1 (1991), p. 18-22, 89.

152 **Recent archaeological research and dates from West Africa.**
Susan Keech McIntosh, Roderick J. McIntosh. *Journal of African History*, vol. 27, no. 3 (1986), p. 413-42. map. bibliog.

Malian sites including Trhaza, Azawad, Tondidarou, and Jenne-jeno are well represented by some 46 radiocarbon dates among the 250 reported in this survey article. Other articles in this series in the *Journal of African History* include: J. E. G. Sutton, 'Archaeology in West Africa: a review of recent work and a further list of radiocarbon dates', vol. 23, no. 3 (1982), p. 291-313 (12 dates from Mali); D. Calvocoressi and N. David, 'A new survey of radiocarbon and thermoluminescence dates for West Africa', vol. 20, no. 1 (1979), p. 1-29 (23 dates from Mali); M. Posnansky and R. McIntosh, 'New radiocarbon dates for northern and western Africa', vol. 17, no. 2 (1976), p. 161-95 (seven dates from Mali); Colin Flight, 'A survey of recent results in the radiocarbon chronology of northern and western

Africa', vol. 14 (1973), p. 531-54; F. Willett, 'A survey of recent results in the radiocarbon chronology of western and northern Africa', vol. 12 (1971), p. 339-70. In the more recent survey 'Current research and recent radiocarbon dates from northern Africa, III', vol. 29, no. 2 (1988), p. 145-76, Angela E. Close discusses calibration issues and mentions twelve dates from five sites in northern Mali.

153 **Recherches archéologiques au Mali: prospections et inventaire, fouilles et études analytiques en Zone lacustre.** (Archaeological research in Mali: explorations and inventory, excavations and analytical studies in the Lacustrine Zone).
Michel Raimbault, Kléna Sanogo.   Paris: Editions Karthala, 1991.
567p. (Archéologies Africaines).

Fifteen scholars authored twenty-eight chapters, each with its own bibliography, in this essential work in French. It is in two parts: Part one, 'L'Inventaire des sites archéologiques depuis 1980' and Part two, 'Une région privilégiée: la zone lacustre'. K. Sanogo, Director of the Institut des Sciences Humaines, Bamako, authored the conclusions on pages 511-16. Annexes (p. 517-60) include a list of radiocarbon dates from thirty-six sites, ninety sites in the Malian Sahara, and drawings of ceramic artefacts. The only non-French, non-Malian scholars included are S. K. and R. J. McIntosh, who authored 'Reconnaissances archéologiques le long du moyen-Niger' (p. 99-120). It was reviewed by Eric Huysecom in *Sahara: prehistory and history of the Sahara* (Milan), vol. 4 (1991), p. 179-80. See also M. Raimbault and Mamadi Dembélé, 'Les ateliers prehistoriques de Manianbugu (Bamako, Mali)', *Bulletin IFAN*, Série B, vol. 45, nos. 3-4 (July-Oct. 1983), p. 219-76, describing the excavation of a lithic workshop site near Bamako in 1977.

154 **Rediscovering the Tellem of Mali.**
Rogier M. A. Bedaux.   *Archaeology*, vol. 35, no. 3 (May/June 1982),
p. 28-34. map. bibliog.

This article, with its photographs, provides one of the clearest, succinct introductions to archaeological research on the Tellem people of the Bandiagara Cliffs of Mali during the period from the eleventh to the sixteenth century. See Bedaux and John Huizinga's 'Anthropological research in Mali' in *National Geographic Society research reports, 1970 projects* (Washington, DC: National Geographic Society, 1979, p. 281-98). And see Bedaux's 'Tellem, reconnaissance archéologique d'une culture de l'ouest africain au moyen âge: recherches architectoniques' (Tellem, archaeological survey of a West African culture of the Middle Ages: architectural studies) in *Journal de la Société des Africanistes*, vol. 42, no. 2 (1972), p. 103-85; and 'Recherches ethno-archéologiques sur la poterie des Dogon (Mali)' (Ethnological archaeological research on Dogon pottery) in *Op zoek naar mens en materiële cultuur* (In search of man and material culture), edited by H. Fokkens, P. Banga and M. Bierma (Groningen: Rijksuniversiteit Groningen, 1986, p. 117-46).

155 **Répertoire général des sites historiques et archéologiques du Mali.**
(General list of historical and archaeological sites in Mali.)
[Bamako?]: Division du Patrimoine Culturel, 1984. 74p.

This useful tool, listing archaeological and historical sites such as village ruins, paintings and inscriptions, graves and necropoli and other historical remains, is the result of bibliographical research, reconnaissance missions over the earth, and analysis of questionnaires completed by district authorities and annual reports of the Bureaux Régionaux du Patrimoine Culturel. Entries are arranged alphabetically by administrative region; approximate locations and geographical coordinates are provided for each entry.

156 **The Sahara in northern Mali: man and his environment between 10,000 and 3500 years BP. (Preliminary results).**

N. Petit-Maire, J. C. Celles, D. Commelin, G. Delibrias, M. Raimbault.

African Archaeological Review, vol. 1 (1983), p. 105-25. map. bibliog.

The authors describe archaeological survey results from the Malian Sahara where they found abundant Acheulian and Aterian Pleistocene materials, as well as Holocene sites. Finds are correlated with Sahelian flora and fauna. They include a map of the region, radiocarbon dates, and ten photographs of artefacts. See also N. Petit-Maire and J. Riser, editors, *Le Sahara malien à l'Holocène* (Paris: C.N.R.S., 1983), and N. Petit-Maire and M. Gayet's 'Hydrologie du Niger (Mali) à l'Holocène ancien' (Hydrology of the Niger River in the early Holocene), *Comptes Rendus de l'Academie des Sciences de Paris*, vol. 298, no. 1 (1984), p. 21-23.

157 **Le Sarnyéré dogon: archéologie d'un isolat, Mali.** (The Sarnyéré Dogon: archaeology of an isolate, Mali.)

Alain Gallay, Claudine Sauvain-Dugerdil. Paris: Editions ADPF, 1981. 242p. maps. bibliog. (Recherche sur les Grandes Civilisations. Mémoire, no. 4).

The author analyses in great detail the technical aspects of present-day pottery, its ethnographic context and its historical evolution from AD 1700 to the present in four Dogon villages of Sarnyéré (Boni District, Douentza Cercle). The text is profusely illustrated with figures of pottery. Appendices (p. 151-66) include carbon-14 dates and a genealogy of a potter's family. In addition, the work includes a bibliography of 33 items, 23 plates of pottery types, and 49 photographic plates of the geographical setting and of pottery details. Among the author's publications is 'La poterie en pays Sarakolé (Mali, Afrique occidentale): étude de technologie traditionnelle' (Sarakole pottery from Mali: a study of traditional technology), *Journal de la Société des Africanistes*, vol. 40, no. 1 (1970), p. 7-84.

158 **Tableau géographique de l'Ouest africain au Moyen Age, d'après les sources écrites, la tradition et l'archéologie.** (Geographical description of West Africa in the Middle Ages according to written, traditional and archaeological sources.)

Raymond Mauny. Dakar: IFAN, 1961. 587p.

In this massive, important work, the author, then Chief of the Archaeology-Prehistory Section of IFAN, examines the geographical setting and economic and human geography of the large West African region during the period from the seventh to the mid-fifteenth century. Of special value are the chapters discussing the Arabic written sources (p. 21-53) and the archaeology of the region (p. 56-187) including 'Soudan (Mali)' (p. 92-137). Among the 111 diagrams, maps, and photographs, is a fold-out map showing 'The Songhay empire at its apogee (about 1520)' in West Africa. The extensive bibliography (p. 547-75) is invaluable for the broad subject coverage. See also Mauny's 'Notes d'archéologie sur Gao', *Bulletin de l'Institut Fondamental d'Afrique Noire*, vol. 13, Series B (1952), p. 837-52.

159 **Tellem: een bijdrage tot de geschiedenis van de Republiek Mali.**
(Tellem: a contribution to the history of the Republic of Mali).
R. Bedaux. Berg en Dal, The Netherlands: Afrika Museum; New York: Oceanic Primitive Arts [distributor], 1977. 104p. map. bibliog.

This well-illustrated catalogue for an exhibition of eighty-seven objects on loan from the Musée National at Bamako is in Dutch (p. 5-69) but has translations into English (p. 72-86) and French (p. 87-101) by J. Le Grand, and a bibliography (p. 102-3). Bedaux describes the Dogon, the Tellem, his archaeological investigations, architecture, the household, burial rituals, statues, and Tellem history. There are 64 black-and-white photos. P. J. Imperato reviewed the volume as a 'major authoritative work . . . the largest and most comprehensive corpus of information on the Tellem, their material culture and their art' (p. 85) in *African Arts*, vol. 11, no. 1 (Oct. 1977), p. 84-85.

160 **Tellem textiles: archaeological finds from burial caves in Mali's Bandiagara Cliff.**
Rita Bolland, with contributions by Rogier M. A. Bedaux and Renée Boser-Sarivaxévanis. Amsterdam: Tropenmuseum/Royal Tropical Institute, 1991. 320p. bibliog. (Mededelingen van het Rijksmuseum voor Volkenkunde, Leiden, no. 27).

This book is a detailed catalogue illustrating and describing some 500 textiles excavated between 1964 and 1974 from Tellem burial caves and dating from the eleventh to the eighteenth century. Bedaux describes 'The Tellem Research Project: the archaeological context' (p. 14-36); Boser-Sarivaxévanis offers 'An introduction to weavers and dyers in West Africa' (p. 37-51). Bolland, a curator at the Tropenmuseum in Amsterdam, discusses the Tellem textiles (p. 52-78) and provides a catalogue (p. 79-292). Appendices (p. 293-304) contain an analysis of dyestuff and fibres by J. H. Hofenk de Graaff (p. 294-96), 'The conservation of the Tellem textiles' by C. J. van Nes (p. 297), and a glossary by Bolland (p. 298-302). The bibliography (p. 316-20) is useful. See also Bedaux and Bolland's 'Medieval textiles from the Tellem caves in central Mali, West Africa', in *Textile Museum Journal*, no. 19/20 (1980/81), p. 65-74, and their *Tellem, reconnaissance archéologique d'une culture de l'ouest africain au moyen âge: les textiles* (Tellem, archaeological survey of a West African culture of the Middle Ages: textiles) ([n.p.], 19 leaves), based on excavations in twenty-nine caves between 1964 and 1974.

161 **Ten years of archaeological research in the Sahara, 1965-1975.**
Gabriel Camps. *West African Journal of Archaeology*, vol. 7 (1977), p. 1-15. map. bibliog.

Several sites from Tilemsi Valley in eastern Mali are mentioned in their regional context. See also M. J. Gaussen's 'Un atelier de burins à Lagreich, Oued Tilemsi (République du Mali)' (A burin workshop in Lagreich, Tilemsi, Mali), *Anthropologie*, vol. 69 (1965), p. 237-48. See also Andrew Brown Smith's 1974 University of California at Berkeley doctoral thesis, 'Adrar Bous [Niger] and Karkarichinkat [Mali]:

examples of post-paleolithic human adaptation in the Saharan and Sahel zones of West Africa' (382p.) and A. Smith's A 'biogeographical consideration of colonization of the lower Tilemsi Valley in the second millennium B.C.' in *Journal of Arid Environments*, vol. 2 (1979), p. 355-61.

162 **Terra d'Africa, terra d'archeologia: la grande scultura in terracotta del Mali Djenné VIII-XVI sec.** (Land of Africa, land of archaeology: the great sculpture in terracotta from Mali, Djenné VIII-XVI centuries.)

Bernardo Bernardi, Bernard de Grunne. Florence, Italy: Alinari, 1990. 62p. maps.

The terracottas of Djenné, located in the Inland Niger Delta Region, are discussed in two essays. Bernardi gives the history, and places the terracottas in their cultural setting. De Grunne focuses on the state of research of the terracottas, analyses their iconography and also relates them to other terracottas found in southern Mali. The plates (largely in colour) show thirty objects dated by the Oxford Laboratory. The text is in Italian and French. For related articles in English by de Grunne, see his 'An art historical approach to the terracotta figures of the Inland Niger Delta', in an issue of *African Arts* – vol. 28, no. 4 (Autumn 1995), p. 70-79, 112 – on protecting Mali's cultural heritage, as well as his 'Ancient sculpture of the Inland Niger Delta and its influence on Dogon art', *African Arts*, vol. 21, no. 4 (Aug. 1988), p. 50-55.

163 **Terres cuites anciennes de l'ouest africain.** (Ancient terracottas from West Africa.)

Bernard de Grunne, Doreen Stoneham, Jacqueline Evrard. Louvain-la-Neuve, Belgium: Institut Supérieur d'Archéologie et d'Histoire de l'Art, Collège Érasme, 1980. 293p. maps. (Publications d'Histoire de l'Art et d'Archéologie de l'Université Catholique de Louvain, no. 22).

There are 250 black-and-white and six colour photographs in this attractive, richly illustrated volume in French, with an English translation by Claire W. Enders. The authors synthesize what is known of the early terracottas of Mali, the Akan of Ghana, Nok, Ife and Benin of Nigeria, and the Sao of Chad. The valuable section on Mali describes the history and archaeology of the Inland Delta, artistic styles, uses and origins of statuettes, horsemen, bronzes and technology, and concludes with a bibliography (p. 52-55). Following the essay is a detailed catalogue of thirty-nine terracottas shown in photographs. Doreen Stoneham contributes 'Some thermoluminescence datings of terracottas from the Inland Delta of the Niger (Mali)' (p. 276-82) and Jacqueline Evrard adds 'Les statuettes en terre cuite du Mali' (p. 283-91). B. de Grunne and George Nelson Preston authored the catalogue *Ancient treasures in terra cotta of Mali and Ghana* (New York: African-American Institute, 1981. 58p. maps. bibliog. 42 photographs) for an exhibition by that name at the African-American Institute, 14 October 1981 to 9 January 1982, and from 30 January 1982 to 27 March 1982 at the Chicago Public Library. Patricia Crane Coronel reviews the above work in *African Arts*, vol. 14, no. 2 (Feb. 1981), p. 82-83, and the catalogue in vol. 15, no. 4 (Aug. 1982), p. 88-89, as does P. J. Imperato in vol. 15, no. 3 (May 1982), p. 80-81.

164 **Le Tilemsi préhistorique et ses abords: Sahara et Sahel malien.**
(Prehistoric Tilemsi and its environs: the Malian Sahara and Sahel.)
Jean Gaussen, Michel Gaussen. Paris: Editions du Centre National de
la Recherche Scientifique, 1988. 270p. (Cahiers du Quaternaire,
no. 11).

This impressive study details surface finds of stone and bone implements and pottery
shards from the Palaeolithic and Neolithic in the large region northeast of Gao. The
study is richly illustrated with 165 figures of the artefacts, four photographs, maps and
a substantial bibliography (p. 265-70).

165 **Vasellame del Mali (X°–XIV° Sec. d.C.) = The pottery from Mali
(10th-14th century A.D.).**
Roberto Ballarini. Milan, Italy: Africa Curio, 1986. 52p. maps.
bibliog.

This catalogue was published to accompany a 1986 exhibition, held in Milan, Italy, of
seventy ancient terracotta vases from Mali. Forty-eight vases are pictured, dating from
between 950 and 1350 AD. Text preceding the illustrations discusses locations of the
pottery finds, ritual earthenware, morphological characteristics of the vases, and
earthenware for domestic use. Some brief historical notes are also included.

166 **West African prehistory.**
Susan Keech McIntosh, Roderick J. McIntosh. *American Scientist,*
vol. 69, no. 6 (Dec. 1981), p. 602-13. maps. bibliog.

This important review article covers climate and palaeoclimate, Late Stone Age
subsistence, herding and hunting, agricultural origins, Iron Age societies, and complex
societies before AD 1000. The Malian sites of Tondidaro, along the Niger Bend, Jenne-
jeno, Kobadi, and Karkarichinkat in the Tilemsi Valley are mentioned. Illustrations of
sites and forty-two references are included. This examination continues in their
'Current directions in West African prehistory', *Annual Review of Anthropology,*
vol. 12 (1983), p. 215-58, which lists 274 references. See also their 'Cities without
citadels: understanding urban origins along the Middle Niger', in *The archaeology of
Africa: foods, metals and towns* edited by T. Shaw, P. Sinclair, B. Andah, A. Okpoko
(London: Routledge, 1993, p. 622-41). Graham Connah highlights the sites of Koumbi
Saleh (on the border of Mauritania), Galia, Doupwil, Niani, Kouga, El-Oualedji and
Jenne in 'An optimal zone: the West African savanna' in *African civilizations:
precolonial cities and states in tropical Africa* (New York: Cambridge University
Press, 1987, p. 97-120).

**The Sahara and the Nile: Quaternary environments and prehistoric
occupation in northern Africa.**
See item no. 88.

History

General and regional

167   The Cambridge history of Africa.
General editors, Roland Oliver, J. D. Fage.   Cambridge, England:
Cambridge University Press, 1975-86. 8 vols. maps. bibliog.

The volumes of this invaluable history, which covers the continent from prehistoric
times to 1975, contain substantial material useful for the study of Mali. This includes,
for example, Nehemia Levtzion's lengthy essay 'The western Maghrib and Sudan' in
volume three, *From c. 1050 to c. 1600* (1977, p. 331-462, 726-31); also Levtzion's
'North-West Africa: from the Maghrib to the fringes of the forest' in volume four,
From c. 1600 to c. 1790 (1975, p. 142-222, 661-66); and M. Hiskett's 'The
nineteenth-century jihads in West Africa' in volume five, *From c. 1790 to c. 1870*
(1976, p. 125-69, 546-49).

168   The conquest of the Sahara.
Douglas Porch.   New York: Fromm International, 1986. 332p. maps.
bibliog.

This vivid account of the conquest of the desert by Arabs and the French includes a
chapter on the Tuareg, 'The people of the veil' (p. 65-82) and the conquest of
Timbuktu by Lt Col. Eugène Bonnier and naval Lt H. G. M. Boiteux and Marshall
Joseph Joffre (p. 132-42).

169 **Corpus of early Arabic sources for West African history.**
Edited and annotated by Nehemia Levtzion, J. F. P. Hopkins, translated
by J. F. P. Hopkins. Cambridge, England: Cambridge University
Press, 1981. 492p. map. bibliog. (Fontes Historiae Africanae. Series
Arabica, no. 4).

This important volume contains sixty-five Arabic documents in translation, written
between AD 846 and 1632, and relevant for the history of the larger region.
Explanatory material, notes on each document, an introductory preface, extensive
bibliography (p. 434-40) and index-glossaries (p. 441-92) for places, tribes, persons,
books and general subjects are included. Notable inclusions are by al-'Umari
(1301-49; p. 252-78), Ibn Battuta (1304-68; p. 279-304), Ibn Khaldūn (1332-1406;
p. 317-42) and al-Maqqari (1591-92 to 1632; p. 370-72). Reviewers of the volume
include: Murray Last, *African Affairs*, vol. 81, no. 324 (July 1982), p. 440-41; D. C.
Holsinger, *African Studies Review*, vol. 24, no. 4 (Dec. 1981), p. 144; and, at length,
H. J. Fisher in 'Early Arabic sources and the Almoravid conquest of Ghana', *Journal
of African History*, vol. 23, no. 4 (1982), p. 549-60.

170 **General history of Africa.**
Paris: UNESCO; London: Heinemann; Berkeley, California:
University of California Press, 1981-93. 8 vols. maps. bibliog.

Numerous essays in this important work contribute to the broad history of Mali: In
Vol. 1, *Methodology and African prehistory*, edited by J. Ki-Zerbo (1981. 819p.) is
C. T. Shaw's 'The prehistory of West Africa' (p. 611-33); in Vol. 2, *Ancient
civilizations of Africa*, edited by G. Mokhtar (1981. 804p.) is B. Wai Andah's 'West
Africa before the seventh century' (p. 593-619); in Vol. 3, *Africa from the seventh to
eleventh century*, edited by M. El Fasi (1988. 869p.) is J. Devisse's 'Trade and trade
routes in West Africa' (p. 367-435); in Vol. 4, *Africa from the twelfth to the sixteenth
century*, edited by D. T. Niane (1984. 751p.) are Niane's 'Mali and the second
Mandingo expansion' (p. 117-71), M. Ly-Tall's 'The decline of the Mali Empire'
(p. 172-86), S. M. Cissoko's 'The Songhay from the 12th to the 16th century'
(p. 187-210), and M. Izard's 'The peoples and kingdoms of the Niger Bend and the
Volta basin from the 12th to the 16th century' (p. 211-37); in Vol. 6, *Africa in the
nineteenth century until the 1880s*, edited by J. F. Ade Ajayi (1989. 861p.) are
S. Baier's 'The Sahara in the nineteenth century' (p. 515-36), A. Batran's 'The
nineteenth-century Islamic revolutions in West Africa' (p. 537-54) and K. Arhin and
J. Ki-Zerbo's 'States and people of the Niger Bend and the Volta' (p. 662-98) which
includes discussion of the Bambara kingdoms of Segu and Kaarta.

171 **Grandes dates du Mali.** (Important dates of Mali.)
Alpha Oumar Konaré, Adam Ba Konaré. Bamako: Editions
Imprimeries du Mali, 1983. 284p. maps. bibliog.

This large, valuable reference tool contains a foreword (p. 7-8) and a detailed, richly
illustrated chronology of dates from the fourth century to December 1981. Annexes
(p. 223-71) contain lists of Malian dynasties, colonial administrators, members of
government, presidents of the council, the Republic, party officials and a table of
journals and periodicals of Mali (p. 260-71). The bibliography (p. 273-76) is followed
by 122 photographs.

172 **Histoire du Sahel occidental malien des origines à nos jours.**
(History of the western Malian Sahel from its origins to the present day.)
Amadou Bâ.   Bamako: Editions Jamana, 1989. 244p.

Amadou Hampaté Bâ, the famous Malian scholar of African oral tradition and culture, has constructed this history of western Mali and its peoples from the writings of Arab and black authors, French military men and colonial administrators, and from the words of the oral traditionalists who travel the Sahelian countries, from the time of the Ghana Empire to independence.

173 **History of West Africa.**
Edited by J. F. A. Ajayi, Michael Crowder.   Harlow, England; New York: Longman, 1985- . 3rd ed. 2 vols. maps. bibliog.

Written by specialist scholars and edited by two internationally prominent African historians, this title is a general reference for all those interested in West African studies. Volume one covers the earliest times to 1800 and emphasizes the theme of state formation and the development of social and political institutions. The second volume of this edition is forthcoming; the latest edition available of volume two is the second (Harlow, England: Longman, 1987. 833p.) and is a significant revision. It covers the nineteenth and twentieth centuries and emphasizes the role of Islamic and European influences in the region. Several essays in this important work pertain to Malian history. J. D. Fage reviews successive editions in *Journal of African History*, vol. 14, no. 1 (1973), p. 129-38; vol. 20, no. 1 (1979), p. 135-36; and vol. 28, no. 2 (1987), p. 305-8. For a more basic, condensed version of West African history, see Crowder's *A history of West Africa A. D. 1000 to the present* (London: Longman, 1979. 222p.).

174 **Le Mali.** (Mali.)
Attilio Gaudio.   Paris: Karthala, 1992. 2nd ed., rev. and updated.
307p. maps. bibliog. (Méridiens).

This informative book covers Mali from prehistoric times to 'the dawn of democracy' in 1992. The remainder of the book surveys cultural traditions; ethnic groups (Bambara, Malinké, Sarakole, Senoufo (Senufo), Dogon, Peul, Songhay, Tuareg, Maure and Arab); Bamako and other cities (Jenne, Mopti and Timbuktu); the problem of famine; and concludes with a short chapter on tourism. The book contains six maps (one of which is of Bamako), twenty photographs of scenes throughout the country, and a brief bibliography (p. 300-3).

175 **Mali, a handbook of historical statistics.**
Pascal James Imperato, Eleanor M. Imperato.   Boston, Massachusetts:
G. K. Hall, 1982. 339p. (A Reference Publication in International Historical Statistics).

Aimed at both the specialist and the general reader, this volume uses historical statistics, complemented by descriptive and explanatory essays, to trace Mali's historical, social, economic and political development. Chapters are divided into the following topics: climate; population; health; migration; education; labour; wages and labour organizations; agriculture; livestock, fisheries, forests and wildlife; mining, energy and industry; transportation; communication; commerce, imports, exports and prices; finances, development plans and foreign aid. Each chapter also contains a generous number of bibliographical references.

176 **The new atlas of African history.**
G. S. P. Freeman-Grenville. New York: Simon & Schuster, 1991. 144p.

Illustrating the history of Africa from prehistoric times to 1990, this atlas contains 103 maps facing 64 pages of accompanying commentary. An index is included. Other invaluable atlases for historical overviews are the incomparable *Historical atlas of Africa* edited by J. F. Ade Ajayi, Michael Crowder, Paul Richards, Elizabeth Dunstan and Alick Newman (London; New York: Cambridge University, 1985. 167p.); *African history in maps* by M. Kwamena-Poh, J. Tosh, R. Waller and M. Tidy (Harlow, England: Longman, 1982. 76p.); and *An atlas of African history* by J. D. Fage (New York: Africana, 1978. 2nd ed. 79p.).

177 **Nouvelles d'hier ... et d'aujourdhui.** (News of yesterday ... and today.)
Mamadou Kaba. Bamako: Editions Jamana, 1989. 209p.

A compilation of the author's journalistic works about important Malians, Malian social and economic conditions, and events in Malian history which appeared in *L'Essor* (q.v.) and *Sunjata* (q.v.) between 1970 and 1980. The articles, reports, interviews, and editorials included cover such topics as Mali's border dispute with Burkina Faso, juvenile delinquency, economic development, President Traoré's anti-corruption campaign initiative, military government, the droughts, and the mission of information and freedom of the press.

178 **Pays du Sahel: du Tchad au Sénégal, du Mali au Niger.** (Countries of the Sahel: from Chad to Senegal, from Mali to Niger.)
Joël Vernet. Paris: Éditions Autrement, 1994. 231p. maps. bibliog.

A history of the countries of the Sahel and Sudan Region, their civilizations and social conditions. For Mali, one finds 'Mali: autour du lac Débo' (Mali: around Lake Debo) by Jean Gallais (p. 139-47), 'Regard Touareg' (The Tuareg point of view) by Hélène Claudot-Hawad (p. 148-53). 'Tombouctou: un défi au Sahara' (Timbuktu: a defiance of the Sahara) by Daniel Grevoz (p. 193-97), and 'Ségou: la ville au bord du fleuve' (Segou: the city on the banks of the river) by J. Vernet (p. 198-203). The volume includes a chronology for the region from 2500 BC to 1993, country data, and a bibliography.

179 **Peoples and empires of West Africa: West Africa in history 1000-1800.**
G. T. Stride, Caroline Ifeka. London: Nelson, 1971. 373p. maps.

This book was produced in order to provide West African examination students with a more accurate evaluation of this region's past and a more balanced presentation of West African and European activities there. A great number of folk traditions have been intentionally included, as well as an excellent index. Sample examination questions are found at the end of each chapter.

180   **Topics in West African history.**
      A. Adu Boahen.   Harlow, England: Longman, 1986. 2nd ed. 202p.
      maps. bibliog.
This valuable, succinct history, written for senior school and first-year university students is especially useful for its account of 'The Sudanese states and empires' (p. 1-53) which contains sections on 'Ancient Ghana', 'The rise and fall of Mali', and 'The Songhai empire'.

Precolonial (to 1883)

181   **After the Jihad: the reign of Ahmad Al-Kabir in the Western Sudan.**
      John Hanson, David Robinson.   East Lansing, Michigan: Michigan State University Press, 1991. 410p. (African Historical Sources, no. 2).
An anthology of Arabic documents, approximately half of which are from the Fonds Archive at the Bibliothèque Nationale in Paris (originally from Segu), which the authors use to reconstruct the reign of Ahmad al-Kabīr, from the 1860s to the 1890s, over the domain he inherited from his father Umar Tal in the Western Sudan. They include a sketch of the life of 'Umar Tal' (p. 27-37), an extensive study of Ahmad al-Kabīr (Aḥmadu Sheku; p. 41-263), a glossary (p. 265-69), bibliography (p. 271-78), index of personal names (p. 279-82) and reproductions of Arabic documents (p. 285-410). Mervyn Hiskett reviews it in 'Umarian jihad', *Journal of African History*, vol. 34, no. 2 (1993), p. 353-54 as an 'invaluable contribution to West African history' (p. 354). Ahmad Alawad Sikainga reviews it in *Research in African Literatures*, vol. 25, no. 2 (Summer 1994), p. 205-7. Of related interest is *The Islamic regime of Fuuta Tooro: an anthology of oral tradition transcribed in Pulaar and translated into English* by Moustapha Kane and David Robinson, with David Dwyer and Sonja Fagerbery (East Lansing, Michigan: Michigan State University, African Studies Center, 1984. 177p.).

182   **The age of Mansa Musa of Mali: problems in succession and chronology.**
      Nawal Morcos Bell.   *International Journal of African Historical Studies*, vol. 5, no. 2 (1972), p. 221-34. bibliog.
The author argues that 'very little of significance is known about the empire' of Mali (p. 234) and that most scholars have relied over-much on the accounts of Ibn Khaldūn. He examines the problems encountered in ascertaining the date of death of Mansa Musa (also known as Kankan Moussa), whose only certain date in AD 1324 when he passed through Cairo to Mecca, and the issue of possible matrilineal succession in the empire of Mali. See also David Conrad's entry 'Mansa Musa' in the *Encyclopedia of Islam* (Leiden, The Netherlands: E. J. Brill, 1988, vol. 6, p. 421-22).

183   **Ancient Ghana and Mali.**
Nehemia Levtzion.   New York and London: Africana, 1980. rev. ed.
289p. maps. bibliog.

This important, lucidly written volume is based especially on Arabic sources. In Part one, Levtzion considers the history of these ancient kingdoms from the eighth to the sixteenth century. Part two concerns government structures and economic bases, gold, the Saharan trades, staple commodities, and Islam. Originally published in 1973 by Methuen, the 1980 edition leaves the main text unchanged but adds a brief second preface and a 'topical survey of recent publications' (p. 277-78). The original bibliography (p. 255-77) is excellent. Maps show 'Ghana and Mali' (p. 2) and 'Trade routes of the Sahara and the Sudan, c. 1000-1500' (p. 138-39), and there is a chart showing 'The genealogy of the kings of Mali based on the chronicle of Ibn Khaldūn' (p. 71).

184   **The Arab conquest of the Western Sahara: studies of the historical events, religious beliefs and social customs which made the remotest Sahara a part of the Arab world.**
H. T. Norris.   Harlow, England: Longman; Beirut, Lebanon: Librairie du Liban, 1986. 309p. maps. bibliog. (Arab Background Series).

This remarkable work of lucid scholarship consists of four parts: 'The tribal tapestry' (p. 2-23); 'The Arabian locust' (p. 26-100); 'The conquest by the pen and the amulet' (p. 103-32); and 'The Arabisation of the Western Sahara' (p. 133-78). In addition to five maps and ten plates there are extensive appendices (p. 179-241), a useful glossary (p. 243-52), notes and references (p. 253-94), and a bibliography (p. 295-97). C. C. Stewart considers the work 'essential' in his review in *Journal of African History*, vol. 30, no. 3 (1989), p. 496-97. See also Norris's 'Sanhaje scholars of Timbuctoo' in *Bulletin of the School of Oriental and African Studies*, vol. 30 (1967), p. 634-40, and C. C. Stewart's 'Southern Saharan scholarship and the *Bilād al-Sūdān*' in *Journal of African History*, vol. 17, no. 1 (1976), p. 73-93 (item no. 210).

185   **The Bamana empire by the Niger: kingdom, jihad, and colonization, 1712-1920.**
Sundiata A. Djata.   Princeton, New Jersey: Markus Wiener, 1997.
251p. maps. bibliog.

Presenting a colourful portrait of the Bamana (Bambara) Empire, this book focuses on the efforts of two foreign powers – one African, the other European – to control the kingdom of Segu. This account, which relies heavily on oral histories and archival resources, is one of the few told from the Bamana point of view.

186   **The economic foundations of an Islamic theocracy: the case of Masina.**
Marion Johnson.   *Journal of African History*, vol. 17, no. 14 (1976),
p. 481-95. map. bibliog.

Johnson describes the economic bases of the Masina state located in the interior Niger Delta south of Timbuktu, and also deals with religious and military aspects, public finance and taxation, the economy, and the creation of the Masina theocracy.

187 **L'Empire peul du Macina. Vol. I (1818-1853).** (The Peul Empire of
Macina. Vol. 1, 1818-1853.)
Amadou Hampaté Bâ, J. Daget.   Paris: Mouton, 1962. Reprinted,
Abidjan: Nouvelles Éditions Africaines, 1984. 306p. maps.

This detailed history, largely based on oral traditions, describes the empire of Cheikou
Amadou (1755-1844), a fundamentalist Islamic cleric, and the period of rule by his
son Amadou Cheikou (d. Feb. 1853). The appendix (p. 287-306) prints Amadou
Wangara's 292-line 'Song of Cheikou Amadou' in Peul (Fulfulde) and French, with
explanatory footnotes. The study originally appeared as volume 3 of *Etudes
soudanaises* (Bamako: IFAN, 1955. 306p.) and has eight maps but neither
bibliography nor index.

188 **L'empire toucouleur, 1848-1897.** (The Toucouleur empire, 1848-97.)
Yves-J. Saint-Martin.   Paris: Le Livre africain, 1970. 189p. maps.
bibliog.

Twenty historical plates, numerous maps, a comparative chronology of the Toucouleur
empire from 1776 to 1908 (p. 180-86) and a useful bibliography (p. 187-90) of
archival and fifty-four printed sources all enhance this history. Saint-Martin has also
written 'Un fils d'El Hadj Omar: Aguibou, roi du Dinguiray et du Macina (1843?-
1907)' (A son of El Hadj Omar: Aguibou, king of the Dinguiray and of Macina),
Cahiers d'Etudes Africaines, vol. 8, no. 29 (1968), p. 144-78, and *L'empire
toucouleur et la France: un demi-siècle de relations diplomatiques (1846-93)* (The
Tukulor empire and France: half a century of diplomatic relations) (Dakar: [n.p.],
1966).

189 **Les empires du Mali: étude d'histoire et de sociologie soudanaises.**
(The empires of Mali: study of Sudanese history and sociology.)
Charles Monteil.   Paris: G.-P. Maisonneuve et Larose, 1968. 157p.
maps. bibliog.

This reprint from the *Bulletin du Comité d'Études Historiques et Scientifiques de
l'Afrique Occidentale Française*, vol. 12, nos. 3-4 (July-Dec. 1929), p. 291-447,
includes a synoptic table of dynasties of the empires of Mali and discusses empires of
northern and central Mali. The author (1870-1949) provides a bibliography of works
from the tenth to the twentieth century (p. 155-57).

190 **From Mande to Songhay: towards a political and ethnic history of
medieval Gao.**
Dierk Lange.   *Journal of African History,* vol. 35, no. 2 (1994),
p. 275-301. bibliog.

The author carries on the debate with John Hunwick (q.v.) over interpretations of the
Gao kinglists, with emphasis on the nature of the Zā dynasty (12th-14th century) and
the circumstances of the introduction of Songhay speech and culture in the fifteenth
century. The bibliography is invaluable for the topic. This article extends his critique
begun with 'Les rois de Gao-Sané et les Almoravides' ('The kings of Gao-Sané and
the Almoravids') in *Journal of African History*, vol. 32, no. 2 (1991), p. 251-75, an
examination of royal tombstones discovered in 1939 in Gao-Sané suggesting there
was no 'conquest' by Berber peoples from outside the kingdom. For additional
material on Gao, see Felix Iroko's doctoral thesis in history under the direction of

Raymond Mauny, 'Gao, des origines à 1591' (Paris: University of Paris, 1973-74. 385 leaves. maps. bibliog.) which traces Gao's origins in the sixth and seventh centuries and through to 1591, and includes (in annexes) oral traditions gathered by the author, documents extracted from other printed sources, and a 25-page selected bibliography at the end. *L'Empire de Gao: histoire, coutumes et magie des Sonrai* (The Gao empire: history, customs and magic of the Songhay) by physician Jean Boulnois of the Colonial Health Corps and Boubou Hama, conseiller de l'Union Française (Paris: Librairie d'Amérique et d'Orient, 1954. 183p. map. bibliog.) is an account of Songhay history, royalty, mythology and magical beliefs.

191 **Gao and the Almoravids revisited: ethnicity, political change and the limits of interpretation.**
John O. Hunwick. *Journal of African History*, vol. 35, no. 2 (1994), p. 251-73. bibliog.

Hunwick offers a detailed response to and critique of Dierk Lange's 1991 critique of Hunwick's 'Gao and the Almoravids: a hypothesis' in *West African culture dynamics: archaeological and historical perspectives*, edited by B. K. Swartz and R. E. Dumett (The Hague: Mouton, 1980, p. 413-30). Among the numerous problems raised are the location of Gao and issues in the interpretation of documents and of ethnic relations in the area during the period AD 1100-1500. See also his 'Religion and state in the Songhay empire, 1464-1591' in *Islam in tropical Africa* edited by I. M. Lewis (London: Oxford University for the International African Institute, 1966, p. 296-317), and 'Ahmad Baba and the Moroccan invasion of the Sudan (1591)' in *Journal of the Historical Society of Nigeria*, vol. 2, no. 3 (1981), p. 311-28.

192 **A glorious age in Africa: the story of three great African empires.**
Daniel Chu, Elliott Skinner. Trenton, New Jersey: Africa World Press, 1990. 120p. (1st AWP ed.)

An ideal selection for the general reader, this book chronicles the successive rise and fall of three powerful West African kingdoms from the eighth to the sixteenth century: Ghana, Mali, and Songhay.

193 **Gold, Salz und Sklaven: die Geschichte der grossen Sudanreiche Gana, Mali, Songhai.** (Gold, salt and slaves: the history of the great empires of the Sudan: Ghana, Mali and Songhay.)
Rudolf Fischer. Tübingen, Germany: Edition Erdmann, 1982. 284p. maps. bibliog.

Those who read German will enjoy this historical overview of the Western Sudan's major empires from about AD 1200 to 1600. The author points out that there are relatively few histories of the region in German, compared to French and English. Supplementing the text are numerous black-and-white and colour photographs, eight maps, a chronology of important dates for each empire (p. 255-56), a historical diagram of important events (p. 257), a glossary (p. 259-61), a bibliography (p. 262), notes (p. 263-70), and an index (p. 271-84).

194 **Histoire des Berbères et des dynasties musulmanes de l'Afrique septentrionale.** (History of the Berbers and of the Islamic dynasties of northern Africa.)
Ibn Khaldoun 'Abd-ar-Rahmân, translated from the Arabic by Baron de Slane. Paris: Librairie Orientaliste, 1968-69. 2nd ed. 4 vols.

Ibn Khaldūn (1332-1382 or 1406) never travelled in the region of today's Mali, but his *Histoire des Berbères* contains accounts of the oral traditions of the early empires of Ghana, Sosso (Susu) and Mali. The original translation from Arabic to French was by William MacGuckin Slane (Algiers, 1852-56. 4 vols) and was published as a new edition by Paul Casanova (Paris: Paul Geuthner, 4 vols). Volume 4 (1969. 628p.) includes a geographical table. See also Ibn Khaldūn's 1377 work *The Muqaddimah: an introduction to history*, translated from the Arabic by Franz Rosenthal (New York: Pantheon, 1958. 3 vols) or the same edition edited and abridged by N. J. Dawood (Princeton, New Jersey: Princeton University Press, 1967).

195 **The holy war of Umar Tal: the western Sudan in the mid-nineteenth century.**
David Robinson. Oxford, England: Clarendon Press; New York: Oxford University Press, 1985. 434p. maps. bibliog. (Oxford Studies in African Affairs).

Through the skilled use of oral traditions and archival sources from Mauritania, Senegal, Côte d'Ivoire, Guinea, Futa Toro, Gajaga, and Bundu in 1967-69 and 1973-74, Mali in 1976 and 1979, and archives in Paris, the author provides a remarkably detailed and lucid reconstruction of the life of Umar Tal (1794-1864). Umar Tal waged a holy war in the Western Sudan from 1852 to 1864 and created the Umarian empire which, at its greatest extent, stretched from Timbuktu to the Senegal River. The exceptional bibliography (p. 376-416) contains archival sources and theses as well as extensive published sources. In addition there are twenty-six tables and nineteen maps. Kathryn L. Green reviews the book in *African Studies Review*, vol. 29, no. 4 (Dec. 1986), p. 105-10; as does Donal B. Cruise O'Brien in *African Affairs*, vol. 85, no. 341 (Oct. 1986), p. 628-30. In 'Umar's jihad', *Journal of African History*, vol. 27, no. 3 (1986), p. 570-73, J. D. Fage reviews the work as 'full of insight' and 'compelling reading'. Robinson's earlier *Chiefs and clerics: Abdul Bokar Kan and Futa Toro, 1853-1891* (Oxford, England: Clarendon Press, 1975. 239p. Oxford Studies in African Affairs) is reviewed by John Ralph Willis in 'Islam and politics on the Senegal', *Journal of African History*, vol. 19, no. 2 (1978), p. 284-85.

196 **The lost cities of Africa.**
Basil Davidson. Boston, Massachusetts: Little, Brown, 1970. rev. ed. 366p. maps. bibliog.

Among the twelve chapters of this highly readable volume is 'Kingdoms of the old Sudan', recounting the general histories of Timbuktu and of the empires of Ghana, Mali and Songhay and the chroniclers who left us records, notably in the *Tarikh es Sudan* and the *Tarikh el fettach*. A new edition of this title is forthcoming (Oxford, England: J. Currey, 1997). In *The African past: chronicles from antiquity to modern times* (New York: Grosset & Dunlap, 1964. 392p.), Davidson excerpts and introduces accounts pertaining to the area which became Mali and to the city of Timbuktu: Al Yakubi, 'The king of Ghana'; Al Bekri, 'Ghana in 1067'; anonymous, 'Sundiata's triumph'; Al Omari, 'Mali in the fourteenth century'; Ibn Battuta, 'Travels in Mali';

Al Maghili, 'Social reform in Songhay'; Kati, 'Bound and free in 1508'; Es-Sa'di, 'Djenné'; Mungo Park, 'To the Niger'; and Heinrich Barth, 'Finding the *Tarikh es-Sudan*' and 'Timbuktu'. See also his *Old Africa rediscovered* (London: Victor Gollancz, 1959).

197 **Love for three oranges, or, the askiya's dilemma: the Askiya, al-Maghili and Timbuktu, c. 1500 A.D.**
Charlotte Blum, Humphrey Fisher. *Journal of African History*, vol. 34, no. 1 (1993), p. 65-91. bibliog.
The authors reinterpret a well-documented era of Songhay history in proposing that the first askiya of Songhay, al-Hajj Muhammad Turi who seized power in 1493, experimented with and ultimately had to choose among three different Islamic identities. He first allied himself with court clerics in Gao, then sought the advice of radical scholar al-Maghīlī, but ultimately chose the 'urbane and tolerant Islamic practice' of Timbuktu (p. 91).

198 **Mali, crossroads of Africa.**
Philip Koslow. New York: Chelsea House Publishers, 1995. 63p. bibliog. (The Kingdoms of Africa).
A history of the kingdom of Mali written for older children, with informative maps and illustrations. An index, glossary and chronology are included. This title would be appropriate for adult readers as well.

199 **'Mande Kaba', the capital of Mali: a recent invention?**
Kathryn L. Green. *History in Africa*, vol. 18 (1991), p. 127-35. bibliog.
The author examines the usual association of the source of the Mande (Malinké) people at Kaba with Kangaba, the capital of the Mali Empire, arguing that 'Mande Kaba did not achieve anything like the reputation it now has until the late nineteenth or early twentieth centuries' (p. 130). 'It simply cannot be used to establish either chronology or actual provenance for Mande lineages' (p. 132). The argument is thoroughly documented.

200 **The mid-fourteenth century capital of Mali.**
J. O. Hunwick. *Journal of African History*, vol. 14, no. 2 (1973), p. 195-208. map. bibliog.
The author describes efforts by scholars to locate the capital of the Mali Empire at the height of its power, and uses a careful analysis of the route of Ibn Battuta, who visited the capital in 1352, to argue that the capital is on the left bank of the River Niger, between Segu and Bamako. In the course of his discussion he reviews the varied names for the capital and disagrees with arguments of Claude Meillassoux in 'L'itinéraire d'Ibn Battuta de Walata à Mali', *Journal of African History*, vol. 13, no. 3 (1972), p. 389-95, who suggests a location for the capital between the Falémé and Gambia rivers, also based on Ibn Battuta's 1352 route.

201 **The pen, the sword, and the crown: Islam and the revolution in Songhay reconsidered, 1464-1493.**
Lasiné Kaba. *Journal of African History,* vol. 25, no. 3 (1984), p. 241-56. bibliog.

The author examines the origins of the Askiya dynasty in Songhay, the alliance between militant clerics ('ulam'), the military during Sonni 'Alī's reign, and especially the political conflict in Timbuktu. See also his 'Archers, musketeers, and mosquitoes, the Moroccan invasion of the Sudan and the Songhay resistance (1591-1612)', *Journal of African History,* vol. 22, no. 4 (1981), p. 457-75, and 'Power, prosperity and social inequality in Songhay (1464-1591)', in *Life before the drought: the savanna-sahel zones of Africa,* edited by Earl P. Scott (Boston, Massachusetts: Allen & Unwin, 1984, p. 29-48).

202 **A reconsideration of Wangara/Palolus, Island of Gold.**
Susan Keech McIntosh. *Journal of African History,* vol. 22, no. 2 (1981), p. 145-58. maps. bibliog.

The author proposes that the Western Sudan's 'Island of gold', known as 'Wangara' to Arab geographers and 'Palolus' to European map-makers, refers to the Inland Niger Delta. She provides extensive discussion of Arabic and European sources and oral traditions, and buttresses the argument with an analysis of early Soninke (Sarakole) long-distance traders known as 'Wangara' and recent excavations at the early trading centre of Jenne-jeno in the Inland Delta, a Soninke settlement of urban size by AD 900.

203 **Recueil des sources arabes concernant l'Afrique occidentale du VIIIe au XVIe siècle: (bilād al-sūdān).** (Collection of Arabic sources on West Africa from the 8th to the 16th century: (land of the black people).)
Edited and translated by Joseph M. Cuoq, preface by Raymond Mauny.
Paris: Éditions du Centre National de la Recherche Scientifique, 1985. 515p. maps. bibliog. (Sources d'Histoire Médiévale).

This major sourcebook in French (originally published in 1975) contains relevant extracts from the works of seventy-two individuals (Wahb b. Munabbih, c. AD 728, to al-Maghīlī, from 1493 and 1496, including al-Bakri, al-Idrisi, Ibn Battuta, al-'Umari, Ibn Khaldūn) with biographical information on each, a full bibliography (p. 439-64, with addenda, p. 487-88) and indexes of Arabic words, authors, toponyms, tribal names and individuals (p. 489-512). In 'New light on Islamic Africa', *Journal of African History,* vol. 19, no. 4 (1978), p. 617-19, Humphrey J. Fisher calls Father Cuoq's volume 'one of the most useful books, . . ., which it has ever been my good fortune to review' (p. 617) and includes a review of Cuoq's *Les musulmans en Afrique* (Muslims in Africa) (Paris: Maisonneuve et Larose, 1975. 522p.).

204 **The role of the Wangara in the economic transformation of the Central Sudan in the fifteenth and sixteenth centuries.**
Paul E. Lovejoy. *Journal of African History,* vol. 19, no. 2 (1978), p. 173-93. map. bibliog.

The author discusses the Wangara, the name frequently used for gold merchants, but here referring to 'Songhay-based merchants and their agents to the east and south'

(p. 176) who were part of the Songhay-oriented commercial diaspora and who played an important role in the economic development of Hausa cities and Borno. A map (p. 178) shows the Songhay Empire in 'West Africa in the sixteenth century'.

205 **The royal kingdoms of Ghana, Mali, and Songhay: life in medieval Africa.**
Patricia McKissack, Frederick McKissack.   New York: H. Holt, 1994.
1st ed. 142p. maps. bibliog.

This fine, well-illustrated history for early high-school students introduces the medieval kingdoms of Ghana (p. 5-40), Mali (p. 41-78) and Songhay (p. 79-118), their leaders, Sundiata, cities (especially Koumbi Saleh, Timbuktu, Gao and Jenne), peoples and political economy. The award-winning authors skilfully integrate oral history, archaeology and historical excerpts with lucid text. They also include a time-line (1,000,000 BC to AD 1884; p. 119-23), notes (p. 124-30), bibliography (p. 131-35) and index (p. 136-41). Daniel Chu and Elliott Skinner co-authored a similar book for junior high-school students, *A glorious age in Africa: the story of three great African empires* (q.v.), illustrated by Moneta Barnett, in which they tell the stories of the empires of Ghana (p. 13-50), Mali (p. 51-78) and Songhay (p. 79-113). The conclusion 'The past shapes the present' (p. 114-18) explains the important role of history. André Clair's *Le fabuleux empire du Mali* (The fabulous Mali Empire) (Paris: Présence Africaine, 1959. 20p.) is a children's book illustrated by Tall Papa Ibra telling the story of the ancient kingdom of Mali and includes a table showing dates for Malian emperors and the history of Mali, AD 1050-1480.

206 **Salts of the western Sahara: myths, mysteries, and historical significance.**
E. Ann McDougall.   *International Journal of African Historical Studies*, vol. 23, no. 2 (1990), p. 231-57. maps. bibliog.

The author examines the importance of salt in the region's economy, the idea of the 'salt-starved interior', the pricing of salt, and specific sources of salt including Tishit, Tegaza and Tawdeni. Maps show 'Principal salt routes and salt sources, ca. 1000-1700' and 'Principal salt routes and salt sources, ca. 1700-1900'. In addition, see her 'Banamba and the salt trade of the western Sudan', in *West African economic and social history: studies in memory of Marion Johnson*, edited by D. Henige and T. C. McCaskie (Madison, Wisconsin: University of Wisconsin, African Studies Program, 1990, p. 151-69) on an important market about 100 kilometres northeast of Bamako in the late nineteenth century; 'Camel caravans of the Saharan salt trade', in *The workers of African trade*, edited by Paul Lovejoy and C. Coquery-Vidrovitch (Beverly Hills, California: Sage, 1985, p. 99-121); 'The Sahara reconsidered: pastoralism, politics and salt from the ninth through the twelfth centuries', *African Economic History*, no. 12 (1983), p. 263-86; and 'The view from Awdaghust: war, trade and social change in the southwestern Sahara, from the eighth to the fifteenth century', *Journal of African History*, vol. 26, no. 1 (1985), p. 1-31. McDougall's 1980 University of Birmingham doctoral thesis was 'The Ijil salt industry: its role in the pre-colonial economy of the western Sudan'. Of related interest is Dominique Meunier's 'Le commerce du sel de Taoudeni' (The salt trade of Taoudeni), *Journal des Africanistes*, vol. 50, no. 2 (1980), p. 133-44. Lovejoy's *Salt of the desert sun: a history of salt production and trade in the central Sudan* (Cambridge, England: Cambridge University Press, 1986. 351p. bibliog.) is essential reading.

207 **The Segu Tukulor Empire.**
B. O. Oloruntimehin. London: Longman, 1972. 357p. maps. biblog.
(Ibadan History Series).

Using archival material from Paris and Dakar, Senegal, oral sources in Dakar, Bamako and Segu and printed resources, the author has reconstructed the history of the Tukulor empire in the Western Sudan from about 1851 to the French conquest in 1893. At its greatest, the empire covered most of present-day Mali, eastern Mauritania, northern Guinea and parts of Senegal. The title emphasizes the spread of the Tukulor from their Futa Toro homeland to incorporate the Bambara Segu empire. The book deals especially with 'the process of political unification, administration and politics in the Western Sudan' (Preface, p. xiii). The four plates, six maps and bibliography are very useful. The work is based on the author's 1966 doctoral thesis at the University of Ibadan, Nigeria, where, at the time of publication, he was in the history department.

208 **Shari'a in Songhay: the replies of al-Maghili to the questions of Askia al-Hajj Muhammad.**
Muhammad ibn 'Abd al-Karim Maghili, Mohammed I. Edited and translated by John O. Hunwick. Oxford, England; New York: Published for the British Academy by the Oxford University Press, 1985. 165p. + 48p. (Arabic). maps. biblog. (Fontes Historiae Africanae. Series Arabica, no. 5).

This excellent study describes 'The Middle Niger before 1500: trade, politics and the implantation of Islam' (p. 1-28); 'Muhammad b. 'Abd al-Karim al-Maghili: his life and influence' (p. 29-48; born between 1425 and 1440, d. 1472-73); 'The replies: introduction to the text and translation' (p. 49-53); 'the replies of Al-Maghili to the questions of Askia al-Hajj Muhammad' (p. 60-95); 'commentary' (p. 96-131). Appendices of published and unpublished sources (p. 132-38), a bibliography (p. 139-50) and an index/glossary (p. 151-65) precede the Arabic text of the Replies (50p.). The volume is a 'completely revised, and largely re-written', version of Hunwick's 1974 doctoral thesis at the University of London, 'Al-Maghili's replies to the questions of Askia al-Hajj Muhammad, edited and translated with an introduction on the history of Islam in the Niger Bend to 1500'. Louis Brenner reviews the book in 'A text for another time', *Journal of African History*, vol. 27, no. 3 (1986), p. 560-62.

209 **Slavery and Muslim society in Africa: the institution in Saharan and Sudanic Africa and the trans-Saharan trade.**
Allan G. B. Fisher, Humphrey J. Fisher. Garden City, New York: Anchor Books, Doubleday, 1972. 219p. maps. biblog.

In the course of this broad study of Muslim society and the trans-Saharan slave trade, the authors include discussion of ancient Mali, Gao, Masina (Macina), Segu, Timbuktu, the Bambara, Fulani (Peul), Songhay and Tuareg. Raymond C. Ganga reviews the work in *African Studies Review*, vol. 16, no. 3 (Dec. 1973), p. 457-58. See also the more recent *Transformations in slavery: a history of slavery in Africa* by Paul E. Lovejoy (Cambridge, England: Cambridge University Press, 1983. African Studies Series, no. 36. 349p.) which places slavery in the area of present-day Mali in a regional context and particularly David C. Conrad's 'Slavery in Bambara society: Segou, 1712-1861', *Slavery & Abolition*, vol. 2 (1981), p. 69-80. Nehemia Levtzion's

'Slavery and Islamization in Africa' (vol. 1, p. 182-98) and J. O. Hunwick's 'Notes on slavery in the Songhay Empire' (vol. 2, p. 16-32) appear in *Slaves and slavery in Muslim Africa*, edited by John Ralph Willis (London: F. Cass, 1985. 2 vols), reviewed at length in 'Of slaves, and souls of men' by H. J. Fisher, *Journal of African History*, vol. 28, no. 1 (1987), p. 141-49.

210 **Southern Saharan scholarship and the *bilād al-sūdān*.**
C. C. Stewart. *Journal of African History*, vol. 17, no. 1 (1976), p. 73-93. map. bibliog.

Using data from the late eighteenth and early nineteenth centuries, the author reconstructs the complex social and economic relations in a large area on the southern and western edge of the Sahara, much of which is in present-day Mali, north of the River Niger. In 'Frontier disputes and problems of legitimation: Sokoto–Masina relations, 1817-1837', *Journal of African History*, vol. 17, no. 4 (1976), p. 497-514, Stewart reconstructs fluctuations in political relations between the caliphates of Hambullahi in Masina and the northern Nigerian caliphate of Sokoto. See also W. A. Brown's 1969 University of Wisconsin doctoral thesis, 'The Caliphate of Hambullahi, c.1818-1864'.

211 **Tarikh el-fettach, ou Chronique du chercheur, pour servir à l'histoire des villes, des armées et des principaux personnages du Tekrour.** (History of the Searcher, or, History for the use of one who seeks knowledge of the history of the cities, armies and principal personages of Tekrour.)
By Mahmoûd Kâti ben El-Hâdj El-Motaouakkel Kâti and one of his sons. French translation, accompanying notes, index and map by Octave Houdas, Maurice Delafosse.   Paris: Librairie d'Amérique et d'Orient, 1981. 2 vols in 1 (361p. (French) + 186p. (Arabic)). map. (Collection UNESCO d'Oeuvres Représentatives. Série Africaine). (Documents Arabes Relatifs à l'Histoire du Soudan). (Publications de l'École des Langues Orientales Vivantes, 5. sér., vol. 9-10).

This important sixteenth- and seventeenth-century history of the Western Sudan, especially of the Songhay empire, is by a resident Soninke (Sarakole) scholar (1468-1593?) of Timbuktu writing about 1519. He accompanied Askia Mohammed to Mecca. The work was originally published in Arabic, edited by Octave Victor Houdas (1840-1916) and Maurice Delafosse (1870-1926), and in French translation by Houdas and Delafosse (both were published in Paris: Ernest Leroux, 1913). The volume is thought to have been completed by a grandson of Kâti about 1600 and brought up to about 1665 by Ibn al-Mukhtar. The UNESCO edition is indexed (p. 343-61). See Imperato's account of the author and the work itself in his *Historical dictionary of Mali* (item no. 7), 1996, 3rd ed., p. 131 and 218-19.

212 **Tarikh es-Soudan.** (History of Sudan.)
Abderrahman ben Abdallah ben 'Imran ben 'Amir es-Sa'di; Arabic text
edited and translated by Octave Houdas, with the collaboration of
Edmond Benoist. Paris: Librairie d'Amérique et d'Orient,
A. Maisonneuve, 1981. 2 vols in 1 (540p., 333p.). bibliog. (Collection
UNESCO d'Oeuvres Représentatives. Série Africaine). (Publications
de l'École des Langues Orientales Vivantes. 4. sér.,
vol. 12-13). (Documents Arabes Relatifs à l'Histoire du Soudan).
This remarkable seventeenth-century history of the Sudanese kingdoms by a scholar
born in Timbuktu in 1596 (d. 1656?) and who worked as a notary in Djenné was
originally published in Arabic (Paris: Leroux, 1898) and in French translation by
Octave Victor Houdas (Paris: Leroux, 1900). Here it is reprinted in a single volume
with the French translation (540p.) including an index (p. 491-534) followed by the
Arabic (333p.). The work is an important source for the history of Djenné (Jenne),
Tombouctou (Timbuktu) and the Songhai (Songhay) Empire and was originally
discovered in Guandu, Nigeria, in 1853 by Heinrich Barth. Imperato calls it 'one of
the most important historical texts written about the western Sudan' in his *Historical
dictionary of Mali* (q.v., p. 219).

213 **'The chronicle of the succession': an important document for the
Umarian state.**
David Robinson. *Journal of African History*, vol. 31, no. 2 (1990),
p. 245-62. map. bibliog.
The author describes, interprets and translates the full text of the 1860 document 'The
chronicle of the succession' in which al-hajj 'Umar Tal tries to resolve conflict among
his sons in favour of the eldest, Ahmad al-Kabir. A map (p. 246) shows the boundaries
of the Umarian state. The document is from the Umarian library and archives once
held in Segu but since 1890 located in Paris. See Noureddine Ghali, Sidi Mohamed
Mahibou with Louis Brenner, compilers, *Inventaire de la Bibliothèque 'Umarienne de
Ségou, conservée à la Bibliothèque nationale, Paris* (item no. 907) (Paris: Editions du
Centre National de la Recherche Scientifique, 1985. 417p.).

214 **A tropical dependency: an outline of the ancient history of the
western Soudan with an account of the modern settlement of
northern Nigeria.**
Lady Lugard. London: J. Nisbet, 1905. 508p. maps.
Lady Lugard (Flora L. Shaw), wife of Sir Frederick Lugard, the chief architect and
colonial administrator of Nigeria, includes at least twenty brief chapters (p. 78-217,
296-321) of interest for Mali's early history, among them 'Ghana and Timbuctoo'
(p. 113-16), 'Mansa Musa' (p. 122-28), 'Meeting of eastern and western influence
upon the Niger' (p. 153-62), 'Songhay under Askia the Great' (p. 190-210), 'The
Moorish conquest' (p. 296-305) and 'The Soudan under the Moors' (p. 306-14). Large
fold-out maps show 'Ancient kingdoms in the Sudan' (no scale) and 'Northern
Nigeria' (scale 1.014 inches to 32 miles).

215 **The vanquished voice: Shaykh Muhammad's defense: a case study from the western Sahara.**
Humphrey J. Fisher.   In: *West African economic and social history: studies in memory of Marion Johnson*, edited by David Henige, T. C. McCaskie.   Madison, Wisconsin: University of Wisconsin, African Studies Program, 1990, p. 47-61. bibliog.

The author provides an insightful textual criticism of a document, the Taysīr al-fattāh, written by Shaykh Muhammad al-Gunah ni, a nineteenth-century cleric of the Kel es-sūq living among the Iwillimmeden Tuareg northeast of the Niger bend. Shaykh Muhammad's library had been captured in a raid and was being held as booty; he argues for its return.

216 **Voilà ce qui est arrivé = Bayân mâ waqaḥa d'al-Ḥâgg 'Umar al-Fûtî: plaidoyer pour une guerre sainte en Afrique de l'Ouest au XIXe siècle.** (Look what happened = Description of what happened by Al-Hajj 'Umar al-Futi: a plea for a holy war in West Africa in the nineteenth century.)
Umar Tal, edited and translated by Sidi Mohamed Mahibou, Jean-Louis Triaud.   Paris: Centre Régional de Publication de Paris, Editions du Centre National de la Recherche Scientifique, 1983. 261p. + 58p. (Arabic). map. bibliog. (Fontes Historiae Africanae. Series Arabica, no. 8).

This model volume of scholarship contains the Arabic text *Bayân mâ waqaa* from the Bibliothèque Nationale, Paris, a French translation (p. 75-156) with 507 notes, detailed indexes, an exceptional bibliography, tables, and twenty-nine plates, following an introduction with 424 notes and a map of al-Hagg Umar's (Umar Tal's) campaigns (1851-62; p. 8-9) in the region of present-day Mali. C. C. Stewart reviews the work in *Journal of African History*, vol. 25, no. 4 (1984), p. 472-73. See also Omar Jah's 'Source materials for the career and the jihad of al-Hajj 'Umar al-Futi (1794-1864)', *Bulletin de l'IFAN*, series B, vol. 41, no. 2 (1979), p. 371-97.

217 **War and servitude in Segou.**
Jean Bazin.   *Economy and Society*, vol. 3, no. 2 (May 1974), p. 107-43. bibliog.

Bazin discusses the issue of 'slavery' in Bambara Segou on the continuum of *jon-horon* (slave or captive) to freeman, emphasizing the important political role of the warrior *jon*. He offers a detailed analysis of the origins, distribution and differentiation of captives. The article is translated into English by Helen Lakner from *Slavery in pre-colonial Africa* and edited by Claude Meillassoux (Paris: Maspéro, 1974). The latter also offers an introductory note.

218 **Warriors, merchants, and slaves: the state and the economy in the Middle Niger Valley, 1700-1914.**
Richard L. Roberts.   Stanford, California: Stanford University Press, 1987. 293p. maps. bibliog.

Based extensively on research conducted for the author's thesis and on fieldwork in Mali in 1976-77, 1981 and 1984, this is an economic history of three successive states in the Middle Niger valley: the Segu Bambara state, 1712-1861; the Umarian state, 1861-1890; and the French colonial state, 1883-1905. In 1905, slaves began a mass exodus from the area, the slave trade was ended and new relations between masters and former slaves were forged. Roberts emphasizes the central role of the state in the structure and performance of the economy and considers the state a 'field of force' in which 'the forces and social relations of production, appropriation, and exploitation were articulated and defended' (p. 212). The bibliography is excellent. See reviews by E. Hodgkin in *Africa*, vol. 59, no. 3 (1989), p. 428-29, and vol. 60, no. 1 (1990), p. 159-61, and by Robin Law who calls it 'a very good book indeed' in *Journal of African History*, vol. 29, no. 3 (1988), p. 550-51. See also Roberts's 'Ideology, slavery, and social formation: the evolution of Maraka slavery in the Middle Niger Valley', in *The ideology of slavery in Africa*, edited by Paul E. Lovejoy (Beverly Hills, California: Sage, 1981, p. 170-99); 'Production and reproduction of warrior states: Segu Bambara and Segu Tokolor, c. 1712-1890', in *International Journal of African Historical Studies*, vol. 13, no. 3 (1980), p. 389-419; and 'The Banamba slave exodus of 1905 and the decline of slavery in the Western Sudan', *Journal of African History*, vol. 21, no. 3 (1980), p. 375-94.

219 **West Africa: the former French states.**
John D. Hargreaves.   Englewood Cliffs, New Jersey: Prentice-Hall, 1967. 183p. map. bibliog. (The Modern Nations in Historical Perspective).

The author offers an historical account of the Francophone region which became Senegal, Mali, Mauritania, Guinea, Ivory Coast (now Côte d'Ivoire), Upper Volta (now Burkina Faso), Dahomey (now Benin), Niger and Togo. He discusses briefly the ancient empire of Mali, the Mali Federation of 1959-60 and the modern republic and well as other relevant topics. 'Suggested readings' (p. 169-73) notes numerous useful works. George E. Brooks, Jr. reviews the book in the *American Historical Review*, vol. 73, no. 2 (Dec. 1967), p. 560. Philip Neres's earlier *French-speaking West Africa: from colonial status to independence* (London: Oxford University Press for the Institute of Race Relations, 1962. 101p. maps. bibliog.) provides a succinct overview of precolonial and colonial history, and traces the rise of political and constitutional change for the large region including French Sudan and Mali.

French colonial (1883-1960)

220 Amkoullel, l'enfant peul: mémoires.
Amadou Hampâté Bâ. Arles, France: Actes Sud, 1991. 409p.

Bâ recounts his childhood adventures and adolescence in this volume of his memoirs. It is continued by *Oui, mon commandant* (Arles, France: Actes Sud, 1994. 396p.). In this autobiography, beginning with the year 1922, Bâ offers a lively and fascinating description of the colonial African era. He tells of his career as a young civil servant of the colonial administration in Upper Volta (now Burkina Faso), his marriage, the start of his family, and his comical adventures, both touching and dramatic. He also recounts how, during a long voyage, he begins to note the oral tales of which he becomes a trustee. An excerpt from *Amkoullel, l'enfant peul* was adapted to produce a children's book, *Le petit frère d'Amkoullel* (Paris: Syros, 1994. 38p.), in which Bâ tells of the birth of his younger brother in a village hospital.

221 The Bambara–French relationship, 1880-1915.
Jennifer Claudette Ward. PhD thesis, University of California, Los Angeles, 1976. 490 leaves. maps. bibliog. (Available from University Microfilms International, Ann Arbor, Michigan, order no. 7712946).

Using data from archives in Paris, Dakar and Mali and interviews in Mali in 1974-75, the author analyses the relationship between Segu and Bèlèdugu Bambara and the French up to and beyond the First World War. The history and comparison of the Segu and Bèlèdugu show how similar cultures evolved different political systems. Both groups allied with the French but for different reasons: the Bèlèdugu needed the French for offensive purposes and the Segu to regain control of their homeland. Ward describes the French advance to Bamako, the conquest of Segu, colonial rule and inter-war events. She includes a chronology of the Bambara kings of Segu from c. 1600 to 1890, four maps, and an extensive bibliography.

222 Campagne dans le Haut Sénégal et dans le Haut Niger, 1885-1886.
(Campaign in upper Senegal and the upper Niger, 1885-1886.)
Henri Nicolàs Frey. Paris: Plon, 1888. 503p.

The author, commandant of the 2nd Regiment of marine infantry, describes in detail the campaign against Samory and Mahmadou Lamine. The three fold-out maps include a 'Carte du Haut-Sénégal et du Haut-Niger' (scale 1:7,500,000).

223 Colonial conscripts: the Tirailleurs Sénégalais in French West Africa, 1857-1960.
Myron J. Echenberg. Portsmouth, New Hampshire; London: Heinemann; Currey, 1991. 236p. maps. bibliog. (Social History of Africa Series).

Echenberg examines the 'Conquest army' (1857-1905), the 'Occupation army' (1905-19), the 'Conscript army' (1919-45) and the period from 1945 to 1960 of the West African troops who helped France win its large territory. A. S. Kanya-Forstner reviews the volume in *Journal of African History*, vol. 34, no. 3 (1993), p. 511-12. This study won the 1992 African Studies Association Herskovits Award. See also 'African military labour and the building of the *Office du Niger* installations,

1925-1950' by Echenberg and Jean Filipovich in *Journal of African History*, vol. 27, no. 3 (1986), p. 533-51 (including maps and bibliog.), describing how more than 50,000 military conscripts worked on the Office du Niger irrigation project for three-year periods. 'Ironically, this new system of forced labour allowed the colonial administration to construct a grandiose irrigation scheme that was destined to fail, chiefly because the sparsely populated colony could not supply enough labour to exploit the irrigated land' (p. 551).

224   **The conquest of the Western Sahara: a study in French military imperialism.**
A. S. Kanya-Forstner.   Cambridge, England: Cambridge University Press, 1969. 297p. maps. bibliog.

Following an informative discussion of the colonial army, the Western Sudan and the background of the conquest, the author presents chapters on 'The revival of the Niger plan, 1876-80', 'The occupation of the Niger, 1880-83', 'The problems of occupation, 1883-6', 'The consolidation of the Sudan and the new African policy', 'The "total conquest" of the Sudan, 1888-93', 'The civilian administration of the Sudan, 1893-5', 'The last years of military rule, 1895-9', and 'Conclusion: French African policy and military imperialism'. An extensive list of archival sources (p. 275-78) and an excellent bibliography (p. 279-88) are included. Kanya-Forstner's 'Mali – Tukulor' in *West African resistance: the military response to colonial occupation*, edited by Michael Crowder (New York: Africana, 1971, p. 53-79. map. bibliog.) is an excellent account of the rise of the empire under Umar b. Said Tall (Umar Tal), his 1852 jihad, succession by his son Ahmadu, and relations with the French, leading to the fall of Segu, the Tukulor capital, in 1890.

225   **Deux campagnes au Soudan Français, 1886-1888.** (Two campaigns in the French Sudan, 1886-88.)
Joseph Simon Gallieni.   Paris: Hachette, 1891. 638p. maps.

The author offers a full account of the first campaign of the French, 1886-87, including the mission of Lt J. E. Caron to Tombouctou (Timbuktu; p. 5-320) and the second in 1887-88 (p. 323-633). The volume contains 163 engravings, a plan of the Fort of Siguiri, on the upper Niger, southwest of Bamako, and two detailed fold-out maps: 'Soudan Occidental' (scale 1:4,000,000) and 'Itinéraires levés dans le Soudan Français par ordre du Lt. Colonel-Gallieni, 1886-1888' (scale 1:5,000,000). He also authored *Mission d'exploration du Haut-Niger; voyage au Soudan français (Haut-Niger et pays de Ségou), 1879-1881* (Paris: Hachette, 1885. 632p. maps. plans). See also G. Grandidier's *Gallieni* (Paris: Plon, 1931).

226   **Djenné, il y a cent ans.** (Djenné, one hundred years ago.)
Bernard Gardi, Pierre Maas, Geert Mommersteeg.   Amsterdam; Paris: KIT Publications; Karthala, 1995. 167p. bibliog.

The photographs and postcards in this historically important work reveal the beauty and mystery of Djenné and the daily life of its inhabitants at the turn of the century. As these images attest, during that period this legendary city was truly rich and prosperous. The iconography of these pictures is especially important considering the fact that old photographs of the interior of the African continent are in general very rare. The book includes an introduction by Malian historian Bintou Sanankoua.

227 **France and Islam in West Africa, 1860-1960.**
Christopher Harrison.   Cambridge, England; New York: Cambridge
University Press, 1988. 242p. map. bibliog. (African Studies Series,
no. 60).

This important contribution to the social, political and intellectual history of French
West Africa focuses on an examination of 'not so much the "problem" of Islam but
rather the "problem" of French understanding of Islam' (p. 2). The study consists of
four chronological parts: '1850-1898: nineteenth-century origins of French Islamic
policy'; '1898-1912: the fear of Islam'; 'French scholarship and the definition of *Islam
noire*'; and '1920-1940: the French stake in *Islam noire*'. The volume includes
detailed notes and a bibliography of archival sources, unpublished monographs and
theses, and published sources. The book is based largely on the author's University of
London doctoral thesis 'French attitudes and policies towards Islam in West Africa,
1900-1940'. Jacques Louis Hymans reviews it as an 'exciting volume', 'a series of
intellectual sketches of European administrators', in *African Studies Review*, vol. 32,
no. 3 (Dec. 1989), p. 155-56. J. D. Hargreaves reviews it in *African Affairs*, vol. 88,
no. 352 (July 1989), p. 459-60, as does David Robinson in *Journal of African History*,
vol. 30, no. 2 (1989), p. 38-40.

228 **Francophone Sub-Saharan Africa, 1880-1985.**
Patrick Manning.   Cambridge, England; New York: Cambridge
University Press, 1988. 215p.

The author paints in broad brush-strokes a century of rapid change for the large
French-speaking area of West and Central Africa which covers thirty-five per cent of
the continent and is home to seventeen modern nations. He traces historical, political
and economic changes in the region as well as social and cultural ones and shows the
impacts of the internationalized world economy, providing regional context for the
emergence of modern Mali. The useful 'Bibliographical essay' (p. 200-5) surveys
books in seven broad categories, in English or translated into English. Thirteen maps
and four figures of data on exports and tax revenue are included. Femi Ojo-Ade
reviews the book in *Journal of Modern African Studies*, vol. 28, no. 1 (1990), p. 167-69;
as do John Hargreaves in *Journal of African History*, vol. 30, no. 1 (1989), p. 180-81;
and Chris Harrison in *African Affairs*, vol. 88, no. 351 (April 1989), p. 291-92.

229 **Les migrations militaires en Afrique occidentale française,
1900-1945.** (Military migrations in French West Africa, 1900-45.)
Myron J. Echenberg.   *Canadian Journal of African Studies*, vol. 14,
no. 3 (1980), p. 429-50. bibliog.

Using numerous data, figures and tables, the author shows the scale of French military
recruitment in West Africa during this period, describing three types of migration:
movement to avoid military service; movement from villages to urban areas and
overseas; and return migration. More men were conscripted in Mali (44,333) during
1920-46 than in any other area of French West Africa.

230 **Papa-commandant a jeté un grand filet devant nous: les exploités des rives du Niger, 1900-1962.** (The colonial administrator has thrown a large net in front of us: the exploitation of the Niger River, 1900-62.) Amidu Magasa, preface by Claude Meillassoux. Paris: F. Maspéro, 1978. 170p. maps. bibliog. (Textes à l'Appui: Série Feux de Brousse).

This account of the role and impact of the Office du Niger skilfully blends first-hand descriptions by participants in the large agricultural scheme with historical analysis of the flawed endeavour. Particularly interesting are the testimonials of eight workmen (p. 57-82) and seventeen settlers (p. 97-112).

231 **Les pionniers du Soudan, avant, avec et après Archinard, 1879-1894.** (The pioneers of Sudan, before, with and after Archinard, 1879-94.)
Jacques Méniaud, preface by M. E. Roume. Paris: Société des publications modernes, 1931. 2 vols. maps.

This work recounts the early penetration of the Western Sudan by the French in 1879 and continues through to Archinard's second campaign of 1889-90, Captain F. Quiquandon's campaign with Tiéba Traoré, King of Kénédougou in the Sikasso area from 1863 to 1893, and the arrival of Dr Crozat in Sikasso. Also covered is the third campaign of Lt-Col. Archinard (1890-91) to his retirement in Villiers-le-Bel in 1919. A list of governors and commandants is given in a table (vol. 1, p. 12-14); the two volumes (573p. and 554p., respectively) include 15 maps and 150 drawings. The author was Secretary-General of Haut-Sénégal-Niger, 1906-9. This is an excellent source on the subject of the French penetration of present-day Mali.

232 **Sikasso, ou, l'histoire dramatique d'un royaume noir au XIXe siècle.** (Sikasso; or, the dramatic history of a black kingdom in the nineteenth century.)
Jacques Méniaud, preface by Jules Brévié. Paris: F. Bouchy, 1935. 208p. maps.

This is a fine colonial product describing the kingdom of Kénédougou (whose capital was Sikasso), French penetration in the area, the mission to the king of Kéné, the siege and conquest of Sikasso in 1898, and consequences of the French vistory. It includes thirty-two plates of period photographs, among them views of Sikasso in 1893, four maps, a plan of Sikasso in April 1898, two engravings and a facsimile of the original order of assault. The volume includes a separate fold-out map of 'Champ d'opérations de la colonne de Sikasso et de la Colonne de Kong' (scale 1 cm to 50 km) showing the dates on which French posts were established in the central Malian region.

233 **Sikasso Tata.** (Fortifications of Sikasso.)
Alpha Oumar Konaré. Bamako: Editions-Imprimeries du Mali, 1983. 100p. maps. bibliog.

This interesting book consists of a brief text, profusely illustrated with photographs from the late nineteenth century and of the battle results, describing the city in southern Mali and its futile defence against French invaders, 15 April to 1 May 1898. Annexes (p. 79-93) include the French general orders, a plan of French bivouac positions, and lists of French personnel. The bibliography has fourteen references. *Tata* refers to fortifications of the city.

234   Les villages de liberté en Afrique noire française, 1887-1910.
(Liberty villages of French black Africa, 1887-1910.)
Denise Bouche.   The Hague: Mouton, 1968. 278p. map. bibliog. (Le
Monde d'Outre-Mer, Passé et Présent. 1. sér.: Études, no. 28).
The author describes the history, creation by Lt-Col. Gallieni in 1887, populations,
financing and administration of liberty villages, and settlements of freed slaves, as
well as the important role of the French Anti-Slavery Society. Bouche begins with a
detailed bibliography of archival sources in Paris, Mali, Dakar, Guinea, Mauritania
and of published works (p. 5-38). The appendix contains a list of *villages de liberté*
(p. 259-73) and a fold-out map of the villages in West Africa.

Timbuktu

235   The background and possible historical significance of a letter and
manuscript of 1798 concerning Timbuktu.
Michael T. Stieber.   *History in Africa*, vol. 8 (1981), p. 271-76.
The author describes the context of a French extract from an Arabic manuscript
recounting the 1591 fall of Timbuktu to 'Moroccan forces'. The Arabic manuscript
was translated for French naturalist Pierre-Auguste-Marie Broussonet who wrote a
cover letter dated September 1798. Stieber translates into English both the letter and
the extract, now located in the Hunt Institute for Botanical Documentation, Carnegie-
Mellon University, Pittsburgh, Pennsylvania.

236   L'occupation de Tombouctou. (The occupation of Tombouctou.)
Gaëtan Bonnier.   Paris: Les Editions du Monde Moderne, 1926. 288p.
This account of the exploits of Lt-Col. E. Bonnier includes a history of Tombouctou to
1893, a description of the French Sudan in 1893, and the actual efforts of Bonnier to
reach and conquer the city. He and numerous men were killed on 15 January 1894 by
Tuaregs at Tacoubao after leaving Tombouctou. Annexes (p. 193-288) include a
biography of Bonnier (1856-94) as well as letters and relevant documents. In addition
there are maps of the region and a small (scale 1:5000) map of Tombouctou in 1894.
Imperato provides a lengthy entry on Bonnier in his *Historical dictionary of Mali*
(q.v., p. 52-53). R. Bluzet, a lieutenant in the forces stationed at Tombouctou in 1894,
provides a brief geographical, social and political description of the region and a
'Carte de la région Tombouctou' (scale 1:500,000), with an insert of 'Le Niger devant
Tombouctou' (scale 1:100,000) in 'La Région de Tombouctou', *Bulletin de la Société
de Géographie* (Paris), Aug. 1895, p. 374-88.

237   The quest for Timbuctoo.
Brian Gardner.   New York: Harcourt, Brace & World, 1968. 212p.
This book is an engaging history of the famous town, 'the most irresistable word
connected with Africa' (p. 52). The author uses published sources and documents
from the Public Record Office, London, and the British Library to tell the stories of
Robert Adams and James Riley, Gordon Laing, René Caillié, Heinrich Barth, Oscar

Lenz and the French conquest of the Western Sudan, Father August Dupuis, Felix Dubois and A. H. Haywood. The volume has a chronology for Timbuctoo from c. 450 BC to AD 1960 (p. 197-200), a bibliography (p. 201-3), and twenty-one illustrations of historical figures and scenes.

238 **Social history of Timbuktu: the role of Muslim scholars and notables, 1400-1900.**
Elias N. Saad. Cambridge, England; New York: Cambridge University Press, 1983. 324p. (Cambridge Studies in Islamic Civilization).

This is probably the best academic study of Timbuktu written in English. Chapter titles reveal the work's emphases: 'Introduction'; 'Genesis of a social tradition'; 'The scholars as a learned elite'; 'The scholars as administrators'; 'The scholars as regional notables'; 'Persistence of the patriciate'; and 'Summary and conclusions'. Appendices (p. 234-53) include fifteen genealogies, lists of judges of Timbuktu and imams of the main mosque, notes (p. 254-95), glossary (p. 296-97), and an excellent bibliography (p. 298-307). Michel Abitbol reviews the book in French in 'The religious élite of Timbuktu', *Journal of African History*, vol. 25, no. 4 (1984), p. 469-72.

239 **Timbuktu.**
Daud Malik Watts. Washington, DC: Afro-Vision, 1986. 12p. map. bibliog. (Positive Image Education Series, vol. 1, no. 2).

This illustrated children's book sketches the history of Timbuktu, the importance of the Niger River, the salt trade and the University of Sankore, located in Timbuktu.

240 **Timbuktu under imperial Songhay: a reconsideration of autonomy.**
Michael A. Gomez. *Journal of African History*, vol. 31, no. 1 (1990), p. 5-24. bibliog.

The author argues, in contrast to most contemporary scholars, that during the period 1464-1591, imperial Songhay dominated Timbuktu and extracted financial profit from it. He believes that Timbuktu had relatively little influence over Gao during this period.

241 **Tombouctou au milieu du xviiie siècle: d'après la chronique de Mawlay al-Qasim B. Mawlay Sulayman. (Dhikr al-wafayat wa-ma hadatha min al-umur al-īzam wa-al-fitan.** (The eighteenth-century milieu of Timbuktu according to the chronicle of Mawlay al-Qasim B. Mawlay Sulayman.)
Paris: G.-P. Maisonneuve et Larose, 1982. 85p. + 18p. (Fontes Historiae Africanae. Series Arabica, no. 7).

Michel Abitbol provides a short introduction (p. vii-xii) to the chronicle of Timbuktu from 1747 to 1801 by Mawlay al-Qasim which he (Abitbol) has translated into French (p. 1-32) and for which he has included detailed notes (p. 33-65) and appendices (p. 68-85). These include a chronology of Timbuktu, 1703-4 to 1833, a list of Pachas of Timbuktu, 1748-96, and a list of titles and genealogies of the leading figures from the chronicle (p. 73-85). Following all this is the Arabic text itself (18p.).

242 **Tombouctou et l'empire Songhay: épanouissement du Soudan Nigérien aux xv-xvi siècles.** (Timbuktu and the Songhay Empire: the flowering of the Nigerian Sudan in the fifteenth and sixteenth centuries.) Sékéné Mody Cissoko. Paris: L'Harmattan, 1996. 243p. maps. bibliog.

The author traces the history of Timbuktu to the accession of the Askia family, the evolution and organization of the Songhay Empire (1493-1592), and describes social, traditional and economic life and the Muslim religion in the sixteenth century. The volume contains four maps, two diagrams and six historical photographs. The author also wrote 'Famines et epidémies à Tombouctou et dans la Boucle du Niger du xvie au xviiie siècle' (Famines and epidemics at Timbuktu and in the Niger Bend from the sixteenth to the eighteenth century) in *Bulletin IFAN*, vol. 30, series B, no. 3 (1968), p. 806-21, and 'Intelligentsia de Tombouctou aux xve et xvie siècles' (The intelligensia of Timbuktu in the fifteenth and sixteenth centuries), *Bulletin IFAN*, vol. 31, series B, no. 4 (1969), p. 927-52.

243 **Tombouctou et les Arma: de la conquête marocaine du Soudan nigérien en 1591 à l'hégémonie de l'empire Peulh du Macina en 1833.** (Tombouctou and its arma: from the Moroccan conquest of the Sudan in 1591 to the hegemony of the Peul Empire of Macina in 1833.) Michel Abitbol. Paris: G.-P. Maisonneuve et Larose, 1979. 295p. bibliog.

In the four parts of this work the author examines: the conquest of the Sudan and the establishment of Pashalik, the period of Moroccan domination of the Niger Bend area; the evolution of Pashalik to the seventeenth century; social and economic life of the Pashalik; and the collapse of the occupied state of Tombouctou. Imperato explains in his *Historical dictionary of Mali* (3rd ed., 1996, p. 193) that 'Arma', derived from 'Rumat' (soldiers carrying firearms), is the term the Songhay 'applied to the Moroccan invaders and their descendants'. The volume concludes with extensive appendices including historical abstracts (p. 240-49), a list of 167 pashas of Tombouctou from 1591 to 1833 (p. 250-54), genealogies (p. 255-58) and a chronology of Pachalik, 1591-1833 (p. 259-62). The book would benefit from a good map and a subject index. Louis Brenner praises the book in his review 'The Arma of Timbuktu', *Journal of African History*, vol. 22, no. 4 (1981), p. 549-60.

244 **The White Monk of Timbuctoo.** William Seabrook. New York: Harcourt, Brace and Company, 1934. 1st ed. 279p.

A biography of Auguste Dupuis-Yakouba, the legendary 'White Monk of Timbuctoo'. Yakouba, a White Fathers missionary, married an African woman and settled in Timbuctoo as its first permanent white citizen. He became fluent in the Songai language (and authored such titles as *Manuel de la langue songay parlée de Tombouctou à Say dans la boucle du Niger* and *Essai de méthode pratique pour l'étude de la langue songoï ou songaï*) and developed an extensive knowledge of the traditions and customs of the many indigenous peoples of the region. This work is useful for the number of historical facts it contains, both in the text and in the appendix.

Historical dictionary of Mali.
See item no. 7.

Atlas historique de la boucle du Niger: synthèse des colloques de Bamako et Niamey, 1975-1976-1977. (Historical atlas of the Niger Bend: a synthesis of the symposia of Bamako and Niamey, 1975, 1976, 1977.)
See item no. 91.

Répertoire général des sites historiques et archéologiques du Mali. (General list of historical and archaeological sites in Mali.)
See item no. 155.

Colonial policy and the family life of black troops in French West Africa, 1817-1904.
See item no. 379.

Freedom and authority in French West Africa.
See item no. 413.

Rulers of empire: the French colonial service in Africa.
See item no. 419.

An economic history of West Africa.
See item no. 473.

The golden trade of the Moors: West African kingdoms in the fourteenth century.
See item no. 504.

The impact of the Western Sudanic empires on the trans-Saharan trade: tenth to sixteenth century.
See item no. 505.

Long distance trade and production: Sinsani in the nineteenth century.
See item no. 507.

Trade and politics on the Senegal and Upper Niger, 1854-1900: African reaction to French penetration.
See item no. 510.

Two worlds of cotton: colonialism and the regional economy in the French Soudan, 1800-1946.
See item no. 511.

Dictionary of African historical biography.
See item no. 849.

L'Encyclopédie coloniale et maritime. (The colonial and maritime encyclopaedia.)
See item no. 853.

Jamana.
See item no. 870.

Population

Population and demography

245 Africa, Mali: selected statistical data by sex.
United States. Agency for International Development. Office of
Development Information and Utilization. Washington, DC: Office
of Development Information and Utilization, US Agency for
International Development, 1981[?]. 48p.

USAID published statistical tables for various Third World countries. The source for
eighteen of the nineteen tables included here is the *Enquête démographique au Mali,
1960-61* (q.v.) and the source for the other table is the *1976 Recensement général de
la population* (see item no. 261). The information includes tables on population, life
expectancy, infant mortality, marital status, urban/rural population, minimum legal
age at marriage, number of households, fertility rates, literacy counts, and
employment. For six of the tables, there are no data. The statistics are available on two
microfiches.

**246 Intégration des variables démographiques dans les plans et les
programmes de développement de la République du Mali: éléments
de méthodologie et la politique de population.** (Integration of
demographic variables into the plans and development programmes of
the Republic of Mali: elements of a methodology and the politics of
population.)
Ministère du Plan, Direction de la Planification. Bamako: Ministère
du Plan, Direction Nationale de la Planification, République du Mali,
1986. 90p. bibliog.

Mali's central government published this report on the methodology of integrated
planning. It includes an analysis of Mali's demographic–economic situation and lists
the factors which define the politics of population.

247 **Inventory of Population Projects in Developing Countries Around the World.**
United Nations Population Fund. New York: United Nations Population Fund, 1973/1974- . annual.

In this current annual publication on population research and projects, the subjects covered under Mali (1995, p. 321-26) include family planning/reproductive health, population education and communication, population policies and dynamics, and population data collection and analysis. For each project, there is a brief description of its purpose, funding agency, the project duration and budget.

248 **Perspectives de population par cercle/arrondissement, 1993-1997.**
(Population perspectives by circle/ward, 1993-97.)
Ministère de l'Economie, des Finances et du Plan, Direction Nationale de la Statistique et de l'Informatique. Bamako: Ministère de l'Economie, des Finances et du Plan, Direction Nationale de la Statistique et de l'Information, 1993. 291 leaves.

This publication, containing statistical tables without text, projects the population of Mali for the period of 1993-97, by region, sex and age. A similar earlier publication exists: *Perspectives démographiques du Mali: estimation de la population de 1963 à 1973* (Demographic perspectives of Mali: population estimates from 1963 to 1973) (Bamako: Service de la Statistique Générale de la Comptabilité Nationale et de la Mécanographie, 1963. 23 leaves).

Migration (internal and external)

249 **Atlas des migrations ouest-africaines vers l'Europe, 1985-1993.**
(Atlas of West African migrations to Europe, 1985-93.)
Nelly Robin. Paris: EUROSTAT and ORSTOM, 1996. 109p. maps. bibliog.

Whereas even recent publications on migrations are often based on census data from the 1970s, this publication's data from 1985 to 1993 is timely. Mali's place in West African migration to Europe is easy to see in the publication's numerous charts, graphs and maps. In 1993, there were 39,131 Malians living in the European Union countries and, not surprisingly, most of them had chosen France: 37,693 in France, 889 in Germany, 275 in Italy, 204 in Spain, and the remaining 70 in Denmark, Greece, Portugal, Finland, and Sweden (p. 95). Malians choosing to emigrate within West Africa prefer Côte d'Ivoire and Senegal. The number of Malians asking for asylum in France has diminished between 1988 (2,703) and 1993 (1,372) (p. 98).

250 **Les clandestins: enquête en France, en Chine et au Mali.** (The clandestine ones: study in France, China, and Mali.)
Jean-Luc Porquet. Paris: Flammarion, 1997. 403p. maps. bibliog.

Malian and Chinese illegal aliens living in France are the subject of this recent study. The author travelled to the region of Fegui, a Soninke village. Porquet secretly interviewed some of the illegal aliens and discusses the reasons for their exile. An interesting chronology of immigration to France from 1945 to February 1997 appears in an appendix (p. 347-90). See also Salim Jay's *101 Maliens nous manquent* (101 Malians are missing) (Paris: Arcantère, 1987. 114p.) about the deportation from France of 101 Malians on 18 October 1986.

251 **Les flux migratoires à Bamako.** (Migratory flows to Bamako.)
Coordinated by Mamadou Diallo Pesg, edited by Mamadou Sarr.
Bamako: AMRAD; Milan, Italy: FOCSIV, 1987. 66, 22 leaves. maps. bibliog.

Internal migration in Mali is tied to economic problems stemming from both the harsh climatic conditions and the physical geography of the country. A brief history of Mali's internal migration (leaves 8-12) is followed by an in-depth look at the case of migration to Bamako in 1987 (leaves 13-57) from the perspectives of geographical, sociological, and psychological realities. Sarr took this research to the next level in his *Migration & espace rural: la région de Segou, in* [sic] *Mali* (Migration and rural space: the region of Segou, in Mali) (Milan, Italy: FOCSIV, 1991. 1 vol.) which describes rural migration in Mali's Segou region.

252 **Gens d'ici, gens d'ailleurs: migrations Soninké et transformations villageoises.** (People from here, people from there: Soninke migration and rural change.)
Catherine Quiminal. Paris: C. Bourgeois, 1991. 222p. maps. bibliog. (Cibles, no. 21).

Based on her research in the 1970s in Guidimaka (the region of Kayes) and in France, the author writes about the anthropology of change. She studied Soninke migrants living in France today and the effects of their lengthy absences on village associations.

253 **L'habitat des familles sahéliennes en Ile de France, originaires des pays riverains du fleuve Sénégal: Mali, Mauritanie, Sénégal: une catastrophe annoncée.** (The housing of Sahelian families in Ile de France, originally from the countries bordering on the Senegal River: Mali, Mauritania, Senegal: a catastrophe waiting to happen.)
Claudette Bodin, Almadane Diakite, Damou Kouyate. Paris: Afrique Partenaires Services, 1995. 129 leaves. bibliog.

Malian, Mauritanian and Senegalese men began their emigration to France during the 1970s droughts in the Sahel. Those immigrants living in Ile de France (Paris) are the subjects of this study. The analysis covers housing characteristics, family regrouping, lodging and social marginalization, housing aspirations, the future of Sahelian families in France, and proposals for improving the lodging situation of Sahelian families.

254 **Les migrations agricoles au Mali.** (Agricultural migrations in Mali.)
Ibrahima Cissé. Louvain-la-Neuve, Belgium: CIDEP: Academia-
Erasme, 1993. 73p. maps. bibliog. (Cahiers du CIDEP, no. 18).

Agricultural migration is here defined as rural–rural migration of at least six months'
duration undertaken to cultivate new lands. In Mali, these migrations flow from north
to south, from the Sahelian and Sudanic regions to pockets of southern Mali. In order
to better balance population and resources, recommendations are made to integrate
existing national population/desertification policies into a 'new indigenous policy of
development relative to internal migration and the agricultural exploitation of fresh
land' (English summary, p. 7).

255 **Migrations et urbanisation en Afrique de l'ouest (MUAO):
résultats préliminaires.** (Migrations and urbanization in West Africa:
preliminary results.)
Edited by Sadio Traore, Philippe Bocquier. Bamako: CERPOD,
1995. 30p. map.

In 1993, the Réseau Migrations et Urbanisations en Afrique de l'Ouest made
simultaneous demographic studies in eight West African countries: Burkina Faso,
Côte d'Ivoire, Guinea, Mali, Mauritania, Niger, Nigeria and Senegal. Using eleven
tables, nine graphs, and two maps as well as some text, this publication analyses each
country's population (total, rural/urban, migrants, schooling, unemployment, foreign
population, internal migration, migration within the region, and emigration).

256 **Pérégrinations sahéliennes: la problématique du changement dans
une société traditionnelle d'Afrique noire: les Dogon du Mali.**
(Sahelian peregrinations: the problematics of change in a traditional
Black African society: the Dogon of Mali.)
Dominique Vialard. Toulouse, France: Institut d'Etudes Politiques,
Université des Sciences Sociales de Toulouse, 1983. 116p. maps.
bibliog.

This is a study of internal migration of the Dogons who inhabit the cliffs along the
Niger River Bend. Some of the changes in Dogon society which impact upon
migration include the process of Islamization, economic factors, tourism, and central
government administration.

257 **La problématique de l'émigration des Soinkés de Kayes, Mali:
quelques aspects des problèmes sociaux du développement rural
intégré.** (The problem of emigration among the Soninke of Kayes
Region, Mali: some aspects of the social problems caused by integrated
rural development.)
Abdoulaye Keita. Quebec, Canada: Centre Sahel, Université Laval,
1996. 35p. bibliog. (Notes et Travaux, no. 35).

The Soninke constitute 42 per cent of the population of the Kayes Region in western
Mali. The origins, driving forces, and consequences of Soninke emigration (internal
and external) are considered here.

258 **Rural out-migration and labor allocation in Mali.**
Robert E. Mazur. In: *Rural migration in developing nations: comparative studies of Korea, Sri Lanka, and Mali.* Edited by Calvin Goldscheider. Boulder, Colorado: Westview Press, 1984, p. 209-88.
In order to understand migration in Mali, Mazur considers the population process in relation to agricultural development. Short- and long-term labour migration do not follow the same processes. 'Larger and more complex households are characterized by higher rates of long-term migration' (p. 279).

259 **The social dynamics of rural population retention: a Malian case study of the link between household social control and the sustained ruralization of Sub-Saharan Africa.**
Michael Tawanda. PhD thesis, Brown University, Providence, Rhode Island, 1994. 228p. bibliog. (Available from University Microfilms International, Ann Arbor, Michigan, order no. 9433455).
This study of migration in the Kayes Region of Mali from 1982 to 1989 tests the link between household authority and the probability and direction of migration.

260 **Women's roles in settlement and resettlement in Mali.**
Dolores Koenig. In: *African feminism: the politics of survival in Sub-Saharan Africa.* Edited by Gwendolyn Mikell. Philadelphia, Pennsylvania: University of Pennsylvania Press, 1997, p. 159-81. bibliog.
Although men have made decisions about population movement patterns, women's production is necessary to improve family welfare and achieve self-sufficiency in food production. Three groups of rural migrants were studied: those affected by the droughts of the 1970s and 1980s, those who were repatriated by international governments, and those who were involuntarily displaced by development projects.

Censuses

261 **Analyse du recensement.** (Analysis of the census.)
Ministère du Plan et de la Coopération Internationale, Direction Nationale de la Statistique et de l'Informatique, Bureau Central de Recensement. [Bamako?]: Bureau Central de Recensement, 1982-85. 7 vols. maps. bibliog.
The first full national census of Mali dates from 1976. This comprehensive analysis also includes a healthy dose of statistical tables. The work is divided into: vol. 1. Principal characteristics; vol. 2. Administrative and technical report; vol. 3. Demographic characteristics; vol. 4. School attendance and level of instruction; vol. 5. Economic activity; vol. 6. Perspectives of the resident population of Mali, 1977-2007; vol. 7. Special studies. For detailed statistical tables, see also *Recensement général de*

la population, décembre 1976, résultats définitifs (General census of the population, December 1976, definitive results) ([Bamako?]: Bureau Central de Recensement, 1980. 3 vols), which covers population, demography, nomads, social series, economic series, and a directory of villages. For an excellent summary of this and all Mali censuses (ending with the 1976 census), see Eliane Domschke and Doreen S. Goyer's *The handbook of national population censuses: Africa and Asia* (New York; London: Greenwood Press, 1986. 1,032p.) in which they state 'the counts previous to this census were all of partial populations which makes them difficult to compare' (p. 267). Mali is covered on pages 263-70.

262 **Enquête démographique au Mali, 1960-1961.** (Demographic study of Mali, 1960-61.)
Mali. Service de la Statistique.   Paris: Secrétariat d'Etat aux Affaires Etrangères; I.N.S.E.E. Service de Coopération, 1969[?]. 349p. maps.

The region north of Timbuktu is excluded from this study as is the Office du Niger territory (primarily the centres of Niono-Molodo and Kokry-Kolougotomo). Tables are grouped by individual and collective data, 'natural' movement, and migratory movement. It includes the standard vital statistics such as age, birthplace, marital status, fertility, as well as ethnic group (indigenous population) or nationality (non-indigenous), education, occupation, and religion. Of further interest from the same author, see *Bamako, recensement 1958, enquête démographique, 1960-61: résultats définitifs* (Bamako, 1958 census, demographic study, 1960-61: definitive results) (Paris, 1969. 97p.) which includes data on sex, age, ethnicity, marital status, religion, occupation, literacy, and industry. Both are available in the microfilm series International Population Census Publications. Africa (Woodbridge, Connecticut: Research Publications, 197-).

263 **Enquête démographique de 1985: résultat préliminaire.**
(Demographic study of 1985: preliminary results.)
Paris: Organisation des Nations Unies, Programme des Nations Unies pour le Développement, Département de la Coopération Technique pour le Développement, 1986. 30 leaves. map.

The entire country was surveyed from June to August 1985 in a joint Government of Mali/UN project. These provisional figures cover the national, regional and local (urban and rural) levels. For the District of Bamako, the commune level is also given. The twenty-two tables cover population, residence, sex, residents present, absent residents, and visitors.

264 **Rapport sur l'évaluation, l'ajustement et l'analyse des données du recensement de la population de décembre 1976: perspectives de population au Mali de 1976 à l'an 2010.** (Report on the evaluation, adjustment and analysis of the population census data of December 1976: population perspectives in Mali from 1976 to the year 2010.)
Patrice Sawadogo.   Addis Ababa: Division de la Population, 1983. 150, 40 leaves. maps.

This is a demographic, economic and social analysis of the 1976 census of Mali.

265 **Recensement général de la population et de l'habitat (1er au 14 avril 1987): principaux résultats d'analyse.** (General census of the population and habitat (1-14th April 1987): principal results of analysis.)
Ministère du Plan et de la Coopération Internationale, Direction Nationale de la Statistique et de l'Informatique, Bureau Central de Recensement. Bamako: Bureau Central de Recensement, 1991. 43p. maps.

This work summarizes the results of the 1987 (second) national census in a brief text, twenty-eight tables and eighteen graphs. Data is given for sex, age, matrimonial status, monogamy and polygamy, schooling, literacy, economic activity, housing characteristics, and population movement (births, fertility, deaths, migration). A complete list of the 1987 census publications (p. 41-43) shows forty volumes already published and three more in preparation. For those readers interested in more detailed data from this census, consult *Recensement général de la population et de l'habitat au Mali: analyse* (General census of the population and habitat of Mali: analysis) (Bamako: Bureau Central de Recensement, 1991-92. 7 vols), in which each volume covers a specific topic such as population movement, economic activities, housing and households, etc.; *Recensement général de la population et de l'habitat: résultats définitifs* (General census of the population and habitat: definitive results) (Bamako: Bureau Central de Recensement, 1990. 9 vols in 12), which provides an analysis for the whole country (volume 0, parts 1-4) and by regions (volumes 1-8).

266 **Soudan: population en 1951 par canton et groupe ethnique: chiffres provisoires.** (Sudan: population in 1951 by canton and ethnic group: provisional figures.)
Haut Commissariat de l'Afrique Occidentale Française, Service de la Statistique Générale. Dakar: Service de la Statistique Générale, 1953. 135 leaves.

Provisional data on the native population, by ethnicity, of the French Sudan is divided into four *cercles*: Cerle du Bassin du Sénégal, Cercle du Niger, Cercle du Sahel et du Delta du Niger, and Cercle de l'Intérieur de la Boucle du Niger. See also *Recensement de la population non autochtone de l'Afrique Occidentale Française en juin 1951* (Census of the non-indigenous population of French West Africa in June 1951) (Dakar: Service de la Statistique Générale, 1955. 69p.) This census of non-indigenous people covers all of French West Africa. Data on Mali is found under 'Soudan' or 'Soudan française'. It covers French citizenship, age, nationality, marital status and children, birthplace, and duration of sojourn. Both are available in the microfilm series International Population Census Publications. Africa (Woodbridge, Connecticut: Research Publications, 197-).

Les migrations militaires en Afrique occidentale française, 1900-1945. (Military migrations in French West Africa, 1900-45.)
See item no. 229.

Infant and child mortality in rural Mali.
See item no. 400.

Changing places?: women, resource management and migration in the Sahel: case studies from Senegal, Burkina Faso, Mali and Sudan.
See item no. 469.

Senoufo migrants in Bamako: changing agricultural production strategies and household organization in an urban environment.
See item no. 536.

Pop Sahel.
See item no. 873.

Ethnic Groups

267 **Arid ways: cultural understandings of insecurity in Fulbe society, central Mali.**
Mirjam de Bruijn, Han van Dijk.   Amsterdam: Thela, 1995. 547p. maps. bibliog. (CERES Series, no. 1).
The droughts in the Sahel over the past two decades have caused social, political and ecological insecurities for the impoverished Fulbe (Peul) pastoralists living in Hayre, central Mali. The authors conclude with a chapter on the 'cultural understandings' of insecurity which can be used to help the pastoralists solve their problems.

268 **Bambara men and women and the reproduction of social life in Sana Province, Mali.**
Maria Luise Grosz-Ngaté.   PhD thesis, Michigan State University, 1986. 249p. bibliog. (Available from University Microfilms International, Ann Arbor, Michigan, order no. 8625025).
Based on research undertaken in a specific Bambara community in the province of Sana, neighbouring communities, and the national archives of Mali and Senegal, this thesis is an analysis of contemporary Sana Bambara society, how it developed historically, and its underlying dynamics.

269 **Bibliographie générale du monde peul.** (General bibliography of the Peul world.)
Christiane Seydou.   Niamey: Institut de Recherches en Sciences Humaines, Université de Niamey, 1977. 179p. (Etudes Nigériennes, no. 43).
Although this bibliography is twenty years old, it is an excellent source of older materials on the Peuls. It is well indexed by subjects, and includes physical anthropology, cultural anthropology, social anthropology and history, as well as other more general works. The geographical index makes it easy to find the 277 works covering Mali.

270 **Boucle du Niger: approches multidisciplinaires.** (Niger Bend: multidisciplinary approaches.)
Kawada Junzo. Tokyo: Institut de Recherches sur les Langues et Cultures d'Asie et d'Afrique, 1988-92. 3 vols. map. bibliog.
This joint Malian–Japanese study took place between 1986 and 1991 and consisted of three broad multi-disciplinary projects. Volume 1 covers 'Homme, matière et technologie; Univers aquatique; Les éleveurs et leurs milieux; Rites et communication'. Volume 2: 'La technologie traditionnelle face au développement; Symbiose et intégration de peuples et civilisations hétérogènes; Espace archéologique, citadin et domestique'. Volume 3: 'L'homme et son milieu; Le corps humain: nature et culture; La société dans l'histoire; La culture orale dans la société malienne contemporaine'. A fourth volume is supposed to have been published, but could not be obtained by the authors.

271 **La célébration de la levée du deuil: les rites du dannyi chez les Dogon de Pelu.** (The celebration of the lifting of mourning: the rites of the Dannyi of the Dogon of Pelu.)
Groupe de Recherche des Coutumes Dogon. Bandiagara, Mali: Groupe de Recherche des Coutumes Dogon, 1989. 172p. map.
This is a description of the funeral rites and chants of the masked Dogon dancers of Pelu. The *Dannyi* is a celebration honouring dead males. The work includes an appendix on the four stages of male initiation rites into the society of masks. Other recent publications on similar topics by the GRCD include: *La fête du bilɛ chez les Dogon du Kamma dans les villages de Pelu et Veje* (The festival of Bilɛ of the Dogon of Kamma in the villages of Pelu and Veje) (1991. 19p.) and *Les funerailles et le yimu-kɔmɔ chez les Dogon du Kamma dans les villages de Pelu et Veje* (Funerals and the yimu-kɔmɔ of the Dogon of Kamma in the villages of Pelu and Veje) (1991. 60p.).

272 **Les chemins de la noce: la femme et le mariage dans la société rurale au Mali.** (The path to the wedding: woman and marriage in Mali's rural society.)
René Luneau. Lille, France: Service de Reproduction des Thèses, Université de Lille III, 1975. 699p. maps. bibliog.
This is a study of the marriage customs of a Bambara people in Béléko Soba, southeastern Mali. Part 1 covers the background information on the daily life and social organization of the villagers. Part two analyses kinship and alliances, and Part 3 describes the good and bad fortunes of conjugal life. Luneau includes an index of Bambara terms (p. 689-95).

273 **La confrérie des chasseurs Malinké et Bambara: mythes, rites et récits initiatiques.** (The brotherhood of Malinke and Bambara hunters: myths, rites, and initiatory tales.)
Youssouf Tata Cissé. Ivry, France: Nouvelles du Sud; Paris: Agence de Coopération Culturelle et Technique, 1994. 390p. map. bibliog.
Donso tòn, the Malinké and Bambara secret hunting society, originated in the ancient kingdom of Wagadu. Soundiata Keita, founder of the Mali Empire, was a member of this society. This study uncovers the myth of the founding of the society, and analyses

its structure, religious beliefs, and rites and ceremonies. The text concludes with two initiatory hunting songs/tales: Flani Boyi (Boyi the twin), performed by Bâla Djimba Diakité, and Boli Nyanan, performed by Bougoba Djiré, published here in Manding and French and Bambara and French respectively.

274 **Les Dogon.** (The Dogons.)
Photographs by Michel Renaudeau, text by Nadine Wanono, preface by Jean Rouch. Paris: Editions du Chêne, 1996. 191p. map. bibliog.
In this lavishly illustrated book on the Dogons, the text is written by a cinematographer who has worked in Dogon country for twenty years, in the region of Sanga. She secured access to pioneering French ethnologist Marcel Griaule's archives at the Université de Paris X and has illustrated the book with contrasting photographs – some recently taken and Griaule's from the 1930s – of the same subjects. The bibliography (p. 191) is largely reliant on the works of Griaule and his associates. The brief filmography (same page) is worth perusing.

275 **Les Dogon de Boni: approche démo-génétique d'un isolat du Mali.**
(The Dogon of Boni: demo-genetic approach of an isolate of Mali.)
Under the direction of Marie-Hélène Cazes (et al.), preface by Albert Jacquard. Paris: Presses Universitaires de France: Editions de l'INED, 1993. 302p. maps. bibliog. (Travaux et Documents, cahier no. 132).
The eight chapters on the social structure and genetics of the Dogons of Boni include an overview of their geography, history, language, cultural and social organization; census data and other collected data; local pathology; preliminary study in Sarnyéré; demographic dynamic; endogamy and matrimonial exchanges; consequences of marriage structure on the genetic evolution of the Dogons; analysis of blood samples.

276 **Les Dogons du Mali.** (The Dogons of Mali.)
Gérard Beaudoin. Paris: A. Colin, 1984. 222p. maps. bibliog.
(Collection Civilisations).
The history, religion, rituals, social and cultural life of the Dogons are contained in this general text for the French reader. It is illustrated with black-and-white photographs and line-drawings.

277 **Encyclopedia of world cultures. Volume IX, Africa and the Middle East.**
David Levinson, editor in chief; John Middleton and Amal Rassam, volume editors. Boston, Massachusetts: G. K. Hall, 1995. 447p. maps. bibliog.
This recent publication, prepared under the auspices of the Human Relations Area Files (HRAF) at Yale University, will give only a taste of all of the ethnic groups found in Mali. Coverage here is limited to Dogon (p. 71-74), Dyula (p. 75-78), Fulani (p. 100-4), Mande (p. 215-16), Songhay (p. 319-20), and Tuareg (p. 366-70) ethnic groups. For each group, ethnonyms, orientation, history and cultural relations, settlements, economy, kinship, marriage and family, sociopolitical organization, religion and expressive culture, and a bibliography are given. For more complete information on the Dogon and Tuareg, see the HRAF microfiles (item no. 281)

278 **Family identity and the state in the Bamako Kafu, c.1800-c.1900.**
B. Marie Perimbam. Boulder, Colorado: Westview Press, 1997.
341p. maps. bibliog. (African States and Societies in History).
Perinbam writes about Mande social history in her exploration of the families who founded the Bamako state and their quest for political power, economic opportunities, and social status. As these families migrated, their ethnic identities changed from Soninke to Marka-Sarakole to Bamana.

279 **Groupes ethniques au Mali.** (Ethnic groups in Mali.)
Bokar N'Diayé. Bamako: Editions Populaires, 1970. 479p. maps.
bibliog. (Collection 'Hier').
Begin here for the most complete analysis of Mali's ethnic groups. The author summarizes the origins and history, political–administrative and judicial organization, economic and social structures, customs, beliefs, arts, and characteristic traits of the Touareg (Tuareg), Maures, Peuls, Bambara, Malinké, Soninke (Sarakole), Songhay, Dogon, Sénufo-Minianka, Bobo, Diawara, Khassonke, Bozo and Somono, Toucouleur (Tukulor), Kagoro, Foulanké, and Diallonké peoples.

280 **Histoire des Bambara.** (History of the Bambara.)
Louis Tauxier. Paris: P. Geuthner, 1942. 226p. maps. bibliog.
This is one of the important older works on the Bambara, written by a former colonial administrator, but not part of the HRAF files (see item no. 281).

281 **Human Relations Area Files: Bambara.**
Human Relations Area Files, Inc. New Haven, Connecticut: HRAF,
1974- . 43 microfiches. maps. bibliog.
The HRAF files are a superb ethnographic resource. They contain the full original text, or in some cases, the English translation, of the most important, older ethnographic works. For Mali, only three ethnic groups are represented, but they include many ethnographic classics. Texts on the Bambara reproduced here are from four sources published between 1900 and 1950, and comprise 1,127 pages of text. They include works by Germaine Dieterlen, Charles Monteil, Viviana Pâques, and Joseph Henry. Hardcopy HRAF paper files have also been published, but are often not as complete as the microfiche collection. HRAF files have also been published on the Dogon (145 microfiches; 23 sources from 1925 to 1970 in 4,645 pages of text), including works by Monserrat Palau Martí, Denise Paulme, Germaine Dieterlen, Marcel Griaule, Solange de Ganay, Paul Parin and others. The Tuareg collection is also of interest, although about the Tuareg of the Algerian Hoggar (54 fiches; 8 sources from 1900 to 1960 in 1,225 pages of text).

282 **Les Khassonké: monographie d'une peuplade du Soudan Français.**
(The Khassonke: monograph on a tribe of French Sudan.)
Charles Monteil. Paris: E. Leroux, 1915. Reprinted, Nendeln,
Liechtenstein: Kraus Reprint, 1974. 528p map. bibliog. (Collection de
la Revue du Monde Musulman).
This ethnology of the Khassonke people of northwestern Mali covers their origins and history, customs, political and social organizations, their partial Islamization, and

language. Monteil is best known for his work with the Bambara (see item no. 281). His comprehensive look at the city of Djenne, entitled *Une cité soudanaise: Djénné, métropole du delta central du Niger* (A Sudanese city: Djenne, metropolis of the central Niger Delta) (Paris: Éditions Anthropos, 1974. 301p.), pays particular attention to its various inhabitants.

283 **La langue secrète des Dogons de Sanga.** (The secret language of the Dogons of Sanga.)
Michel Leiris. Paris: Institut d'Ethnologie, 1948. Reprinted, Paris: J.-M. Place, 1992. 530p. bibliog. (Cahiers de Gradhiva, no. 19).

As a member of Marcel Griaule's research team in the 1930s, Leiris, a philologist and ethnologist, studied the Dogons' secret language of rites and ceremonies, particularly the *Sigui* (celebration of a new generation of men every 60 years) as well as funerary practices. The text concludes with a *Sigui* grammar and vocabulary.

284 **Malinke.**
C. O. Nwanunobi. New York: Rosen Publishing Group, 1996. 1st ed. 64p. maps. bibliog. (The Heritage Library of African Peoples).

This book is aimed at the juvenile reader and discusses the history, culture, religion, traditions and daily life of the Malinké, West African people who live in the Manding Highlands near the upper Niger River. Also available in this series are: Chukwuma Azuonye's *Dogon* (1996); Pat I. Ndukwe's *Fulani* (1995); Tunde Adeleke's *Songhay* (1996); and C. Nwanunobi's *Soninke* (1996).

285 **Masked dancers of West Africa: the Dogon.**
Stephen Pern and the editors of Time-Life Books, photographs by Bryan Alexander. Amsterdam: Time-Life Books, 1982. 168p. map. bibliog. (Peoples of the Wild).

This is an excellent introductory text on the Dogon people aimed at the general reader. Pern and Alexander lived in the heart of Dogon country in the village of Tireli, part of the 120-mile-long Bandiagara escarpment. Using many beautiful colour photographs, they describe the physical setting, family life, ceremonies, social structures such as 'the compulsion towards conformity and harmony' (p. 122) and life during the rainy season.

286 **Masques dogons.** (Dogon masks.)
Marcel Griaule. Paris: Institut d'Ethnologie, 1983. 3rd ed. 896p. maps. bibliog. (Travaux et Mémoires de l'Institut d'Ethnologie, no. 33).

Perhaps the most important work by the pioneering French ethnologist, and based on his research on the Dogon in the area of Bandiagara between 1931 and 1937. Recent scholars have criticized his methodology. For example, B. DeMott states, 'As ethnographic surveys, these descriptions of Dogon culture are extremely valuable. However, the unity of approach, the homogeneity of the informants, the suppression of critical analysis, and the lack of attribution of specific field data to individual informants constitute the major problems with these pre-war sources.' (B. DeMott, *Dogon masks*, p. 10, q.v.). For more information, see Walter E. A. van Beek's article,

'Dogon restudied: a field evaluation of the work of Marcel Griaule', in *Current Anthropology*, vol. 32, no. 2 (April 1991), p. 139-67. Also available in English translation in the Human Relations Area Files (q.v.). Some of Griaule's other important works on the Dogon include *Conversations with Ogotemmêli* (q.v.) and *The pale fox* (q.v.).

287 **Mélanges maliens.** (Malian miscellanea.)
Edited by Jean-Loup Amselle. Paris: Editions de l'Ecole des Hautes Etudes en Sciences Sociales. *Cahiers d'Etudes Africaines*, vol. 36, no. 144 (1996), p. 559-853.
This issue of the important French-based journal *Cahiers d'Etudes Africaines* is entirely devoted to articles about Mali, with a focus on the Mande people and civilization. About half of the articles are in English; those in French have English summaries.

288 **Organisation sociale des Dogon.** (Social organization of the Dogon.)
Denise Paulme. Paris: Domat-Montchrestien, 1940. Reprinted, Paris: J.-M. Place, 1988. Corrected reprint. 603p. map. bibliog. (Cahiers de Gradhiva, no. 3).
This is one of the classic studies on the Dogon people, dating from the colonial era and based on the author's fieldwork in Sanga in 1935. It covers aspects of social organization such as family life, economy, households, marriage, polygamy, etc. An English translation by Frieda Schütze appeared in the HRAF files (see item no. 281) in 1969.

289 **Peoples of the world. Africans south of the Sahara.**
Joyce Moss, George Wilson. Detroit, Michigan: Gale Research, 1991. 443p. maps. bibliog.
This English-language general work on Sub-Saharan ethnology covers only thirty-four African ethnic groups (including Fulani, Malinké, and Tuareg) and five 'old cultures' (including Ghana, Mali and Songhai). It contains an overview of Mali on pages 365-69.

290 **Peoples of West Africa.**
Diagram Group. New York: Facts on File, 1997. 112p. maps. (Peoples of Africa).
In this look at thirteen West African ethnic groups, aimed at middle- and high-school students, the region is described in terms of land, climate, vegetation and wildlife. For Mali, the ethnic groups include the Bambara and Malinké, Dogon, Fulani and Moors (Maures) and the survey covers their history, language, ways of life, social structure, and culture and religion. The reader should also peruse the 'special features' (such as 'Four medieval empires' (p. 38-41) and 'Superstars of the West African music scene' (p. 92-93) for Malian content. There are numerous two-colour line-drawings and the glossary (p. 102-7) is useful.

291 **Petit atlas ethno-démographique du Soudan entre Sénégal et Tchad.** (Little ethno-demographic atlas of Sudan between Senegal and Chad.)
Y. Urvoy. Paris: Larose, 1942. 46p. maps. (Mémoires de l'Institut Français d'Afrique Noire, no. 5).
The three large folding maps (map no. 1, scale 1 cm to 50 km) show population density, ethnic groups, and Islam and animism. They cover the region from the Senegal–Mali border on the west to the Nigeria–Chad border on the east. The interesting parts of the accompanying text include chapters (with line-drawings) on the types of housing and 'tribal scars' found in the region.

292 **Peuls et Mandingues: dialectique des constructions identitaires.**
(Peuls and Mandings: dialectic of identity constructions.)
Edited by Mirjam de Bruijn, Han van Dijk. Paris: Karthala; Leiden, The Netherlands: Afrika-Studiecentrum, 1997. 286p. maps. bibliog.
(Collection 'Hommes et Sociétés').
Conference proceedings of the 1995 Mande Studies Association, held in Leiden, on the subject of inter-ethnic relations between the Peuls and the Mandings. The disciplines included are anthropology, archaeology, geography, history, linguistics, and literature. All but one of the eleven papers discusses one or both ethnic groups in Mali (see map on page 16). All four of the English-language papers have a French summary. The papers are all interesting and each is followed by an excellent up-to-date bibliography.

293 **The reluctant spouse and the illegitimate slave: marriage, household formation, and demographic behaviour amongst Malian Tamesheq from the Niger Delta and the Gourma.**
Sara Randall, Michael Winter. London: Overseas Development Institute, Agricultural Administration Unit, 1986. 30p. bibliog.
This paper examines the role marriage plays in determining the low rate of fertility among the Tamasheq and the high rate among the Bambara.

294 **The reproductive ecology of the Dogon of Mali.**
Beverly Ilse Strassmann. PhD thesis, University of Michigan, 1990. 176 leaves. bibliog. (Available from University Microfilms International, Ann Arbor, Michigan, order no. 9116303).
The Dogon women of Sangui, Mali, are the subject of this dissertation. By studying the women who, by custom, must sleep in a menstrual hut during menses, the author determined that women do not synchronize their menstrual cycles, menstrual segregation promotes the confidence of paternity, and conception varies because of factors such as age, nursing status, and marital duration, not because of factors such as nutrition, polygamy, or the variability of menstrual cycles.

295 **Retour aux Dogon: figure du double et ambivalence.** (Return to the Dogons: figure of the double and of ambivalence.)
Françoise Michel-Jones. Paris: Le Sycomore, 1978. 157p. bibliog.

The concept of the 'double' or twin is well known in Dogon cosmology. Here the author proposes that the principle of duality always operates with a logical contradition, asymmetry. The inequality of social positions within Dogon society encourages ambivalences. The author writes of bisexuality (p. 67-91), woman–mother ambivalence (p. 93-131), and ambivalence of age (p. 133-46).

296 **Rite et société à travers le Bafili: une cérémonie d'initiation à la géomancie chez les Bambara du Mali.** (Rites and society through the Bafili: a divination initiatory ceremony of the Bambara of Mali.)
Pascal Baba F. Couloubaly. Bamako: Jamana, 1995. 67p. bibliog.

Geomancy or divination used in Bambara initiation rites is the subject of this work. The Bafili, an initiation rite using geomancy, is a religious rite which the ruling clan uses to tighten control over the other clans. The work includes a summary in English (p. 7-8). In additon to writing a novel, *Les angoisses d'un monde* (The anguishes of a world) (Dakar: Nouvelles Editions Africaines, 1980. 125p.), Couloubaly has also authored *Une société rurale bambara à travers des chants de femmes* (A rural Bambara society through women's songs) (Paris: IFAN-Dakar, 1990. 103p.) as well as 'The narrative genre among the Bamana of Mali', *Research in African Literatures*, vol. 24, no. 2 (Summer 1993), p. 47-60.

297 **Les Sénoufo (y compris les Minianka).** (The Senufo (including the Minianka).)
B. Holas. Paris: Presses Universitaires de France, 1966. 2nd rev. ed. 183p. maps. bibliog. (Monographies Ethnologiques Africaines).

First published in 1957, this is a comprehensive look at the Senufo of Mali, Côte d'Ivoire and Burkina Faso. The portions specifically relevant to Mali are found under Cercle de Dan, Cercle de Koutiala, Cercle de Sikasso, Cercle de Bougouni. The social organization of the Minianka (who are related to the Senufo) is discussed separately (p. 111-23). The book includes a fold-out map.

298 **Sensuous scholarship.**
Paul Stoller. Philadelphia, Pennsylvania: University of Pennsylvania Press, 1997. 166p. bibliog. (Contemporary Ethnography).

Although Stoller has done all of his fieldwork on the Songhay in Niger, this book also pertains to the Songhay of Mali. In Chapter 1, he uses 'sensuous description as well as logical exposition to argue that one learns about Songhay sorcery not through the assimilation of texts, but through the mastery of the body – through the vicissitudes of pain and illness' (p. xvi). In Chapter 2, he analyses the role of the West African griot [bard]. He maintains that history 'consumes the bodies' of Songhay griots. Chapter 6, 'Artaud, Rouch, and the cinema of cruelty', is of interest for its critical perspective on Jean Rouch's ethnographic films, particularly *Les maîtres fous* about the Songhay of the Gold Coast (Ghana). Stoller's other important works on the Songhay of Niger include *In sorcery's shadow* (Chicago, Illinois: University of Chicago Press, 1987. 235p.) and *Fusion of the worlds* (same publisher, 1989. 243p.).

299 **La société minyanka du Mali: traditions communautaires et développement cotonnier.** (Minyanka society of Mali: community traditions and the development of cotton farming.)
Danielle Jonckers. Paris: L'Harmattan, 1987. 234p. map. bibliog. (Connaissance des Hommes).

The Minyanka (Minianka), located in southeastern Mali, are subsistence farmers who have been growing cotton as a cash crop. Jonckers analyses their daily life, family structures, social and political organization, and economic conditions in order to observe their recent change in market economy. Her related dissertation from the Université Libre de Bruxelles (1981) is entitled: 'Organisation socio-économique des Minyanka du Mali' (Socio-economic organization of the Minyanka of Mali). The author has recently published a chapter (p. 55-80) entitled, 'Puissance, sacralité et violence des pouvoirs chez les Minyanka bamana du Mali' (Might, sacredness, and the violence of power in the Bamana Minyanka of Mali) in *Religion et pratiques de puissance* (Paris: L'Harmattan, 1997. 360p.).

300 **La société Soninké (Dyahunu, Mali).** (Soninke society (Dyahunu, Mali).)
Eric Pollet, Grace Winter. Brussels: Editions de l'Institut de Sociologie, Université Libre de Bruxelles, 1972, ©1971. 566p. maps. bibliog. (Etudes Ethnologiques).

In this excellent ethnographic work on the Soninke (Sarakole) people of Dyahunu (northwest Mali on the border with Mauritania), the authors analyse their history, economy, political and social organization, land tenure, family organization, religion, economic development and social evolution.

301 **Les sociétés Songhay-Zarma, Niger–Mali: chefs, guerriers, esclaves, paysans.** (The Songhay-Zarma societies, Niger–Mali: leaders, warriors, slaves, farmers.)
Jean-Pierre Olivier de Sardan. Paris: Karthala, 1984. 299p. maps. bibliog. (Hommes et Sociétés).

Although the research took place primarily in Niger, this study of the Songhay-Zarma people located in eastern Mali and western Niger still contains valuable information for those studying the culture and civilization of Mali's ethnic groups. The precolonial social structure is examined in order to understand the changes brought about during the colonial era. See also the author's cultural encyclopaedia on the Songhay-Zarma, entitled *Concepts et conceptions songhay-zarma: histoire, culture, société* (Songhay-Zarma concepts and conceptions: history, culture, society) (Paris: Nubia, 1982. 445p.).

302 **Les Sorko (Bozo), maîtres du Niger: étude ethnographique.** (The Sorkos (Bozos), masters of the Niger: ethnographic study.)
Z. Ligers. Paris: Librairie des Cinq Continents, 1964-77. 5 vols.

The Sorkos, or Bozos, are fishermen of the middle Niger River who live in Mali and Niger and seasonally move up and down the river. This in-depth ethnographic study covers (vol. 1) harvesting and hunting, (vol. 2) fishing, (vol. 3) the habitat (i.e., villages and encampments, housing, cooking), (vol. 4) navigation and the life of children, and (vol. 5) life of young people. All the volumes together contain 128 pages of plates, nearly all of which are photographs.

303 **Status and identity in West Africa: *nyamakalaw* of Mande.**
Edited by David C. Conrad, Barbara E. Frank. Bloomington, Indiana: Indiana University Press, 1995. 204p. maps. bibliog. (African Systems of Thought).

The *nyamakalaw* (professional castes of artists and artisans) 'have long been recognized for the essential roles they play in Mande society, yet they remain its most misunderstood social group' (p. 1). Although the entire collection of papers is relevant to the study of Mali, three chapters in particular focus in on Malian leather-makers, potters, and griots: Barbara E. Frank's 'Soninke *garankéw* and Bamana-Malinke *jeliw:* Mande leatherworkers, identity, and the Diaspora' (p. 133-50); Adria LaViolette's 'Women craft specialists in Jenne: the manipulation of Mande social categories' (p. 170-81); and Cheick Mahamadou Chérif Keita's '*Jaliya* in the modern world: a tribute to Banzumana Sissoko and Massa Makan Diabaté' (p. 182-96).

304 *Togu na*: **the African Dogon: 'house of men, house of words'.**
Tito Spini, Sandro Spini. New York: Rizzoli, 1977. 251p. maps. bibliog.

Togu na, the 'great shelter' (or as the subtitle indicates, 'house of men' and 'house of words'), is the first building to be erected in a Dogon village. As it structures their society, it serves many male communal functions, from the administration of justice and other collective decisions to a meeting and resting place. In this well-illustrated publication, forty-seven *togu na* in thirty-two Dogon villages are examined in the contexts of their physical setting, architecture and place in Dogon society and mythology.

305 **Touaregs: un peuple du désert.** (Tuaregs: a people of the desert.)
Edmond Bernus, Jean-Marc Durou, preface by Théodore Monod.
Paris: R. Laffont, 1996. 331p. map. bibliog.

In this illustrated book on the nomadic Tuaregs of the Sahara, the authors take a comprehensive look at Tuareg civilization (e.g., history, art, language, literature, economics, ethnicity, social relations, medicine, etc.) from the point of view of commonalities and diversities. The last chapter discusses the Tuaregs in the post-colonial era, particularly the Malian revolts of the Kel Adagh (1963-64) and the revolts of the 1990s in the Adrar des Ifoghas.

306 **The Tuaregs: the blue people.**
Karl-G. Prasse. Copenhagen: Museum Tusculanum Press, University of Copenhagen, 1995. 85p. maps. bibliog.

The author, a linguist noted for his studies of the Tuareg language, states that he hopes this book will help bring international pressure to end Tuareg persecution. In this fine book Prasse describes the Tuaregs (Berbers living primarily in Mali and Niger), their social structure, daily life, culture, economy, and history. Of particular note is the chapter on the Tuaregs since independence (1960) which discusses their repression by and subsequent rebellion against the two ruling black governments (p. 52-67). Because of the revolt which began in 1990, 90 per cent of Malian Tuaregs have fled to other countries, primarily Algeria. The book is amply illustrated with thirty-five pages of plates and two maps.

307 **Words and the Dogon world.**
Geneviève Calame-Griaule, translated from the French by Deirdre
LaPin.   Philadelphia, Pennsylvania: Institute for the Study of Human
Issues, 1986. 704p. bibliog.

First published in French in 1965 under the title *Ethnologie et langage,* this translation
makes available to the English-speaking community important research in the
ethnography of speaking. Through extensive contact with and research on the Dogons,
the author formulated a Dogon 'theory of speech' (Part I). Part II, the mythology of
speech, includes discussion of the speech of the Nommo (the Dogon mythical saviour)
and the fox (his brother-enemy). Part III is a discussion of speech in Dogon society.

Fishing in the Pondo.
See item no. 82.

**Pérégrinations sahéliennes: la problématique du changement dans une
société traditionnelle d'Afrique noire: les Dogon du Mali.** (Sahelian
peregrinations: the problematics of change in a traditional Black African
society: the Dogon of Mali.)
See item no. 256.

Villages perchés des Dogon du Mali: habitat, espace et société. (Perched
villages of the Dogon of Mali: habitat, space and society.)
See item no. 673.

Languages and Dialects

General

308 **Bibliographie analytique des langues parlées en Afrique subsaharienne, 1970-1980.** (Analytical bibliography of the languages spoken in Sub-Saharan Africa, 1970-80.)
Jean-François Bourdin, Jean-Pierre Caprile, Michel Lafon.   Paris: AELIA, 1982, ©1983. 556p.

In this well-organized bibliography of Sub-Saharan languages, the languages of Mali are found in the geographical index under Mali (40 citations) as well as in the language index under each language name (e.g., there are 24 entries under Bambara, 9 under Dogon, etc.). Most of the citations include keywords and a brief annotation.

309 **Language map of Africa and the adjacent islands.**
David Dalby.   London: International African Institute, 1977.
Provisional ed. 63p.

In this detailed and comprehensive linguistic map of Africa (scale 1:5,000,000), Dalby updates Joseph Harold Greenberg's classification and mapping of African languages. Mali is covered in its entirety on the northwest sheet, and an insert covering the southeast region of Mali (around Sikasso) appears on the southwest sheet. The accompanying handbook, which clarifies the languages spoken in Mali, is difficult for the layman to use, but still provides valuable information. As a companion to the map, see Michael Mann and David Dalby's *A thesaurus of African languages: a classified and annotated inventory of the spoken languages of Africa* (London: H. Zell, 1987. 325p.) which uses the same language names but a 'less controversial' level of language classification. On pages 190-91, Mali's languages are classified by language family, and a table shows the number of speakers, use of the language in the media and in schools, and its status as a national or official language. In Section 2, the reader will find notes on each language, their variant names and the printed source consulted.

310 **Stratégies communicatives au Mali: langues régionales, bambara, français.** (Communicative strategies in Mali: regional languages, Bambara, French.)
Gérard Dumestre with the collaboration of Cécile Canut (et al.).
Aix-en-Provence, France; Paris: Institut d'Etudes Créoles et
Francophones, URA 1041 du CNRS, Université de Provence, 1994.
364p. maps. bibliog. (Collection 'Langues et Développement').
This is an up-to-date study of the language situation in Mali. Chapters focus on southern Mali (Minyanka country), the Manding languages zone (cities of Kita, Sagabari and Bamako), Dogon country (from the east of Mopti to Bandiagara and the plain of Séno), and Kassonke country (city of Kayes), as well as the role of Bambara in the oral press and the current situation of the written press in Mali. Other recent publications in the same series include: Cécile Canut's *Dynamiques linguistiques au Mali* (Linguistic dynamics in Mali) (Paris[?]: CIRELFA-Agence de la Francophonie, 1996. 360p.), an analysis of plurilingualism in Mali using linguistic theory to study the Manding, Fulah (Fulfulde) (region of Mopti), Songhay (Songai) (region of Gao) and Tamasheq (region of Kidal) zones of Mali; and André Marcel d'Ans (et al.) *Langues et métiers modernes ou modernisés au Mali: santé et travail du fer* (Languages and modern or modernized trades in Mali: health and ironworking) (same publisher, 1992. 213p.), discussing the economic aspects of language, development and health in Mali.

French, the official language

311 **Inventaire des particularités lexicales du français au Mali.**
(Inventory of French usage specific to Mali.)
A. Queffélec, F. Jouannet, and members of the team.   Paris[?]:
Groupe de travail IFM de l'AELIA, 1982. 273p. bibliog. (Publications de l'AELIA, no. 2. Série Langues Parlées en Afrique).
Written by French and Malian scholars, this standard work contains a lexicon of French spoken in Mali. It includes idiomatic usages of French words, Arabic and English loanwords, and other words borrowed from Malian languages as well as derivations and quotations from sources in which they are found. The bibliography (p. 259-71) is the key to locating the original source cited.

312 **La situation du français au Mali = (The situation of French in Mali.)**
Jacques Blondé.   In: *Le Français hors de France.*   Paris:
H. Champion, 1979, p. 377-83.
Although by now dated, this is still the best source on the state of the official language of Mali, French. French is used by the intellectual élite and is the language used by Malians outside of Mali. However, Bambara is also taught to the labouring classes and is the language of national communication.

National languages

313 **An ka bamanankan kalan, introductory Bambara.** (We are studying the Bamara language, introductory Bambara.)
Charles Bird, John Hutchison, Mamadou Kanté. Bloomington, Indiana: Indiana University Linguistics Club, 1977. 3rd ed. 298p.
This standard Bambara language textbook was written for Peace Corps training programmes in 1972-73. For the more advanced student, Charles Bird and Mamadou Kanté also published *An ka bamanankan kalan, intermediate Bambara* (Bloomington, Indiana: Indiana University Linguistics Club, 1976). The culturally oriented topics which are part of each lesson include 'major life ceremonies such as births, deaths, marriages, etc.' (p. iii).

314 **Atlas international de la vitalité linguistique = International atlas of language vitality.**
Under the direction of Grant D. McConnell, Jean-Denis Gendron.
Quebec, Canada: Centre International de Recherche en Aménagement Linguistique, Université Laval, Québec, 1995. (Publication, G-15).
In Volume 3, *West Africa*, the reader will find maps, graphs and tables of linguistic geography for thirteen countries including fifty-nine languages spoken in the region. The languages of Mali covered here are Bamanankan (Bambara), Dogoso (Dogon), Pulaar (Fulfulde), Songoy ciini (Songai), and Soninke. Bamanankan is clearly emerging over the other languages in the domains of schools, mass media, administration, courts, legislature, industrial manufacturing, and sales and service industries.

315 **Le Bambara du Mali : essais de description linguistique.** (Bambara of Mali: linguistic essays.)
Gérard Dumestre. Paris: Université La Sorbonne Nouvelle, 1987. 585p. bibliog.
The subjects of this Sorbonne dissertation are the grammar, morphology and phonology of the Bambara language spoken in the large cities of Mali.

316 **Bambara–English, English–Bambara student lexicon.**
Charles Bird, Mamadou Kanté. Bloomington, Indiana: Indiana University Linguistics Club, 1977. 84p.
Designed to be used in conjunction with the authors' two textbooks *An ka bamanankan kalan* (q.v.), this two-way lexicon is not intended to be exhaustive. The particular value of this book is the English to Bambara section since the Bambara to English terms are also contained in the textbooks.

317 **Cours pratique de bambara.** (Practical course in Bambara.)
Charles Bailleul.   Bobo-Dioulasso, Upper Volta: Librairie La Savane,
1977-84.
This slim set (4 bibliographical volumes but 3 physical volumes) is a Bambara
textbook for those who speak French. It covers Bambara sounds and tones (volumes 1-
2) as well as the construction of sentences (volumes 3-4).

318 **Daɲɛgafe kɛrɛnkɛrɛnnen: bamanankan–tubabukan,
tubabukan–bamanankan.** (Specialized lexicon: Bambara–French,
French–Bambara.)
Moussa Diaby.   Bamako: Ministère de l'Education de Base,
République du Mali, 1993. 46p.
Political science and economics are the specializations covered by this two-way
Bambara–French lexicon. The author's name appears in French (Moussa Diaby) and
Bambara (Musa Jaabi).

319 **Le dialecte senoufo du minianka: grammaire, textes et lexiques.**
(The Senufo dialect of Minianka: grammar, texts, lexicons.)
Georges Chéron.   Paris: P. Geuthner, 1925. 167p. maps.
The Minianka (Mamara) dialect (of the Senufo group of Gur languages) is spoken by
the Minianka people in the region of Koutiala (southeastern Mali). This early text
consists of a grammar, texts (songs, fables, and tales), and a two-way Minianka–French
lexicon.

320 **Dialectes manding du Mali.** (Manding dialects of Mali.)
Direction Nationale de l'Alphabétisation Fonctionnelle et de la
Linguistique Appliquée.   Paris: Agence de Coopération Culturelle et
Technique; Bamako: DNAFLA, 1983. 409p. maps. bibliog. (Promotion
des Langues Manding et Peul: MAPE).
The sounds, morphology and syntax, and brief sample text are given for each of the
twenty-seven dialects of Manding (Mande or Mandekan) described here, roughly
corresponding to traditional regions of Mali. Hand-drawn maps identify towns where
each dialect is spoken.

321 **The dialects of Mandekan.**
Charles S. Bird.   Bloomington, Indiana: African Studies Program,
Indiana University, 1982. 423p. bibliog.
The dialects of Mandekan are spoken in West Africa from southern Mauritania to the
Côte d'Ivoire and from central Burkina Faso to the Atlantic coast. This survey is based
on subjects from the rural areas of Mali. Bambara (from Mali, Guinea and Côte
d'Ivoire) comprises the first region, Dyula (from Burkina Faso and Côte d'Ivoire) is the
second region, and Maninka-Mandinka (from southern Mali to eastern Guinea and
from Kita to the sea) is the third region. The purpose of this book is to give a
comparative grammar of the various dialects covered. See also *La langue mandingue et
ses dialectes: malinke, bambara, dioula* (Manding language and its dialects: Malinke,
Bambara, Dioula) (Paris: P. Geuthner, 1929-55. 2 vols) by noted French linguist and
ethnologist Maurice Delafosse for a grammar and two-way French–Manding lexicon.

322 **Dictionnaire bambara–français.** (Bambara–French dictionary.)
Gérard Dumestre. Paris: G. Dumestre, 1981-91. 9 vols. bibliog.
The first nine fascicules of this scholarly dictionary cover half of the Bambara alphabet, A–N. (See *Lexique bambara–français* (item no. 341) for the correct alphabetical order of the Bambara language.) It is based on the standard Bambara, spoken in the large cities of Mali as well as on Radio-Mali. Over 200 publications (ranging from books, articles, dissertations, archives, unpublished manuscripts, recordings of griots, interviews, etc.) have been consulted in order to create the dictionary. Most entries include an illustration of the use of the word in a Bambara text. The source for the text is given in the form of a two-letter code, where the most complete list appears in fascicule 6 (p. I-IX). It appears that no more fascicules have been published in recent years.

323 **Dictionnaire bambara–français, précédé d'un abrégé de grammaire bambara.** (Bambara–French dictionary preceded by an abridged Bambara grammar.)
Mgr. H. Bazin. Paris: Imprimerie Nationale, 1906. Reprinted, Ridgewood, New Jersey: Gregg Press, 1965. 693p.
An early important one-way dictionary and brief grammar which, of course, predate official Malian orthography of 1967.

324 **Dictionnaire boomu–français.** (Bomu–French dictionary.)
Bernard de Rasilly. San, Mali: [n.p], 1995. 667p. map. bibliog.
This is a revised edition of a publication written by a White Father, and first appearing in fascicules from 1963 to 1971 under the title: *Lexique bore–français* (Bore–French lexicon). Bomu is spoken in Burkina Faso and in southeastern Mali. Several sections at the end of the alphabetical dictionary cover numerals, the human body, names of mammals, birds, and medicinal plants.

325 **Dictionnaire dogon: dialecte toro. Langue et civilisation.** (Dogon dictionary: Toro dialect. Language and civilization.)
Geneviève Calame-Griaule. Paris: C. Klincksieck, 1968. 332p. map. bibliog. (Langues et Littératures de l'Afrique Noire, no. 4).
One-way dictionary (Toro–French) of the Dogon language dialect of Toro, which is spoken by approximately 30,000 people living in the region of the Bandiagara cliffs. The introductory chapter includes a section on phonology and grammatical structures. There is also included a brief French–Dogon lexicon (p. 317-29), as well as eight plates illustrating Dogon cultural life with photographs of musical instruments, architecture and dress.

326 **Dictionnaire dogon–français donno so: région de Bandiagara.** (Dogon–French dictionary: region of Bandiagara.)
Marcel Kervran. Brussels: R. Deleu, 1993. 643p. map. bibliog.
This new edition of the Dogon language dictionary, 130 pages longer than the 1982 edition, includes corrections to the original text. Kervran is a member of the Pères Blancs (White Fathers) and lived in Bandiagara for a number of years.

327 **Dictionnaire élémentaire fulfulde–français–English = elementary dictionary.**
Centre Régional de Documentation pour la Traduction Orale.
Niamey: CRDTO, 1971. 166p. (Langues Africaines, no. 4).
In order to improve national literacy campaigns in West Africa, this trilingual Fulfulde–French–English dictionary was based on work by David W. Arnott, of the University of London's School of Oriental and African Studies, and a team of Unesco experts including two Fulanis, Eldridge Mohamadou and Alfâ Ibrâhim Sow. It includes about 5,000 Fulfulde basic words from the Gombe region of Nigeria as well as some entries from the 'Eastern group' (Adamawa, Sokkoto, Kano, Eastern Niger) and the 'Western group (Futa-Jalon, Futa-Toro, Masina, Upper Volta and Western Niger). For a more recent detailed trilingual dictionary, see Osborne's *A Fulfulde (Maasina)–English–French lexicon* (item no. 332).

328 **Eléments de grammaire du soninke.** (Elements of Soninke grammar.)
Yacouba Diagana.   Paris: Association Linguistique Africaine, 1994.
2 vols. bibliog. (Documents de Linguistique Africaine, no. 2).
This is an in-depth grammar of the Soninke language, as spoken in the author's hometown of Kaëdi, in southern Mauritania, on the Senegal River. Although it has borrowed from the Fulfulde language because of its location in Peul country, it is still an excellent intermediate-to-advanced grammar and therefore of interest to Soninke speakers in Mali.

329 **English–Fula dictionary: Fulfulde, Pulaar, Fulani: a multidialectal approach.**
Paul P. de Wolf.   Berlin: D. Reimer, 1995. 3 vols. bibliog. (Sprache und Oralität in Afrika, Band 18).
This excellent extensive dictionary of the Fula (Fulfulde) language is unusual in that it takes a multi-dialect approach to the language, including the dialects of Mali (e.g., Macina, Bandiagara, Futa Toro or Pulaar, etc.). The one-way English–Fula dictionary is preceded by a 'grammatical summary' (p. xxv-cxiv) and a bibliography (p. cxv-cxxx). Galina Zoubko's *Dictionnaire peul–français* (Peul–French dictionary) (Osaka, Japan: National Museum of Ethnology, 1996. 552p.) has also gathered many dialects for its one-way Fula–French dictionary.

330 **Form and meaning in Fulfulde: a morphophonological study of Maasinankoore.**
J. O. Breedveld.   Leiden, The Netherlands: Research School CNWS, 1995. 508p. maps. bibliog. (CNWS Publications, no. 32).
Based on data collected in Mali in 1987-88, this is a scholarly study of the morphology and phonetics of the Fulfulde dialect spoken in Maasina (Masina), in the Inner Niger Delta and in the Haayre. Maasinankoore is the dominant language spoken in Maasina.

331 **Fula–russko–frantsuzskii slovar' = Kamuusu pular**
(Fulfulde)–Riisinkoore–Farankoore = Dictionnaire peul
(fula)–russe–français: Okolo 25000 slov. (Fula–Russian–French
dictionary: approximately 25,000 words.)
G. V. Zubko, Nyaalibuuli Bureyma, Mamadu Jeng. Moscow:
'Russkii Iazyk', 1980. 600p.

A unique trilingual dictionary, in Fula (Fulfulde), Russian, and French, followed by a
study of Fula grammar (p. 567-600) written in Russian. The authors' names in French
are spelled: Gnalibouly Boureima, Dieng Mamadou, and G. V. Zoubko.

332 **A Fulfulde (Maasina)–English–French lexicon: a root based**
compilation drawn from extant sources followed by
English–Fulfulde and French–Fulfulde listings.
Donald W. Osborn, David J. Dwyer, Joseph I. Donohoe, Jr. East
Lansing, Michigan: Michigan State University Press, 1993. 688p.
bibliog.

The Fulfulde of Masina (central Mali) is the subject of this recent three-way lexicon
(Fulfulde–English–French, English–Fulfulde, French–Fulfulde). The authors have
gathered the Masina Fulfulde vocabulary from numerous published and unpublished
sources (see the bibliography on pages 681-88).

333 **Grammaire et vocabulaire de la langue poul à l'usage des**
voyageurs dans le Soudan. (Grammar and vocabulary of the Peul
language for use by travellers in the Sudan.)
Le Général Faidherbe. Paris: Maisonneuve, 1882. 2nd ed. 164p. map.

In this early work, Faidherbe includes a grammar and phrase-book, a comparison of
Fula (Fulfulde) to Wolof and Serer as well as a French–Fula lexicon. He also includes
a map showing the regions of West Africa where Fula is spoken.

334 **Guide de transcription et de lecture du bambara.** (Guide to the
transcription and reading of Bambara.)
Direction Nationale de l'Alphabétisation Fonctionnelle et de la
Linguistique Appliquée. [Bamako?]: Ministère de l'Education
Nationale, DNAFLA, 1979. 60p. bibliog.

This government publication on the Bambara language is one of a series geared at
fostering literacy of the national languages of Mali. Others published by the DNAFLA
include *Guide de transcription et de lecture du fulfulde* (1986. 94p.), *Guide de
transcription et de lecture du soɲoy* (1986. 49p.), *Guide de transcription du tamasheq*
(1986. 16p.), *Guide de transcription et de lecture du dogon* (1982. 38p.), *Guide de
transcription et lexique bozo* (1982. 127p.), and *Guide de transcription du bomu*
(1980. 138p.). See also *Grammaire de la phrase bambara* (Grammar of the Bambara
sentence) (Bamako: Centre National de l'Alphabétisation Fonctionnelle, 197[-?].
44p.), aimed at 'Bambaraphones' wishing to understand the structure of their mother
tongue.

335 **Influences de l'arabe sur la langue bambara.** (Influences of Arabic
     on the Bambara language.)
     Michel Lagarde. Falajè, Mali: Centre d'Etude de Langue Bambara de
     Falajè, 1988. 48p.
This study by White Father Lagarde consists of a list of Bambara words borrowed
from Arabic, thematic classification (e.g., Muslim religious life) of Bambara words
from Arabic, and linguistic assertions concerning the passage from Arabic to
Bambara. In order to reach a broad audience, all of the Arabic words appear in
romanized form.

336 **Initiation à la linguistique africaine par les langues du Mali:
     manuel programmé.** (Initiation to African linguistics among the
     languages of Mali: programmed manual.)
     Direction Nationale de l'Alphabétisation Fonctionnelle et de la
     Linguistique Appliquée du Mali. Paris: ACCT; Bamako: DNAFLA;
     Paris: Editions Karthala, 1980. 93p. map.
This unique self-guided teaching manual (with questions and answers) will be of use
to any French-speaker interested in learning about the languages of Mali. Languages
spoken in Mali consist of the Hamito-Semitic family including Tamasheq and Arabe
hassanya (Maure) as well as the Negro-African language family including the Mande
group (Mande: Kassonke, Maninka (Malinké), Bambara, Jula, etc.), the Voltaic group
(Bobo-fing, Senufo-Minyanka, Boré (Bobo-Wule), Pana, Kurumba, Mosi (Moore), the
West Atlantic group (Fulfulde), and unclassified languages (Soɲoy, Dogon). Part I
covers the sounds of language. An extremely helpful feature for the uninitiated
Western reader is the comparative table on the alphabet of the nine national languages
of Mali (p. 27-28), for each language has its individual alphabet amongst the fifty-five
possible Malian written letters! Other useful charts include the phonology of the
International African Institute (p. 37) as well as a chart of the four major languages of
Mali (Bamanan (Bambara), Fulfulde, Soɲoy, Tamasheq). Part II is a discussion of
syntax or the structure of language, using the national languages of Mali as examples.

337 **Jam tan: initiation à la langue peule: méthode d'auto-
     enseignement.** (In total peace: initiation to the Peul language: self-
     instruction method.)
     Roger Labatut, Djibi M'Bodj, Mohamadou Aliou. Paris: BPI, Centre
     Georges Pompidou: INALCO, 1987. 388p. map.
The Peul (Fulfulde) language, spoken by the Peuls and Toucouleurs of Senegal,
Mauritania, northern Guinea and western Mali, has preserved a remarkable structural
unity enabling the speakers to understand each other even when they are from regions
fairly far from each other. In this textbook of grammar, which is accompanied by five
cassette tapes, each lesson has exercises, a Peul text and its translation into French, as
well as 'particularités d'emploi' (hints for proper usage).

338 **La langue bozo.** (The Bozo language.)
J. Daget, M. Konipo, M. Sanankoua. Bamako: Institut Français d'Afrique Noire, Gouvernement du Soudan, 1953. 277p. (Etudes Soudaniennes, no. 1).

Part I covers the phonetics and grammar of the Bozo (Boso) language, including its dialects. In Part 2, Bozo proverbs, tales and folklore illustrate each of the dialects of Mopti, Débo, Korondougou, Diafarabé. Part 3 is a Bozo–French lexicon.

339 **La langue des Peuls ou Foulbé; lexique français–peul.** (The language of the Peuls or Fulfulde; French–Fulfulde lexicon.)
H. Labouret. Dakar: IFAN, 1955. 160p. bibliog. maps. (Mémoires de l'Institut Français d'Afrique Noire, no. 41).

Although Fulfulde (or Fula), the lingua franca of Mali's Inland Delta, is the main subject of this important monograph, the author begins with a bibliography on the Peul, covering linguistics, history, physical anthropology, animal breeding, and maps. Chapter I discusses the origins of the Peuls and their migrations, Chapter II proposes the place of Fulfulde language in the classification of African languages. Appendices discuss Peul family and kinship as well as listing useful plants and animals. The work concludes with a French–Fulfulde lexicon. Labouret is also the author of *La langue des Peuls ou Foulbé* (Dakar: IFAN, 1952. 268p.) which includes an analysis of the grammar and morphology of the language, folktales of several dialects, and a French–Peul, Peul–French lexicon.

340 **La langue sonay et ses dialectes.** (The Songai language and its dialects.)
A. Prost. Dakar: IFAN, 1956. 627p.

The Songai language is spoken from Mopti to Gaya on the Niger River, in eastern and northeastern Mali. This comprehensive book contains a grammar, twenty-two texts from Gao in Songhay and French, and a lengthy Songai-to-French dictionary as well as a brief French-to-Songai lexicon. The author's 1977 supplement to the dictionary is located in a pocket in the back of the volume.

341 **Lexique bambara–français: (bamanan kan ni tubabu kan danyègafè).** (Bambara–French lexicon.)
Direction Nationale de l'Alphabétisation Fonctionnelle et de la Linguistique Appliquée. Bamako: Ministère de l'Education Nationale, DNAFLA, 1980. 3rd ed. 79p.

In an effort to promote functional literacy efforts, the government of Mali has thus far published bilingual lexicons of seven of its national languages. The Bambara lexicon presents itself as a skeleton or outline of the Bambara language, hoping that it will serve as the basis for future lexical research. Here the alphabetical order follows the official 1967 order of: a, b, d, j, e, è, f, g, h, i, k, l, m, n, ny, ɲ, o, ò, p, r, s, sh, t, c, u, w, y, z. The other volumes published are *Lexique dogon–français* (Dogon–French lexicon) (1986. 144p.), using the Tòrò-Sò dialect of Dogon spoken on the plains surrounding Sangha and Madougou as the 'standard Dogon'; *Lexique fulfulde–français* (Fulfulde–French lexicon) (1993. 314p.), containing 7,107 entries; *Lexique mamara–français* (Mamara–French lexicon.) (1983. 46p.), spoken by the Minianka people, using Nafanra as its 'standard' dialect; *Lexique soninke–français: (soninken do tubabun qanne sefetanu)* (Soninke–French lexicon) (1979. 100p.), which updates Abdoulaye Bathily and Claude Meillassoux's *Lexique soninké–français* (Dakar: CLAD, 1976) and predates the decree which fixed the Soninke alphabet, affecting two letters, the "nw" and the "x"; *Lexique soɲay–français = Kalima citaabu so ayannasaara senni* (Songhay–French lexicon) (1995. 175p.), authored by Youssouf Mohamed Haïdara, Youssouf Billo Maïga, Mohamed Bagna Maïga and John P. Hutchison; *Lexique tamasheq–français* (Tamasheq–French lexicon) (1986. 127p.), using the dialects Tawellemmedt, spoken mainly in Menaka and in Niger, and Taneslemt, spoken in Mali. Also of interest from the DNAFLA is *Phonologie du tamasheq* (Phonology of Tamasheq) (1987. 68 leaves).

342 **Lexique médical: bambara–français, français–bambara.** (Medical
    lexicon: Bambara–French, French–Bambara.)
    Marijke Huizinga, Mamadou Keita.   Amsterdam: Free University
    Press, 1987. 112p.

This two-way medical dictionary also includes Bambara neologisms. The term 'medical' is broadly conceived and includes names of diseases, the parts of the body and some terms used for symptoms or traditional medicine cures, as well as occasional mention of the social connotations of a particular Bambara word.

343 **Mali: langues nationales, nouvelle donné[e].** (Mali: national
    languages, new concept.)
    Ismaïl Maiga.   *Diagonales,* vol. 34 (May 1995), p. 42-43.

Although Mali has twelve national languages and an official language, French, the most important languages are Bambara, Songhoi (Songai), Peul (Fulfulde), and Soninke. The Ministry of Education proposes that primary school students should learn to read and write their national language for the first two years of school, adding French during the third year.

344 **Mande languages and linguistics.**
    Raimund Kastenholz.   Hamburg, Germany: H. Buske Verlag, 1988.
    274p. (African Linguistic Bibliographies, vol. 4).

The Mande family of languages covered in this broadly conceived bibliography include all the Mande languages spoken in Mali. The very brief annotations, when given, are ôf some use. The work includes a lengthy section on Bambara (p. 108-48), as well as shorter sections on Soninke, Bozo, Mandinka (Mande), etc. See also *Bibliographie mandingue* (Manding bibliography) (Bamako: DNAFLA, 1982. 53p.) as well as the similar title about the Fulfulde language, *Bibliographie fulfulde* (Fulfulde bibliography) (Bamako: DNAFLA, 1982. 57p.).

345 **Mandenkan.**
    Paris: INALCO, 1981- . semi-annual.

An important periodical on the study of Mande languages in West Africa. Nearly all of the articles are written in French. Number 9 (Spring 1985) is a bibliography of Mande languages and linguistics. Other periodicals of interest to Africana linguists include *Journal of African Languages and Linguistics* (Dordrecht, The Netherlands: Foris Publications for Department of African Linguistics, University of Leiden,

1979-); *Journal of West African Languages* (London: Published by the Cambridge University Press in association with the Institute of African Studies, University of Ibadan, 1964-).

346 **Manuel de la langue songay parlée de Tombouctou à Say dans la boucle du Niger.** (Manual of the Songai language spoken from Timbuktu to Say in the Niger Bend.)
RR. PP. Hacquard and Dupuis. Paris: J. Maisonneuve, 1897. 253p.

In this pioneering work on the Songai language, the authors, who were White Father missionaries in Timbuktu, have included a pronunciation guide, grammar, lists of common words by category, and some Songai texts, fables and tales. The bulk of the book is a two-way lexicon (p. 101-253). See also A. Dupuis-Yakouba's *Essai de méthode pratique pour l'étude de la langue songoï ou songai, langue commerciale et politique de Tombouctou et du Moyen-Niger, suivie d'une légende en songoï avec traduction et d'un dictionnaire songoï français* (Essay on a practical method of studying the Songai language, the commercial and political language of Timbuktu and the Middle Niger) (Paris: E. Leroux, 1917. 210p.) which complements the 1897 *Manuel.*

347 **The new Bambara grammar.**
Centre de Littérature Evangélique. Bamako: Centre de Littérature Evangélique, between 1980 and 1983[?]. rev. ed. 3 vols.

This is a good text on Bambara grammar for the English-speaker. Volume 3 contains a vocabulary.

348 **Un parler dogon, le donno so: notes de grammaire.** (A Dogon language, the Donno So: grammatical notes.)
Marcel Kervran, André Prost. Bandiagara, Mali: Paroisse Catholique, 1986. 188p. map.

This grammar of the Donno So dialect of Dogon, spoken in the region of Bandiagara, updates Prost's *Les parlers dogons: 1. Donno so* ([n.p.], 1969). In addition to the thorough grammatical analysis, it also includes the transcription of two tales.

349 **Parlons soninké.** (Let's speak Soninke.)
Christian Girier. Paris: L'Harmattan, 1996. 311p. maps. bibliog. (Collection 'Parlons').

Soninke is spoken in the region of Kayes in western Mali as well as in southern Mauritania and eastern Senegal. It is also the most frequently used language among African immigrants in France. The author has lived in Bamako and worked on the transcription of Soninke since 1974. This recently published scholarly look at the Soninke language includes its phonetics, writing and grammar, and it is not designed for the beginning student. It also covers Soninke (Sarakole) society, its social structure, family names and forenames. The section on French–Soninke vocabulary (p. 245-69) is organized by categories (e.g., parts of speech, time, geography, family, eating and drinking, social relations, health, religion, animals, plants, etc.). The Soninke–French vocabulary (p. 270-300) is, however, given in alphabetical order. Girier also wrote *Enseignement du Soninké (Sarakole): grammaire et syntaxe* (The teaching of Soninke (Sarakole): grammar and syntax) (Paris: Centre de Recherches et d'Enseignement du Soninke, 197-[?] 95 leaves), a textbook for the beginner. See also a textbook designed for the literate Soninke public, *Enseignement du soninke: manuel de lecture et écriture* (The teaching of Soninke: reading and writing manual) (Montreuil, France: Centre de Recherches et d'Enseignement du Soninke, 1977. 100p.).

350 **Petit dictionnaire bambara–français, français–bambara.** (Little Bambara–French, French–Bambara dictionary.)
Charles Bailleul. Amersham, England: Avebury Publishing Co., 1981. 339p.

This two-way dictionary is the result of fifteen years of work by Father Charles Bailleul. It is destined for the reader who is already familiar with Bambara phonology, syntax, and tonology. This is 'common' or *'forobakan'* Bambara from the regions of Falajè, Banan, and Bèlèko. Considered by Mary Jo Arnoldi, author of *Playing with time* (q.v.) to be 'one of the most complete published sources for current spelling of Bamana words'.

351 **Petit dictionnaire français–bambara et bambara–français.** (Little French–Bambara and Bambara–French dictionary.)
Moussa Travélé. Paris: P. Geuthner, 1913. Reprinted, 1944. new ed. 281p.

The first dictionary written by a native Malian, Travélé's pocket-size dictionary is also notable because it is a two-way dictionary, unlike Bazin's *Dictionnaire bambara–français* (see item no. 323). Six brief tales, in Bambara and French, conclude the volume. See also Travélé's *Petit manuel français–bambara* (Little French–Bambara manual) (Paris: P. Geuthner, 1947. 89p.) which is a Bambara phrasebook and vocabulary for the French-speaker and also contains a Bambara tale, fable, short songs, and a few proverbs.

352 **Quelques donnés sociolinguistiques sur le Mali.** (Some sociolinguistic data on Mali.)
Adama Ouane. In: *Inventaire des études linguistiques sur les pays d'Afrique noire d'expression française et sur Madagascar.* Established under the direction of Daniel Barreteau. Paris: Conseil International de la Langue Française, 1978, p. 375-87. maps.

Ouane describes the linguistic situation for each of the following languages spoken in Mali: Bambara, Fulfulde, Tamasheq, Songai, Senufo-Minyanka group, Soninke, Dogon, Bobo (Bore, Bwamu), Bozo (Boso), and Maure (Arabic). An interesting table (p. 378) lists the various uses of the language, such as secret language, religious services, literature, education, etc.

353 **Règles d'orthographe des langues nationales.** (Rules of orthography of the national languages.)
Direction Nationale de l'Alphabétisation Fonctionnelle et de la Linguistique Appliquée. Bamako: DNAFLA, [between 1981 and 1993]. 71 leaves.

Because Mali's national languages did not have a written form until recently, rules of orthography were established in 1967 and revised in 1979. The alphabet and alphabetical order, rules of transcription, segmentation, and notation of tones are given for each of the following languages: Bambara (Bamanankan), Bozo (Boso), Dogon, Peul (Fulfulde), Soninke, Senoufo-Minyanka, and Tamasheq.

354 **Tableaux morphologiques: dialecte touareg de l'Adrar du Mali (berbère) = Tesaten en-tmawiten: Tamashaq, Adagh, Mali.**
(Morphological tables: Tuareg dialect of the Adrar of Mali (Berber).)
Karl-G. Prasse, Ekhya agg-Albostan ag-Sidiyan. Copenhagen: Akademisk Forlag, 1985. 62p.

This is one of the few studies on the Tamasheq language of Mali, spoken by the Tuareg nomads of northern Mali (Gao, Kidal, and Timbuktu). A dictionary of note from the same publisher is the *Lexique touareg–français* (Tuareg–French lexicon) (Copenhagen: Akademisk Forlag, 1980. 284p.) by Ghoubeïd Alojaly. Sidiyan also publishes under the form of name: Ehya Ag Sidiyene.

355 **Writing and publishing in national languages today.**
Robert C. Newton. In: *Preserving the landscape of imagination: children's literature in Africa.* Edited by Raoul Granqvist and Jürgen Martini. Amsterdam; Atlanta, Georgia: Rodopi, 1997, p. 315-25. (Matatu 17-18).

Recent literacy efforts in Mali have been far from successful. Newton states that rather than focus on literacy alone, literature and literacy must develop simultaneously in order to be successful. The primary publisher of materials in Malian national languages, the Direction Nationale de l'Alphabétisation Fonctionnelle et de la Linguistique Appliquée (DNAFLA), has failed to engage the readers in the way that works of oral tradition continue to entertain Malians today. Newton describes the work of two authors writing in the Bambara language, Ismaila Traoré and Berehima Wulale.

Aperçu de la situation ethno-linguistique du Mali. (Survey of the ethnolinguistic situation in Mali.)
See item no. 587.

Language policy and literacy development: a study of the two west African countries of Ghana and Mali.
See item no. 597.

Religion

356 The Bambara.
Dominique Zahan. Leiden, The Netherlands: Brill, 1974. 32p.
42 plates. bibliog. (Iconography of Religions. Section VII: Africa,
fascicule 2).

This slim volume in a well-regarded series is an excellent introduction to the religion
of the Bambara people. Zahan describes their system of 'ancestor worship', including
their supreme God, Ngala or Bemba, various ancestor-worship cults, and the role of
initiatory societies in Bambara society. The black-and-white plates illustrate many of
the rituals. See also the author's *La viande et la graine: mythologie dogon* (Meat and
seeds: Dogon mythology) (Paris: Présence Africaine, 1969. 178p.) and his *Sociétés
d'initiation bambara: le n'domo, le korè* (Bambara initiatory societies: the n'domo
and the kore) (Paris: Mouton, 1960. 438p.).

**357 Buffoons, queens, and wooden horsemen: the Dyo and Gouan
societies of the Bambara of Mali.**
Pascal James Imperato, with a foreword by Irwin Hersey. New York:
Kilima House, 1983. 57p. map. bibliog.

The Dyo and Gouan secret religious societies of the southern Bambara are nearly
extinct. Imperato, who was able to research these cultures from 1966 to 1974, became
interested in them because of the large female statues or 'Bambara queens' fashioned
by the Bambara. This book was written to help correct errors made in art publications
written in the 1970s. It includes thirty-five black-and-white photographs of which
twenty-three are of wood or iron sculptures.

358 **A case of fundamentalism in West Africa: Wahabism in Bamako.**
Jean-Loup Amselle, translated by Donald Taylor. In: *Studies in religious fundamentalism.* Edited by Lionel Caplan. Albany, New York: State University of New York Press, 1987, p. 79-94. bibliog.

The purpose of Wahabism, an Arab and Islamic religious and political movement dating from the eighteenth century, was to 'restore Islam to its original purity by driving out all innovations and superstitions and adopting a policy of expansion' (p. 80). This article discusses the growth of this Islamic fundamentalist sect in Bamako after the Second World War, its growth among the merchants of Bamako, its anti-marabout [Muslim hermit] views, and its nationalist and pro-Arab perspectives. Amselle is better known for his work on ethnicity, such as *Au coeur de l'ethnie: ethnies, tribalisme et état en Afrique* (At the heart of ethnicity: ethnic groups, tribalism and state in Africa) (Paris: Découverte, 1985. 225p.).

359 **Les chemins de Nya: culte de possession au Mali.** (The roads of Nya: posession cult in Mali.)
Jean-Paul Colleyn. Paris: Editions de l'Ecole des Hautes Etudes en Sciences Sociales, 1988. 221p. maps. bibliog. (Anthropologie Visuelle, no. 1).

This is an in-depth look at Minyanka society and its Nya possession cult. Twice a year, Nya, a powerful religious force, takes possession of certain men and talks through their mouths. This communication brings together God, Nya, the ancestors and the living. He is nourished by the blood of sacrifices. The work includes the transcription of a film (p. 32-56) with the same title by Jean-Paul Colleyn and Jean-Jacques Péché.

360 **Conversations with Ogotemmêli: an introduction to Dogon religious ideas.**
Marcel Griaule, with an introduction by Germaine Dieterlen. London and New York: Oxford University Press for the International African Institute, 1970, ©1965. 230p. map. bibliog.

In this translation of *Dieu d'eau: entretiens avec Ogotemmêli* (Paris: Editions du Chêne, 1948. 263p.), the English-language speaker can read one of Marcel Griaule's important pioneering works on the cosmology, myth, religion and philosophy of the Dogon people. A new French edition has just been published (Paris: Fayard, 1997. 233p.). Several of Griaule's works have also been incorporated into the HRAF files (see item no. 281). Another work on Dogon cosmology is Eric Guerrier's *Essai sur la cosmogonie des Dogon: l'arche du Nommo* (Essay on the cosmogony of the Dogons: Nommo's arch) (Paris: R. Laffont, 1975. 249p.).

361 **Eglise et pouvoir colonial au Soudan français: les relations entre les administrateurs et les missionnaires catholiques dans la Boucle du Niger, de 1885 à 1945.** (The Church and colonial power in French Sudan: the relations between administrators and Catholic missionaries in the Niger Bend, from 1885 to 1945.)
Joseph-Roger de Benoist. Paris: Karthala, 1987. 539p. maps. bibliog. (Hommes et Sociétés).

This is the history of missions in the French Sudan from the arrival of the White Fathers to the end of the Second World War. Close attention is paid to the relations between Church and state.

362 **An essay on the religion of the Bambara = Essai sur la religion bambara.**
Germaine Dieterlen, translated from the French by Katia Wolf. New Haven, Connecticut: Human Relations Area Files, 1960. 293 leaves.

Written by Marcel Griaule's associate, this is an important work on the Bambara religion dating from the colonial period. It was first published in French (Paris: Presses Universitaires de France, 1951. 240p.). Dieterlen has also written numerous books on the Dogons – e.g., *The pale fox* (co-authored with Griaule) (q.v.) – and has made ethnographic films on the Dogons with Jean Rouch. Several of her works have been translated into English and appear in the HRAF files (see item no. 281).

363 **Etudes sur l'Islam et les tribus du Soudan.** (Studies on Islam and the tribes of Sudan.)
Paul Marty. Paris: E. Leroux, 1920-21. 4 vols. maps. bibliog.

The history of Islam is recounted for various regions (i.e., the East, Timbuktu, Djenne, Macina, the Sahel, and Kayes) and ethnic groups (i.e., the Kounta, Berabich, Iguellad, Songhai, Peul, Maure, Bambara, and Nioro) of the former French Sudan. In the appendices are included numerous genealogies as well as fascimiles in Arabic script of the handwriting of important tribal chiefs. The work is also available on microfim (1 reel).

364 **The expansion of Islam among the Bambara under French rule, 1890-1940.**
Stephen Albert Harmon. PhD thesis, University of California, Los Angeles, 1988. 548p. maps. bibliog. (Available from University Microfilms International, Ann Arbor, Michigan, order no. 8907544).

Although the Bambara had resisted the Islamization of West Africa since medieval times, they began to convert to Islam during the French colonial era. The reasons for this conversion stem from socio-economic factors of colonial rule, for the French developed a new class of wage-earners (shifting away from subsistence farming), expanded commerce, ended slavery and forced labour, and created a cash-based economy.

365 **Genii of the River Niger.**
Jean-Marie Gibbal, translated by Beth G. Raps, with a foreword by
Paul Stoller. Chicago, Illinois; London: University of Chicago Press,
1994. 204p. bibliog.
In this translation of *Génies du fleuve* (Paris: Presses de la Renaissance, 1988. 257p.),
Gibbal describes his trip down the Niger River where he observed the Ghimbala
possession rites performed between Mopti and Timbuktu in the inland delta of the
Niger River by the Songhay people. Although the original French edition contains two
maps which are lacking in the English translation, the latter has ten pages of
photographs lacking from the French edition. The author's other books on Mali
include *Tambours d'eau* (Paris: Le Sycomore, 1982. 354p.), about a possession cult in
western Mali, and *Guérisseurs et magiciens du Sahel* (Paris: A. M. Métailié, 1984.
160p.), about three Malian Songhay healers/magicians.

366 **In the path of Allah: the passion of Al-Hajj 'Umar, an essay into
the nature of charisma in Islam.**
John Ralph Willis. London: F. Cass, 1989. 255p. map. bibliog.
This biography and study of the nature of charismatic personality examines the life of
mystic Shaykh al-Hajj 'Umar (Umar Tal) who developed a religious community
(Jama'a) during the period 1849-64 stretching over a vast area of the Western Sudan,
covering present-day Guinea, Mali and Mauritania. His passion was 'a dramatic re-
enactment of circumstances contained in the life of Muhammad' (Preface, p. xi). The
work includes a glossary (p. 228-33) and a bibliography (p. 234-46). Willis's related
1970 doctoral thesis at the University of London, School of Oriental and African
Studies was '''Al-Hajj 'Umar b. Sa'id al-Futi al-Turi (c. 1794-1864) and the doctrinal
basis of his Islamic reformist movement in the Western Sudan'.

367 **The innocent sorcerer: coping with evil in two African societies
(Kapsiki & Dogon).**
Walter E. A. van Beek. In: *Religion in Africa.* Edited by Thomas D.
Blakely, Walter E. A. van Beek, Dennis L. Thomson. London:
J. Currey; Portsmouth, New Hampshire: Heinemann, 1994, p. 197-228.
bibliog. (Monograph Series of the David M. Kennedy Center for
International Studies at Brigham Young University, no. 4).
The Kapsiki of northern Cameroon and the Dogon of Mali are the subjects of this
article on the concept of evil. Van Beek asserts that evil is applicable outside the
Judaeo-Christian sphere. He compares and contrasts the two religions and their notion
of evil.

368 **Islam and Christianity in West Africa.**
Toyin Falola, Biodun Adediran. Ile-Ife, Nigeria: University of Ife
Press, 1983. 137p. bibliog.
The history of Islam and Christianity are each discussed in separate sections of this
general study which follows the syllabus of the West African Examination Council.

369 **Islam in the Banamba region of the eastern Beledugu, c. 1800 to c. 1900.**
B. Marie Perinbam. *International Journal of African Historical Studies,* vol. 19, no. 4 (1986), p. 637-57. map. bibliog.

The author shows there was extensive interaction and co-existence between Muslims and non-Muslims in the Banamba region of the eastern Beledugu, northeast of Bamako. She argues that Islamic animist 'mixing' or pluralism involved a complex interaction of political, social and economic elements. '. . . Islamic beliefs and practices (in one form or another) were so diffused in numerous cultural norms that many were simply accepted, believed in and practiced by eastern Beledugu populations, regardless of whether Niger-bend Islamic traditions, which the French later adopted, regarded them as Muslim or not' (p. 657).

370 **Islamisme contre 'naturisme' au Soudan français: essai de psychologie politique coloniale.** (Islamism versus 'naturism' in French Sudan: essay on political colonial psychology.)
J. Brévié, preface by Maurice Delafosse. Paris: E. Leroux, 1923. 320p.

This is an early French work on the history of Islam and animism (here roughly synonymous with 'naturism') in Mali.

371 **La mission catholique auprès des Bwa avant et après l'indépendance du Mali, 1888-1988.** (The Catholic mission to the Bwas before and after the independence of Mali, 1888-1988.)
D. Y. Pierre Diarra. Milan, Italy: Federazione Organismi Cristiani di Servizio Internazionale Volontario; Centro Studi e Richerche Africa, 1993. 2 vols. maps. bibliog. (Collana Contributi, no. 26).

The Bwas are the only Malian people to convert to Catholicism in large numbers. Volume 1 covers the history of Catholic missions in Mali. Volume 2 examines the attitudes of the Church. Since the missionaries did not encourage the Bwa to take responsibility for the future of their own country, few Catholic Bwas are active in deciding Mali's future. The work includes a chronology contrasting the Church and state from 1888 to 1991 (p. 599-602) and a lengthy bibliography (p. 603-25).

372 **The origins of clericalism in West African Islam.**
Lamin Sanneh. *Journal of African History,* vol. 17, no. 1 (1976), p. 49-72. map. bibliog.

In the twelfth and thirteenth centuries, Serakhullé (Sarakole or Soninké) clerics – known as Jakhanké and led by Al-Hajj Salim – disavowed jihād and established travel as a part of clerical life. Sanneh focuses on the work of 'Abd al-Rahmān Jakhité who eventually settled in Kano in the fifteenth century, and traces the role of these peaceful clerics in Islam's spread in the region.

Religion

373 **The pale fox.**
Marcel Griaule, Germaine Dieterlen, translated from the French by
Stephen C. Infantino. Chino Valley, Arizona: Continuum
Foundation, 1986. 560p. maps.

This is the classic study on Dogon cosmology (creation of the world) by noted anthropologists Griaule and Dieterlen, translated into a very readable English. Dogon myth, thought, symbolism and social organization are revealed. Numerous illustrations (especially drawings which explain symbolism) are scattered throughout the text. The work, which includes lists of animals, plants and heavenly bodies (p. 541-47), was originally published in French as *Le renard pâle* (Paris: Institut d'Ethnologie, 1965).

374 **Paroles de nouvel an: témoignages de l'Eglise catholique malienne.**
(Words for the new year: testimonial of the Malian Catholic Church.)
Luc Sangaré. Bamako: Jamana, 1988. 216p. maps.

Marking the centennial of the Catholic Church in Mali, this publication by Archbishop Luc Sangaré, includes a twenty-five-year compilation of his letters to the president of Mali and six letters by Mali's bishops marking the occasion of the centennial. There are also numerous photos of Malian church officials, and descriptions of the six dioceses (including their work with schools, libraries, social/cultural organizations, and health care), of the male and female Catholic religious orders in Mali, and of religious associations in Mali. In 1988, it was estimated that there were between 75,000 and 100,000 Catholics out of a total Malian population of 8 million.

375 **La religion et la magie Songhay.** (Songhay religion and magic.)
Jean Rouch. Brussels: Editions de l'Université de Bruxelles, 1989.
2nd rev. and augmented ed. 377p. (Anthropologie Sociale).

First published in 1960, this is one of several works the famous French ethnologist and film-maker wrote on the Songhay of Niger (also pertaining to the Songhay of Mali). The religion is centred on a cult of possession which includes trances and a dance of the possessed.

376 **The spiritual economy of Nioro du Sahel: Islamic discourses and practices in a Malian religious center.**
Benjamin F. Soares. PhD thesis, Northwestern University, Evanston,
Illinois, 1997. 2 vols. map. bibliog. (Available from University
Microfilms International, Ann Arbor, Michigan, order no. 9731342).

This recent dissertation examines the changing 'spiritual economy' (or economy of religious practice) of a west Malian town, Nioro du Sahel, known for its Muslim religious leader Shaykh Hamallah (1883?-1943), founder of a branch of the Tijaniyya (Tijaniyah) Sufi order. Hamallah was exiled to France in 1941and died there soon after, although his followers in Africa believe he will some day return. See also *Le temps des marabouts: itinéraires et stratégies islamiques en Afrique occidentale française v. 1880-1960* (The time of marabouts: itineraries and Islamic strategies in French West Africa from 1880 to 1960) (Paris: Karthala, 1997. 583p.), edited by David Robinson and Jean-Louis Triaud; it contains six chapters on Muslim marabouts (clerics) in Mali, including several chapters on Hamallah.

377 **West Africa and Islam: a study of religious development from the 8th to the 20th century.**
Peter B. Clarke.   London: E. Arnold, 1982. 275p. maps. bibliog.
In this study of Islam in West Africa, Islam's development is traced from the eighth century through to 1980. There are numerous informative historical maps of the region, a glossary (p. 263-64) and a 'select bibliography' (p. 268-70), as well as useful footnotes following each chapter. Another older but still useful text is J. Spencer Trimingham's *A history of Islam in West Africa* (London; New York: Oxford University Press, 1970. 262p.). A recent text on this topic is Mervyn Hiskett's *The course of Islam in Africa* (Edinburgh: University of Edinburgh, 1994. 218p.) which contains an excellent chapter on West Africa (p. 92-134), especially the section 'Medieval empires of the Sahel (c. 220/835 to c. 1060-1650)' (p. 92-104).

378 **West African Sufi: the religious heritage and spiritual quest of Cerno Bokar Saalif Taal.**
Louis Brenner.   Berkeley, California: University of California Press, 1984. 215p. maps. bibliog.
In this biography of Cerno Bokar, spiritual leader and teacher in Bandiagara, and convert to the Hamalliya (a branch of the Tijaniyah Sufi order), the author describes the order's origins and development. Another prominent biography of this leader is Amadou Hampâté Bâ's *Vie et enseignement de Tierno Bokar: le sage de Bandiagara* (Life and teachings of Tierno Bokar: the sage of Bandiagara) (Paris: Seuil, 1980. 254p.).

Antilopes du soleil: arts et rites agraires d'Afrique noire. (Antelopes of the sun: arts and agrarian rites of Black Africa.)
See item no. 644.

The artfulness of M'Fa Jigi: an interview with Nyamaton Diarra.
See item no. 659.

Soudan français: contes soudanais. (French Soudan: Sudanese tales.)
See item no. 762.

Islam in the oral traditions of Mali: Bilali and Surakata.
See item no. 774.

Society and Social Conditions

379 **Colonial policy and the family life of black troops in French West Africa, 1817-1904.**
J. Malcom Thompson. *International Journal of African Historical Studies*, vol. 23, no. 3 (1990), p. 423-53. map. bibliog.
The author provides an interesting account of the associations and roles of women and families of African soldiers in French West Africa and of the creation of *tirailleur sénégalais* villages such as Kayes and Siguri in Mali. The 'military gradually encouraged its African garrisons to marry and establish households near French forts' (p. 423).

380 **Femmes du Mali: statut, image, réactions au changement.** (Women of Mali: stature, image, reactions to change.)
Danielle Bazin-Tardieu. Montreal, Canada: Leméac, 1975. 259p. bibliog. (Collection Francophonie Vivante).
The author, a sociologist who lived in Mali for a number of years, provides readers with a description and analysis of the status and situation of women in Mali's traditional society.

381 **Histoire des classes sociales dans l'Afrique de l'ouest. I.: Mali.**
(History of social classes in West Africa. I.: Mali.)
Majhemout Diop. Paris: L'Harmattan, 1985. 260p. bibliog. (Logiques Sociales).
This first volume of a two-volume set is devoted to Mali (the second is about Senegal) and contains a historical study of socio-professional groups and classes in Malian

society during the precolonial, colonial, and post-colonial periods. It shows how this society was entirely restructured and became organized into new social classes founded on a previously established hierarchy.

382 **Material world: a global family portrait.**
Peter Menzel, Charles C. Mann. San Francisco, California: Sierra Club Books, 1994. 255p.

Using superb photographs, statistical profiles and text to present a comparative study of families from thirty countries around the world, this fascinating book captures 'both the common humanity of the peoples inhabiting our Earth and the great differences in material goods and circumstances that make rich and poor societies.' The Natomo family of Kouakourou, Mali, comprising a father, two wives and eight children, is featured.

383 **Nomads of the Sahel.**
Patrick Marnham. New York: Minority Rights Group, 1979. rev. ed. 19p. map. bibliog. (Minority Rights Group Report, no. 33).

Marnham, a journalist, has reported from various African countries for several publications, making visits to the Sahel in 1973-74 and again in 1976 for the Minority Rights Group. This highly critical document begins with a description of the Sahelian land, its nomads and other peoples, and the traditional economy. This is followed by a discussion of the 1973 drought crisis and how the nomads were affected, including their mistreatment by Mali and other countries. A critique of inappropriate and destructive development programmes follows, as well as a section about the status of the Sahelian nomads and their way of life since the drought. Marnham asserts that climatic conditions have a lesser impact than development policies and programmes on the continuation of nomadic transhumance in this region. Two appendices, a bibliography, and a filmography of selected documentaries is included. This title is part of the critically acclaimed Minority Rights Group Report series.

384 **Les paysannes du Mali: espaces de liberté et changements.** (Female farmers of Mali: times of freedom and changes.)
Chantal Rondeau. Paris: Editions Karthala, 1994. 362p. map. bibliog.

The literature on women in development often emphasizes the constraints which they suffer. In effect, however, being dominated does not prevent women from securing a certain degree of liberty. To study this liberty, it is necessary to analyse the control that women exercise on their lives, work, etc. Written for a broad audience, and based on field studies made of 188 Malian women, this book demonstrates that, in spite of their inferior social position in three partriarchal societies (Dogon, Minyanka (Minianka) and Senufo), rural Malian women successfully manage to attain their freedom. The author's 1980 University of Paris VII doctoral dissertation was 'La société senufo du sud Mali (1870-1950) de la 'tradition' à la dépendance' (Senufo society in southern Mali (1870-1950), from 'tradition' to dependence).

385   **Urbanization of an African community: voluntary associations in Bamako.**
Claude Meillassoux.   Seattle, Washington: University of Washington Press, 1968. 165p. maps. bibliog.

Meillassoux's study describes the capital city of Bamako and its inhabitants, culture, history and social conditions. Various types of associations (regional, religious, youth, political, etc.) that existed in Bamako during the colonial period are also discussed, as well as the ways their role and purpose have evolved since independence.

386   **Where camels are better than cars: a locality study in Mali, West Africa for Key Stage 2.**
John Snyder, Sarah Snyder, Catherine McFarlane.   Birmingham, England: Development Education Centre, Gillett Centre; London: Save the Children, 1992. 2 vols. maps. bibliog.

This information packet is designed for use by teachers but is an excellent resource for anyone interested in learning about Malian society. Consisting of two books accompanied by twenty-four colour photographs and a poster, the materials offer insight into the lives of four Malians of different ethnic groups (Sonrai (Songhay), Dogon, Bozo, Tuareg) who live in and around the multicultural town of Douentza.

387   **Women in slavery in the Western Sudan.**
Martin A. Klein.   In: *Women and slavery in Africa.* Edited by Claire C. Robertson, Martin Klein.   Madison, Wisconsin: University of Wisconsin Press, 1983, p. 67-92. map. bibliog.

As part of this description of women in slavery in the western Sudan, Klein assesses Claude Meillassoux's argument that female slaves were more highly valued because of their capacity for work and not because of their ability to reproduce.

388   **Women in the material world.**
Faith D'Aluisio, Peter Menzel.   San Francisco, California: Sierra Club Books, 1996. 255p.

This book, a companion volume to the best-selling *Material world: a global family portrait* (q.v.), reveals the hopes, joys, sorrows, and aspirations of women in twenty disparate lands at the close of the twentieth century. The remarkable stories are complemented by 375 colour photographs and a wealth of pertinent statistics. Two co-wives from Mali are featured in pictures and interviews in a separate section (p. 166-79).

389   **Women's work and women's property: household social relations in the Maraka textile industry of the nineteenth century.**
Richard Roberts.   *Comparative Studies in Society and History,* vol. 26, no. 2 (April 1984), p. 229-50.

The Maraka (Marka), a 'Malinkized Soninke' who migrated from ancient Ghana and spoke only Bambara, produced two types of cloth, 'plain white and indigo dyed, with the symbols of the struggles between Maraka men and women' (p. 230). Roberts describes changes in the 'gender–property connection' related to changing social relations within the Maraka household as they became more patriarchal. This is an excellent social and economic history of an African handicraft which changed while textile technology remained the same.

Pays du Sahel: du Tchad au Sénégal, du Mali au Niger. (Countries of the Sahel: from Chad to Senegal, from Mali to Niger.)
See item no. 178.

Dancing skeletons: life and death in West Africa.
See item no. 393.

Socialism and social change in rural Mali.
See item no. 430.

Cattle, women, and wells: managing household survival in the Sahel.
See item no. 517.

Descendants and crops: two poles of production in a Malian peasant village.
See item no. 519.

Gens de la parole: essai sur la condition et le rôle des griots dans la société malinké. (People of the word: essay on the condition and role of griots in Malinke society.)
See item no. 773.

Compendium of Social Statistics and Indicators, 1988.
See item no. 838.

World handbook of political and social indicators.
See item no. 842.

Medicine, Health and Nutrition

390 **African folk medicine: practices and beliefs of the Bambara and other peoples.**
Pascal James Imperato. Baltimore, Maryland: York Press, 1977. 251p. bibliog.

Imperato, a specialist in public health and tropical medicine, was sent to Mali in 1966 by the United States Public Health Service to establish and direct a programme to eradicate smallpox and control measles. During his six-year stay, and subsequent visits in 1973-74, he studied and gathered extensive information on traditional Bambara medicine. The result is this 'compilation of the knowledge of Bambara healers, herbalists, Koranic teachers, diviners, patients and old sages', aimed at both the general reader and those specifically interested in the subject of this detailed and fascinating work. Following introductory chapters on the country and the Bambara people, the therapeutic process, African beliefs in links between disease causation and the spirit world, and folk medicine as practised among rural and urban Bambara, there are chapters dealing with mental illness, fertility and reproduction, childhood diseases, measles, adult communicable diseases, chronic diseases, etc. A glossary, full index, and separate name index are included.

391 **Breastfeeding, weaning, and other infant feeding practices in Mali and their effects on growth and development.**
Katherine A. Dettwyler. PhD thesis, Indiana University, 1985. 378p. maps. bibliog. (Available from University Microfilms International, Ann Arbor, Michigan, order no. 8526996).

Dettwyler's goal in undertaking this study is to determine how Malian women's beliefs concerning breastfeeding, infant feeding and weaning affect the growth and development of their children. Study results indicate that children's nutritional status could possibly be improved without major changes in the belief system and without massive donations of foreign aid. This research has made available the first complete set of anthropometric data for Malian infants. Barbara Cashion has completed a study on the growth and development of older children in rural Mali, 'Creation of a local growth standard based on well-nourished Malian children and its application to a village sample of unknown age' (PhD thesis, Indiana University, 1988. Available on microfiche from University Microfilms International, 1989).

392 **Cost recovery in public health services in Sub-Saharan Africa.**
Brian Nolan, Vincent Turbat. Washington, DC: World Bank, 1995. 106p. bibliog. (EDI Technical Materials).

Pressures on health and health-care financing are intense in Sub-Saharan Africa, and this continent possesses special characteristics that must be considered when assessing the potential of health-care cost recovery. This study seeks to identify the tools necessary to assess cost recovery programmes and apply them to this region of Africa. See also the chapter on Mali in *Recurrent costs in the health sector: problems and policy options in three countries*, edited by B. Abel-Smith and A. Creese (Geneva: World Health Organization; Washington, DC: USAID, 1989. 165p.).

393 **Dancing skeletons: life and death in West Africa.**
Katherine A. Dettwyler. Prospect Heights, Illinois: Waveland, 1994. 172p. map. bibliog.

Dettwyler, a physical anthropologist whose research interests focus primarily on nutrition, has compiled a vibrant, moving, and introspective account of a 1989 trip to Mali, during which she conducted fieldwork among malnourished children. She paints a vivid portrait of Malian people, places, and society, and explores such diverse topics as culture shock, population control, breastfeeding, female circumcision, the role of women, the meaning of disability and child death, and issues and problems associated with anthropological fieldwork. Designed for use in introductory-level anthropology classes, this work is a unique contribution to the small body of published literature on Malian ethnography.

394 **The ecology of malnutrition in the French-speaking countries of West Africa and Madagascar.**
Jacques Meyer May, Donna M. McMellan. New York: Hafner, 1968. 1st ed. 433p. (Studies in Medical Geography, vol. 8).

Each chapter of this study is devoted to a country; Mali is covered on pages 277-321. Following a general profile of the country, there is a detailed consideration of food production and consumption, food industries, trade, food supply, diet, and malnutrition and other nutrition-related diseases. Tables, maps and short bibliographies supplement the text.

395 **Enquête démographique et de santé au Mali, 1987.** (Mali demographic and health survey, 1987.)
Baba Traoré, Mamadou Konaté, Cynthia Stanton. Bamako: Centre d'Etudes et de Recherches sur la Population pour le Développement, Institut du Sahel; Columbia, Maryland: Institute for Resource Development/Westinghouse, 1989. 2 vols. bibliog.

This document presents the results of a survey conducted by the Centre d'Etudes et de Recherche sur la Population pour le Développement (CERPOD) of the Sahel Institute. The first volume (187p.) discusses detailed statistical information collected about fertility rates; knowledge of, attitudes towards, and use of contraception; and maternal and infant health in Mali. The second volume (20p.) is a summary of survey results. Many tables and graphs are included; the bibliography consists of 11 citations. A second, expanded survey was conducted which takes into account developments and changes in health demographics (e.g., the spread of AIDS); its title is *Enquête démographique et de santé, Mali 1995-1996* (q.v.).

396 **Enquête démographique et de santé, Mali 1995-1996.** (Mali demographic and health survey, 1995-96.)
Salif Coulibaly (et al.). Bamako: Cellule de Planification et de Statistique du Ministère de la Santé, de la Solidarité et des Personnes Agées; Direction Nationale de la Statistique et de l'Informatique, 1996. 375p. bibliog.

This document presents the results of a survey conducted in 1995-96 by the Cellule de Planification et de Statistique du Ministère de la Santé, de la Solidarité et des Personnes Agées (CPS/MSSPA) and the Direction Nationale de la Statistique et de l'Informatique (DNSI). Following a chapter containing general information about Mali and the methodology of the survey, it discusses the detailed statistical information which was collected about fertility rates; marriage and pregnancy; knowledge of, attitudes towards, and use of contraception; maternal and infant health; child and maternal mortality; lactation and nutrition; female genital mutilation; sexually transmitted diseases and AIDS; and available family planning and maternal and infant health services. Many tables and graphs complement the text. A first survey is also available, *Enquête démographique et de santé au Mali, 1987* (q.v.). Both surveys are an important source of information for establishing programmes on maternal and infant health and family planning campaigns.

397 **Family mediation of health care in an African community (Mali).**
Kathleen O. Slobin. PhD thesis, University of California, San Francisco, 1991. 330p. bibliog. (Available from University Microfilms International, Ann Arbor, Michigan, order no. 9205237).

The author focuses on how families in a rural Malian town and village mediate traditional, Islamic and biomedical treatments when caring for family members who are ill. She suggests that the country's national health policy should embrace family-based lay health care along with the traditional and biomedical therapies it currently supports.

398 **Field research in Macina for vitamin A communications, March 5-22, 1990.**
Katherine A. Dettwyler, Claudia Fishman, with the collaboration of Kanté Dandara Touré (et al.). Washington, DC: Nutrition Communication Project, Academy for Educational Development, 1990. 80p.

This report describes a nutritional study designed by Dettwyler and undertaken by herself and a research team in the Macina circle of Segu in March 1990. Material was collected on such topics as dietary practices, child-feeding practices and attitudes, suggested food behaviour changes, and appropriate avenues of communication for rural populations using questionnaires, market surveys and focus group interviews. The team's findings are summarized and recommendations are presented which are geared to increasing consumption of foods rich in Vitamin A as well as improving general nutritional status. Recommendations were also drafted for a communications strategy that would be appropriate for achieving these goals.

399   **The Hosken report: genital and sexual mutilation of females.**
Fran P. Hosken.   Lexington, Massachusetts: Women's International Network News, 1993. 4th rev. ed. 439p. bibliog.

The objective of this publication is 'to provide a comprehensive record of female genital mutilation (FGM) from a global perspective'. The substance of the report is contained in a compilation of detailed country case-histories, including one for Mali (p. 211-32) which reveals the extent of female genital mutilation in that country and how the lives and health of female children are sacrificed in the name of tradition and to fulfil religious 'requirements'. Malian women relate their experiences with genital mutilation and Malian midwives describe what they observe during the course of their work about the reality of women who undergo genital mutilation and about their lives in Malian society. The work also includes an overview of this practice and the related health dangers, a discussion of the politics of female genital mutilation, and a section that documents positive initiatives being taken in Africa and other parts of the world to eradicate it.

400   **Infant and child mortality in rural Mali.**
Allan G. Hill, Sara C. Randall, Marie-Louise van den Eerenbeemt. London: Centre for Population Studies, London School of Hygiene and Tropical Medicine, 1983. 45p. map. bibliog. (CPS Research Paper, no. 83-5).

The authors present in this study an analysis of some new data gathered on child mortality among three distinct Malian ethnic groups with contrasting ways of life: the Bambara, Fulani (Peul), and Kel Tamasheq. The data were collected during a programme of surveys conducted by a team of demographers from the London School of Hygiene and Tropical Medicine, working together with the International Livestock Centre for Africa and the Malian Direction de la Statistique et de l'Informatique.

401   **L'infection par le virus de l'immunodéficience humaine (VIH) au Mali.** (Infection by the human immunodeficiency virus (HIV) in Mali.)
E. Pichard (et al.).   *Médecine Tropicale*, vol. 48, no. 4 (Oct.-Dec. 1988), p. 345-49. bibliog.

A review and summary of epidemiological and clinical data on HIV infection in forty-six cases in Mali. The data are compared with those for other countries in Africa. Consult also a discussion of HIV infection in the West African region (p. 68-72) in *AIDS: an African perspective* (Boca Raton, Florida: CRC Press, 1992. 363p.) by A. Olufemi Williams.

402 **Maternal income-generation activities and child nutrition: the Bambara of Mali.**
June Neff. PhD thesis, Cornell University, 1995. 178p. bibliog.
(Available from University Microfilms International, Ann Arbor, Michigan, order no. 9509458).

This study examines the relationship between maternal food production and the trading activities of Bambara women in rural Mali and the nutritional status of children one to three years of age.

403 **'People are not the same': leprosy, identity, and community in colonial and post-colonial Mali.**
Eric Silla. PhD thesis, Northwestern University, Evanston, Illinois, 1995. 2 vols. maps. bibliog.

Silla's research, which relies extensively on patient perspectives, describes how the lives of leprosy sufferers were transformed during particular points in Mali's history, how they achieved a collective identity, and the reaction of Malian societies to the disease and those afflicted by it. Sources include interviews with over 190 former leprosy patients, professionals, and healers, as well as Arabic manuscripts, colonial archives, and mission records.

404 **Primary health care in Africa: a study of the Mali Rural Health Project.**
Clive S. Gray (et al.). Boulder, Colorado: Westview Press, 1990. 177p. (Westview Special Studies in Social, Political, and Economic Development).

The Mali Rural Health Project (Projet Santé Rurale), conducted from 1978 to 1982, was an initiative within the US foreign aid programme to establish a workable, cost-efficient, primary health-care programme that could be replicated throughout rural Mali. This volume describes the project and assesses the successes that were achieved as well as its shortcomings. Unfortunately, the project failed to achieve its immediate goals because it proved too costly to implement nationwide.

405 **Public health problems in 14 French-speaking countries in Africa and Madagascar: a survey of resources and needs.**
Washington, DC: Division of Medical Sciences, National Academy of Sciences, National Research Council, 1966. 2 vols. maps. bibliog.

This two-volume set, prepared for the Agency of International Development, presents an inventory of the major public health problems afflicting those countries of Africa which were formerly under French administration. The first volume contains information about organizations and programmes, communicable diseases and the other main health problems, and medical education and training – all pertinent to these nations as a whole or to groups of them. The second volume supplements this general information with details about each individual country; Mali is found on pages 269-86.

406   **Quel usage des plantes médicinales au Mali aujourd'hui?** (What use
       of medicinal plants in Mali today?)
       Denis Malgras.   Bamako: Centre Djoliba, 1993. 23 leaves. bibliog.

The purpose of this work is to compile information on the rich traditions associated
with the great variety of vegetable species and their uses in medicine, which risk being
lost. In order to better understand how medicinal plants are used in Mali, Malgras
attempts, in the first part, to describe how these plants were and are still used in
traditional medicine; in the second part the practical modality of using these plants in
Mali today is discussed. The author is an agronomist who has lived in Mali for over
forty years and who has completed a detailed study and inventory of medicinal trees
and shrubs from the Mali savannahs, *Arbres et arbustes guérisseurs des savanes
maliennes* (Paris: A.C.C.T.: Editions Karthala, 1992. 478p.). This contains a chapter
about traditional medicine but is botanical in nature.

407   **Revue de Médecines et Pharmacopées Africaines.** (Review of
       African Medicine and Pharmacology.)
       Eysines, France: A.C.C.T., G.R.I.P.T., 1987- . semi-annual.

Intended to serve as a link between specialists and the francophone world, this
periodical occasionally contains articles about traditional medicine and pharmacology
as these topics relate to Mali and West Africa. Its title has changed: from 1987 to 1990
it was called *Médecine Traditionnelle et Pharmacopée*; the present title dates from
vol. 5, no. 1 (1991).

408   **Satisfaction of food requirements in Mali to 2000 A.D.**
       Jacqueline Mondot-Bernard, Michel Labonne.   Paris: Development
       Centre of the Organisation for Economic Co-operation and
       Development, 1982. 213p. (Development Centre Studies).

The authors, one a nutritionist, the other an agro-economist, worked closely to
produce this study. The first part is an analysis, based on field survey data, of Mali's
problematic food intake and nutritional situation. A balanced diet is suggested which
would meet the nutritional requirements of the people and at the same time conform to
their food habits. In the second part, 'Agricultural policy and satisfaction of food
requirements in Mali', the country's potential to produce both food and non-food
agricultural products is assessed, based on its natural, human, and technological
resources. In the light of this assessment, a method for building a model of Malian
agriculture is described.

409   **A wind in Africa: a story of modern medicine in Mali.**
       Pascal James Imperato.   St. Louis, Missouri: W. H. Green, 1975.
       363p. bibliog.

An autobiographical narrative of the author's many and unique experiences as the
leader of a medical mission sent to Mali in 1966 by the United States government to
conduct a smallpox eradication/measles control programme. The work covers the six
years Imperato spent in Mali, during which time he worked closely with members of
Mali's national mobile medical service, the Service des Grandes Endémies, and
gained access to parts of the country little-known to foreigners. This rich and
fascinating story is complemented by photographs taken by the author; an index is
included.

Bulletin de l'Association des Naturalistes du Mali. (Bulletin of the Association of Malian Naturalists.)
See item no. 102.

Medicinal plants in tropical West Africa.
See item no. 116.

Les Dogon de Boni: approche démo-génétique d'un isolat du Mali. (The Dogon of Boni: demo-genetic approach of an isolate of Mali.)
See item no. 275.

Lexique médical: bambara–français, français–bambara. (Medical lexicon: Bambara–French, French–Bambara.)
See item no. 342.

Food strategies in four African countries: a study on food policy formulation and implementation in Kenya, Mali, Rwanda and Zambia.
See item no. 523.

The healing drum: African wisdom teachings.
See item no. 695.

Representation of female circumcision in *Finzan*, a dance for the heroes.
See item no. 723.

Politics

General and regional

410 Aoua Kéita and the nascent women's movement in the French Soudan.
Jane Turrittin. *African Studies Review*, vol. 36, no. 1 (April 1993), p. 59-89.
Kéita, the first woman elected deputy to the Republic of Mali's national assembly, is an extraordinary figure who has been largely ignored by historians. Turrittin's article is therefore a welcome contribution to the literature on Malian women and politics. Following a synopsis of Kéita's life and a discussion of the development of her political and feminist beliefs, Turrittin examines the platform of the nascent women's movement in the French Soudan and contrasts Soudanese and Guinean women's support of and participation in the independence movements which emerged simultaneously in their countries.

411 Creating political order: the party-states of West Africa.
Aristide R. Zolberg. Chicago, Illinois: Rand McNally, 1966. 168p.
Zolberg, who has conducted extensive fieldwork in Mali, examines political life in that country and four other 'one-party states' of West Africa: Ivory Coast (Côte d'Ivoire), Ghana, Senegal, and Guinea.

412 Femme d'Afrique: la vie d'Aoua Kéita racontée par elle-même.
(Woman of Africa: the life of Aoua Kéita as told by herself.)
Aoua Kéita. Paris: Présence Africaine, 1975. 397p.
Kéita, who lived from 1912 to 1979, was a pioneering midwife (she contributed to the establishment of the first maternity clinic) and political militant in the Union Soudanaise-Rassemblement Démocratique Africain (US-RDA). Written in exile following the 1968 coup, this intriguing autobiography is valuable for a number of

reasons. In addition to providing a portrait of the difficulties of women in Malian society, it is an account of the independence movement in the French Sudan as seen and experienced by an African female élite. It is especially revealing concerning the role of women in decolonization as well as the nature of women's political organizations in the twentieth century.

413 **Freedom and authority in French West Africa.**
Robert Louis Delavignette. London: F. Cass, 1968. 152p.

Delavignette, himself a colonial official who served as governor of the French Cameroons, surveys French colonial administrative practices in West Africa. Chapters discuss the commandant, colonial society, the native territories, native policy, the chiefs, law and custom, religion, the peasant community, and modernization of the African world. Of particular value in this work are the insights it offers into the way French colonial administrators viewed their role during the early post-war period. See also his 'French colonial policy in black Africa, 1945 to 1960' in *Colonialism in Africa 1870-1960, volume 2. The history and politics of colonialism, 1914-1960*, edited by L. H. Gann and Peter Duignan (Cambridge, England: Cambridge University Press, 1970, p. 251-85).

414 **Mali.**
Thomas Hodgkin, Ruth S. Morgenthau. In: *Political parties and national integration in tropical Africa.* Edited by James S. Coleman, Carl G. Rosberg, Jr. Berkeley, California: University of California Press, 1964, p. 216-58.

This essay, primarily concerned with Soudan–Mali political life from 1945 to 1964, presents a description and analysis of the Malian political party system in its historical and social context.

415 **Nation-building in Mali: art, radio, and leadership in a pre-literate society.**
Charles Hickman Cutter. PhD thesis, University of California, Los Angeles, 1971. 370 leaves. bibliog. (Available from University Microfilms International, Ann Arbor, Michigan, order no. 725823).

Cutter analyses the dynamics of nation-building in Mali, a country in search of a national identity. Art – specifically music, drama, and poetry – is examined as a form of communication, as an instrument of political power, and as an essential aspect of the nation-building process.

416 **One-party government in Mali: transition toward control.**
Frank Gregory Snyder. New Haven, Connecticut: Yale University Press, 1965. 178p. bibliog. (Yale College Series, no. 4).

Snyder's work traces the origins, growth and development of the Union Soudanaise-Rassemblement Démocratique Africain (US-RDA), an anti-colonialist political party, from 1936 to 1964. Founded by Mamadou Konaté and Modibo Keita, it was able to effectively mobilize the political support of the masses and become the only political party in the French Sudan by 1959. The question of whether the party will be able to adapt, post-independence, to its new responsibilities and meet the demands of the Malian people is considered.

417 **Political parties in French-speaking West Africa.**
Ruth S. Morgenthau. Oxford, England: Clarendon Press, 1964. 445p.
maps. bibliog. (Oxford Studies in African Affairs).

Moving from the specific to the general, Morgenthau relates the history of political parties in the countries of French-speaking West Africa in detail, focusing primarily on Mali, Senegal, the Ivory Coast (Côte d'Ivoire) and Guinea. The chapter entitled 'Teachers and chiefs in Mali', is a descriptive history of the Union Soudanaise-Rassemblement Démocratique Africain (US-RDA). More information about Malian politics scattered throughout the book can be located through the index under 'Mali Republic', 'Mali Federation', and 'Soudan'. This is the most exhaustive account that exists of political development in French West Africa before independence.

418 **Political revival in Mali.**
Aristide Zolberg. *Africa Report*, vol. 10, no. 7 (July 1965), p. 15-20.

An assessment of Mali's political and economic scene on its fourth anniversary in September 1964, when Malians celebrated their 'revival' by commemorating the 1960 decision to create the Republic of Mali following the breakup of the Mali Federation. As the reader of this article will surmise, there was at the time it was written more reason to be optimistic about Mali's future.

419 **Rulers of empire: the French colonial service in Africa.**
William B. Cohen. Stanford, California: Hoover Institution Press, 1971. 279p. maps. bibliog.

A study of the history and evolution of the French colonial administration, with emphasis on French West Africa, from its early beginnings in Algeria and Senegal until its demise upon independence (1960). The author surveys its structure, functions, methods of recruiting and training officials, the men themselves who exercised French authority overseas, and the ways it adapted to social, economic and political changes unleashed throughout the nineteenth century and up until after the end of the Second World War. Scholars and administrators who contributed greatly to the study of the region and its peoples are discussed, such as Henri Labouret, Maurice Delafosse and Louis Faidherbe. A valuable bibliography lists a variety of sources, including archives, colonial memoirs, fiction of the period, and standard academic resources.

420 **The Tuareg rebellion.**
Jacky Rowland. *Africa Report*, vol. 37, no. 4 (July/Aug. 1992), p. 43-45.

Rowland outlines the long-running dispute between the Tuaregs and the Malian government, which began in earnest in 1990 with Tuareg strikes against government targets. The conflict escalated to attacks on Tuaregs in the north by other Malian ethnic groups and massacres of entire Tuareg villages by government soldiers. A tenuous ceasefire was signed three months before this article was published, but the author notes it will take a great deal of trust and political goodwill on both sides before some thirty-five thousand refugees, who fled to Mauritania, will be induced to return to Mali. An excellent and current (1995) book about the Tuaregs is Karl-G. Prasse's *The Tuaregs: the blue people* (q.v.), which discusses their repression by and subsequent rebellion against the two ruling black governments (p. 52-67).

421 **Vers la Troisième République du Mali.** (Towards the Third Republic of Mali.)
Cheick Oumar Diarrah. Paris: L'Harmattan, 1991. 233p.

In producing this work, Diarrah wanted the youth of Mali, who will be responsible for building a democractic government, to know and understand their nation's political past. He provides an account of Malian political history from 1946 to 1960, discusses the administration of Modibo Keita and the Première République (First Republic) (1960-68), the presidency of General Moussa Traoré and the Deuxième République (Second Republic), and chronicles the inevitable fall of Traoré in 1991 and the aftermath. A final chapter focuses on political renewal in Mali with the creation of a democracy under the Troisième République (Third Republic).

Independence, Modibo Keita and Malian socialism (1960-68)

422 **The coup and after: continuity or change in Malian politics?**
Michael G. Schatzberg. Madison, Wisconsin: African Studies Program, University of Wisconsin, 1972. 12, 6 leaves. bibliog.

The author of this paper first examines the ideological, economic and political initiatives of Modibo Keita in order to provide an understanding of his 1968 overthrow and the political path chosen by his successor, Moussa Traoré. Following this is a comparison of the political thought of the two leaders during their first two years in office, achieved through an analysis of the content of their speeches. Schatzberg concludes that with Traoré's accession to power, there has generally been more continuity than change in Malian politics.

423 **Dependency and conservative militarism in Mali.**
Miles D. Wolpin. [n.p.]: [n.p.], 1974[?]. 66 leaves. bibliog.

Policy changes and events that resulted in the downfall of Modibo Keita's leftist government in 1968 are analysed from a class perspective. Wolpin also examines the problems associated with a transition from state capitalism to state socialism.

424 **Economics of the coup.**
William I. Jones. *Africa Report*, vol. 14, no. 3-4 (March-April 1969), p. 23-26, 51-53.

Jones analyses the economic factors that played such an important role in Keita's fall from power in 1968, including the concentration of political power in towns and the ranks of government employees; the expense of operating the government; and problems with the 'socialist option', the Five-Year Plan of 1961, and the balance of payments.

425 **An era ends in Mali.**
Francis G. Snyder. *Africa Report*, vol. 14, no. 3-4 (March-April 1969), p. 16-22.

Two years previous to the overthrow of President Modibo Keita, few observers of the African political scene would have imagined it would occur. This article summarizes characteristics of the Keita regime, background events which led to the 1968 military takeover, the new government's desire to partially dismantle the socialist structure, and foreign reaction to the coup. Concluding this discussion is an examination of why the coup took place.

426 **Le Mali de Modibo Keïta.** (The Mali of Modibo Keita.)
Cheick Oumar Diarrah. Paris: L'Harmattan, 1986. 187p. (Collection Points de Vue).

This work is an account of the endeavour undertaken by former President Modibo Keita to establish a socialist state in Mali following independence in 1960, an endeavour which was ended by a military *coup d'état* in 1968. The author, who does not hide his sympathies for Keita, reveals the work of a leader who is often presented as a utopic visionary or a dogmatic politician by his enemies. In the introduction, he examines Mali's passage through decolonization to independence from France and the failure of the Mali Federation which Keita desired. The first part of the book discusses Mali's achievement of genuine independence and the Congrès Extraordinaire of 22 September 1960, which formally adopted a socialist programme. The second part of the book focuses on the economic and political problems that followed.

427 **Mali: the prospects of 'Planned Socialism'.**
Kenneth W. Grundy. In: *African socialism.* Stanford, California: Published for the Hoover Institution on War, Revolution, and Peace by Stanford University Press, 1964, p. 175-93.

This chapter examines the variety of African socialism practised in Mali and how it functions. Following a discussion of Malian attitudes toward capitalism and socialism is an analysis of Mali's first Five-Year Plan (1961-65) and the government's apparent intent to bring various sectors of the economy under state control. Completing the discussion, there are observations, conclusions, and predictions about the operation of African socialism in general and Mali's 'planned socialism' in particular.

428 **Marxian socialism in Africa: the case of Mali.**
John N. Hazard. *Comparative Politics*, vol. 2, no. 1 (Oct. 1969), p. 1-15. bibliog.

This essay examines how Keita adapted the Soviet model of Marxism to Malian politics, economics and society, yet firmly preserved more of the 'core' concepts than his neighbours, Touré of Guinea and Senghor of Senegal. Successes and failures of his attempt to introduce orthodox Marxism-Leninism to Mali are analysed, and a number of problems are identified as playing a part in Keita's overthrow in 1968, such as the resulting economic decay and grievances created by the people's militia. The author concludes by making some predictions about Mali's immediate political and economic future following Keita's exit from power.

429 **The political thought of Modibo Keita.**
Francis G. Snyder. *Journal of Modern African Studies*, vol. 5, no. 1
(May 1967), p. 77-106. bibliog.

This essay provides the reader with an introduction to President Keita's thoughts on politics and related topics, as well as a background for further and more detailed research. Although Keita had played an important role in African as well as Malian politics, at this time little research or writing had been done on this subject.

430 **Socialism and social change in rural Mali.**
Nicholas S. Hopkins. *Journal of Modern African Studies*, vol. 7,
no. 3 (1969), p. 457-67. bibliog.

Based on fieldwork completed by the author in an area near the town of Kita in 1964-65, this article considers the kinds of social change that took place in rural Mali in reaction to the socialist policies and programmes enacted by the central political and administrative authorities after independence.

Dictatorship of Moussa Traoré (1968-91)

431 **Downfall of a dictator.**
Pascal James Imperato. *Africa Report*, vol. 36, no. 4, (July-Aug.
1991), p. 24-27.

Imperato analyses how the ousted President Traoré managed to survive twenty-two years in power despite the burdens of Mali's weak economy and large foreign debt, grinding poverty and two serious droughts. He describes the pro-democracy demonstrations and riots protesting at Traoré's heavy-handed rule, his attempts to end the crisis, his overthrow, and succeeding events. The author concludes that Traoré's downfall resulted in part because he underestimated the pro-democracy groups and the inspiration they found in multi-party movements in other parts of Africa and the Eastern European Communist bloc after the events of 1989.

432 **Mali: people topple Traoré.**
Jane Turrittin. *Review of African Political Economy*, no. 52 (Nov.
1991), p. 97-103.

Turrittin describes how the democracy movement and popular demonstrations in Mali were fuelled by government corruption and mismanagement, culminating in President Traoré's 1991 overthrow. The article concludes with an assessment of Mali's future prospects under a new regime.

433 **Mali: soldiers as politicians.**
David P. Rawson. In: *The performance of soldiers as governors: African politics and the African military.* Washington, DC: University Press of America, 1980, p. 265-312.

Rawson first traces Mali's martial–political tradition and history from the time of the golden empires to independence. The remainder of this paper is devoted to a discussion of the programme, politics and policies of the military government established by President Traoré and the Military Committee for National Liberation following the 1968 coup, as well as Traoré's gradual attempts to establish a new, more democratic political order.

434 **Military government in Mali.**
Valerie Plave Bennett. Washington, DC: US Department of State, 1979. 10p.

This paper briefly traces the path of conflict and conspiracy that fractured the army command and military junta formed during the 1968 coup, the Military Committee for National Liberation. Following this is a discussion of leader Moussa Traoré's restructuring of Malian political life, starting in 1976, and a brief analysis of Mali's foreign policy in 1979.

Democratization and the presidency of Alpha Oumar Konaré (1991-)

435 **Le défi démocratique au Mali.** (The democratic challenge in Mali.)
Cheick Oumar Diarrah. Paris: L'Harmattan, 1996. 313p. (Points de Vue Concrets).

The author, currently the Malian ambassador to the United States, analyses the difficulties marking the consolidation of pluralistic democracy in Mali in the past. He writes about the problems Mali faced following the end of the Traoré regime in 1991; the democratic elections of 1992, during which the Third Republic was born under President Konaré; democracy under construction after his election; and Mali's position in the West African geopolitical sphere.

436 **Democracy and civic community in Mali.**
Zeric Kay Smith. Master's thesis, University of North Carolina at Chapel Hill, 1993. 92p. map. bibliog.

Applying the concepts of civic community and political culture, Smith demonstrates how combined aspects of Malian history, culture and society created conditions favourable to the democratization process which transformed Malian politics in the early 1990s.

437 **Democratic transition and electoral systems in Africa: a preliminary comparison of Ghana, Mali, and Niger.**
Shaheen Mozaffar. Boston, Massachusetts: African Studies Center, Boston University, 1995. 33p. bibliog.

Mozaffar's paper compares newly installed electoral systems in Mali, Ghana and Niger. He examines the politics that influenced the choice of electoral institutions in each country, and how these institutions have impacted on the emerging party system, as well as the strategies and behaviours of politicians. He also considers the degree to which these institutions contribute to the consolidation of democracy in each country.

438 **An exemplary transition.**
Allison Boyer. *Africa Report*, vol. 37, no. 4 (1992), p. 40-42.

Boyer describes the first democratic election of 1992, in which the charismatic Alpha Oumar Konaré was elected president with a 69 per cent majority. The transition to democracy was smoothed by Lieutenant Colonel Amadou Touré, who overthrew Moussa Traoré the previous year and kept his promise to restore power to the people. Because the tasks which faced Konaré were monumental and expectations were high, the author concludes that Malians may turn to the popular Touré if things go wrong.

439 **'From demons to democrats': Mali's student movement 1991-1996.**
Zeric Kay Smith. *Review of African Political Economy*, vol. 24, no. 72 (June 1997), p. 249-63. bibliog.

The Association of Students and Pupils of Mali (AEEM) played a key role in bringing down Moussa Traoré's dictatorial regime in 1991. Conflict between students and the Malian government continued through the Third Republic to the present, erupting at times into violence. Smith traces the evolution of this post-Traoré conflict with a focus on the violent events that occurred from December 1995 to January 1996 and the peaceful resolution to those conflicts in February and March of that same year. A brief overview of AEEM activities during the recent 1996/97 school year is included. Consult Louis Brenner's essay, 'Youth as political actors in Mali' in the forthcoming *Political transitions in Africa: expanding political space* (edited by Catharine Newbury, Pearl Robinson, Mamadou Diouf) for a view of the AEEM's role in Malian politics that is less positive.

440 **Governance and the transition to democracy: political parties and the party system in Mali.**
Richard Vengroff. *Journal of Modern African Studies*, vol. 31, no. 4 (Dec. 1993), p. 541-62.

Vengroff examines the nature of the party system in Mali and analyses the results of the 1992 municipal, legislative, and presidential elections. Emphasized throughout the article are the strengths and weaknesses of Mali's transition in the early 1990s from a highly authoritarian regime to a sound, modern, liberal democracy.

The Bamana empire by the Niger: kingdom, jihad, and colonization, 1712-1920.
See item no. 185.

France and Islam in West Africa, 1860-1960.
See item no. 227.

L'Etat de droit: sources d'information sur vingt pays d'Afrique et Haïta. (Law of the State: information sources on 20 countries of Africa and Haiti.) *See* item no. 443.

Implementing in law post-Keita Mali's retreat from 'scientific socialism'. *See* item no. 444.

Mali.
See item no. 446.

Mali's socialism and the Soviet legal model.
See item no. 447.

Les textes fondamentaux de la IIIe République du Mali. (The fundamental texts of the Third Republic in Mali.) *See* item no. 448.

Pan-Africanism: evolution, progress and prospects.
See item no. 456.

From French West Africa to the Mali Federation.
See item no. 457.

Political integration in Africa: the Mali Federation.
See item no. 458.

Mali, bilan d'une gestion désastreuse. (Mali, record of a disastrous administration.) *See* item no. 480.

Planning and economic policy: socialist Mali and her neighbors.
See item no. 484.

The political use of economic planning in Mali.
See item no. 485.

Socialism, economic development and planning in Mali, 1960-1968.
See item no. 488.

Mali and the U.M.O.A: a case-study of economic integration.
See item no. 497.

Trade and politics on the Senegal and Upper Niger, 1854-1900: African reaction to French penetration.
See item no. 510.

National governments, local governments, pasture governance and management in Mali.
See item no. 529.

Politics. Democratization and the presidency of Alpha Oumar Konaré (1991-)

Trade unions and politics in French West Africa during the Fourth Republic.
See item no. 553.

The politics of music in Mali.
See item no. 704.

World handbook of political and social indicators.
See item no. 842.

Journal Officiel de la République du Mali.
See item no. 872.

Law

441 **The case of Faama Mademba Sy and the ambiguities of legal
jurisdiction in early colonial French Soudan.**
Richard Roberts. In: *Law in colonial Africa.* Edited by Kristin Mann,
Richard Roberts. Portsmouth, New Hampshire: Heinemann; London:
J. Currey, 1991, p. 185-201. bibliog.

Roberts examines important issues of legal jurisdiction that were raised in French
Sudan in 1899, when African king and colonial administrator Faama Mademba Sy was
charged with administrative misconduct and abuse of power. The case highlighted the
question of whether Mademba's actions were justified by African customary law and
practice, as he claimed, or if it was appropriate he be held accountable for his actions
according to French law, as argued by the prosecuting authority.

442 **Coutumiers juridiques de l'Afrique occidentale française.**
(Customary law in French West Africa.)
Paris: Larose, 1939. 3 vols. maps. bibliog. (Publications du Comité
d'Etudes Historiques et Scientifiques de l'Afrique Occidentale
Française, Série A, nos. 8-10).

This multi-volume set is a standard source of information on customary law in
colonial French West Africa. The second volume, which covers the Soudan, has
chapters about the customary law of the Bambara, Bozo, Marka-Sarakollé (Sarakole),
Toucouleur (Tukulor), Sonraï (Songhay), Kado (Dogon), and Maure peoples. The first
volume is devoted to Senegal, and the third to Mauritania, Niger, Côte d'Ivoire,
French Guinea and Dahomey (Benin). The bibliography is found in volume one
(p. 43-54).

443 **L'Etat de droit: sources d'information sur vingt pays d'Afrique et Haïti.** (Law of the State: information sources on 20 countries of Africa and Haiti.)
Talence, France: Centre d'Etude d'Afrique Noire; Paris: IBISCUS, 1997. 316p. bibliog. (Réseaux Documentaires pour le Développement).

For each country covered, including Mali, this valuable resource provides a summary of the nation's democratic process, political institutions, legal system, politics of decentralization, political parties and syndicates, human rights, and law of the written press. Also included is a chronology of important dates in history since independence; information about the principal legal and judiciary organizations and institutions and their documentary resources; and a bibliography of recent books and articles which reflect the political history of the country and its special features and problems.

444 **Implementing in law post-Keita Mali's retreat from 'scientific socialism'.**
John N. Hazard. *African Law Studies,* vol. 7 (Dec. 1972), p. 1-26. bibliog.

The author reviews legal changes during the four years following Modibo Keita's being ousted from the presidency of the Republic of Mali on 19 November 1968. Topics covered include the rise of political parties, the return to capitalism, labour unions, state companies, taxation, customary law and the Supreme Court.

445 **The legal system of Mali.**
Karyl T. Spriggs. In: *Modern legal systems cyclopedia.* Edited by Kenneth Robert Redden. Buffalo, New York: William S. Hein, 1989, vol. 6, p. 6.320.1-17.

This marvellous synopsis, periodically updated, covers the background, the system of government, the judiciary, legal education and the legal profession. The bibliography lists 17 books and 18 articles.

446 **Mali.**
Amos J. Peaslee. In: *Constitutions of nations. Vol. 1: Africa.*
The Hague: Martinus Nijhoff, 1965, p. 532-45. 3rd ed.

Contains the text of the Constitution of 22 September 1960 of the Republic of Mali, modified on 29 January 1961. This version replaces the Federal Constitutions of 21 January 1959, which was ratified by Soudan and Senegal (the Mali Federation) on 18 June 1960. It also replaces the Soudanese Constitution of 23 January 1959 (at which time Mali was known as the Sudanese Republic). A summary which introduces the document is divided into the following sections: 'International status'; 'Form of national government'; 'Source of sovereign power'; 'Rights of the people'; 'Legislative department'; 'Executive department'; 'Judicial department'; and 'Area, population, etc.'.

447 **Mali's socialism and the Soviet legal model.**
John N. Hazard. *Yale Law Journal*, vol. 77, no. 1 (Nov. 1967),
p. 28-69. bibliog.
The author explores the impact and adaptations of orthodox Marxism in Mali under
Modibo Keita. Topics covered include leadership; party–state relations; economic
planning and financial credit; industry and commerce; civil, commercial and
customary law; labour and the civil service; criminal law; the judicial system; French
influence; and the 'road ahead'.

448 **Les textes fondamentaux de la IIIe République du Mali.**
(The fundamental texts of the Third Republic in Mali.)
Compiled by Sékou Mamadou Chérif Diaby. Bko [i.e. Bamako]:
Librairie Bah, 1992[?]. 126p.
Includes the text of Mali's constitution of 25 February 1992, the electoral code and the
charter of the parties, both passed into law on 10 October 1991. A useful glossary and
analytical table of contents (p. 86-113) allows the reader to locate topics within the
text of the constitution.

**Recommendations for a new Malian forest code: observations from the
Land Tenure Center's study of land and tree tenure in Mali's Fifth
Region.**
See item no. 574.

**Proverbes et contes bambara, accompagnés d'une traduction française et
précédés d'un abrégé de droit coutumier bambara et malinké.** (Bambara
proverbs and tales, . . . preceded by a summary of Bambara and Malinke
customary law.)
See item no. 770.

International Relations

General and regional

449 **Affaire du différend frontalier (Burkina Faso/République du Mali): ordonnance du 9 avril 1987, designation d'experts. Cour Internationale de Justice = Case concerning the frontier dispute (Burkina Faso/Republic of Mali): order of 9 April 1987, nomination of experts. International Court of Justice.**
International Court of Justice. The Hague: International Court of Justice, 1987. 1 vol. (various pagings).
Text of an order handed down at the International Court of Justice in 1987 nominating three experts (of French, Algerian and Dutch nationality) to assist the Malian and Burkinabe governments in the demarcation of a disputed border.

450 **African boundaries: a legal and diplomatic encyclopaedia.**
Ian Brownlie. London: C. Hurst; Berkeley: University of California Press for the Royal Institute of International Affairs, 1979. 1,355p. maps. bibliog.
This valuable reference work focuses on the legal status of African boundaries. Each of the five parts concerns boundaries within a specific region; each boundary has its own section in which it is discussed in terms of its general provenance, alignment, the evidence for its existence, demarcation (rivers, etc.), and current issues. Brief bibliographies are also found in each section. An introduction discussing various aspects of boundaries, a list of maps, and a table of cited documents (dated from 18 March 1845 to 13 January 1975) constitute the prefatory material. Mali is paired with her neighbours (Algeria, Guinea, Ivory Coast (Côte d'Ivoire), Mauritania, Niger, Senegal, Burkina Faso) in parts one and two for treatment of her boundaries with each.

144

451 **Burkina–Mali war: is Nigeria still a regional power?**
Segun Johnson. *India Quarterly*, vol. 42, no. 3 (July-Sept. 1986),
p. 294-306.

Providing comprehensive coverage of the conflict, this article describes and appraises
Nigeria's participation in mediating a settlement to the 1985 war between Mali and
Burkina Faso, and analyses why this large, rich, and influential West African state was
expected to play a major and successful leadership role in bringing the crisis to a
logical conclusion.

452 **Conflict management in the West African sub-region: the case of
the war between Burkina Faso and Mali (1985).**
R. O. Ladipo. *Nigerian Journal of Political Science*, vol. 5, no. 1-2,
(1987), p. 58-72.

The author analyses the events which led to a border dispute and then war between
Mali and Burkina Faso in 1985. Nigeria and Côte d'Ivoire led the inititative to
mediate the confrontation, but only diplomatic efforts by the latter country succeeded
in helping to bring the war to a close. Ladipo examines the conditions which
hampered Nigeria's role in the mediation process and the factors which proved to be
decisive in securing a diplomatic resolution to the conflict.

453 **The foreign policy of Mali.**
Modibo Keita. *International Affairs*, vol. 37, no. 4 (Oct. 1961),
p. 432-39.

The text of a speech given in French at Chatham House on 7 June 1961 by President Keita,
in which he defines Mali's position regarding the confrontation between the Eastern and
Western power blocs. Keita also speaks, in some detail, of his attitudes towards African
unity. A short summary of the discussion following the speech is included.

454 **The Ghana–Guinea–Mali Union: a bibliographic essay.**
Mark W. DeLancey. *African Studies Bulletin*, vol. 9, no. 2 (Sept.
1966), p. 35-51.

From 1960 to 1963, Mali, Ghana and Guinea were part of an organization known as
the Union of African States (UAS). Because the Union functioned quietly and for such
a short period of time and was relatively unimportant in the development of Pan-
Africanism, very little has been written about it. DeLancey has successfully managed,
however, to compile for this essay a number of works that are useful in securing
information about the UAS as well as Malian politics.

455 **The Organisation of Senegal River States.**
Ronald Bornstein. *Journal of Modern African Studies*, vol. 10, no. 2
(1972), p. 267-83.

Bornstein examines the history, nature and experience of the sub-regional grouping
established in 1968, which included the nations of Mali, Guinea, Mauritania and Senegal.
Its main goal was to coordinate the development of the Senegal River Basin, but political
and economic differences combined to stifle any successes it may have achieved. Guinea
withdrew its membership in 1972 and the three remaining states formed the Organisation
pour la Mise en Valeur du Fleuve Sénégal (OMVS) that same year.

456 **Pan-Africanism: evolution, progress and prospects.**
Adekunle Ajala. London: A. Deutsch, 1973. 442p. bibliog.
This study presents the breakup of the Mali Federation (p. 181-90) as an example of one of Pan-Africanism's failures, and discusses the Ghana–Guinea–Mali Union and the regional economic grouping known as the Organisation des États Riverains du Sénégal (Organization of Senegal River States), of which Mali was a member. Other information about Pan-Africanism and Mali scattered throughout the book can be located through the index.

Mali Federation

457 **From French West Africa to the Mali Federation.**
William J. Foltz. New Haven, Connecticut: Yale University Press, 1965. 235p. maps. bibliog. (Yale Studies in Political Science, no. 12).
Deriving most of his information from African political party programmes, records, speeches, newspapers and government publications, plus interviews and conversations with both African and foreign political participants and observers, Foltz seeks to answer two specific questions: Why was the Mali Federation formed and why did it fail? The work focuses particularly on 'the contributions of the colonial period to institutions and patterns of behavior that affected the area's capabilities for federation, and its effect on the way Africans think and act about the whole issue of federation'. The bibliography (p. 215-28) is excellent. In theory, this study is dated but remains the standard work on the topic.

458 **Political integration in Africa: the Mali Federation.**
Donn M. Kurtz. *Journal of Modern African Studies*, vol. 8, no. 3 (1970), p. 405-24.
Kurtz examines one of the first attempts at economic and political integration in Africa, the Mali Federation. He writes about its background, why it was thought possible, conditions at the time of union, and the reasons for its failure. Kurtz states that both leaders who formed the Federation, Keita of Mali and Léopold Sédar Senghor of Senegal, were committed to its success but concludes that neither wished to risk erosion of his power base at home while promoting it. Comments on the breakup of the Mali Federation can be found in the introduction of Senghor's *On African socialism* (New York: Praeger, 1964).

ECOWAS (Economic Community of West African States)

459 ECOWAS and the economic integration of West Africa.
Uka Ezenwe. New York: St. Martin's Press, 1983. 210p. bibliog.
A general work discussing the history, development and experience of economic cooperation and integration schemes in West Africa, with an emphasis on ECOWAS (Economic Community of West African States). The performance of ECOWAS and other regional organizations is evaluated, and prospects for the future are assessed. The author views economic integration as a crucial part of the development and industrialization process, but this will require nations to relinquish elements of their political sovereignty.

460 Liberalising trade.
Paxton Idowu. *West Africa*, no. 3851 (1-7 July 1991), p. 1075.
This concise article identifies several issues of concern to and the main goals of ECOWAS, such as: the threat of an integrated European market, the danger of economic collapse resulting from Africa's marginalization by the international community, shrinking export earnings coupled with huge debts, efforts at trade liberalization within ECOWAS, preparation of an industrial master-plan, and the question of monetary union. The author concludes that growth is occurring, in spite of problems, but full potential is much greater than what has been achieved in the sub-region.

461 Toward regional development: a transactional analysis of regional integration in the Economic Community of West African States (ECOWAS).
Kalu Ndukwe Kalu. PhD thesis, Texas Technical University, 1994. 203p. bibliog. (Available from University Microfilms International, Ann Arbor, Michigan, order no. 9517228).
One of the main objectives of ECOWAS is to encourage and increase intra-regional trade and reduce external trade dependency, but this has not been realized and truly effective regional integration has been held in check. This study offers possible explanations as to why specific factors have affected the level of intra-regional trade and limited the success of ECOWAS as a regional integration scheme. See also Charles Kwarteng's dissertation, 'Challenges of regional economic cooperation among the ECOWAS states of West Africa' (Available from University Microfilms International, Ann Arbor, Michigan, 1989. 345p. order number 8924306).

Relations with developed countries

462 **Continuity and change in Franco-African relations.**
Guy Martin. *Journal of Modern African Studies*, vol. 33, no. 1 (1995), p. 1-20.
A general survey of the state of France's relations with its former colonies. Signs of change have begun to appear since 1990 in particular, but, in the end, economic ties between the two continue to be of great importance, and there is evidence that France selectively supports those democratic movements which serve its economic and political interests.

463 **French African policy: towards change.**
Tony Chafer. *African Affairs*, vol. 91, no. 362 (1992), p. 37-51.
A survey of French policy toward Sub-Saharan Africa in the early 1990s. The author discusses the premises on which this policy is based and why, despite internal and external pressures for change, major obstacles limit the opportunities for adapting it to a new international situation.

464 **Material on Soviet relations with West Africa: problems involved and a specimen bibliography, with special reference to Mali.**
Gordon Harris. *Library Materials on Africa*, vol. 10, no. 1 (1972), p. 26-64.
This paper, written as an exercise for a librarianship degree, systematically assesses bibliographical control of this subject and provides 96 briefly annotated entries (p. 39-58) from 32 English, French and Soviet periodicals for the period 1960-70. It is indexed by author and country of the article's origin. Robert Legvold examines Soviet policies primarily in Guinea, Ghana and Mali during the period 1960 to 1968 in *Soviet policy in West Africa* (q.v.).

465 **Soviet policy in West Africa.**
Robert Legvold. Cambridge, Massachusetts: Harvard University Press, 1970. 372p.
A study of the foreign policy of the former Soviet Union in Mali and five other countries of West Africa: Guinea, Ghana, Côte d'Ivoire, Nigeria and Senegal.

Military government in Mali.
See item no. 434.

Mali and the U.M.O.A.: a case-study of economic integration.
See item no. 497.

The Economy and Economic Development

466 **The A.I.D. economic policy reform program in Mali.**
Michael A. Rugh (et al.). Washington, DC: Agency for International Development, 1990. 19p.
This paper analyses the success of the Mali Economic Policy Reform Program (EPRP) from 1985 to 1989. Supported by the US Agency for International Development (AID), this programme was designed to encourage private-sector development and increase efficiency in the public sector.

467 **Adjustment programs in Africa: the recent experience.**
Justin B. Zulu, Saleh M. Nsouli. Washington, DC: International Monetary Fund, 1985. 37p.
Examines the experience of African countries from 1980 to 1983 with the design and implementation of structural adjustment programmes supported by resources of the International Monetary Fund (IMF). A case-study of Mali is included which illustrates how adopting adjustment measures helped significantly improve the country's overall economic and financial picture.

468 **Africa Review.**
Saffron Walden, England: Africa Guide Co., 1976- . annual.
This annual publication briefly reviews the current state of politics and the economy for each African country. Also included are key facts, key indicators, a country profile, and a summary of information valuable to the business traveller under the headings 'Business guide' and 'Business directory'. Mali is found on pages 126-29. It was published as *Africa Guide* from 1977 to 1984.

469 **Changing places?: women, resource management and migration in the Sahel: case studies from Senegal, Burkina Faso, Mali and Sudan.**
Rosalind David. London: SOS Sahel International, 1995. 169p. bibliog.

Based on research carried out from July to October 1993, a section of this volume examines the livelihoods of Dogon farmers and traders in two villages of southeastern Mali, and the strategies they use to manage their resources in response to the effects of migration.

470 **Colonial rural development: French policy and African response at the Office du Niger, Soudan français (Mali), 1920-1960.**
Monica M. van Beusekom. PhD thesis, Johns Hopkins University, 1989. (Available from University Microfilms International, Ann Arbor, Michigan, order no. 9018637). 247p. bibliog.

This dissertation examines the history of one of the first large-scale development projects in Sub-Saharan Africa, the Office du Niger. A rice and cotton irrigation project in the Niger River Valley in French Sudan, the Office du Niger implemented only a fraction of the original development plan. Its failures were rooted in the project managers' refusal to recognize the needs, priorities and expertise of Africans who settled at the project.

471 **Country Profile: Côte d'Ivoire, Mali.**
London: Economist Intelligence Unit, 1986- . annual.

This specialized publication is an annual supplement to the Economist Intelligence Unit's *Country Report: Côte d'Ivoire, Mali* (q.v.). It is an excellent source of current background information pertinent to business and economic research. Text and statistical information are provided on the following topics: politics; population and society; currency; the economy; national accounts; employment; wages and prices; agriculture, livestock and fishing; mining; energy; manufacturing; construction; tourism; transport and communications; finance; foreign trade; external payments and debt; exchange, trade and investment regulations.

472 **Country Report: Côte d'Ivoire, Mali.**
London: Economist Intelligence Unit, 1993- . quarterly.

Carefully monitors, analyses and forecasts economic and political trends, in a coherent and readable style. Charts, graphs, and statistics that provide varied information about the economy supplement the text. This work is useful in providing introductory material on Mali or for those who wish to keep informed of developments in major sectors. Before 1993, Mali is covered by previous titles of this serial publication: *Quarterly Economic Review of Guinea, Mali, Mauritania*, 1985-1986, no. 1; *Country Report. Guinea, Mali, Mauritania*, 1986, no. 2-1992, no. 4.

473 **An economic history of West Africa.**
A. G. Hopkins. New York: Columbia University, 1973. 337p. maps.
bibliog. (Columbia Economic History of the Modern World Series).

A highly regarded, comprehensive account of the region incorporating anthropological, economic and geographical perspectives in an effort 'to direct attention away from the adventures and triumphs of great leaders, past and present, and towards the activities of the overwhelming majority of Africans' (p. 296). Professor Hopkins describes traditional domestic economies and their encounters with external and colonial trade up to 1960, keeping to the study's central theme of 'the interaction of the various internal and external factors which have determined the structure and performance of the market economy' (p. 293). The bibliography (p. 297-326) is excellent.

474 **Evaluation of Netherlands aid to India, Mali and Tanzania.**
Translated from the Dutch by Sandra Johnson. The Hague: Ministry of Foreign Affairs, Directorate General International Cooperation, Operations Review Unit, 1995. 218p. bibliog. (Summary Evaluation Report, 1995).

This volume contains the summary results of three reports which evaluate the effectiveness, efficiency and relevance of Dutch bilateral aid to Mali, Tanzania and India from 1980 to 1992. A comparison of findings which the three reports had in common is included. The separate report on Mali (p. 106-43) states that most aid projects implemented were reasonably successful, but predicts results will probably be unsustainable once aid ceases, because of the government's lack of resources and limited management capacity.

475 **Foreign Economic Trends and Their Implications for the United States.**
Washington, DC: US Department of Commerce, Industry and Trade Administration, 1969- . annual.

Issues of this document are devoted to individual countries, and one about Mali is available. It summarizes the current state of and dominant trends in the Malian economy, and analyses economic relations with the United States.

476 **The informal sector and microfinance institutions in West Africa.**
Edited by Leila Webster, Peter Fidler. Washington, DC: World Bank, 1996. 365p. maps. bibliog. (World Bank Regional and Sectoral Studies).

This volume is a study of the informal sector of twelve West African countries, initiated by the World Bank to secure information that would enable it to offer greater assistance to low-income populations of this region. Following four overview chapters is a profile of the informal sectors of these countries; Mali is found on pages 153-66. The work also contains information about the effective delivery of credit and savings services to the poor, and evaluations of nine microfinance institutions in the region considered to be the most effective and possible partners for the World Bank, including two from Mali, Kafo Jiginew and Caisses Villageoises d'Epargne et de Crédit Autogerées du Pays Dogon. Implications for the World Bank are outlined based on the findings of the research presented here.

477 **International Conference of Donors for the Economic Recovery and Development of the Republic of Mali.**
Bamako: Ministry of Planning, National Directorate of Planning, 1982. 2 vols. maps.

Embodied in this document is a request for economic aid that was submitted by the Malian government to the international community following the United Nations Conference on the Least Developed Countries, held in 1981. The first volume is a summary report which discusses such topics as Mali's potential, principal obstacles to development, development objectives and strategies, including the 1981-85 Five-Year Development Plan, aid needed for development, and anticipated results. The second volume describes seventy-nine economic development projects that were selected according to defined priorities and submitted as part of the request for aid.

478 **Listening to one's clients: a case study of Mali's famine early warning system – the Système d'Alerte Précoce (SAP) – and rural producers.**
Jindra Monique Cekan. PhD thesis, Tufts University, Medford, Massachusetts, 1994. 394p. bibliog. (Available from University Microfilms International, Ann Arbor, Michigan, order no. 9427331).

Cekan examines the Système d'Alerte Précoce (SAP), a famine early-warning system in Mali, and analyses whether or not it successfully predicts the onset of famine. She also assesses to what degree its recommendations sustainably prevent the escalation of the famine process.

479 **Mali.**
Prepared by the Regional and Country Studies Branch. Vienna: United Nations Industrial Development Organization, 1986. 71p. bibliog. (Industrial Development Review Series).

Provides an overview and brief analysis of Mali's industrial sector. A graphical presentation of manufacturing trends and statistical and other appendices are included.

480 **Mali, bilan d'une gestion désastreuse.** (Mali, record of a disastrous administration.)
Cheick Oumar Diarrah. Paris: L'Harmattan, 1990. 203p.

Published a year before the collapse of General Moussa Traoré's government, this is an analysis of the political and economic evolution that occurred in Mali following his rise to power in 1968. The first part discusses the reasons for the coup which ended Keita's rule, as well as political changes and aspects of external politics under the Deuxième République (Second Republic). The second part outlines Mali's economic and financial crises which developed under the the Traoré administration. A concluding chapter discusses changes that need to occur in order to provide Mali with a viable economic future.

481 **Mali, recent economic developments.**
A. Tahari (et al.). Washington, DC: International Monetary Fund, 1994. 88p. bibliog. (IMF Staff Country Report, no. 94/11).

Prepared by a team of staff of the International Monetary Fund, this report contains chapters on income and production; prices, wages, and employment; development planning; government finance; the public enterprise sector; money and banking; the external sector; the exchange and trade system; and environmental issues. Tables and charts complement the text and an appendix entitled 'Summary of tax system as of June 30, 1994' is included.

482 **Mali, women in private enterprise: final report.**
Sydney A. Lewis, Karen Russell. Washington, DC: Ernst & Young, 1989. 169 leaves. bibliog.

Women entrepreneurs in Mali's private sector are usually less visible than men, and are therefore often ignored by agencies which offer assistance through development programmes. The authors have gathered valuable data on women-owned enterprises in Bamako for the US Agency for International Development, so that it may consider gender issues and integrate them into its projects and programmes. The work includes interesting profiles of thirty-four women entrepreneurs who were interviewed as part of the study. This report for the Bureau for Private Enterprise, US Agency for International Development, USAID/Mali and PPC/WID, is based on interviews with thirty-four female entrepreneurs in business sectors of Bamako. Chapters cover: 'The context: Bamako'; 'The policy environment for women entrepreneurs'; 'Women entrepreneurs in the formal sector'; 'Women entrepreneurs in the informal sector'; and 'Recommendations for USAID/Mali'. Annexes include 'Profiles of women entrepreneurs in Bamako' (leaves 49-138), a 'List of individuals interviewed' (l. 139-44), bibliography (l. 145-47), scope of work (l. 148-50) and 'A.I.D. program for women in development: a user's guide to the Office of Women in Development (FY 90)' (l. 151-69).

483 **Men, women, and market trade in rural Mali, West Africa.**
Jane Sawyer Turrittin. East Lansing, Michigan: Michigan State University, 1986. 17p. bibliog.

Based on data collected during fieldwork in a Bambara village in 1982-83, this paper examines differential participation by men and women in market and intra-village trade. The author explains how women's access to the market is restricted and their bargaining power reduced, leaving them at a disadvantage despite a situation of market expansion.

484 **Planning and economic policy: socialist Mali and her neighbors.**
William I. Jones. Washington, DC: Three Continents Press, 1976. 422p. bibliog.

Focusing on Mali's Five-Year Economic and Social Development Plan of 1961-66, the author first examines the country's economic and political conditions and describes and analyses the plan. Jones then compares Mali's plan with those of other West African governments.

485 **The political use of economic planning in Mali.**
Aristide R. Zolberg. In: *Economic nationalism in old and new states.*
Edited by Harry G. Johnson. Chicago, Illinois: University of Chicago
Press, 1967, p. 98-123.

A case-study which illustrates how the economic policy formulated by Malian leaders
in the late 1950s shifted from an approach that was sensible, rational and international
in outlook, to one that was unrealistic and designed to define and strengthen the image
and identity of the nation-state.

486 **The politics of integrating gender to state development processes:**
trends, opportunities and constraints in Bangladesh, Chile,
Jamaica, Mali, Morocco, and Uganda.
Anne Marie Goetz. Geneva: United Nations Research Institute for
Social Development, 1995. 62p. bibliog. (Occasional Paper, no. 2).

Drawing on in-country interviews, national and sectoral policy statements, documents
from multilateral and bilateral agencies, and secondary literature, this paper assesses
efforts to incorporate the needs of women into state development processes in Mali,
Bangladesh, Chile, Jamaica, Morocco and Uganda.

487 **Rapport sur le plan quinquennal de développement économique et**
social de la République de Mali, 1961-1965. (Report on the Five-
Year Plan of Economic and Social Development of the Republic of
Mali, 1961-65.)
Mali. Ministère du Plan et de l'Economie Rurale. Paris[?]: [n.p.],
1961. 42p. map.

Presents the text of Mali's ambitious first Five-Year Plan, in which an annual growth
rate of 8 per cent is projected and parastatals are established. In reality, the country's
socialist economy exhibited a 2 per cent annual growth rate for most of the decade and
most parastatals operated with significant losses. Coupled with government spending
that reached 12 per cent, the negative impact on the economy was significant. In the
1987-91 plan, however, *Plan quinquennal de développement économique et social,
1987-1991* (Bamako: République du Mali, Ministère du Plan, Direction Nationale de
la Planification, 1988. 2 vols), growth of the GDP is targeted at 3.4 per cent, a figure
which was narrowly missed.

488 **Socialism, economic development and planning in Mali, 1960-1968.**
Guy Martin. *Canadian Journal of African Studies*, vol. 10, no. 1
(1976), p. 23-46.

Following a review of Mali's political history and social structure and a discussion of
socialist planning in the Malian context, Martin examines the economic and sociopolitical causes of the failure of socialist policies implemented as part of the Malian
Five-Year Plan (1961-66).

489 **A study of the business climate in Mali.**
Petr Hanel, William Grant. Springfield, Virginia: NTIS, 1988. 190p.

This study, conducted between 10 July and 10 August 1988 for USAID and based on interviews with eighteen private-sector firms and officials from two dozen organizations, 'analyses the climate for business investment and looks at the most promising sectors (textiles, skins and hides, dairy, agricultural machinery and farm implements) to identify their constraints' (Preface, p. i). The authors estimate that urban unemployment will rise from 25.7 per cent in 1988 to 34.3 per cent in 1995; they include twenty-three tables of data on the economy and employment, a bibliography and eleven annexes. Among the annexes are: import/export statistics; industrial enterprises in Mali in 1987; and the Malian tax system. The authors make several recommendations for investment.

490 **Women and development in Mali: an annotated bibliography.**
Susan Caughman. Addis Ababa: United Nations, Economic
Commission for Africa, 1982. 34p. (Bibliography Series, no. 6).

This very useful annotated compilation of selected recent works is organized into sections on: 'Bibliographies' (10 works, not annotated); 'Women and development in other Sahelian zones' (7); 'Ethnographic sources on Malian cultures' (15, not annotated); 'Rural development and women' (47); 'Population studies' (19); 'Education and training' (7); 'Urban development and women' (3)'; 'Women's situation' (12); and 'Women's organizations' (1).

491 **Women and sustained development in the Sahel: an analysis of national and aid agencies' policies in Burkina Faso and in Mali.**
Marthe Doka Diarra, Marie Monimart. Paris: OECD: Club du Sahel;
[Ouagadougou]: CILSS, 1989. 43p. bibliog.

Prepared for an anti-desertification programme known as the Segou (Mali) Regional Encounter on Sahelian Village Land Management, this study examines the situation in Mali and Burkina Faso regarding the integration of women and women's issues into rural development. It includes an analysis of both countries' national policies and how they regard and affect women, and an evaluation of major aid agency policies and their record of including Malian and Burkinabè women in development programmes. A concluding chapter defines issues and questions aimed at helping the Regional Encounter improve women's participation in the fight against desertification.

492 **Women at work in Mali : the case of the Markala Cooperative.**
Susan Caughman. Boston, Massachusetts: African Studies Center,
1981. 35 leaves. bibliog.

The author profiles and evaluates the Markala Cooperative, founded in 1975 by a group of twenty poor women in rural Mali. Their goals were to earn a regular income and acquire marketable skills. Since its inception, its principal revenue base has been cloth dyeing, but a number of secondary activities have been attempted also, including soapmaking (see item no. 493). This cooperative differs from most development projects in that it was designed and implemented by its beneficiaries, and not a donor or government agency. See also the author's *New skills for rural women* (Philadelphia, Pennsylvania: American Friends Service Committee, 1977. 19p.).

493 **Women finding suitable assistance: soapmaking in Mali.**
Susan Caughman, Mariam N'diaye Thiam. In: *Experiences in
appropriate technology*. Ottawa: Canadian Hunger Foundation, 1980,
p. 65-71.

The authors describe the soapworks formed by the Markala Cooperative. These had
greater success than the cloth-dyeing activities which became the cooperative's
principal revenue base in its first year.

The economic foundations of an Islamic theocracy: the case of Masina.
See item no. 186.

**Warriors, merchants, and slaves: the state and the economy in the
Middle Niger Valley, 1700-1914.**
See item no. 218.

Material world: a global family portrait.
See item no. 382.

Women in the material world.
See item no. 388.

**Maternal income-generation activities and child nutrition: the Bambara
of Mali.**
See item no. 402.

Political revival in Mali.
See item no. 418.

Economics of the coup.
See item no. 424.

Mali: the prospects of 'Planned Socialism'.
See item no. 427.

Marxian socialism in Africa: the case of Mali.
See item no. 428.

The Organisation of Senegal River States.
See item no. 455.

Pan-Africanism: evolution, progress and prospects.
See item no. 456.

ECOWAS and the economic integration of West Africa.
See item no. 459.

Liberalising trade.
See item no. 460.

**Toward regional development: a transactional analysis of regional
integration in the Economic Community of West African States
(ECOWAS).**
See item no. 461.

Continuity and change in patterns of trade in southern Mali.
See item no. 502.

Adaptable livelihoods: coping with food insecurity in the Malian Sahel.
See item no. 512.

Cattle, women, and wells: managing household survival in the Sahel.
See item no. 517.

The impact of direct taxation and government price policies on agricultural production in a developing African country: an empirical study of Mali.
See item no. 525.

The role of the state in food production and rural development: lessons from Opération Riz-Ségou in Mali.
See item no. 534.

Survival in the Sahel: an ecological and developmental challenge.
See item no. 539.

Land-locked countries of Africa.
See item no. 541.

Emploi, potentialités et priorités au Mali: rapport présenté au Gouvernement du Mali. (Employment, potentials and priorities in Mali: report presented to the Government of Mali.)
See item no. 548.

Politiques d'emploi, politiques commerciales et financières: étude de cas comparés de Madagascar et du Mali. (Politics of employment, commercial politics and finances: comparative case-study of Madagascar and Mali.)
See item no. 551.

The Sahara, ecological change and early economic history.
See item no. 576.

Mali: éducation et développement au Mali, bibliographie selective des documents disponibles au Centre de documentation de l'IIPE. (Mali: education and development in Mali, selective bibliography of documents held at the IIPE Documentation Centre.)
See item no. 600.

African Statistical Yearbook, 1992/93. Volume 1, Part 2, West Africa.
See item no. 835.

Finance and Banking

494 Access to credit for poor women: a scale-up study of projects carried out by Freedom from Hunger in Mali and Ghana.
Jeffrey Ashe (et al.). Bethesda, Maryland: Growth and Equity through Microenterprise Investments and Institutions, 1992. 1 vol. (various pagings). bibliog. (GEMINI Technical Report, no. 33).

An evaluation by a team from Growth and Equity through Microenterprise Investments and Institutions (GEMINI) of a pilot project implemented in Mali and Ghana by Freedom from Hunger. This project, in which credit is extended to the rural poor in combination with hunger-prevention education, was implemented in Mali's Sikasso region because of its economic potential, proximity to urban markets, and prevailing health and nutrition problems. Comparisons are made between the success of the project in the two countries.

495 The AED African Financial Directory.
London: Africa Economic Digest, 1987- . irregular[?]

In the country section, 'Mali' (p. 121-24) includes general information, central bank authority data and a list of banks and financial institutions. Introductory materials describe 'International financial institutions in Africa', Banking systems in Africa', 'The franc zone', and the 'African Development Bank'. The first issue, the 1987 edition, is apparently the only one that has been published to date.

496 African economic and financial data.
World Bank, Trade and Finance Division, Africa Technical Department. New York: United Nations Development Programme; Washington, DC: World Bank, 1989.

This single volume is an excellent source for economic and financial data of all types for 1980-87, relating to fifty countries. The tables of data are grouped in seven chapters: 'National economic indicators'; 'External sector'; 'Debt and related flows'; 'Government finance'; 'Agriculture'; 'Public enterprise'; and 'Aid flows'. The document was prepared by a large team led by Charles Humphreys, with Dan Swanson as supervisor of publication. There is a main introduction and each section has its own brief introduction; technical notes (p. 199-201) and references (p. 203-4) are appended. Two other annual World Bank publications provide excellent sources of economic, demographic and social statistical data: *The World Bank Atlas* and *World Development Report*.

497 **Mali and the U.M.O.A.: a case-study of economic integration.**
David Leith Crum. *Journal of Modern African Studies*, vol. 22, no. 3 (Sept. 1984), p. 469-86.
In 1962, Mali issued her own national currency and left the Union Monétaire Ouest-Africaine (West African Monetary Union), but the development of serious economic problems forced it to seek re-entry within five years. This study of the readmission process illustrates how political factors, such as the Oudalan ownership dispute with Burkina Faso (then Upper Volta), and some of the difficulties inherent in African economic integration kept Mali out of the Union until 1984.

498 **The Malian experience in financing the cereals trade.**
Jonathan Coulter. *African Review of Money, Finance and Banking*, no. 1 (1993), p. 27-45. bibliog.
Describes Mali's implementation of donor-supported credit schemes as a method of providing increased bank credit to the private cereals trade.

499 **Women's economic activities and credit opportunities in the Opération Haute Vallée (OHV) zone, Mali.**
Andrea Luery. [n.p.]: [n.p.], 1989. 51 leaves. bibliog.
Although women constitute a large percentage of the agricultural labour force in Mali, their access to institutionalized credit is limited, and they have developed their own support network in response. This report is the first of a two-part study of rural women's economic resources and credit opportunities in the Opération Haute Vallée region of Mali.

The informal sector and microfinance institutions in West Africa.
See item no. 476.

Trade and Commerce

500 **Commerce and community: paths to success for Malian merchants..**
Richard L. Warms. *African Studies Review*, vol. 37, no. 2 (Sept. 1994), p. 97-120.
In Malian society, it is believed that the key to success and escape from poverty is a prosperous career as a trader. In this article, Warms examines the commercial community in the southern Malian town of Sikasso, what individuals are most likely to succeed as merchants, and the reasons why.

501 **Comparative advantage, trade flows and prospects for regional agricultural market integration in West Africa: the case of Côte d'Ivoire and Mali.**
Abdoul Wahab Barry. PhD thesis, Michigan State University, 1994. 298p. bibliog. (Available from University Microfilms International, Ann Arbor, Michigan, order no. 9431212).
The author of this thesis has chosen Mali and Côte d'Ivoire to explore issues associated with intra-regional trade. Although they differ in terms of geographical location and level of economic development, agriculture is the most important sector in both countries. This study evaluates each country's comparative advantage in producing and marketing cotton, maize, millet/sorghum and rice, as well as actual trade flows of these commodities.

502 **Continuity and change in patterns of trade in southern Mali.**
Richard Lee Warms. PhD thesis, Syracuse University, New York State, 1987. 511p. bibliog. (Available from University Microfilms International, Ann Arbor, Michigan, order no. 8806708).
A study of the present-day trading community in the city of Sikasso, and its history. The author analyses how this community has been affected by changes over time, its

present social component, and how it compares economically to African traders discussed in other studies. This work 'illustrates the importance of the community and private trade to the future development of Mali, and the impact of government policy on trading communities and national development'.

503　The emergence of a grain market in Bamako, 1883-1908.
Richard Roberts. *Canadian Journal of African Studies*, vol. 14, no. 1 (1980), p. 55-81. maps.

This article examines 'the nature and operation of the Bamako grain market between 1883 and 1908 . . . [and explores] how, in the absence of agricultural innovations, so much grain entered the market and what, if any, changes in the structure and organization of production occurred as a result of increased grain trade' (p. 37). Additional topics include pricing and profits, the impact of the railway, the quantity of rice and millet produced, and the impacts of slave emancipation and the army.

504　The golden trade of the Moors: West African kingdoms in the fourteenth century.
Edward William Bovill. Princeton, New Jersey: M. Weiner Publishers, 1995. 299p. maps. bibliog.

Robin Hallett revised this classic, originally published in 1958, and added material following the author's death in 1966. Bovill aims 'to show how the trans-Saharan trade routes had woven ties of blood and culture between the peoples north and south of the desert, and to win a measure of recognition for the part which Western Sudanese have played in the history of civilization' (Preface, p. v). Notable for the history of Mali are chapters on 'Mansa Musa of Mali', 'Ibn Battuta: a fourteenth-century traveller in the Sudan', 'The Songhai', 'Leo Africanus: an early sixteenth-century traveller in the Sudan', and 'The fall of Songhai'. References are extensive (p. 252-68); the select bibliography (p. 269-71) is too brief. This famous work is based on Bovill's classic account of the development of the trans-Saharan trade, *Caravans of the old Sahara: an introduction to the history of the Western Sudan* (London: Oxford University Press, 1933).

505　The impact of the Western Sudanic empires on the trans-Saharan trade: tenth to sixteenth century.
Samir M. Zoghby. PhD thesis, Georgetown University, Washington, DC, 1966. 358 leaves. bibliog. (Available from University Microfilms International, Ann Arbor, Michigan, order no. 6612832).

This dissertation examines the influence of the major empires of Ghana, Mali and Songhay on the dynamic trans-Saharan trade of the precolonial period.

506　Liberalisation of agricultural markets: an institutional approach.
Anne M. Thomson, Lawrence D. Smith. Glasgow, Scotland: Centre for Development Studies, University of Glasgow, 1991. 35p. bibliog. (CDS Occasional Paper, no. 8).

Following a discussion of the movement to liberalize agricultural markets in developing countries within an institutional context, this paper analyses the success of the Cereals Market Restructuring Project in Mali, the main goals of which were to increase consumer and producer prices and bring them into parity with parallel market prices, to liberalize the grain trade by abolishing the monopoly enjoyed by the Office Malien des Produits Agricoles [i.e., Office des Produits Agricoles du Mali (OPAM)] and increasing the private sector's role, and to increase OPAM's efficiency and reduce its operating costs.

507 **Long distance trade and production: Sinsani in the nineteenth century.**
Richard Roberts. *Journal of African History*, vol. 21, no. 2 (1980), p. 169-88. map. bibliog.

This history examines trade up and down the Niger and Bani rivers of the Middle Niger valley from the town of Sinsani (Sansanding in French sources) and describes influences of the desert-side trade, the link between Maraka (Marka) trade and local plantation production and the roles of canoes and caravans in the trade.

508 **Revue des Douanes du Mali: Bulletin Trimestriel des Douanes Maliennes.** (Review of Malian Customs: Quarterly Bulletin of Malian Customs.)
Bamako: Douanes Maliennes, 1984- . quarterly.

This publication covers customs administration, laws and legislation pertaining to customs, tariffs and customs statistics. The first issue (no. 1, 24p.) contains an introduction by M. Drissa Keita, Minister of Finance, and discusses several customs declarations.

509 **Sub-Saharan agriculture: synthesis and trade prospects.**
Shamsher Singh. Washington, DC: World Bank, 1983. 157p.

Agricultural commodities account for high percentages of export earnings in many Sub-Saharan African countries, including Mali, making agricultural production the most important cause of economic growth in this area of the world. This paper is divided into three parts: Part one summarizes the state of agriculture in Sub-Saharan Africa in the early 1980s and discusses the constraints hindering its development at that time; Part two is a summary of the price, trade, and consumption outlook for major Sub-Saharan agricultural commodities; and Part three presents brief projections for individual commodities into the mid-1990s. While this work is somewhat dated, it is useful for information on the history of Sub-Saharan agricultural trade from mid-century to the time of publication.

510 **Trade and politics on the Senegal and Upper Niger, 1854-1900: African reaction to French penetration.**
Barbara Marie Perinbam. PhD thesis, Georgetown University, Washington, DC, 1969. 305 leaves. maps. bibliog. (Available from University Microfilms International, Ann Arbor, Michigan, order no. 705927).

Explores the expansion of French trade and control in the Western Sudan in the nineteenth century and the resulting Franco-African and inter-African power struggles. See also Robert Griffeth's 1968 Northwestern University PhD thesis, 'Varieties of African resistance to the French conquest of the Western Sudan, 1850-1900'.

511   **Two worlds of cotton: colonialism and the regional economy in the French Soudan, 1800-1946.**
Richard L. Roberts.   Stanford, California: Stanford University Press, 1996. 381p. bibliog.

This book contains a study of French colonial cotton policy in the French Soudan, the part of Africa in which they focused their most intense efforts to develop cotton production for export to France. Roberts argues that French failure to develop and control the cotton harvest can be directly linked to the persistence of the domestic precolonial handicraft textile industry, to which, along with the West African continental market, the majority of the annual cotton supply flowed.

Salts of the western Sahara: myths, mysteries, and historical significance.
See item no. 206.

Slavery and Muslim society in Africa: the institution in Saharan and Sudanic Africa and the trans-Saharan trade.
See item no. 209.

ECOWAS and the economic integration of West Africa.
See item no. 459.

Liberalising trade.
See item no. 460.

Toward regional development: a transactional analysis of regional integration in the Economic Community of West African States (ECOWAS).
See item no. 461.

Africa Review.
See item no. 468.

Men, women, and market trade in rural Mali, West Africa.
See item no. 483.

The Malian experience in financing the cereals trade.
See item no. 498.

Economic analysis of traders' response to cereals market reforms in Mali.
See item no. 520.

Trade routes of Algeria and the Sahara.
See item no. 545.

Agriculture

512 **Adaptable livelihoods: coping with food insecurity in the Malian Sahel.**
Susanna Davies. Basingstoke, England: Macmillan Press; New York: St. Martin's Press, 1996. 335p. bibliog.

This work is based on information gathered in the Malian Sahel and Inner Niger Delta by the Suivi Alimentaire Delta Sèno (SADS), a local food-monitoring system. It examines how people in these areas feed themselves during periods of critical food shortages, and shows how this information can be used by governments, donors, and non-governmental organizations to make decisions regarding food security when drought and food aid cease but food shortages and hunger continue.

513 **Agribusiness and public sector collaboration in agricultural technology development and use in Mali: a study of the mechanization of cotton production.**
Phil Serafini, Boubacar Sada Sy. Bethesda, Maryland: Abt Associates, 1992. 69 leaves. bibliog.

This detailed case-study of the mechanization of Malian cotton production is used to test and refine a number of hypotheses relating to proposed greater public- and private-sector collaboration in developing and using agricultural technology. Following an overview of Malian cotton production, the report discusses the demand for mechanical technology; the impacts of mechanical technology and its inputs; research support for mechanical technologies; and the Malian economic, business and regulatory environment. Generalizations, conclusions, and recommendations regarding the application of mechanized technology to cotton production in Mali conclude the report.

514   **Agricultural development policy and grassroots democracy in Mali.**
R. James Bingen.   *African Rural and Urban Studies*, vol. 1, no. 1 (1994), p. 57-72.

In this essay, Bingen discusses the political significance of events that launched the Malian farmers' movement following Moussa Traoré's overthrow in 1991, and identifies how these events transformed relations between the government and certain groups of agricultural producers. Bingen also argues that strengthening the technical, managerial and negotiating skills and capacities of these producers will contribute to their continued success in exerting popular pressure to effect change in Malian agricultural and rural development policy.

515   **Agricultural research impact assessment: the case of maize technology adoption in southern Mali.**
Duncan Boughton, Bruno Henry de Frahan.   East Lansing, Michigan: Dept. of Agricultural Economics, Michigan State University, 1994. 95p. bibliog.

This study evaluates the impact of maize research in southern Mali within the context of a broader study of the maize subsector. Following an overview of this subsector is a brief history of maize research in Mali, a discussion of the diffusion of maize technology in southern Mali, and a comparison of costs incurred and benefits derived from maize technology development and diffusion. A concluding section analyses the strengths and weaknesses of maize technology development and prospects for replicating its success in the future.

516   **Bibliographie sur les systèmes de production: Burkina Faso, Mali, Niger.** (Bibliography on production systems: Burkina Faso, Mali, Niger.)
Réseau de Recherche sur la Résistance à la Sécheresse, Comité de Coordination Documentaire.   Montpellier, France: CIRAD-CA; Bamako: INSAH/RESADOC, 1993. 146p.

This bibliography of materials about the agricultural systems of Mali, Burkina Faso and Niger contains 484 citations divided among the following chapters: 'Systèmes d'exploitation agricole'; Méthodes et systèmes d'élevage'; Systèmes agropastoraux'; Recherche développement'. Author and keyword indexes are included.

517   **Cattle, women, and wells: managing household survival in the Sahel.**
Camilla Toulmin.   Oxford, England: Clarendon Press; New York: Oxford University Press, 1992. 295p. bibliog.

This study presents the results of research undertaken in Kala and other neighbouring Bambara farm villages between 1980 and 1982. It is an attempt to understand the choices faced by farm households (e.g., what crops to grow, how to adapt to changing climatic conditions, how to manage the household workforce) and the constraints that limit those choices. These constraints are examined to determine how and why some individuals and households survive and prosper more successfully than others in such a harsh environment.

518 **Changes in drought-coping strategies in the Segu Region of Mali.**
Roy Cole. PhD thesis, Michigan State University, 1991. 265p.
bibliog. (Available from University Microfilms International, Ann
Arbor, Michigan, order no. 9216291).
Cole examines, in relation to location, economic status and ethnic group, the drought-coping strategies employed by Sudano-Sahelian farmers, agropastoralists and fishermen during the droughts of 1973 and 1984.

519 **Descendants and crops: two poles of production in a Malian
peasant village.**
John Van Dusen Lewis. PhD thesis, Yale University, 1979.
487 leaves. maps. bibliog. (Available from University Microfilms
International, Ann Arbor, Michigan, order no. 8002728).
An anthropological and historical study of how the technology of farming production is manipulated by ties of kinship and descent among Bambara subsistence farmers of the central Malian savannah.

520 **Economic analysis of traders' response to cereals market reforms
in Mali.**
Niama Nango Dembélé. PhD thesis, Michigan State University,
1994. 208p. bibliog. (Available from University Microfilms
International, Ann Arbor, Michigan, order no. 9524918).
Mali's grain trade is in need of expansion following cereal market reforms which resulted in excess production and depressed producer prices. However, expansion is hindered by inadequate investment in grain storage and cereals exports. The main objective of this study is to analyse what factors determine investment in grain storage and cereals exports by traders. Dembélé also examines how the choice of structures available to manage their interdependence (referred to as 'coordination mechanisms') affects their investment behaviour.

521 **Family social structure, farm operation characteristics and the
adoption of new technologies for sustainable farming systems in
Mali.**
Mahamadou Tangara. PhD thesis, Iowa State University, 1992. 101p.
bibliog. (Available from University Microfilms International, Ann
Arbor, Michigan, order no. 9234851).
Focusing on the rural farming communities of the Opération Haute Vallée area, this study attempts to determine to what degree family social structure and farm operation characteristics affect the adoption of new farming technologies.

522 **Farming systems in the Niger Inland Delta, Mali.**
Derrick J. Thom, John C. Wells. *Geographical Review*, vol. 77, no. 3
(July 1987), p. 328-42. maps. bibliog.
The authors examine traditional farming systems of the Inland Delta, hydrology, natural flood irrigation, flood-control irrigation, recessional cultivation (rice, sorghum,

millet), the irrigation project of the Office du Niger, and pastoralism. Nine maps of the area accompany the article, one showing the Office du Niger project and its settlements.

523 **Food strategies in four African countries: a study on food policy formulation and implementation in Kenya, Mali, Rwanda and Zambia.**
Prepared for the Commission of European Communities by the Royal Tropical Institute. Amsterdam: The Institute, 1984. 71p.

This study, a review of food policy in Mali, Kenya, Rwanda and Zambia, identifies priorities for policy revision and recommends programmed action to meet food and nutrition objectives in these four countries.

524 **Household income and agricultural strategies in the peri-urban zone of Bamako, Mali.**
Yacouba Konaté. PhD thesis, State University of New York at Binghamton, 1994. 237p. maps. bibliog. (Available from University Microfilms International, Ann Arbor, Michigan, order no. 9432090).

Kalabancoro, a Bamana (Bambara) village whose farmlands have been engulfed by the expanding capital city of Bamako, is the focus of this study. The author examines its production systems, changes that are occurring due to the loss of farmland, and the range of income-earning and agricultural strategies households in this peri-urban environment are mixing to survive and/or prosper.

525 **The impact of direct taxation and government price policies on agricultural production in a developing African country: an empirical study of Mali.**
Bacari Koné. PhD thesis, State University of New York at Albany, 1983. 245p. bibliog. (Available from University Microfilms International, Ann Arbor, Michigan, order no. 8325610).

The primary goal of this study was to assess quantitatively how direct government taxation and price policies impact on agricultural production in rural areas of Mali. The period covered extends from 1969 to 1979. During this time, the major taxes levied in the agricultural sector were vestiges of colonial practice and were administered as they had been under colonialism.

526 **Informing food security policy in Mali: interactions between technology, institutions and market reforms.**
Josué Dioné. PhD thesis, Michigan State University, 1989. 402p. bibliog. (Available from University Microfilms International, Ann Arbor, Michigan, order no. 8923842).

Relying on primary data collected from 190 farm households and 118 cereal wholesalers, the author examines constraints – such as rigid head taxes, poor access to financing and market regulations – to Malian farmers' and grain traders' ability and willingness to invest in order to improve the coarse grain production and distribution system.

527 **Irrigation and the Soninke people: organizational and management problems: current situation and prospects.**
Georges Diawara. London: Irrigation Management Network (Africa edition), ODI, 1992. 25p. bibliog.

This study examines the organizational problems associated with selected irrigation schemes established in areas inhabited by the Soninke (Sarakole) people – problems that inhibit expansion of irrigation schemes in this and other areas of Mali.

528 **The Malian Union of Cotton and Food Crop Producers: its current and potential role in technology development and transfer.**
Jim Bingen, Diana Carney, Edmond Dembelé. London: Overseas Development Institute; The Hague: ISNAR, 1995. 32p. maps. bibliog.

This case-study examines the technology-related activities of the Malian Union of Cotton and Food Crop Producers, or SYCOV (Syndicat des Producteurs de Coton et Vivriers), a national farmers' organization composed mainly of those who have scarce resources and operate on a small scale. SYCOV's marked success just four years after its creation in 1991, during a new era of Malian democracy, makes it especially interesting as the object of a study such as this.

529 **National governments, local governments, pasture governance and management in Mali.**
James T. Thomson. Burlington, Vermont: Associates in Rural Development, 1993[?]. 23p. bibliog.

Focusing on the village of Yaguinébanda in northwestern Mali, this paper considers whether administrative changes inaugurated by the government of the Third Republic in 1992 can have any positive impact on pasture governance and management.

530 **On building a partnership in Mali between farmers and researchers.**
Marie-Hélène Collion. London: Overseas Development Institute, 1995. 22p. bibliog.

This paper describes the efforts of Mali's Institut d'Economie Rurale (IER) to establish a partnership with farmers' organizations. The role of non-governmental organizations is highlighted, as well as changes in Mali's political climate since 1991, which have made conditions favourable to such an endeavour.

531 **Pesticides on millet in Mali.**
N. D. Jago. Chatham, England: Natural Resources Institute, 1993. 45p. maps. bibliog.

Pest damage to millet, the principal crop in Mali's Sahelian zone, is significant. This case-study presents the results of the Mali Millet Pest Project, executed in northwestern Mali between 1985 and 1991; the observation, field trials and socio-economic research that made up this scientific endeavour have yielded a wealth of information both on pests themselves and on the practicality and effectiveness of current pest control methods.

532 **Productivity of transhumant Fulani cattle in the Inner Niger Delta of Mali.**
K. T. Wagenaar, A. Diallo and A. R. Sayers. Addis Ababa: International Livestock Centre for Africa, 1986. 57p. map. bibliog. (ILCA Research Report, no. 13).

Data collected on 2,550 Sudanese Fulani Zebu cattle in the Inner Niger Delta from December 1978 to March 1983 are the basis for this evaluation of their performance traits and productivity. Results indicate moderate milk production, low reproductive performance and high calf mortality. Proposals to increase the cattle's overall productivity include improvements of pastures to provide higher-quality forage for milking cows, and feed supplementation to increase calf survival and growth rates.

533 **Research for rural development: experiences of an anthropologist in rural Mali.**
Dolores Koenig. In: *Anthropology and rural development in West Africa.* Edited by Michael M. Horowitz, Thomas M. Painter. Boulder, Colorado: Westview Press, 1986, p. 29-60.

Koenig discusses her role as a development specialist/anthropologist while participating in research programmes for agricultural development between 1977 and 1980 in rural Mali. She includes a detailed presentation of the research itself, research results, and some problems she experienced with data collection and analysis, interdisciplinary collaboration, and the scale of project operations.

534 **The role of the state in food production and rural development: lessons from Opération Riz-Ségou in Mali.**
James R. Bingen. PhD thesis, University of California, Los Angeles, 1983. 327p. maps. bibliog. (Available from University Microfilms International, Ann Arbor, Michigan, order no. 8312004).

This study is an assessment of Opération Riz-Ségou, a state-sponsored rural development project designed to improve rice production and irrigated agriculture in Mali. The author traces the evolution of Malian agricultural policies and the government's approaches to rural development from 1960 to 1980.

535 **Sansanding: les irrigations du Niger.** (Sansanding: the Niger River irrigations.)
Georges Spitz. Paris: Société d'Editions Géographiques, Maritimes et Coloniales, 1949. 237p. maps.

The author, at the time Honorary Governor of the Colonies, discusses aspects of a major (56,000-hectare) irrigation scheme for cotton and rice cultivation begun in 1932 with the diversion of water from the River Niger at Sansanding. These include social and health issues, problems of rice and cotton production, and financing. There are twenty-one photographs of the project and two maps.

536 **Senoufo migrants in Bamako: changing agricultural production strategies and household organization in an urban environment.**
Steven P. Dettwyler. PhD thesis, Indiana University, 1985. 453p. maps. bibliog. (Available from University Microfilms International, Ann Arbor, Michigan, order no. 8526997).

This study examines how Senufo migrant farmers adapt, socially and economically, to an urban, commercial agricultural environment in Bamako.

537 **The social organization of agricultural labour among the Soninke (Dyahunu, Mali).**
Eric Pollet, Grace Seddon. In: *Relations of production: Marxist approaches to economic anthropology*, edited by David Seddon. London; Totowa, New Jersey: F. Cass, 1978, p. 331-56. bibliog.

Focusing on the Soninke (Sarakole) people living in an area of extreme western Mali, this essay is a detailed discussion of traditional and contemporary social organization of agricultural labour. Of greatest importance is the essay's 'careful delineation of the relations of production in a specific formation and its discussion of the question of slavery and its precise status in the analysis of pre-capitalist modes of production within the context of Marxist models of social development . . .'.

538 **Social stratification and labor allocation in peanut farming in the rural Malian household.**
Dolores Koenig. *African Studies Review*, vol. 29, no. 3 (Sept. 1986), p. 107-25.

Based on farming systems research conducted in 1977-78 in Kita, this paper examines the different production strategies of affluent, middle and poor Malinke farmers, and their effect on labour allocation in the major cash crop of the region: peanuts.

539 **Survival in the Sahel: an ecological and developmental challenge.**
Edited by Klaus M. Leisinger and Karin Schmitt and the International Service for National Agricultural Research (ISNAR). The Hague: ISNAR, 1995. 211p. bibliog.

Aimed at the general reader with little or no prior knowledge of the subject, *Survival in the Sahel* examines how this region's deteriorating environment and socio-economic conditions have resulted, in part, because of past external development strategies. The first part of the work discusses the Sahel in general, including its history, geography, environment, climate and natural resources, agricultural production, conditions of women, and socio-economics. Part II is a detailed account of the case of Mali, which illustrates the problems and situations of a typical Sahelian country, as discussed in Part I. Also included in this volume are some of the Sahel's development success stories, recommendations for new development approaches, and a discussion of alternative solutions to the Sahel's present environmental and development problems.

540 **Women farmers in Africa: rural development in Mali and the Sahel.**
Lucy E. Creevey. Syracuse, New York: Syracuse University Press, 1986. 1st ed. 212p. bibliog. (Contemporary Issues in the Middle East).
This volume consists of eleven papers presented at the 1983 Bamako Workshop on Training and Animation of Rural Women, sponsored by the Food Corps Programs International (CILCA) and the Union of Malian Women. Most of these papers discuss actual projects established and operating among rural women in Mali, and were written by the Malian women who direct these projects. All who contributed to this book share a common belief: that rural women in the Sahel make essential contributions in agriculture and have been neglected by those active in agricultural development.

Mali.
See item no. 13.

Les migrations agricoles au Mali. (Agricultural migrations in Mali.)
See item no. 254.

Women's roles in settlement and resettlement in Mali.
See item no. 260.

Satisfaction of food requirements in Mali to 2000 A.D.
See item no. 408.

Colonial rural development: French policy and African response at the Office du Niger, Soudan français (Mali), 1920-1960.
See item no. 470.

Women's economic activities and credit opportunities in the Opération Haute Vallée (OHV) zone, Mali.
See item no. 499.

Comparative advantage, trade flows and prospects for regional agricultural market intergration in West Africa: the case of Côte d'Ivoire and Mali.
See item no. 501.

The emergence of a grain market in Bamako, 1883-1908.
See item no. 503.

Liberalisation of agricultural markets: an institutional approach.
See item no. 506.

Sub-Saharan agriculture: synthesis and trade prospects.
See item no. 509.

Agroclimatology of West Africa: Mali.
See item no. 555.

Fighting the famine.
See item no. 562.

Antilopes du soleil: arts et rites agraires d'Afrique noire. (Antelopes of the sun: arts and agrarian rites of Black Africa.)
See item no. 644.

Transport

541 **Land-locked countries of Africa.**
Edited by Zdenek Cervenka. Uppsala, Sweden: Scandinavian
Institute of African Studies, 1973. 369p. maps. bibliog.
The problems land-locked African countries face involving transport, administration
and economics are discussed in this book. Two chapters in particular are relevant to
the study of Mali: 'The land-locked countries of Afrique Occidentale Française
(AOF): Mali, Upper Volta and Niger', by Pierre Alexandre; and 'Problems and
prospects of the seven land-locked countries of French-speaking Africa: Central
African Republic, Chad, Mali, Niger, Upper Volta, Rwanda and Burundi', by Louis
Sabourin.

542 **Mali and Senegal and the Dakar–Niger railroad: economic
diplomacy in the New Africa.**
Victor D. Du Bois. *Fieldstaff Reports* (American Universities, West
Africa Series), vol. 6, no. 4 (1963), 10p.
In 1960, with the collapse of the Mali Federation, the Dakar–Niger railway line
linking Senegal and Mali was severed along with diplomatic and trade relations
between the two countries. Du Bois explores the transport alternatives considered and
adopted by Mali, the economic consequences of cutting the Dakar–Niger line for both
countries, and events which led to its reopening in 1963.

543 **A Sahel transportation survey: a regional profile.**
Thomas Philippi. Washington, DC: Office of Foreign Disaster
Assistance, Agency for International Development, 1979. 137p.
(OFDA Country Profiles).
A survey containing information derived primarily from two studies on transportation
in the Sahel which were commissioned to examine transportation's role in this region
and to assess the transport problems by which all Sahelian countries are plagued. Data
on Mali can be found throughout, but are concentrated on pages 48-64.

544 **Study on the co-ordination of transport and communications.**
Prepared for ECOWAS by the United Nations Economic Commission
for Africa. Lagos: Economic Community of West African States,
1980. 2 vols. maps.

A study carried out by the Economic Commission for Africa, which reviewed the existing
transportation and telecommunications systems in Mali and the other fifteen members of
the Economic Community of West African States (ECOWAS). Recommendations are
included regarding a system of efficient, integrated transportation to facilitate movement
of persons, goods and services, and the most efficient telecommunications and postal
network. The second volume contains draft outline development projects, included as
part of the study where appropriate.

545 **Trade routes of Algeria and the Sahara.**
Benjamin E. Thomas. Berkeley, California: University of California
Press, 1957, p. 165-287. maps. bibliog.

The second part of this book focuses on the western Sahara, where Thomas examines
the development of trade routes in the region and their interrelations with the physical,
economic and political geography. Camel, motor and air transport are all discussed,
and emphasis is placed on more recent history, particularly the impact of the Second
World War on transportation. There is a section entitled 'The rise and decline of
Timbuktu' on pages 240-44.

546 **Trucking in Sub-Saharan Africa: what deregulation?**
Alain Bonnafous. In: *Regulatory reform in transport: some recent
experiences.* Edited by José Carbajo. Washington, DC: World Bank,
1993, p. 106-11.

This paper is based on the results of a 1988/89 study of trucking costs that was
conducted in three franc-zone countries of West Africa: Mali, Côte d'Ivoire and
Cameroon. Trucking costs in these countries, which are high, are compared on several
occasions to those in France in order to interpret some of the statistical information
that was gathered by the two surveys that were part of the study. Bonnafous also
examines what level of transport regulation would be desirable.

The French West African railway workers' strike, 1947-1948.
See item no. 549.

God's bits of wood.
See item no. 621.

Labour, the Labour Movement and Trade Unions

547 **Baarakèla.** (Barakela.)
Bamako: Union Nationale des Travailleurs du Mali, [196-?]- .
monthly.
The organ of Mali's national labour union, the Union Nationale des Travailleurs du Mali (National Union of Malian Workers).

548 **Emploi, potentialités et priorités au Mali: rapport présenté au Gouvernement du Mali.** (Employment, potentials and priorities in Mali: report presented to the Government of Mali.)
Jobs and Skills Programme for Africa.   Addis Ababa: Bureau International du Travail, Programme des Emplois et Compétences Techniques pour l'Afrique, 1984. 1st ed. 266p.
During October and November 1980, thirteen mission members of the International Labour Organization (ILO) examined employment issues in Mali. Their report describes the potential, constraints and continuity of Mali's economy, regional self-sufficiency and the politics of employment in rural communities and mechanized agriculture. The report offers numerous recommendations for increasing decentralization and participation. Annexes include a statistical summary of the economy (p. 257-66).

549 **The French West African railway workers' strike, 1947-1948.**
J. Suret-Canale.   In: *African labor history*. Edited by Peter C. W. Gutkind, Robin Cohen, Jean Copans.   Beverly Hills: Sage Publications, 1978, p. 129-54. bibliog.
Describes the railways of French West Africa when the strike began, followed by a discussion of the origins and development of the strike; pressure and repression levied against the strikers; the press, political parties and the strike; worker solidarity; economic consequences of the strike; and the end of the five-month-long conflict.

Worker demands were not entirely satisfied, but this strike is significant in that the colonial administration's efforts to stifle the union movement and question the right to strike were checked.

550 **Mali, dissolution of the Provisional Consultative Committee of the National Union of Malian Workers (UNTM).**
West Africa (31 Oct. 1970), p. 1300.

Featured in the 'Update' section of *West Africa*, this short article details accusations and criticisms levelled against the National Union of Malian Workers by the Traoré government, and the resulting action it took against the organization.

551 **Politiques d'emploi, politiques commerciales et financières: étude de cas comparés de Madagascar et du Mali.** (Politics of employment, commercial politics and finances: comparative case-study of Madagascar and Mali.)
Philippe Hugon, Olivier Sudrie.   Geneva: International Labour Office, 1989. 1st ed. 131p. bibliog. (World Employment Programme Research Working Paper. WEP 2-46, International Employment Policies, WP 28).

This authors of this study have chosen to analyse the similar economic situations in Mali and Madagascar in order to assess the degree of freedom their governments have to manoeuvre in their efforts to increase employment in the face of exterior constraints and opportunities.

552 **Strike movements as part of the anticolonial struggle in French West Africa.**
J. Suret-Canale.   *Tarikh*, vol. 5, no. 3 (1977), p. 44-56.

Suret-Canale, a leading French Marxist historian of West Africa, briefly discusses the relatively infrequent strikes that occurred between the colonial conquest and 1936, and the reasons there were few during that period of time. He argues that they became increasingly important later as a means of protest against the colonial situation and in the struggle for independence.

553 **Trade unions and politics in French West Africa during the Fourth Republic.**
Guy Pfeffermann.   *African Affairs*, vol. 66, no. 264 (July 1967), p. 213-30.

The author analyses the attitudes of West African trade unions between 1945 and 1960 in an attempt to assess their political motivations, determine their main political orientation, and identify factors within the unions which prevented greater involvement in politics.

Papa-commandant a jeté un grand filet devant nous: les exploités des rives du Niger, 1900-1962. (The colonial administrator has thrown a large net in front of us: the exploitation of the Niger River, 1900-62.)
See item no. 230.

The social organization of agricultural labour among the Soninke (Dyahunu, Mali).
See item no. 537.

Social stratification and labor allocation in peanut farming in the rural Malian household.
See item no. 538.

Environment, Ecology and Urban Studies

Environment and ecology

554   Africa's Sahel: the stricken land.
William S. Ellis.   *National Geographic,* vol. 172, no. 2 (Aug. 1987),
p. 140-79. map.

The article, illustrated with dramatic photographs by Steve McCurry, covers the broad region of Senegal, Mauritania, Niger, Chad and especially Mali. This is an excellent source for showing the process of desertification and includes photographs of handpumps in Mali, Timbuktu, irrigated rice, the Hombouri Mountians and discusses the Dogon. The earlier, related *National Geographic* article and photographs by George Gerster, 'River of sorrow, river of hope' (vol. 148, no. 2 (Aug. 1975), p. 152-89. map) includes aerial views of the Inland Delta and Timbuktu, hippo hunting, the mosque at Mopti, salt trading and huge gold Fulani (Peul) earrings, all from Mali. Robin Welcomme's 'The Niger falters', *Geographical Magazine,* vol. 60 (July 1988), p. 40-45, provides a broad overview of the effects of recurrent droughts on that important river, and includes nine photographs and a map.

555   Agroclimatology of West Africa: Mali.
M. V. K. Siva Kumar, M. Konate, S. M. Virmani.   Patancheru, India:
International Crops Research Institute for the Semi-Arid Tropics, 1984.
294p. maps. bibliog.

The first 48 pages of this work, designed to assist in agricultural planning, contain the text, numerous maps and a few tables. There are analyses of rainfall variabilities in Mali from weekly, monthly and annual measurements. The bulk of the publication consists of the appendices (p. 51-294) which are tables of rainfall analysis, maximum and minimum air temperature, and water balance analysis. To compare Mali's rainfall with that of her neighbours, see *Etude des pluies journalières de fréquence rare au Mali, en Mauritanie et au Sénégal* (Study of daily rainfall of rare frequency in Mali, Mauritania, and Senegal) (Ouagadougou: CIEH, 1984. 129p.) by A. Degoulet.

556 **Amélioration des pays arides du Mali: la théorie et la pratique: déliberations d'un atelier tenu à Bafoulabé, Mali, du 13 au 18 septembre 1993.** (Improvement of arid areas of Mali: theory and practice: deliberations of a workshop held in Bafoulabé, Mali, from 13 to 18 September 1993.)
Arne Olav Oyhus. Aas, Norway: NORAGRIC: NLH, Agricultural University of Norway, 1994. 140p. map. (NORAGRIC Occasional Papers. Series C, Development and Environment, no. 14).

This is a summary of a workshop which discussed five non-governmental development projects occurring in Mali. The goals of the projects included improving food production and security as well as improving the natural ecology.

557 **Changes in land use and vegetation in the ILCA/Mali Sudano-Sahelian project zone.**
Mark Haywood. Addis Ababa: International Livestock Center for Africa, 1980. 187p. maps.

This volume, 'based on the work of Mark Haywood' (title page) compares a 1975 aerial survey of the project area with similar coverage in 1952 to assess changes in land use and vegetation over the 23-year period. The text (p. 1-14) describes the study objectives, methodology, the map legend, water resources and the situations in 1952 and 1975. 'The most outstanding feature is the enormous increase in degraded area' (a 534 per cent increase) (p. 14). The study recorded 712 archaeological sites, some of large size. The bulk of the volume consists of sectional maps (p. 15-166) and diagrams and data analysis (p. 167-87).

558 **The climates of West Africa.**
Oyediran Oyo. London; Ibadan, Nigeria: Heinemann, 1977. 218p. maps. bibliog.

Most of Mali is included in this valuable regional study. Data on solar radiation and sunshine, temperature, evaporation, atmospheric moisture, rainfall, winds, regional climatic patterns, microclimatology, bioclimatology and palaeoclimatology appear in the discussions, numerous tables and maps of the region. The bibliography (p. 210-14) is detailed.

559 **Conservation of large mammals in the Republic of Mali.**
J. A. Sayer. *Biological Conservation,* vol. 12 (1977), p. 245-63. maps. bibliog.

Based on information gathered in 1972-74 while the author worked for the Food and Agriculture Organization of the United Nations as adviser on wildlife conservation to the Forestry Service of the Republic of Mali, Sayer describes the present status of thirty-four large mammals and the ways in which they are affected by human settlement and the livestock industry. Of special interest is his account of giant eland in the Mandingue mountains, giraffe in the Baoulé National Park, and addax and oryx in the desert.

560 **Desertification control and renewable resource management in the Sahelian and Sudanian zones of West Africa.**
Edited by François Falloux, Aleki Mukendi. Washington, DC: World Bank, 1988. 119p. bibliog. (World Bank Technical Paper, no. 70).

This volume includes six papers presented at the Workshop on Desertification Control and Renewable Resource Management held in Oslo, Norway, in June 1986, and focuses on resource depletion in Burkina Faso, Chad, Gambia, Mali, Mauritania, Niger and Senegal. Following the 'Overview' (p. 1-9) the papers are: 'Land tenure as a tool for rational resource management', by F. Falloux and A. Rochegude (p. 10-27); 'Mechanisms to enhance effective popular participation', by Thomas M. Catterson (p. 28-41); 'Management of pastoral production in the Sahel – constraints and options', by Angelo M. Bonfiglioli (p. 42-57); 'Water management: problems and potentials in the Sahelian and Sudanic zones', by Shawki Barghoutial and Dominique Lallement (p. 58-71); 'Household energy issues in West Africa', by Willem Floor and Jean Gorse (p. 72-98); and 'Irrigation and settlement of new lands', by René Rochette (p. 99-119). This study's conclusions support the findings of the earlier World Bank Technical Paper, no. 61, *Desertification in the Sahelian and Sudanian zones of West Africa* (1985. 60p.) by J. E. Gorse and D. R. Steeds.

561 **Draft environmental report on Mali.**
Compiled by A. Paige Grant, with D. F. Stotz. Arid Lands Information Center, Office of Arid Lands Studies, University of Arizona; Washington, DC: US National Committee for Man and the Biosphere, Department of State, May 1980. 70 leaves. maps. bibliog.

Following an introduction to the country, the study describes Malian natural resources (water, soils, vegetation, wildlife and protected areas, and minerals), environmental problems and projects. Numerous references are listed (leaves 35-37). Appendices (l. 38-70) describe environmental legislation, USAID projects in Mali and include a lengthy bibliography (l. 60-70). The report is available from the AID/MAB Project, Department of State, Washington, DC 20520. See also the Club du Sahel's *The Ségou experience: landmarks to guide concerted action. Regional encounter in Ségou (Mali) on local level natural resources management, May 22-27, 1989* (Paris: Club du Sahel, OECD; Ouagadougou: Comité Permanent Inter-Etats de Lutte Contre la Sécheresse dans le Sahel, 1989. 8p. map). This brochure describes the Segou Regional Encounter at which rural population groups, local and central government organizations and international aid agencies met to develop practical solutions to local-level management of natural resources. It lists eight 'Landmarks to guide concerted action'.

562 **Fighting the famine.**
Nigel Twose, Mike Goldwater. London: Pluto Press, 1985. 96p. map. bibliog.

Twose, who worked for Oxfam in the Sahel from 1979 to 1983, argues that famine has human causes, especially cash cropping which prevents agricultural independence. The book examines 'The Sahel' (p. 12-45), in which pictures by M. Goldwater and discussion of Mali are prominent, and features 'The Horn of Africa' (p. 46-91). It was also published in San Francisco by the Institute for Food and Development Policy, 1985.

563   **La gestion des ressources naturelles au Mali.** (The management of
natural resources in Mali.)
Comité de Coordination des Actions des ONG au Mali.   Bamako:
Sahélienne and EPES, 1995. 95p. (Série ONG-Communautés-
Développement).

This recent look at the management of Mali's natural resources includes chapters on
decentralized management by non-government organizations, water resource
management, case-studies of three Malian rural production systems, local land
institutions, and the Village Hydraulic Project of Macina.

564   **The grazing land ecosystems of the African Sahel.**
Henry Noël Le Houérou.   Berlin; Heidelberg; New York; London;
Paris; Tokyo; Hong Kong: Springer-Verlag, 1989. 282p. maps. bibliog.

A vast amount of information on climate, geology, soils, flora, vegetation, wildlife,
livestock, constraints and limits of the region, and general conclusions on the
ecological management of Sahelian ecosystems appears in this volume. A brief section
considers 'The sedentary agropastoral systems of central Mali' (p. 141-42). The
bibliography is one of the best for Sahelian ecosystems (p. 241-68). There are indexes
(p. 269-82) of subjects and of plant and animal scientific names.

565   **Guide pour la lutte contre les feux de brousse.** (Guide for fighting
brush fires.)
Nampaa N. Sanogho.   Bamako: Ministère de l'Environnement et de
l'Elevage, Direction Nationale des Eaux et Forêts, 1988. 54p. bibliog.

This illustrated booklet explains the causes and consequences of brush fires in Mali
and offers detailed advice on their prevention and control. A brief bibliography (p. 42)
notes six previous documents on the subject.

566   **Influence du barrage de Sélingué dans la cuvette du Niger.** (The
influence of the Selingué Dam in the Niger Basin.)
Amadou Ballo.   *Les Cahiers d'Outre-Mer* (Bordeaux), vol. 42,
no. 167 (July-Sept. 1989), p. 257-70. map. bibliog.

The author analyses hydrometric data from 1952 to 1989 to show how the Selingué
Dam on the Niger River in the extreme southwest of Mali is useful in boosting the
flow of water downstream when the river is at its lowest level. The work includes an
English-language summary (p. 257).

567   **Irrigation du delta central nigérien: cartes et plans.** (Irrigation in
the Inland Niger Delta: maps and plans.)
Office du Niger.   Ségou, Mali: Office du Niger, 1955. maps.

This volume contains eleven coloured folding maps, most at a scale of 1:50,000,
showing detailed plans of the irrigation systems of the Inland Niger Delta. A larger
map 'Vallée du Niger entre Bamako et Tombouctou' (scale 1:1,000,000) shows the
region.

568 **Une lutte de longue haleine: aménagements anti-érosifs et gestion de terroir.** (A long-drawn-out fight: erosion prevention programme and land-use management.)
Jan Hijkoop, Piet Van der Poel, Bocary Kaya.   Bamako: IER; Amsterdam: KIT, 1991. 154p. map. bibliog. (Systèmes de Production Rurale au Mali, vol. 2).

Soil conservation in the northern part of Southern Mali has been the focus of research by the Division de Recherche sur les Systèmes de Production Rurale (Bamako) and the Compagnie Malienne pour le Développement des Textiles. The Projet Lutte Anti-Erosive, established in 1986, is described and recommendations are made to move towards sustainable exploitation of natural resources. The work includes a summary in English (p. 13). Other recent titles on the subject of conservation not mentioned elsewhere include *Mali-sud: d'un aménagement anti-érosif des champs à la gestion de l'espace rural* (Southern Mali: from the management of anti-erosion efforts to the administration of rural space) (Amsterdam: Institut Royal des Tropiques, 1989. 52p.) by Jan Hijkoop (et al.); and Will Critchley's *Looking after our land: soil and water conservation in dryland Africa* (Oxford, England: Oxfam, 1991. 84p.)

569 **Mali biological diversity assessment.**
Peter Warshall.   Washington, DC: Agency for International Development, Bureau of Africa, Office of Technical Resources, Natural Resources Branch, Natural Resource Management Support Project, 1989. 95 leaves. maps. bibliog.

This important document, 'the first review of its kind ever written for Mali' is essential reading for the appreciation of Mali's fauna and flora and efforts to protect them. It has four parts: 'Status and management of the preservation of biological diversity' (leaves 5-32); 'Biological diversity and conservation development' (l. 33-58); 'Social, political and economic incentives and biological diversity' (l. 59-72); and 'Projects proposals and US aid' (l. 73-78). An appendix lists projects (l. 79-87) and persons contacted (l. 88) and there is an extensive bibliography (l. 89-95). Informative illustrations and educational side-bars are found throughout. Maps show Mali's biotic zones and protected areas. Twenty-one tables include lists of mammals, birds and trees protected by Malian law, forest reserves, forestry projects, proposed projects, and national laws concerning biodiversity.

570 **Plan national de lutte contre la desertification et l'avancée du désert, 1985-2000.** (National plan to fight against desertification and the advance of the desert, 1985-2000.)
Ministère Chargé des Ressources Naturelles et de l'Elevage, Direction Nationale des Eaux et Forêts.   Bamako: Ministère des Ressources Naturelles et de l'Elevage, Direction Nationale des Eaux et Forêts, 1985. 28, 16 leaves. maps.

This document is an action plan by the government to stop desertification (the destruction of the land that leads to desert conditions) and desertization (the transformation of pre-desert land into deserts).

571   **The politics of natural disaster: the case of the Sahel drought.**
Edited by Michael H. Glantz, foreword by Walter Orr Roberts.   New
York: Praeger, 1976. 340p. maps. bibliog. (Praeger Special Studies in
International Economics and Development).

Fourteen essays divided into 'Social science contributions' and 'Natural science
contributions' explore facets of complex Sahelian issues: M. Glantz, 'Nine fallacies of
natural disaster: the case of the Sahel' (p. 3-24); H. Sheets, R. Morris, 'Disaster in the
desert' (p. 25-76); M. El-Khawas, 'A reassessment of international relief programs'
(p. 77-100); L. Wiseberg, 'An international perspective on the African famines'
(p. 101-27); D. Shear, R. Stacy, 'Can the Sahel survive? Prospects for long term
planning and development' (p. 128-44); P. E. Lovejoy, S. Baier, 'The desert-side
economy of the central Sudan' (p. 145-75); R. Baker, 'Innovation technology transfer
and nomadic pastoral societies' (p. 176-85); D. Winstanley, 'Climatic changes and the
future of the Sahel' (p. 189-213); N. H. MacLeod, 'Dust in the Sahel: cause of
drought?' (p. 214-31); W. G. Matlock, E. L. Cockrum, 'Agricultural production
systems in the Sahel' (p. 232-55); B. E. Norton, 'The management of desert grazing
systems' (p. 256-66); H. N. Le Houérou, 'Ecological management of arid grazing
lands ecosystems' (p. 267-81); P. J. Imperato, 'Health care systems in the Sahel:
before and after the drought' (p. 282-302); and M. H. Glantz, W. Parton, 'Weather and
climate modification and the future of the Sahara' (p. 303-24).

572   **Profil d'environnement Mali-Sud: état des ressources naturelles et
potentialités de développement.** (Environment profile, Southern Mali:
state of natural resources and development potentialities.)
Abou Lamine Berthe (et al.).   Bamako: Institut d'Economie Rurale;
Amsterdam: Institut Royal des Tropiques, 1991. 79p. maps. bibliog.

Southern Mali is here defined as all of the Sikasso administrative region and a part of
the regions of Koulikoro and Segou, and represents 32 per cent of Mali's total
population, or 2.5 million inhabitants. The first part of this book covers the region's
physical, socio-economic, food and health, and administrative and legal frameworks.
Part 2 covers the region's natural resources: agricultural, animal breeding, forests,
fauna, and fish, hydraulic, and their integrated use. Part 3 consists of an analysis of
development perspectives as well as ecological and socio-economic constraints which
have an impact on conservation and development. Also included is a list of French and
Bambara terms of animal and plant species in the zone (p. 76-79).

573   **Projet Bois de Villages, Burkina Faso and Mali.**
Paul Kerkhof, edited by Gerald Foley, Geoffrey Barnard.
In: *Agroforestry in Africa: a survey of project experience.*
London: Panos Publications, 1990, p. 87-95. map. bibliog.

A village forestry project was implemented in Segou, central Mali, in approximately
1985. Fuelwood shortages, initially viewed as a serious problem, do not appear to be a
high priority for villagers. Nor have communal woodlots elicited much interest. Mali's
Forest Department would have to 'change its attitudes' if the Project were to proceed
further. The text is written in English.

574 **Recommendations for a new Malian forest code: observations from the Land Tenure Center's study of land and tree tenure in Mali's Fifth Region.**
Rebecca J. McLain. Madison, Wisconsin: Land Tenure Center, University of Wisconsin-Madison, 1992. 45p. map. bibliog. (LTC Research Paper, no. 109).

Because the peasants believe they should have access to trees they consider their own, there is antagonism between them and the foresters who maintain the state forestry code (Republic of Mali. *Textes forestiers* (Forestry texts). Bamako: Ministère du Développement Rural, Service des Eaux et Forêts, 1986. 54p.), making it difficult to sustain the natural resources. The University of Wisconsin has studied the situation in the *cercles* of Mopti, Bandiagara and Koro, and made recommendations that the government change the code to permit individuals and groups the rights to non-forest areas (e.g., farms) and private forests. *Politique forestière nationale* (National politics of forests) (Bamako: Ministère Chargé du Développement Rural, Direction Nationale des Eaux et Forêts, 1982. 105p.) describes the politics of forests and its application to conserve renewable natural resources. See also Derek W. Brinkerhoff and James D. Gage's *Forestry policy reform in Mali: an analysis of implementation issues* (Washington, DC: US Agency for International Development, Bureau for Research & Development, 1993. 43p.) which looks at the process of forestry policy reform and implementation and includes an excellent bibliography (p. 34-43).

575 **République du Mali, précipitations journalières de l'origine des stations à 1965.** (Republic of Mali, daily rainfall from the founding of the stations to 1965.)
Comité Interafricain d'Etudes Hydrauliques. Paris: République Française, Ministère de la Coopération, 1974. 1,081p.

In this detailed statistical compendium of rainfall in Mali, measurements at some stations began as early as 1895 (Kayes) and 1907 (Bandiagara, Segou and Sikasso) and are recorded through to 1965.

576 **The Sahara, ecological change and early economic history.**
Edited by J. A. Allan, with contributions by G. Barker (et al.). Outwell, England: Middle East & North African Studies Press, 1981. 146p. maps. bibliog. (Menas Monographs, no. 1).

A useful collection of papers presented at the School of Oriental and African Studies, London, in October 1978, gives a broad context to the geographical region and its earliest human habitation. Mali appears as part of the whole region rather than being singled out. Numerous figures, plates and tables are included. Notable is Thurstan Shaw's 'The Late Stone Age in West Africa' (p. 93-130) relating archaeological finds to climate, ecology and early economy, and including an extensive bibliography (p. 107-15).

577 **Seeds of famine: ecological destruction and the development dilemma in the west African Sahel.**
Richard W. Franke, Barbara H. Chasin. Montclair, New Jersey: Allanheld, Osmun, 1980. 266p. maps. bibliog. (Landmark Studies).
Mali is well represented in this comprehensive study of the West African famine of 1968-74. It consists of three parts: 'The making of the Sahel famine' (p. 19-108); 'Responding to the famine' (p. 109-64); and 'Projects for development or new seeds of famine: contradictions in Sahel development' (p. 165-239). The authors discuss 'Mali: ecological degradation' (p. 103-4), the 'Gao Rice and Sorghum Project' (p. 204-5), 'Gao, Mali' (p. 205-7), 'Timbuktu: the Isle of Peace Project' (p. 232-33) and 'Gao: relaunching the herders' cooperatives' (p. 233-34). Maps, figures, tables and an extensive bibliography (p. 240-56) add to the volume's usefulness.

578 **Selective bibliography on the famines and the drought in the Sahel.**
Compiled by Jean Roch, with Bernard Hubert, Emmanuel Ngyrie and Patricia Richard. *Environment in Africa*, vol. 1, no. 2 (April 1975), p. 94-116.
Mali, Chad, Mauritania, Niger, Senegal and (then) Upper Volta are featured in this unnumbered, unannotated list of references. Jonathan Derrick's 'The great West African drought, 1972-74', in *African Affairs*, vol. 76, no. 305 (Oct. 1977), p. 537-86, provides an excellent discussion and bibliography. In 'Drought-related changes to geo-morphologic processes in central Mali', *Geological Society of America Bulletin*, vol. 100 (March 1988), p. 352-61, P. A. Jacobberger describes the drought period of 1968-86 as 'a single event of fluctuating severity' (p. 352). A table shows precipitation in Mopti, 1921-85, and there are eleven satellite photographs of the study region of Tombouctou to Jenne. See also Jacobberger's 'Geomorphology of the upper Inland Niger Delta', *Journal of Arid Environments*, vol. 13 (1987), p. 95-112.

579 **Towards better woodland management in the Sahelian Mali.**
J. Skinner. London: Agricultural Administration Unit, Overseas Development Institute, 1988. 17p.
Skinner offers a case-study of a project of the International Union for the Conservation of Nature (IUCN) in the Inland Niger Delta near Bouna (Cercle de Mopti, Arrondissement de Kona). The project, as described in October 1987, attempts to establish and enforce local rules on woodcutting by Bozo and Somono fishermen and Peul, Tamasheq and Bella herders using the isolated woodland. See also F. M. J. Ohler's 'Fuelwood production of wooded savanna fallows in the Sudan zone of Mali', *Agroforestry Systems* (The Hague), vol. 3, no. 1 (1985), p. 15-23.

580 **Traditional soil and water conservation on the Dogon Plateau, Mali.**
Armand Kassogué, Jean Dolo, Tom Ponsioen. London: International Institute for Environment and Development, 1990. 18p. (Issues Paper, no. 23).
The Dogons use a combination of traditional and new techniques to combat soil and water erosion. To prevent a further rural exodus of population, the Project for Popularising Agricultural Methods has suggested methods of improving conservation techniques.

581 **West Africa: a study of the environment and of man's use of it.**
Ronald James Harrison Church. London: Longman, 1980. 8th ed.
526p.

Chapter 15, 'Mali: Marxian socialism in an inland state' (p. 244-63, 500-1) provides an historical outline, information on climate and vegetation, geology and relief, major regions and economic resources in this highly regarded geography book first published in 1957. Part one, 'The physical basis of West Africa' (p. 1-90) discusses geology, relief and drainage, climate, vegetation and soils; Part two, 'The resources and their development' (p. 91-179) describes agriculture, livestock and fisheries, minerals, fuels and power, and industry, transport and population; Part three, 'The political divisions' covers Mali and fourteen other countries, with bibliographies for each at the end (p. 485-516). Maps, tables, diagrams and 118 plates enhance the volume. 'Mali – land of the Middle Niger' (p. 30-32) receives succinct attention in Church's *West Africa: environment and policies* (New York: Van Norstrand, 1976. 2nd ed. 125p.) which examines the political economy of the region in the light of its geographical and historical background.

Urban studies

582 **Aménagements en quartiers spontanés africains: République du Mali, Burkina Faso.** (Management of African squatter quarters: Republic of Mali, Burkina Faso.)
ACCT, Direction Générale de la Coopération Scientifique et Technique. Paris: Agence de Coopération Culturelle et Technique, 1986. 296p. maps. bibliog.

The first part (p. 17-92) deals with a case-study of Bamako, including urban planning and the rehabilitation operation of a district of Bamako called Sabalibougou. Other recent publications on urban planning include, 'L'insertion urbaine à Bamako: présentation de la recherche et de la méthodologie de l'enquête' (Urban insertion into Bamako: presentation of research and the methodology of the study), by R. Marcoux (et al.), in *La ville à guichets fermés?* ([n.p.]: IFAN: ORSTOM, 1995, p. 27-37); and 'Développement urbain et décentralisation dans le nord-est du Mali: l'exemple de Gao' (Urban development and decentralization in the northeast of Mali: the example of Gao), by Anne Ouallet, in *Petites et moyennnes villes d'Afrique noire*, edited by Monique Bertrand and Alain Dubresson (Paris: Karthala, 1997, p. 125-43).

583 **La France et les villes d'Afrique francophone: quarante ans
d'intervention (1945-1985): approche générale et études de cas:
Niamey, Ouagadougou et Bamako.** (France and African francophone
cities: 40 years of intervention (1945-1985): general approach and
case-studies: Niamey, Ouagadougou and Bamako.)
Sophie Dulucq, preface by Catherine Coquery-Vidrovitch. Paris:
L'Harmattan, 1997. 438p. maps. bibliog. (Villes et Enterprises).
This is a study of the effects of forty years of France's colonization on three West
African capital cities. It includes a general section on France's political and financial
investments in the cities as well as several chapters specifically on France's role in the
management of and financial investments in Bamako.

584 **Mopti: tradition in the present: elements for reflection and action
in medium-sized cities in Africa.**
Jean-Jacques Guibbert. In: *Reading the contemporary African city:
proceedings of seminar seven in the series Architectural
transformations in the Islamic world, held in Dakar, Senegal,
November 2-5, 1982.* Singapore: Concept Media Pte Ltd. for the Aga
Khan Award for Architecture, 1983, p. 101-12.
Medium-sized cities (population of 20,000 to 100,000) in francophone West Africa
have drained the surrounding rural areas rather than building up their regional
development. Many recent city plans in Africa have not been implemented because of
the reliance on a technology that is either inappropriate for the African environment or
too expensive. A 1981 meeting of Malian and international experts found a number of
problems with the 1967 Mopti preliminary development plan. Mali's medium-sized
cities will in future have summary schemes for development and city planning that use
appropriate technology and participative group consultation and management. The
methodology for upgrading Mopti's sanitation system was outlined.

585 **Schéma directeur d'aménagement et d'urbanisme de Bamako et
environs.** (Master plan of development and urbanism of Bamako and
environs.)
Ministère des Travaux Publics de l'Urbanisme et de la Construction,
Direction Nationale de l'Urbanisme et de la Construction, République
du Mali. Bamako: Ministère des Travaux Publics de l'Urbanisme et
de la Construction, Direction Nationale de l'Urbanisme et de la
Construction, République du Mali, 1990. 1st revision. 79 leaves.
In this development plan of Bamako, recommendations are made to improve traffic
patterns and build bridges, as well as to improve sanitation, water, electricity,
telephone, and urban transportation. Related titles produced and published by the
government of Mali include: *Schéma directeur d'aménagement et d'urbanisme de
Tombouctou et environs* (1989. 70 leaves), *Schéma sommaire d'aménagement et
d'urbanisme de Bougouni et environs* (1989. 87 leaves), *Schéma sommaire
d'aménagement et d'urbanisme de la commune de Mopti et environs* (1990. 76 leaves)
and *Schéma directeur de mise en valeur des ressources en eau du Mali* (1990. 2 vols).

Camping with the Prince.
See item no. 56.

The Sahara and the Nile: Quaternary environments and prehistoric occupation in northern Africa.
See item no. 88.

The last Sahelian elephants.
See item no. 115.

Arid ways: cultural understandings of insecurity in Fulbe society, central Mali.
See item no. 267.

Nomads of the Sahel.
See item no. 383.

Listening to one's clients: a case study of Mali's famine early warning system – the Système d'Alerte Précoce (SAP) – and rural producers.
See item no. 478.

Cattle, women, and wells: managing household survival in the Sahel.
See item no. 517.

Changes in drought-coping strategies in the Segu Region of Mali.
See item no. 518.

Survival in the Sahel: an ecological and developmental challenge.
See item no. 539.

Education

586 **An analysis of educational reforms in Mali, 1962-1992.**
Mamadou Chérif Bane. PhD thesis, University of Kansas, 1994.
219 leaves. bibliog. (Available from University Microfilms
International, Ann Arbor, Michigan, order no. 9518954).
After Mali achieved her independence, educational reform became a top priority of the government. Despite reform efforts that took place during the past three decades, a number of goals remain unmet and Malian parents and students alike are disenchanted with Malian schools. This dissertation is a descriptive and historical analysis of the Malian educational system as well as an evaluation of the reforms that took place in 1962 and under the Second Republic. Little research has been done on Mali's educational system in general and her educational reforms in particular, so this study is an important contribution towards filling those gaps.

587 **Aperçu de la situation ethno-linguistique du Mali.** (Survey of the ethno-linguistic situation in Mali.)
Minabe Diarra. Paris: Organisation des Nations Unies pour l'Education, la Science et la Culture, Département de l'Education, 1977. 29p. (Documentation Linguistique pour les Pays en Développement: Cas, Problèmes, Solutions).
This brief paper summarizes efforts to promote functional literacy in Mali since independence. For each of the four national languages, Tamashek (Tamasheq), Songhay (Songai), Fulfulde and Bamana (Bambara), the ethno-linguistic situation plays an important role in achieving functional literacy in Mali. Only the Bamana language has seen rapid gains in literacy. The author discusses the role of newspapers and radio in the linguistic plan.

Education

588   **A comparative survey of seven adult functional literacy programs in Sub-Saharan Africa.**
Edmun B. Richmond.   Lanham, Maryland: University Press of America, 1986. 107p. maps. bibliog.

The author surveys national efforts to develop 'basic reading, writing and arithmetic skills which people need on an everyday basis' (p. 3) in The Gambia, Liberia, Rwanda, Burundi, Kenya, the Seychelles and Mali, the only country with its own chapter, 'Adult functional literacy in Mali: a longitudinal examination, 1959-1988' (p. 53-77). Illustrations from literary materials and a useful bibliography are included. In *Higher education and social change: promising experiments in developing countries. Volume 1: reports by Kenneth W. Thompson and Barbara R. Fogel* (New York: Praeger, 1976. 224p. bibliog.) appear brief discussion of 'Higher education in Mali' and basic statistics on education in Mali in the 'African regional report' (p. 139-65). See also Bernard Dumont's *Functional literacy in Mali: training for development* (Paris: Unesco, 1973. 67p. Educational Studies and Documents, no. 10) and Jerry B. Bolibaugh's *Educational development in Guinea, Mali, Senegal and Ivory Coast* (Washington, DC: United States Office of Education, Institute of International Studies, 1972. 141p.).

589   **Contact.**
Bamako: Institut Pédagogique National du Mali, Ministère de l'Education Nationale, 1970- . irregular.

Each issue includes general information, articles and practical suggestions on pedagogy, folktales and official documents. This serial may have ceased with no. 40/41, which was published in 1990.

590   **Education.** (Education.)
Pascal Hué.   Paris: Agence de Francophonie; IBISCUS, 1997. 277p. bibliog. (Informations Pour le Développement, no. 3).

This information guide presents the following information for each francophone country listed, including Mali: an account of the most important topics in education, a list of addresses of specialized organizations (ministries, research institutes, universities) and a bibliography of important resources. Sections on Mali and some other nations also include introductory text, written by an expert, which summarizes the history and state of education in the country.

591   **Education and society: the Malian school system in transition.**
Cheick O. Sidibe.   PhD thesis, State University of New York at Buffalo, 1982. 144p. bibliog. (Available from University Microfilms International, Ann Arbor, Michigan, order no. 8303244).

Focusing on primary-level schools, this study aims to determine what political and/or cultural motivations influenced educational policies in French Sudan and independent Mali. A special emphasis is placed on how well educational policies matched educational outputs under both governments.

592 **Education in Mali.**
Ahmadou Toure.   In: *Education in Africa: a comparative study.*
Edited by A. Babs Fafunwa, J. U. Aisiku.   London; Boston,
Massachusetts: Allen & Unwin, 1982, p. 188-204.

A synthesis of educational developments in Mali under colonialism and during the post-independence era, written from an African viewpoint.

593 **'Elite' education in French West Africa: the era of limits, 1903-1945.**
Peggy R. Sabatier.   *International Journal of African Historical Studies,* vol. 11, no. 2 (1978), p. 247-66. bibliog.

Among the élite regional schools described by the author is the Higher Technical School (Ecole Technique Supérieur) at Bamako, established in 1940 for students in science and mathematics. By 1945, only thirty had graduated, becoming topographers, overseers and draughtsmen; the top two graduates in each class could continue education in France. The author describes the contributions of the schools, their limitations and the successful policy of the French educational system. 'Thus somewhat ironically colonial education in the era of limits did create, in an ambiguous and often impermanent fashion, a few loyal if second-class black Frenchmen' (p. 265-66).

594 **An evaluation of educational radio programmes for primary school teachers in Mali.**
Moussa Sidibe.   Nairobi: ACO Project, 1983. 69 leaves. (African
Studies in Curriculum Development & Evaluation, no. 122).

The study, partially fulfilling requirements for a post-graduate Diploma in Curriculum Development at the University of Nairobi, September 1983, uses questionnaire data from 234 primary school teachers to determine their attitudes towards the educational radio programmes, the sources of the attitudes and to suggest ways to create more interested and sympathetic listeners. A bibliography of nine sources and the questionnaire in French and English are included.

595 **Inefficiency in education: the case of Mali.**
J. R. Hough.   *Comparative Education,* vol. 25, no. 1 (1989), p. 77-85.
bibliog.

The author interviewed the seven directors of Mali's Grandes Ecoles during a recent visit. Here, he describes the educational system, offers statistics for 1984-86, and notes a host of problems, including: low enrolment rates, high drop-out and repetition rates, few educational supplies, the use of French as the language of instruction for young children, only three per cent of the GNP devoted to education, an out-dated French-based system, and a costly system with too many teachers relative to students in school and too many non-teaching staff.

596 **Integrated literacy in Mali.**
Jane Turrittin.   *Comparative Education Review,* vol. 33, no. 1 (Feb.
1989), p. 59-76. bibliog.

The author describes in detail an integrated literacy project of Unesco's Experimental World Literacy Program administered by the Malian Textile Company (Compagnie

Malienne de Textile, CMDT) in a small Bambara village during her fieldwork (June 1982 to June 1983). The successful project encourages villagers to promote their own interests, reinforces villagers' shared class identity, expresses and reinforces class distinctions and enhances institutional networks. See also Jean Moisset, 'Les politiques d'intégration des systèmes économiques et scolaires dans les pays africains: le cas du Mali', *Canadian Journal of African Studies*, vol. 13, no. 3 (1980), p. 461-69.

597 **Language policy and literacy development: a study of the two west African countries of Ghana and Mali.**
Ousmane Minta. PhD thesis, Ohio University, 1980. 257p. bibliog.
(Available from University Microfilms International, Ann Arbor, Michigan, order no. 8110497).

Minta's thesis compares the language policies adopted by Mali and Ghana, and the problems associated with the development of literacy in both countries.

598 **Learning strategies for post-literacy and continuing education in Mali, Niger, Senegal and Upper Volta: outcomes of an international research project of the Unesco Institute for Education.**
Edited by R. H. Dave, D. A. Perera, A. Ouane. Hamburg, Germany: Unesco Institute for Education, 1984. 206p. (UIE Studies on Post-literacy and Continuing Education, no. 2).

Adama Ouane contributed the chapter 'Rural newspapers and other learning strategies for post-literacy and basic education in Mali' (p. 1-59) which describes the Malian educational system, the leading rural newspaper *Kibaru*, educational radio, provides education statistics for 1973-74, 1978-79 and 1981, and offers useful references (p. 59). The Unesco Institute for Education also published *Basic education in the Sahel countries* by M. Botti, M. D. Carelli and M. Saliba (1978. 130p. bibliog. UIE Monograph, no. 6) in which 'Experimental basic education activities in Mali' (p. 89-100) are discussed. See also Mamadou Bagayoko's 1987 doctoral thesis at the University of Southern California, 'Education and development of non-formal education in urban areas as a national development strategy for Mali: a case study of the District of Bamako, the capital city' (345 leaves).

599 **Mali.**
Edited by George Thomas Kurian. In: *World Education Encyclopedia*. New York and Oxford: Facts on File, 1988. p. 1530-32. bibliog.

This fine resource supplies basic data, history and background, constitutional and legal foundations, an overview of the educational system, brief descriptions of primary, secondary and higher education, administration and finance, non-formal education and the teaching profession. It reports Mali's literacy rate as ten per cent.

600   **Mali: éducation et développement au Mali, bibliographie selective des documents disponibles au Centre de documentation de l'IIPE.**
(Mali: education and development in Mali, selective bibliography of documents held at the IIPE Documentation Centre.)
Françoise Du Pouget.   Paris: Unesco, 1981. 21p.

This bibliography, which is divided into two parts, lists approximately 100 items held by the International Institute for Educational Planning (IIPE) in Paris. Part one includes titles about education; part two includes titles about economic and social development. Items cited, which are in either French or English, include development plans and official reports, statistical works, conference proceedings, and other materials.

601   **Mali: educational options in a poor country.**
Fakoney Ly.   In: *Education for rural development: case studies for planners.* Edited by Manzoor Ahmed, Philip H. Coombs.   New York: Praeger, 1975. p. 217-48. (Praeger Special Studies in International Economics and Development).

The author describes the Bambara majority of the population and the formal education system with its attempts at 'ruralization' of schools, but emphasizes a variety of non-formal education programmes: functional literacy programmes, the role of the press and radio, Comités Culturels et de Plein Air (CCPA), the Pioneer Movement, Science Circles, the Women's Movement, and education for training in agriculture. The author was Director of Literacy and Basic Education, Ministry of National Education, Bamako, at the time of publication. See also Boubacar Mody Guindo's 1991 doctoral thesis at the University of Arizona, 'A feasibility study for the preparation of educational administrators in the Republic of Mali' (239 leaves).

602   **National goals, social mobility and personal aspirations: students in Mali.**
Vera L. Zolberg.   *Canadian Journal of African Studies,* vol. 10, no. 1 (1976), p. 125-42. bibliog.

The author describes Mali's educational system and reports on questionnaire data gathered from 371 secondary school students during the period from January to July 1964 in Bamako, Ségou and Markala. In the only such study reported for the period 1960-68, she describes students' fathers' occupations, educational level of parents and students' attitudes towards work, wealth and aspirations, and compares the Malian findings with similar data from Ghana and the Ivory Coast (Côte d'Ivoire). See the related 1991 University of Laval (Canada) doctoral thesis by Mamadou Diop, 'Stratégies de résolution du conflit du choix vocationnel en contexte malien' (Strategies for resolving conflict over vocation choice in Mali. 194 leaves).

603 **Political and educational reform in French-speaking West Africa: a comparative study of Mali and the Ivory Coast.**
Boniface I. Obichere. In: *Education & politics in tropical Africa.* Edited by Victor C. Uchendu. Owerri, Nigeria; New York: Conch Magazine, 1979, p. 196-210. bibliog.

The author offers dramatic contrasts between the educational policies of Félix Houphouët-Boigny in the Ivory Coast (Côte d'Ivoire), who continued a conservative educational system inherited from France, and Modibo Keita, who sought a socialist model for Mali's educational system. Vera L. Zolberg offers critical commentary on the article (p. 211-16). See also Soumaïla Diakité's 1985 doctoral thesis at Stanford University, 'Education, the state and class conflict: a study of three education policies in Mali' (267 leaves) and Cheick O. Sidibe's 1982 doctoral thesis at the State University of New York at Buffalo, 'Education and society: the Malian school system in transition' (item no. 591).

604 **The Republic of Mali.**
International Institute for Adult Literacy Methods. In: *Functional literacy pilot projects: Iran, Madagascar, Mali and Zambia.* Tehran: International Institute for Adult Literacy Methods, 1972, p. 100-19. bibliog.

Describes the origins, objectives, and execution of the Mali Functional Adult Literacy Project, implemented in 1967 within the framework of the World Experimental Literacy Programme. A comparison of the project's objectives and results concludes the chapter.

605 **A study of the causes and effects of pupils' dropout in the fundamental school level in Mali.**
Male Lamine. Nairobi: ACO Project, 1983. 63 leaves. bibliog. (African Studies in Curriculum Development & Evaluation, no. 111).

The author submitted this study as work towards a post-graduate diploma in curriculum development at the University of Nairobi, Kenya. He collected questionnaire and interview data from 100 dropped-out pupils, fifty educators, and fifty parents and tutors. He concludes that Mali's 22.5 per cent drop-out rate in the first grade and 45 per cent rate in the last grade is due to the 'low socio-economic level of the parents or tutors; poor pedagogical condition in which the pupils must learn; [and] disturbed psychological climate of the child's family' (l. 48). The final chapter offers 'Conclusions and recommendations' (l. 56-59). He includes a copy of the questionnaire in French (l. 61-63).

Literature

606   **Abubakari II: théâtre.** (Abubakari II: theatre.)
      Gaoussou Diawara.   Carnières, Belgium: Lansman, 1992. 37p.

One of Mali's foremost playwrights, Diawara's subject here is a mythical story of the discovery of America by Abubakari II, Emperor of the Mandingos. Other works by Diawara include: *L'aube des béliers* (Dawn of the rams) (Paris: Radio-France-Internationale, 1975. 80p.); *Afrique, ma boussole; suivi de La terre et le pain* [poems] (Africa, my compass; followed by Earth and bread) (Bamako: Librairie Populaire du Mali, 1980. 186p.). Diawara has also written an excellent critical work on Malian theatre, *Panorama critique du théâtre malien dans son évolution* (q.v.).

607   **African literature in French: a history of creative writing in French from West and Equatorial Africa.**
      Dorothy S. Blair.   Cambridge, England; New York: Cambridge University Press, 1976. 348p.

Although only four Malians are covered in this literary criticism text, it does have the advantage of being written for the English-language speaker. Malians covered are Seydou Badian, Mamadou Gologo, Yambo Ouologuem and Fily-Dabo Sissoko.

608   **L'archer bassari.** (The Bassari archer.)
      Modibo S. Keita.   Paris: Karthala, 1984. 198p.

Keita, former President of Mali from 1959 until he was deposed in 1968, was a supporter of socialist economic and political reforms which drove the country into economic crisis in 1967. Keita died suddenly in 1977, under mysterious circumstances. In this novel, a commissioner hunts for the murderer of several grain suppliers and a journalist tries to report honestly on the country's drought and famine. This posthumous detective novel was the winner of the 1984 Grand Prix Littéraire d'Afrique Noire.

609 **Bibliographie commentée des écrivains contemporains.** (Annotated bibliography of contemporary writers.)
Opération Lecture Publique, Réseau Malien de Documentation.
Bamako: O.L.P., REMADOC, 1996. 115p.

This up-to-date partially annotated bibliography on Francophone Malian literature includes 346 titles by 156 authors, published between 1950 and 1995. It concentrates on material not covered in *Littérature malienne* (q.v.). Each section of the bibliography is preceded by an informative essay on the topics covered, namely: literature and oral tradition (including tales, epics, history, oral literature, proverbs, riddles), poetry, novels/short stories, theatre, and essays. The author and title indexes cover the actual bibliography but not the essays that precede each section. Please note that non-Malians who have written literary criticism on Mali or who have collected works of Malian oral tradition are outside the scope of this publication.

610 **Bound to violence.**
Yambo Ouologuem, translated by Ralph Manheim. New York: Harcourt Brace Jovanovich, 1971. 182p.

Translation of *Le devoir de violence* and winner of the Prix Renaudot (France) in 1968, this historical novel has sparked great controversy for two reasons. First, Africans are portrayed as utterly evil, perverted and violent; and second, Ouologuem was accused of plagiarizing from numerous sources, among them Graham Green's *It's a battlefield* (London: Heinemann, 1934), André Schwarz-Bart's *Le dernier des justes* (Paris: Editions du Seuil, 1959), and Aimé Césaire's *Cahier d'un retour ay pays natal* (Paris: Bordas, 1947). In an excellent article by Eric Sellin, 'The unknown voice of Yambo Ouologuem', *Yale French Studies* (no. 53 (1976), p. 137-62), Sellin sheds light on the controversey and states that the African sensibility of oral tradition, which adopts and even copies works of art, makes the charge of plagiarism irrelevant.

611 **Les boutures du soleil: poèmes.** (The buds of the sun: poems.)
Hamadoun Ibrahima Issébéré. Paris: Editions Saint-Germain-des-Prés; Agence de Coopération Culturelle et Technique, 1981. 132p.

Recipient of the 1978 Prix Littéraire de l'Agence de Coopération Culturelle et Technique, this collection of poems is notable for its return to ancient Dogon legends and philosophy. The anguished poet evokes the hero of the past resisting colonization, and hopes to find a better present.

612 **Chronique d'une journée de répression.** (Chronicle of a day of repression.)
Moussa Konaté. Paris: L'Harmattan, 1988. 143p. (Collection Encres Noires, no. 47).

This work of fiction is representative of a trend in Malian fiction dating from the 1980s in which the primary theme is a criticism of the political regime in post-independent Mali. Konaté is a prolific author, including novels such as *Les saisons* (The seasons) (Bamako: Jamana, 1990. 149p.), plays such as *Un appel de nuit* (An appeal of the night) (Carnières-Morlanwelz, Belgium: Editions Lansman, 1995. 44p.), children's books such as *Le chat et les souris, ou, le danger de l'ignorance* (The cat and the mouse, or, the danger of ignorance) (Ouagadougou: Imprimerie Nationale, 1994. 17p.), and political essays such as *Mali, ils ont assassiné l'espoir* (Mali, they have assassinated hope) (Paris: L'Harmattan, 1990. 143p.). Other novelists writing of this same theme of repression include: Mandé Alpha Diarra, author of *Sahel! Sanglante sécheresse* (Sahel! Bloody dryness) (Paris: Présence Africaine, 1981. 170p.), Massa Makan Diabaté, author of *Le boucher de Kouta* (The butcher of Kouta) (Paris: Hatier, 1982. 158p.), and Nagognimé Urbain Dembele, author of *La saga des fous* (The saga of the crazy people) (Bamako: Jamana, 1991. 133p.).

613   **Comme une piqûre de guêpe.** (Like the sting of a wasp.)
       Massa M. Diabaté.   Paris: Présence Africaine, 1980. 159p.

Massa Makan Diabaté, nephew of the renowned griot Kèlè Monson Diabaté, continued the griot tradition by writing more than a dozen major works, many of them based on Malinké oral traditions. They include *Comme une piqûre de guêpe*, a story about circumcision rites among the Mandingo, and winner of the Prix de la Fondation Senghor in 1987; *Kala Jata* (Bamako: Editions Populaires, 1970. 95p.) and *L'aigle et l'épervier, ou, la geste de Sunjata* (The eagle and the sparrow-hawk, or the epic of Sunjata) (Paris: Oswald, 1975. 90p.) – both titles tell the epic story of Sunjata; *Janjon et autres chants populaires du Mali* (Janjon and other popular songs from Mali) (q.v.); and a humorous trilogy of novels about the imaginary town of Kouta, *Le lieutenant de Kouta* (The lieutenant of Kouta) (Paris: Hatier, 1979. 127p.), *Le coiffeur de Kouta* (The hairdresser of Kouta) (Paris: Hatier, 1980. 160p.), *Le boucher de Kouta* (The butcher of Kouta) (Paris: Hatier, 1982. 158p.). For critical works on Diabaté published in English, see Cheick M. Chérif Keita's 'Fadenya and artistic creation in Mali: Kèlè Monson and Massa Makan Diabaté' in *Research in African Literatures* 21, no. 3 (1990), p. 103-14, 'Jaliya in the modern world: a tribute to Banzoumana Sissoko and Massa Makan Diabaté' in *Ufahamu* (vol. 17, no. 1 (1988), p. 57-68) as well as Peter van Lent's 'Initiation rites as literary motif in the fiction of Massa Diabaté and other Francophone writers' in *Commentaries on a creative encounter* (New York: African-American Institute, 1988, p. 39-51). Keita's in-depth look at Diabaté was recently published as *Massa Makan Diabaté: un griot mandingue à la rencontre de l'écriture* (Massa Makan Diabaté: a Mandingo griot meets writing) (Paris: L'Harmattan, 1995. 152p.). Mamadou Bani Diallo's doctoral thesis 'L'univers littéraire de Massa Makan Diabaté' (The literary universe of Massa Makan Diabaté) (Lille, France: Université Charles de Gaulle Lille III, 1991) is available in microfiche and his chapter, 'L'histoire de Soundiata et ses différents traitements dans la littérature d'inspiration orale chez Massa Makan Diabaté' (The history of Soundiata and its different treatments in the orally inspired literature of Massa Makan Diabaté) was published as pages 13-22 of *Littératures africaines et histoire* (Paris: Nouvelles du Sud, 1991).

614   **Concours de la meilleure nouvelle en langue française: (édition 1993).** (Competition for the best short story in the French language: 1993 edition.)
       Direction Régionale de la Jeunesse, des Sports, des Arts et de la Culture du District de Bamako.   Bamako: Jamana, 1994. 77p.

Competition results from 1993 and 1991 were published. The 1993 publication includes stories by Klessigué Sanogo, Tangara Bafily called 'Djelika', Tinzanga Koné, and Ousmane Diarra. The 1991 competition results published under the same title (Bamako: Jamana, 1992. 64p.) include stories by Sindiak (i.e., Mahamadou Sintédia Diakité) and Mamadou Somé Coulibaly.

615 **Dictionnaire des oeuvres littéraires africaines de langue française.**
(Dictionary of African literary works in the French language.)
Pius Ngandu Nkashama. Ivry-sur-Seine, France: Editions Nouvelles
du Sud, 1994. 745p.

Although there are serious faults with this recent dictionary, it is still the most
complete reference source available on Malian literature. The work is divided into
three categories: novels, poetry, and theatre. Unfortunately, the indexes, which refer to
one of the three sections and fail to give page numbers, are not to be trusted. By
scanning the author index, the reader finds listings under 41 Malian authors and their
respective 88 works. However, the book actually contains entries for only 26 Malian
authors and their 50 works. The author supplies a brief summary of each work. The
Malians actually included are: Amadou Oumar Ba, Amadou Hampaté Bâ, Seydou
Badian, Siriman Cissoko, Pascal Baba Coulibaly, Nagognimé Urbain Dembele, Sidiki
Dembele, Massa Makan Diabaté, Yoro Diakité, Mande-Alpha Diarra, Mamadou
Lamine Diawara, Doumbi-Fakoly, Hamadoun Ibrahima Issébéré, Alkaly Kaba, Diama
Kaba, Sounkalo Modibo Keita, Moussa Konaté, Sory Konaké, Ibrahima Ly, Ibrahima
Mamadou Ouane, Yambo Ouologuem, Fily-Dabo Sissoko, Mamadou Soukouna,
Ismaïla Samba Traoré, Issa Baba Traoré, and Seydou Traoré.

616 **Dictionnaire des oeuvres littéraires négro-africaines de langue
française des origines à 1978.** (Dictionary of Black African literary
works in the French language from the earliest times to 1978.)
Under the direction of Ambrose Kom. Sherbrooke, Canada: Editions
Naaman; Paris: Agence de Coopération Culturelle et Technique, 1983.
671p. (Collection 'Dictionnaires', no. 1).

By browsing through the entire alphabetical index of authors, the reader can ascertain
that this dictionary contains entries for the following thirteen important Malian literary
authors: Amadou Hampaté Bâ's *L'étrange destin de Wangrin*; Seydou Badian's *La
mort de Chaka*; *Noces sacrées*; *Le sang des masques*; *Sous l'orage*; Siriman Cissoko's
Ressac de nous-mêmes (Undertow of ourselves); Sidiky Dembele's *Inutiles* (Useless);
Massa Makan Diabaté's *L'aigle et l'épervier ou la geste de Sunjata*; *Janjon et autres
chants populaires du Mali*; *Kala Jata*; *Si le feu s'éteignait*; *Une si belle leçon de
patience*; Yoro Diakité's *Une main amie* (A friendly hand); Mamadou Lamine
Diawara's *Les élucubrations sauvages* (The savage lucubrations); Alkaly Kaba's
Contes de l'Afrique noire; *Les hommes du bakchich*; *Mourir pour vivre*; *Walanda*;
Sory Konaké's *Le grand destin de Soundjata*; Ibrahima Mamadou Ouane's *Le collier
de coquillages* (The necklace of shells); *Drame de Déguembéré* (Drama of
Déguembéré); *Fadimâtâ, la princesse du désert* (Fadimâtâ, the princess of the desert);
Yambo Ouologuem's *Le devoir de violence*; Fily-Dabo Sissoko's *Crayons et
portraits*; *Poèmes de l'Afrique noire*; *Feux de brousse*; *Harmakhis*; *Fleurs et
chardons*; *La savane rouge*; and Seydou Traoré's *Vingt-cinq ans d'escalier ou la vie
d'un planton* (Twenty-five years of steps, or the life of an orderly).

617 **Domestiquer le rêve: poèmes.** (To domesticate the dream: poems.)
Abdoulaye Ascofaré. Bamako: Editions Populaires, 1976. 78p.

In this single collection of poems, Ascofaré represents both themes of post-
independent Mali: the disillusioned poet and the poet of love.

618 **Duel dans les falaises: contes et récits du terroir.** (Duel in the cliffs: tales and stories from the soil.)
Falaba Issa Traoré. Abidjan: Nouvelles Editions Africaines, 1987. 2nd ed. 176p.

First published under the title *Contes et récits du terroir* (Bamako: Editions Populaires, 1970. 223p.). Traoré won the 1987 Sankofa prize at Fespaco for his film based on the title story, here called 'Kiri Kara Wattita'. The protagonists are virtuous people living in difficult times. His novel *L'ombre du passé* (Shadow of the past) (Bamako: EDIM, 1970[?]. 150p.) in which a young teacher criticizes the colonial administration, won the Grand Prix National des Lettres in 1971. The author also publishes under the name of Issa Traoré and Issa Baba Traoré.

619 **Faces of Islam in African literature.**
Edited by Kenneth W. Harrow. Portsmouth, New Hampshire: Heinemann; London: J. Currey, 1991. 332p. map. bibliog. (Studies in African Literature. New Series).

This is the first volume in English on Sub-Saharan African literature of 'Islamic inspiration' or dealing with Islamic beliefs and cultural practices. Part III on West Africa includes four chapters on Mali, including David Robinson's 'An approach to Islam in West African history' (p. 107-29), Thomas A. Hale's 'Can a single foot follow two paths? Islamic and Songhay belief systems in the Timbuktu chronicles and the epic of Askia Mohammed' (p. 131-40), Gabriel Asfar's 'Amadou Hampâté Bâ and the Islamic dimension of West African oral literature' (p. 141-50), and Denise Asfar's 'Kaïdara: Islam and traditional religion in a West African narrative of initiation' (p. 151-62).

620 **The fortunes of Wangrin.**
Amadou Hampaté Bâ, translated from the French by Aina Pavollini Taylor, with an introduction by Abiola Irele. Ibadan, Nigeria: New Horn Press, 1987. 282p.

In this eloquent, classic work of fiction, Bâ, distinguished scholar of oral tradition, tells the story (or writes the biography) of Wangrin, an interpreter working for the French colonial administration. The fact that Bâ presents the work as a true account of a real person has confused readers since its publication. 'The work seems to propose a new category, if not a new form, of imaginative discourse in Africa' (p. v) as it simultaneously incorporates elements of 'historical discourse . . . realistic fiction . . . and fable' (p. xi). It includes an interesting essay by Irele entitled 'Wangrin: a study in ambiguity' (p. iii-xvi). Winner of the Grand Prix Littéraire de l'Afrique Noire, 1976, it was originally published under the title: *L'étrange destin de Wangrin, ou, les roueries d'un interprète africain* (Paris: Union Générale d'Éditions, 1976). For a list of some of his other important works, see the annotation under *Kaidara* (item no. 743).

621 **God's bits of wood.**
Sembène Ousmane, translated by Francis Price. Oxford, England; Portsmouth, New Hampshire: Heinemann, 1995. 248p. (African Writers Series).

Senegal's leading writer sets this historical novel around the construction of the Dakar–Bamako railway line during the strike of 1947-48. The African workers make a stand for better wages and equal rights while the European bosses fight them with all of their power. This is a reflection of traditional African values colliding with technology. *Les bouts de bois de Dieu* (Paris: A. Dumont, 1960. 381p.) is the original title.

622 **Le grand destin de Soundjata.** (The great destiny of Soundiata.)
     Sory Konaké. Paris: ORTF-DAEC, 1973. 89p.

This historical play about the great Soundjata (Soundiata), founder of the Mali Empire (in the thirteenth century), inspires pride in Mali's past. Winner of the Prix des Auditeurs du Concours Théâtral Interafricain 1971.

623 **Littérature malienne.** (Malian literature.)
     Notre Librairie. Paris: CLEF, 1986. 2nd ed. 251p. bibliog.
     (Littératures Nationales, no. 75-76).

This indispensable book, written primarily by prominent Malian authors, goes beyond 'literature' in the strict sense. It includes essays on oral traditions and published literary works as well as chapters on literacy in Mali and Malian cultural life. The section on Arabic-language writings (p. 101-3) is a rare and helpful find for those who do not read Arabic. The bibliographies cover historical works and travellers' accounts (p. 229-31), social sciences (p. 232-37), and literature (p. 238-42). It should be used in conjunction with *Bibliographie commentée des écrivains contemporains* (q.v.) for a nearly complete survey of Malian literature.

624 **Littératures francophones d'Afrique de l'Ouest: anthologie.**
     (Francophone literatures from West Africa: an anthology.)
     Under the direction of Jean-Louis Joubert with the participation of:
     Léopoldo Victor T. Amado, Agbéko Amegbleame, Andrée-Marie
     Diagne, Mamadou Bani Diallo, Oumar Drame, Beugré Emieme,
     Amadou Hamidou, Adrien Huannou, Catherine Pacéré. Paris: Agence
     de Coopération Culturelle et Technique; Nathan, 1994. 255p.

In this anthology aimed at teachers and students of African secondary and higher education, Mali is covered on pages 128-57. In addition to the two-page introduction on Malian literature, there are also one-to-two-page excerpts (including a brief biography) from the representative works of Fily Dabo Sissoko, Hamadoun Ibrahima Issébéré, Amadou Hampâté Bâ, Seydou Badian, Ibrahima Ly, Massa Makan Diabaté, Aoua Kéita, Mandé-Alpha Diarra, Moussa Konaté, Nagognimé Urbain Dembélé, M'Bamakan Souckɔ, Alkaly Kaba, and Gaoussou Diawara. A similar work, Jacques Chevrier's *Littérature africaine: histoire et grands thèmes* (African literature: history and great themes) (Paris: Hatier, 1990) covers Malians Seydou Badian, Massa Makan Diabaté, Amadou Hampâté Bâ, Yambo Ouologuem, and Abdou Traoré.

625 **Moktar Cissé: roman.** (Moktar Cissé: a novel.)
     R. A. Costins. Abidjan: CEDA, 1988-89. 2 vols. (CEDA Fiction).

Costins, a Frenchman working in French West Africa for more than twenty-five years, wrote this historical novel about the Mali Empire of the fourteenth century in which the protagonist is a young Soninke (Sarakole) prince. Costins's real name was Raoul Cosson. For a list of novels written primarily by non-Malians, primarily of the colonial era, see P. J. Imperato's *Historical dictionary of Mali* (item no. 7, p. 303).

626 **Mon coeur est un volcan.** (My heart is a volcano.)
[Mamadou] Gologo. Moscow: Editions en Langues Etrangères,
1961[?]. 27p.
Gologo was the first Malian to write against colonization. The poems in this revolutionary collection cry out for political independence.

627 **Narrating the Mande: West African identity production and the Mande Francophone novel.**
James Reed McGuire. PhD thesis, Northwestern University,
Evanston, Illinois, 1994. 2 vols. bibliog. (Available from University
Microfilms International, Ann Arbor, Michigan, order no. 9433888).
McGuire's thesis concerns the African concept of nationhood and how that concept defines the West African francophone novel. Western literary scholarship often looks along narrow political borders instead of broadly, by regions, to define literary identity. McGuire compares the oral Sunjata epic with two written novels, (Malian) Massa Makan Diabaté's *Le boucher de Kouta* and (Ivoirian) Ahmadou Kourouma's *Monnè, outrages et défis*, to demonstrate their fluidity.

628 **Nègres, qu'avez-vous fait?: tragédie en 3 actes.** (Negroes, what have you done?: tragedy in 3 acts.)
Alkaly Kaba. Bamako: Editions Populaires, 1972. 70p.
Winner of the Grand Prix du Mali, this first play by Kaba concerns all Africans, including Africans in the diaspora. The protagonists, two African-American men living in Harlem, are victims of racism. They exile themselves to Guinea-Bissau, then to Conakry, always in pursuit of a better life. What have Blacks done to improve their lives? Other works by Kaba include *Les hommes du bakchich* (Men of baksheesh) (co-authored with Diama Kaba) (Paris: ORTF-DAEC, 1973. 154p.); *Walanda = La leçon: récit* (The lesson) (Paris: Editions Saint-Germain-des-Prés, 1976. 76p.); *Mourir pour vivre* (To die in order to live) (Paris: Editions Saint-Germain-des-Prés, 1976. 85p.); and *Contes de l'Afrique noire* (Tales of Black Africa) (Ottawa: Naaman, 1973. 74p.)

629 **A new reader's guide to African literature.**
Edited by Hans M. Zell, Carol Bundy, Virginia Coulon. New York:
Africana Publishing Co., 1983. 2nd competely rev. and expanded ed. 553p.
In this survey of African literature, the literature of Mali (p. 254-59) includes English-language summaries as well as occasional brief excerpts of book reviews (in English or French) of 53 works by 22 authors. Also included are informative biographical sketches of Massa Makan Diabaté (p. 373-75), Seydou Badian (p. 359-60), and Yambo Ouologuem (p. 455-57).

630 **Nouvelles d'ici.** (Short stories from here.)
Collectif. Bamako: Jamana, 1995. 107p.
Contains twelve short stories, including two which have won prizes, by promising young Malian authors Mamadou Somé Coulibaly, Diop Kady Guissé, Hamidou Berthé, M'Bamakan Soucko Bathily, and Thierno Ahmed Thiam. The Collectif also published *Poèmes d'ici* (Poems from here) (Bamako: Jamana, 1995. 93p.) which contains poems by Kansoumbaly Fofana, Lassana Ballo, Sawadogo Songré Etienne,

Literature

Mamadou Dia, and Hamidou Berthé. Another publication written by children from Bamako upon the occasion of an annual writing and drawing contest from 1990 to 1993 is *A l'écoute des enfants* (Listening to children) (Bamako: Editions La Ruche à Livres, 1995. 85p.). The stories are written by children in the ninth year of school and the illustrations are from children in their sixth year.

631 **Le personnage de l'ancien dans le roman sénégalais et malien de l'époque coloniale.** (The character of the ancient one in the Sengalese and Malian novel of the colonial era.)
Béatrice Grosskreutz. Frankfurt, Germany: Verlag für Interkulturelle Kommunikation, 1993. 255p. bibliog. (Studien zu den Frankophonen Literaturen Ausserhalb Europas, Band 3).
The author puts into its socio-economic context the role of the venerable elder in Senegalese and Malian colonial novels. The eight novels used as examples include two from Mali: *Kaïdara*, by Amadou Hampaté Bâ and *Sous l'orage*, by Seydou Badian. The six Senegalese authors are Ahmadou Mapaté Diagne, Bakary Diallo, Ousmane Socé, Abdoulaye Sadji, Cheikh Hamidou Kane, and Sembène Ousmane.

632 **Poèmes de l'Afrique noire: Feux de brousse, Harmakhis, Fleurs et chardons).** (Poems from Black Africa: Brush fires, Harmakhis, Flowers and thistles.)
Fily Dabo Sissoko. Paris: Debresse-Poésie, 1963. 170p.
Sissoko was the only Malian poet from the precolonial era. His first collection, *Harmakhis*, first published in 1955 (Paris: Editions de la Tour du Guet) and here reprinted along with two of his other collections, refers to the Great Sphinx of Giza, symbol of precolonial Africa. He has published numerous other collections of poetry and an autobiographical novel, *La savane rouge* (The red savannah) (Paris: Les Presses Universelles, 1962. 139p.), as well as many essays on subjects ranging from folklore to language to socialism in Africa.

633 **Recueil de littérature manding.** (Anthology of Manding literature.)
Agence de Coopération Culturelle et Technique. Paris: Agence de Coopération Culturelle et Technique, 1980. 239p.
The collection includes poems in Mandingo with parallel French translations.

634 **Le roman et l'évolution sociale au Mali.** (The novel and social evolution in Mali.)
Cheickh Mahamadou Cherif Keïta. PhD thesis, University of Georgia, 1984. 182p. bibliog. (Available from University Microfilms International, Ann Arbor, Michigan, order no. 8504610).
Keïta uses sixteen novels by eleven Malian authors to demonstrate the social evolution of Mali. He explains that the role of the griot is to bring about social cohesion, while conversely, the role of the novelist is to cast doubt and stir controversy. The novelists covered are Amadou Hampaté Bâ, Amadou Oumar Bâ, Seydou Badian, Sidiki Dembélé, Massa Makan Diabaté, Mande-Alpha Diarra, Mamadou Gogolo, Moussa Konaté, Ibrahima Ly, Yambo Ouologuem, and Ismaïla Samba Traoré. An English-language summary is included (p. ii-iv).

635 **Les sanglots du Songhoy: recueil de nouvelles.** (The sobs of Songhoy: collection of short stories.)
Abdoul Traoré. Bamako: Jamana, 1995. 102p.

A surgeon in Bamako, Traoré is also the co-founder of the Jamana Cooperative. In the eight stories the reader can see great suffering as well as hope for the future. Other recent literary works not covered elsewhere in this section include Doumbi-Fakoly's *Certificat de contrôle anti-SIDA* (a novel) (Anti-AIDS certificate of authority) (Paris: Publisud, 1988. 128p.); Mahamadou Somé Coulibaly's *Les murmures du vent* (The murmurs of the wind) (Bamako: Jamana, 1989. 62p.); Kassim Dembélé's *Pays de kaolin* (Country of clay) (Bamako: Editions-Imprimeries du Mali, 1982[?]. 31p.); Madjoun Traore's *Au-delà de la peur: une aube nouvelle* (Beyond fear: a new dawn) (Bamako: M. Traore, 1994. 90p.); and Mamadou Kani Konaté's *Fresques intérieures: recueil de poèmes* (Interior frescoes: collection of poems) (Bamako: Jamana, 1995. 58p.).

636 **Sanglots et dédains: recueil de poèmes.** (Sobs and disdain: collection of poems.)
Albakaye Ousmane Kounta. Bamako: Jamana, 1995. 135p.

Although Kounta has written tales such as *Contes de Tombouctou et du Macina* (Paris: L'Harmattan, 1987-89. 2 vols) (q.v.) and children's stories such as *Corbeille de paroles: poèmes pour enfants* (Basket of words: poems for children) (Bamako: Jamana, 1996. 24p.), he is known primarily as a poet. This recent collection consists of 'Fleurs de nénuphar', 'Que revienne la rosée sur les oasis oubliées', and 'Juillet-Juillet', of which the second title was first separately published in Bamako by Editions Populaires in 1976. The poem 'Le soir' is lacking in the 1995 anthology.

637 **Segu: a novel.**
Maryse Condé, translated from the French by Barbara Bray. New York: Viking, 1987. 499p. maps.

In this best-selling novel by Guadeloupian author Condé, the plot concerns the history of a Malian family from the precolonial Kingdom of Segu. Volume 2 has been translated as *Children of Segu* (New York: Viking, 1989. 429p.). The work was originally published in French as: *Ségou* (Paris: R. Laffont, 1984. 2 vols).

638 **Songs of lonely river: (poems).**
Moussa Kanoute. Bamako: Jamana, 1989. 24p.

Kanoute, a native of Bamako and a French teacher, wrote this unique collection of poems in English. His French poems, *Terres australes* (Southern lands) ([n.p.]: [n.p.], 1985) is a denunciation of apartheid, and won the Grand Prix des Lettres du Mali in 1984. Also on the same subject, *Apartheid: poèmes* (Apartheid: poems) (Bamako: Jamana, 1989. 40p.) contains poems by fifteen Malian poets.

639 **Sous l'orage: (Kany) roman.** (Caught in the storm: a novel.)
Seydou Badian. Paris: Présence Africaine, 1963. 152p.

Physician Seydou Badian Kouyaté was deported after the military coup of 1968, but returned to Mali in 1991. In 1997, he was a candidate for President of Mali. In his literary works, he writes of the struggle between tradition and modernity. Kany's traditional father wants her to marry an old, rich merchant, while she is in love with a

Literature

young man, Samou. An English translation by Marie-Thérèse Noiset is expected to be published in early 1998 as: *Caught in the storm* (Colorado Springs, Colorado: Three Continents Press, 1998. 120p.). His other great works, *Le sang des masques* (Blood of the masks) (Paris: R. Laffont, 1976. 250p.) and *Noces sacrées* (Sacred weddings) (Paris: Présence Africaine, 1977. 149p.) also incorporate the theme of tradition versus modernity. Reprinted with *La mort de Chaka* (Paris: Présence Africaine, 1972. 253p.) which is based on Thomas Mofolo's *Chaka*, the story of the founder of the Zulu nation, and was published in translation as *The death of Chaka* (Nairobi: Oxford University Press, 1968. 47p.). For an analysis of the author's works, see S. M. Battestini's *Seydou Badian: écrivain malien* (Seydou Badian: Malian writer) (Paris: F. Nathan, 1968. 63p.).

640 **Toiles d'araignées.** (Spiders' webs.)
Ibrahima Ly. Paris: L'Harmattan, 1982. 344p. (Collection Encres Noires, no. 16).

In his book which was the winner of the Prix de la Fondation Léopold Sédar Senghor in 1985, Ly writes about a young woman who is imprisoned and tortured for refusing to marry the man her parents have chosen for her. Ly spent four years in Malian jails for actively opposing the government and then exiled himself to Dakar, Senegal. For more information, see his *Paroles pour un continent* (Words for a continent) (Paris: L'Harmattan, 1990. 245p.) which contains several excerpts from his unpublished works, published literary criticism of his works (p. 53-115), a biography (p. 117-62), and the tributes to Ly upon his death (p. 163-234).

641 **Who's who in African literature: biographies, works, commentaries.**
Janheinz Jahn, Ulla Schild, Almut Nordmann. Tübingen, Germany: Horst Erdmann, 1972. 406p. bibliog.

Although this basic reference source is now twenty-five years old, it still contains valuable one-page bio-bibliographies of nine Malian authors: Amadou Hampaté Bâ, Seydou Badian, Siriman Cissoko, Sidiki Dembele, Massa Makan Diabaté, Mamadou Gologo, Ibrahima-Mamadou Ouane, Yambo Ouologuem (with a portrait on plate VI), and Fily Dabo Sissoko.

The Arts

Visual arts

General

642 African art of the Dogon: the myths of the cliff dwellers.
Jean Laude. New York: Brooklyn Museum in association with the
Viking Press, 1973. 60, 71p. bibliog.
The 103 Dogon objects in this exhibition and catalogue were collected by Lester
Wunderman in the 1960s and early 1970s. Laude's essay, 'The myths of the cliff
dwellers', first discusses historical background, style and attribution, then the various
carving techniques (i.e., modelling in clay, ironwork, wood carving, and the
blacksmith), and classifies Dogon art into seventeen themes (e.g., figures with raised
arms, stools with caryatids, women with children, etc.) which are the organizing
principle of the actual black-and-white catalogue of objects.

643 African Arts.
Los Angeles: African Studies Center of the University of California,
1967- . quarterly.
In this important journal published by the African Studies Center of the University of
California, the reader will often find well-illustrated articles of interest. The August
1988 issue (vol. 21, no. 4) is entirely devoted to Dogon art and includes nine articles
by important art scholars (i.e., Kate Ezra, R. M. A. Bedaux, Denise Paulme, Bernard
de Grunne, Dominique Zahan, Walter E. A. van Beek, Paul J. Lane, and Allen F.
Roberts).

644 **Antilopes du soleil: arts et rites agraires d'Afrique noire.**
(Antelopes of the sun: arts and agrarian rites of Black Africa.)
Dominique Zahan. Vienna: A. Schendl, 1980. 195p., 101p. of plates.
maps. bibliog.

The Bambara *Tyi Wara* initiatory society concerns itself with the knowledge of crops
and traditional agricultural techniques. This in-depth monumental study is followed by
101 plates containing line-drawings of 538 antelope head-dresses used in ritual
ceremonies.

645 **L'art africain contemporain: guide = Contemporary African art:
guide.**
Nicole Guez. Paris: Association Afrique en Créations, 1996. 2nd ed.
421p.

Mali is covered on pages 138-43 of this recently updated African art directory. The
names, addresses and telephone numbers are given for forty-six contemporary artists,
three artists living abroad (in France and Italy), eight cultural institutions, five
associations, two cooperatives, five galleries, three foreign cultural centres, and one
exhibition hall.

646 **The Arts of Africa: an annotated bibliography.**
Compiled by Janet L. Stanley. Atlanta, Georgia: African Studies
Association, 1989- . 5 vols. (to date).

This is an outstanding, comprehensive bibliography of recent books, chapters of
books, and periodical articles on African art, compiled by the Branch Chief of the
National Museum of African Art in Washington, DC. Chapters are geographically
arranged with coverage beginning in 1986. Each volume also includes a basic list of
books recommended for academic libraries developing their collections on African art.
It also contains four indexes, including a detailed subject index, which makes finding
the citations on Mali more convenient.

647 **Coiffures traditionnelles et modernes au Mali = Traditional and
modern hairstyles of Mali = Traditionelle und moderne Frisuren in
Mali.**
Text and photos by Mamadou Koné. Bamako: Editions Populaires du
Mali, 197-[?]. 160p. map.

All of the major ethnic groups are represented in this book of Malian traditional and
modern hairstyles for women and girls. The illustrations are in black and white and all
captions are in French, English and German. There is no explanation given for why
the front and back endpapers consist of a tourist map of Mali (scale 1:2,500,000),
including ten suggested itineraries for travel within Mali.

648 **Dogon: exposition placée sous le haut patronage du Ministre de la Coopération, Paris, Musée Dapper, 26 octobre 1994 – 13 mars 1995.** (Dogon: exposition placed under the high patronage of the Ministry of Cooperation, Paris, Musée Dapper, 26 October 1994 – 13 March 1995.)
Musée Dapper (Paris, France). Paris: Musée Dapper, 1994. 285p. bibliog.
In this large recent exhibition catalogue are included six essays on Dogon art by Jean-Louis Paudrat, Christiane Falgayrettes-Leveau, Jean Laude, Jacky Bouju and Michel Leveau. Also included are an interesting chart of carbon dating of twenty-two objects, four maps, respectively of Dogon dialects, Dogon ethnic groups and their neighbours, pre-Dogon groups, and the major Dogon villages, as well as an excellent bibliography on Dogon art and culture (p. 265-83).

649 **Dogon masks: a structural study of form and meaning.**
Barbara DeMott. Ann Arbor, Michigan: UMI Research Press, 1982. 202p. map. bibliog. (Studies in the Fine Arts. Iconography, no. 4).
The symbolism of Dogon masked dances of the Awa society is the topic of this important study. Through the use of symbolism, the Dogon express the duality of nature (male) and culture (female). There are forty-six black-and-white illustrations which include photographs or line-drawings of twenty-five masks. For a representative sampling of Mali's masks (Dogon, Bambara, Malinké, Marka, Bozo and Manianka), see E. A. Dagan's *The spirit's image: the African masking tradition: evolving continuity* (Quebec: Galerie Amrad African Art, 1992 (p. 146-58)).

650 **A human ideal in African art: Bamana figurative sculpture.**
Kate Ezra. Washington, DC: Published for the National Museum of African Art by the Smithsonian Institution Press, 1986. 48p. map. bibliog.
This exhibition catalogue of Bambara sculpture includes important text and forty-five black-and-white photographs. The work that first introduced Bambara sculpture to the Western general public is *Bambara sculpture from the Western Sudan* (New York: Museum of Primitive Art, 1960. 64p.). See also Ezra's dissertation 'Figure sculptures of the Bamana of Mali' (Evanston, Illinois: Northwestern University, 1983. 265p.).

651 **Die Kunst der Dogon: Museum Rietberg, Zürich.** (Art of the Dogon: Museum Rietberg, Zurich.)
Edited by Lorenz Homberger, with contributions by Kate Ezra, Alain Gallay, Eric Huysecom, Anne Mayor. Zurich: Museum Rietberg, 1995. 136p. map. bibliog.
The catalogue of an exhibition at the Museum Rietberg, 7 May to 3 September 1995. The first essay, 'Zur Kunst der Dogon' (p. 9-18), by Ezra, briefly describes the cosmology and religion of the Dogon, Dogon sculpture and masks, and the history of Dogon art. The second essay, 'Archéologie, histoire et traditions orales: trois clés pour découvrir le passé dogon' (p. 19-43), by Gallay, Huysecom and Mayor, takes a chronological approach to the archaeology of the Dogons, from prehistory to modern times. The large colour illustrations include 109 objects ranging from the 10th century

to the early 20th century, and consist primarily of wooden sculptures and masks as well as a few iron sculptures and yellow metal rings made of a brass, bronze, and zinc alloy. See also Ezra's earlier work, *Art of the Dogon: selections from the Lester Wunderman collection* (New York: Metropolitan Museum of Art, 1988. 116p.).

652 **The making of Bamana sculpture: creativity and gender.**
Sarah C. Brett-Smith. Cambridge, England; New York: Cambridge University Press, 1994. 352p. maps. bibliog. (RES Monographs in Anthropology and Aesthetics).

This book, based on five years of fieldwork in Mali, studies the relationship between the sculptural process and gender in Bamana (Bambara) society. In choosing an artist for a commission of a ritual object, the Bamana consider the sculptor's personal life and moral character as well as his aesthetic skill. Creation is perceived as 'female' in character, and often exacts a violent toll on the artist. In Chapter 6, the author suggests that the process of creating ritual objects is equivalent to sexual intercourse and childbirth. Frequent quotations from her four informants (given in English in the text and in the original Bamana or Malinke in the notes) help put the data into their proper context.

653 **Mali.**
Paris: Agence de Coopération Culturelle et Technique; Dessain et Tolra, 1979, ©1977. 112p. map. (L'Artisanat Créateur).

The primary focus of this book is the variety of handicrafts made in Mali. The principal artistic centres are identified (p. 35-38). The milieu, history, economy, social life, religion, and culture are discussed for each of Mali's major ethnic groups (Bambara, Malinké Dogon, Sarakolé (Soninké), Touareg, Peul, Sénufo, Songhaï (Songhay), Bobo, Dioula, Maure, Toucouleur). The particular handicrafts for each ethnic group are described and illustrated (e.g., the huge gold earrings of Peul women).

654 **Le masque et la parole: analyse d'un masque 'auditif' de la société initiatique du Komo Minyanka, Mali.** (The mask and the word: analysis of a 'hearing' mask from the Komo Minianka initiation society, Mali.)
Philippe Jespers. In: *Objets-signes d'Afrique.* Texts gathered by Luc de Heusch on the occasion of the exhibition 'Trésors cachés du Musée de Tervuren'. Contributions by V. Baeke (et al.). Tervuren, Belgium: Musée Royal de l'Afrique Centrale, 1995, p. 37-56. map. bibliog. (Annales. Sciences Humaines, vol. 145).

This is a study of Minianka secret initiatory societies and their masks.

655 **Sculpture of the Tellem and the Dogon.**
Text by Jacques Damase, translated by Tony White. New York: Pierre Matisse Gallery, 1960. 32p.

Black-and-white exhibition catalogue, containing brief descriptions of sixty-five Dogon and Tellem sculptures and twenty-three illustrations.

656 **Secret sculptures of Komo: art and power in Bamana (Bambara) initiation associations.**
Patrick R. McNaughton. Philadelphia, Pennsylvania: Institute for the Study of Human Issues, 1979. 55p. map. bibliog. (Working Papers in the Traditional Arts, no. 4).

The author focused his research on the Bambara regions immediately east and west of the Niger, between Bamako and Bougouni. The first part describes Bamana initiation associations in general, and the secretive and powerful Komo association in particular. The second part is a discussion of Komo sculpture, masks and aesthetics. The meanings and functions of the masks are examined from the point of view of age, spirit companions, symbolism, and dance/theatre components.

657 **Seydou Keita.**
Introduction by Youssouf Cissé. Paris: Centre National de la Photographie, 1995. 1 vol. (unpaged). (Photo-Poche, no. 63).

Photographer Seydou Keita took striking black-and-white portraits of the men and women of Bamako from 1945 until his retirement in 1977. He carefully arranged their traditional and Western attire with elegance and simplicity. This volume contains sixty-four portraits of the approximate size of 10 × 15 cm. For seventeen larger-sized portraits (most of them are also contained in this small 1995 publication), see *Seydou Keita* (Paris: Fondation Cartier pour l'Art Contemporaine, 1994). Twelve of the portraits are also found in the Autumn 1995 issue of *African Arts* (p. 90-95).

658 **Statuaire Dogon. (Dogon statuary.)**
Hélène Leloup, William Rubin, Richard Serra, Georg Baselitz, with photographs by Roger Asselberghs, Jerry L. Thompson. Strasbourg, France: D. Amez, 1994. 635p. maps. bibliog. (Art & Ethnologie).

In this lavishly illustrated, massive book on Dogon statuary, Hélène Leloup, expert on Dogon art, analyses the origin and meaning of Dogon statues. She identifies eleven Dogon statuary styles which are all located on a single linguistic map of Mali (p. 116-17), described in her text and illustrated with colour plates. The 140 Dogon statues range in age from the tenth century (Tellem) to the nineteenth century. The excellent bibliography (p. 607-23) ranges far beyond art and ethnology. See also a recent exhibition catalogue with a preface by Leloup, *Dege: l'héritage dogon* (Nantes, France: Chapelle de l'Oratoire, 1995. 64p.).

Metalwork

659 **The artfulness of M'Fa Jigi: an interview with Nyamaton Diarra.**
Translated, edited and with an introduction by Sarah Brett-Smith, recorded and conducted by Adama Mara. Madison, Wisconsin: African Studies Program, University of Wisconsin-Madison, 1996. 149p. map. bibliog.

Bamana (Bambara) informant Nyamaton Diarra was interviewed about the ancient 'semi-mythical 'father of blacksmiths', M'Fa Jigi' (p. 1), a powerful artist tied to traditional Bamana religious institutions such as the secret Komo society. The author explores Bamana and Malinke artistic creativity. The interview is transcribed in Bamana and English.

660 **Les arts des métaux en Afrique noire.** (Metal arts of Black Africa.)
Laure Meyer. Saint-Maur, France: Sepia, 1997. 175p. map. bibliog.

Copper has been mined in Nioro du Sahel (northwest Mali) since the fourteenth century. Chapter 2 concerns ancient copper objects from West Africa, and Mali is featured on pages 36-42. Many of the colour photographs are enlarged so that the reader can see in some detail the surface created by the artist. The beautiful ornament featured on its dust jacket and on page 37 is also described in detail (in English and French) in an article by Timothy F. Garrard, 'Un ornement royal en bronze de l'Empire du Mali = A royal bronze ornament from the Mali Empire', in *Art tribal* (1987, no. 1, p. 3-9). Other publications of interest include two exhibition catalogues featuring Malian metal art objects: *Red gold: copper arts of Africa* (South Hadley, Massachusetts: Mount Holyoke College Art Museum, 1984. 56p.) which contains seventeen Malian objects (sculptures, jewellery and vessels) and *The art of metal in Africa* (New York: African-American Institute, 1982. 159p.) which features a chapter by Jack D. Flam, entitled 'Signs and symbols in traditional metal art of the Western Sudan' (p. 19-30), which focuses on the Dogon and Bambara.

661 **Gold aus Mali.** (Gold from Mali.)
Thomas Schunk, with a report by Barbara Armbruster. Frankfurt am Main, Germany: Museum für Völkerkunde, 1991. 225p. map. bibliog. (Roter Faden zur Ausstellung, no. 18).

The authors give the history of the gold trade in the Sahara and describe the process of goldmining, goldworking and gold jewellery-making in Mali. The illustrations include gold earrings, goldworking tools and numerous photographs of artists in the various stages of work.

662 **The Mande blacksmiths: knowledge, power, and art in West Africa.**
Patrick R. McNaughton. Bloomington, Indiana: Indiana University Press, 1988. 241p. maps. bibliog. (Traditional Arts of Africa).

The Mande blacksmith holds a special place among the castes of Mali. His artistic abilities and creations give him the power to act as sorcerer, healer and mediator, and result in his being greatly feared by Mande society. Amply illustrated with eighty-five photographs of the artist's forge, his tools and the carved or forged objects created. The author's dissertation from Yale University (1977) is entitled: 'The Bamana blacksmiths: a study of sculptors and their art'.

Bogolanfini, or painted mud cloth

663 **Bogolan et arts graphiques du Mali.** (Bogolan and graphic arts of Mali.)
Commissioners of the exhibition, Fallo Baba Keita, Lucette Albaret.
Paris: ADEIAO, Musée National des Arts Africains et Océaniens, 1990. 64p. map. (Cahier de l'ADEIAO, no. 9).

Bogolanfini, or Malian mud cloth painting, has traditionally been performed by rural women from the Bambara, Malinke, Senufo, Bobo and Dogon ethnic groups. The Bogolan Kasobane Group, in Bamako, uses traditional techniques but has brought changes to the medium by opening it to male painters and by painting contemporary figurative subjects on the cloth. The artists featured in this 1990 Paris exhibition are Kandioura Coulibaly, Fallo Baba Keita, Boubacar Doumbia, Souleymane Goro, Néné Thiam, and Kélétigui Dembélé.

664 **Nakunte Diarra, bògòlanfini artist of the Beledougou.**
Tavy D. Aherne. Bloomington, Indiana: Indiana University Art Museum, 1992. 46p. bibliog.

Published in conjunction with a 1993 exhibition held at the Indiana University Art Museum, this catalogue of the work of Nakunte Diarra illustrates her traditional geometrical bògòlanfiniw (sing.: bògòlanfini) and explains the symbolism of forty-two traditional patterns. See also the journal *African Arts* for a review of the exhibition by P. J. Imperato (vol. 27, no. 2 (April 1994), p. 78-79) as well as a letter from Sarah Brett-Smith (vol. 27, no. 4 (Autumn 1994), p. 16-17, 90) correcting some inaccuracies in Aherne's text.

665 **Pama Sinatoa: Malian mud-cloth paintings.**
Betty LaDuke. In: *Africa through the eyes of women artists.*
Trenton, New Jersey: Africa World Press, 1991, p. 55-64.

Pama Sinatoa, from Djenne, creates non-traditional bogolanfiniw (painted mud cloth) with panoramic scenes from her Moslem heritage, scenes from village subsistence activities such as pounding millet and planting crops, and scenes of Dogon life and ceremonies. In 1981, Sinatoa organized the Djenne Women's Cooperative, through which various craft projects are created and sold. Black-and-white illustrations of several of her cloths are featured.

Architecture

666 **African architecture: evolution and transformation.**
Nnamdi Elleh. New York: McGraw-Hill, 1997. 382p. maps. bibliog.

Elleh uses Ali Mazrui's concept of the triple heritage (indigenous, Western and Islamic influences), and applies it to the architecture of Africa. In the chapter on West Africa, the author reviews the history of Mali's architecture (p. 247-55), summarizes the important written sources such as Tarikh al-Soudan, René Caillié, Félix Dubois, on the history of the mosques at Jenne (Djenné), and also discusses the houses of the Dongon (Dogon) people. Bamako was planned like a late nineteenth-century French city.

667 **Architecture soudanaise: vitalité d'une tradition urbaine et monumentale: Mali, Côte-d'Ivoire, Burkina Faso, Ghana.**
(Sudanese architecture: vitality of an urban and monumental tradition: Mali, Côte-d'Ivoire, Burkina Faso, Ghana.)
Sergio Domian.   Paris: L'Harmattan, 1989. 191p.

The architecture of Mali is covered here throughout the text, for example in individual chapters on Djenné, Mopti, Timbuktu and Gao, as well as those on mosques of the Inland Niger Delta, houses of the Delta, and Bozo architecture.

668 **Djenné: chef d'oeuvre architectural.** (Djenné: architectural masterpiece.)
Pierre Maas, Geert Mommersteeg, with the collaboration of Wolf Schijns, contributions by Arie van Rangelrooy, Wim van Unen, Rik van der Velden and photographs by Rob van Wendel de Joode.
Bamako: Institut des Sciences Humaines, 1992. 224p. maps. bibliog.

This is a comprehensive study of the architecture of the city of Djenne, from the geographical, demographic, historical, and socio-economic points of view. Djenne's architecture differs from that of Timbuktu, which has more of a North African influence, because of the strong influence of the indigenous black population. Part 4 (p. 190-216) concentrates on recent changes in the city and its buildings. The work includes a glossary (p. 220-21) of terms for house plans, 'Soudanese' façade, construction elements, and types of clay in the Sonray (Soninke) dialect of Djenne as well as in French. Well illustrated with black-and-white photographs, dozens of drawings of plans, and two maps.

669 **Drawn from African dwellings.**
Jean-Paul Bourdier, Trinh T. Minh-Ha.   Bloomington, Indiana: Indiana University Press, 1996. 308p. bibliog.

Although research was carried out in six countries, Senegal is the focus for this fine study of traditional West African architecture, social organization and cosmology. Because several of the peoples studied here spill out beyond those borders, much of this text also relates to Mali. The Fulbe (Peul) and Tokolor (Tukulor) are featured in the text and the Soninke (Sarakole) and Mandingo (Manding) are featured in the detailed drawings. See also Bourdier's 'Houses of light', *Mimar* (no. 39 (June 1991), p. 60-67) which is about rural mosques in Senegal and Mali.

670 **Les établissements humains au Mali.** (Human settlements in Mali.)
Gérard Brasseur.   Dakar: IFAN, 1968. 549p. maps. bibliog.
(Mémoires de l'Institut Fondamental d'Afrique Noire, no. 83).

This superb, comprehensive study on human settlements, dwellings and human geography in Mali begins with a general overview of the physical features which shape the country. Habitat (primarily villages) and habitation (dwellings) are analysed generally and within regional variations. Ethnic groups covered are: White nomads (Maure, Touareg), Songhay, Peul, Soninké (Sarakole), Khassonké, Malinké, Foula ('sedentary' Peul), Bambara, Bozo, Senufo, Minianka, Bobo and Dogon. The work contains a vocabulary of terms related to habitat in the language of each ethnic group (p. 544-45), 50 photographs on plates, 100 illustrations and 2 fold-out maps. It also includes an English-language summary (p. 533-36).

671 **Hatumere: Islamic design in West Africa.**
Labelle Prussin. Berkeley, California; Los Angeles; London:
University of California Press, 1986. 306p. maps. bibliog.

This is an interesting study of Islamic architecture in West Africa, arranged by space
(physical, behavioural and conceptual environments) and time (medieval West African
empires, Manding and Fulbe diasporas, and the Asante confederacy). See also
Prussin's important dissertation entitled, 'The architecture of Djenne: African
synthesis and transformation' (Yale University, 1973. 426 leaves).

672 **Spectacular vernacular: the adobe tradition.**
Text by Jean-Louis Bourgeois, photographs by Carolee Pelos,
historical essay by Basil Davidson. New York: Aperture Foundation,
1989. 191p. bibliog.

Mali figures prominently in this book of adobe architecture from the arid parts of the
world. Basil Davidson's introduction covers the cultural history of Islam in the
African Sahel as well as in Southwest Asia. Although references to Mali occur
throughout the book (see the index), Chapter 11, on the history of Djenné's mosques,
is notable because it gives credit for the architecture to Africans, not Frenchmen.
Many dramatic colour photographs of the architecture and people of Mali are included
as is a bibliography which contains oral sources (interviews conducted in 1983-84 in
Djenné) and written sources. See also Bourgeois' article, 'The history of the great
mosques of Djenné', in *African Arts* (vol. 20, no. 3 (May 1987), p. 54-63, 90-92).

673 **Villages perchés des Dogon du Mali: habitat, espace et société.**
(Perched villages of the Dogon of Mali: habitat, space and society.)
Jean-Christophe Huet. Paris: L'Harmattan, 1994. 191p. maps.
bibliog. (Collection Géographie et Cultures).

This study of the Dogons, living in the cliffs of the Bandiagara, concerns their habitat
and use of space. It covers aspects related to geography and environment, migration,
dwellings, social conditions, spatial organization and architecture.

Performance, theatre and dance

674 **ACROAMA's dancers of Mali (National Ensemble of the Republic
of Mali.)**
New York: Dunetz & Lovett, 1972. 16p.

This large-format, illustrated booklet was produced for the touring National Dance
Ensemble of Mali, 'a company of dancers, acrobats, warriors, singers, drummers,
musicians'. It lists the members and describes the dancers, the National Ensemble and
its repertoire. A smaller English-language 24-page version was also published, under
the title: *Les danseurs africains: l'Ensemble National du Mali* (same publisher, no
date).

675 **Danze dogon e bambara: il linguaggio simbolico dinamico tra rito, ammaestramento e spettacolo.** (Dogon and Bambara dance: the symbolic dynamic dialogue between rite, teaching and spectacle.) Giovanna Salvioni. Milan, Italy: F. Angeli, 1984. 183p. bibliog.

For those who read Italian, this anthropological study of Dogon and Bambara dance includes a lengthy section on Marcel Griaule and contemporary critics (p. 129-69).

676 **Kolokèlen: théâtre et folie.** (Kolokèlen: theatre and madness.) Texte d'Adama Bagayoko, introduction by Michel Valmer, commentaries by Dominique Paquet (et al.). Nice, France: Z'éditions, 1996. 95p. bibliog. (Sciences, Techniques, Cultures).

Inspired by traditional Malian (Bambara) theatre, in recent years the *koteba* has also been used as a form of therapy to treat mental illnesses. This publication includes two 'therapeutic' *koteba* plays by Adama Bagayoko, *Kolokèlen*, a play about mental illness, and *Jama Jigi*, a play about the prevention of AIDS, as well as numerous essays on the topic. Brief bibliographies are found on pages 18 and 70.

677 **Le kòtèba et l'évolution du théâtre moderne au Mali.** (The *koteba* and the evolution of modern theatre in Mali.) Sada Sissoko. Bamako: Jamana, 1995. 59p.

The *koteba* (great snail) is traditional theatre performed by the Bambara and an integral part of their folklore and cosmogony. Its origins, functions and impacts on modern Malian theatre are discussed. The *koteba* has two parts: the popular folklore part which is open to all people of the village, and the secret part, open to men only, comprised of the *komo*, *nama and kore* secret societies. The author summarizes the best *koteba* performances, from 1958 to 1968, when they were performed at the Semaine de la jeunesse, and beginning in 1970, when they were performed at the Biennale artistique et culturelle.

678 **Marionnettes du Mali.** (Marionettes of Mali.) Werewere Liking. Abidjan: Nouvelles Editions Africaines; Paris: ARHIS, 1987. 63p. (Statuettes Peintes d'Afrique de l'Ouest) (Collection Traditions Africaines).

In this volume on the marionettes of Mali, the colour illustrations stand out, rather than the analysis of the theatre (its social role, performance, etc.).

679 **Notes sur le théâtre total.** (Notes on total theatre.) Moussa Kanoute. Bamako: Jamana, 1989. 38p.

In 1979, the Biennale de la Jeunesse was officially proclaimed and the State effectively institutionalized the concept of national and regional theatre. 'Total theatre' is composed of up to seven elements: a play, ballet, traditional dance, chorus, solo song, instrumental ensemble, and modern orchestra. Usually the play is the primary medium in which the other six elements also have a part. This publication looks at the spectacles of the 1980s.

680   **Panorama critique du théâtre malien dans son évolution.** (Critical overview of Malian theatre in its evolution.)
Gaoussou Diawara.   Dakar: Sankoré, 1981. 109p.

The six sections of this book by the noted Malian playright cover the full range of theatre in Mali, including the sacred theatre, the *koteba* (traditional popular theatre), theatre of the Ecole Normale William Ponty, the period from after the war to independence, the Semaines and Biennales de la Jeunesse (1960 until today), and modern Malian theatre. The author also wrote the chapter on Malian theatre (p. 69-80) in the *Bibliographie commentée des écrivains contemporains* (Annotated bibliography of contemporary writers) (q.v.), which covers the period up to 1995.

681   **Playing with time: art and performance in central Mali.**
Mary Jo Arnoldi.   Bloomington, Indiana; Indianapolis, Indiana: Indiana University Press, 1995. 227p. bibliog. (Traditional Arts of Africa).

This is the definitive work on Segou masquerade theatre by the curator in the Smithsonian Institution's National Museum of Natural History. She analyses the puppet theatre as an artistic event and performance process while also focusing on the 'production of meaning' in performance. A useful glossary (p. 205-8) is followed by a masquerade list (p. 209-11) in which are given the Bamana (Bambara) name, the English name and the page on which it is illustrated. The author has written several articles on this topic as well as her dissertation, 'Puppet theatre in the Segou Region in Mali', Indiana University, 1983 (275, 58p., 109p. of plates).

682   **Pré-théâtre et rituel: National Folk Troupe of Mali.** (Pre-theatre and ritual: National Folk Troupe of Mali.)
Jean Decock.   *African Arts*, vol. 1, no. 3 (Spring 1968), p. 31-37.

This article, published in parallel columns of French and English, describes and praises the National Folk Troupe of Mali as 'the synthesis of art genres in a total pre-theatre' (p. 37). Decock emphasizes the multi-ethnic (Peul, Bambara, Dogon) nature of the performances.

683   **The spirit's dance in Africa: evolution, transformation and continuity in Sub-Saharan Africa.**
Edited by Esther A. Dagan, introduction by Simon Ottenberg.
Westmount, Canada: Galerie Amrad African Arts, 1997. 350p. maps. bibliog.

In this well-illustrated, sweeping survey of African dance, three chapters are particularly relevant here: 'Traditional music and dance of Mali', by Bah Diakité (p. 136-39); 'Of dancing masks and men: visible and hidden dancers of the Bamana and Bozo (Mali)', by Elisabeth Den Otter (p. 140-43); and 'Dance as metaphor in Chewa, Yoruba and Dogon folklore', by Laurel Birch de Aguilar (p. 128-30).

684 **Théâtre africain, théâtres africains?: actes du Colloque sur le Théâtre Africain, Ecole Normale Supérieure, Bamako, 14-18 novembre 1988.** (African theatre, African theatres? acts of the African Theatre Colloquium, Ecole Normale Supérieure, Bamako, 14-18 November 1988.)
Paris: Silex, 1990. 246p.

Numerous chapters from this conference on African theatre – Semaine du Théâtre Africain (1988: Ecole Normale Supérieure, Bamako, Mali) – pertain to Mali, including: Gassou Diawara's 'Le théâtre rituel malien en tant qu'acte social' (p. 51-58); Cheick Oumar Dembele's 'Massa Makan Diabaté: de la littérature au théâtre moderne' (p. 105-8); Victoria Diawara's 'Le théâtre africain: vers une ouverture sur le théâtre de l'universel' (p. 157-60); Hamadoun Kassogue's 'L'adaptation d'oeuvres classiques mondiales à la scène africaine, une nécessité pour un développement social' (p. 161-62); Philippe Dauchez's 'Historique de l'expérience: le koteba d'après Massa Makan Diabaté' (p. 181-86); and Baba Koumare's 'Essai d'utilisation thérapeutique d'une animation traditionelle' (p. 187-92).

685 **Théâtre populaire de marionnettes en Afrique sud-saharienne.**
(Popular marionette theatre in Sub-Saharan Africa.)
Olenka Darkowska-Nidzgorska. Bandundu, Zaïre: Centre d'Etudes Ethnologiques; St. Augustin, Germany: Diffusion hors-Zaïre, Steyler Verlag, 1980. 259p. bibliog. (Publications (Ceeba). Série II, vol. 60).

Mali figures prominently in this publication on the marionette theatre of Sub-Saharan Africa. Bambara marionette theatre 'occupe une place exceptionnelle dans l'histoire de la marionnette africaine' (occupies an exceptional place in the history of African marionettes). The author describes the major marionette characters of the Bambara as well as the Bozo, Somono and Marka of Mali (p. 25-46). She also provides a black-and-white illustration and an explanation for each of sixty-six Malian marionettes (p. 46-90).

686 **Videos of African and African-related performance: an annotated bibliography.**
Carol Lems-Dworkin, with Edward Gogol, technical consultant, and illustrated by Dean Alexander. Evanston, Illinois: C. Lems-Dworkin, 1996. 331p.

'Performance' is here defined not in the Western sense of 'performing arts' (dance, drama and music), but more like 'performance process' or 'Africans doing in cultural ways'. For example, the author was not concerned with masks in museums, but with masks being made, masks being used' (p. xii). Therefore, some videos on history, politics, geography and other primary subjects are, by design, excluded, if Africans are not 'doing'. In this well-indexed annotated bibliography, sixty-nine videos on Mali appear under the heading 'Mali' (with numerous sub-headings) as well as under the main ethnic groups (e.g., Bambara people, Dogon people, etc.), and 'masks and masking', 'music', 'griots and griottes', 'ceremonial greetings', etc. Using this publication, it is possible to distinguish Jean Rouch's ethnographic films which were made not in Niger, but in Mali (numbers 148, 294, 324, 456, 504, 816, 1148, and finally 1252 (where Rouch and G. Dieterlen are the protagonists)).

687 **The world encyclopedia of contemporary theatre. Volume 3, Africa.**
Don Rubin. London and New York: Routledge, 1997. 426p. bibliog.
An excellent source in English to begin the study of the theatre in Mali (p. 183-90), this broad look at the topic includes the history of performance and the theatre in Mali, national theatre companies, important dramatists, theatre for youth, puppet and mask theatre, set designers, theatrical training, research and publications.

Music

688 **African music: a pan-African annotated bibliography.**
Carol Lems-Dworkin. London and New York: H. Zell, 1991. 382p.
In this annotated bibliography of African music and musical instruments, 'Mali' has only four entries in the subject index. Items may be located by searching for the ethnic group in the subject index (mostly qualified by West Africa not Mali) such as Mande people, etc. An unannotated bibliography by John Gray also appeared simultaneously: *African music: a bibliographical guide to the traditional, popular, art, and liturgical musics of Sub-Saharan Africa* (New York: Greenwood Press, 1991. 499p.). Since Mali is unfortunately not listed in the subject index, the reader must look under West Africa in each chapter. A roundabout method of getting to Mali's entries is to use the ethnic group index (e.g., Bambara, Bozo, Dogon, etc.) which also lists the country where the ethnic group is located. Mali is covered in the chapter on African traditional music (p. 103-6) but not in the African popular music chapter.

689 **Anthologie de chants mandingues: Côte d'Ivoire, Guinée, Mali.**
(Anthology of Mandingo songs: Côte d'Ivoire, Guinée, Mali.)
Kaba Mamadi. Paris: L'Harmattan, 1995. 238p. bibliog.
The Ivoirian author heard most of these Mandingo songs from 1934 to 1942, but only recently decided to translate them into French. They are not divided into geographical regions but by the following: 'chants d'expression animiste'; 'chants d'expression islamique'; 'chants d'expression coloniale'. The many footnotes place the songs in their proper context.

690 **The Bamana women drummers.**
Kate Modic. In: *Drums, the heartbeat of Africa.* Edited by Esther A. Dagan. Montreal, Canada: Galerie Amrad African Art, 1993, p. 78-79.
Bamana (Bambara) women drummers are not usually paid for their services. They play *ji dunun* (water drums), *ntamanin* (small drums), and *yakoro* (gourd shakers) at various festivals and non-ritual occasions. Men are recognized by Bamana society as drummers but women are called 'women who play drums'.

691 **Beat King Salif Keita.**
Quincy Troupe. *New York Times Magazine* (29 Jan. 1995), p. 24-27.

The author profiles Salif Keita, born 1949 in Djoliba, French Sudan, as 'one of a handful of great African singers and musicians encompassed by the umbrella 'world music' (p. 24). He describes Keita's early struggles as an albino, his musical development in Mali and his emergence as a renowned musician and vocalist. Keita has four albums released in the US: The mansa of Mali (1994, Island Records), Amen (1992), Ko-yan (1989) and Soro (1987). In 'Youssou N'Dour and Salif Keita' (*Africa Report*, vol. 33, no. 5 (Sept.-Oct. 1988), p. 66-69), Daphne Topouzis provides a brief biography of Salif Keita, the forty-year old mansa (king) of Mali's musical scene, his band Les Ambassadeurs and his musical style which he describes as Malian, not Malinké or Bambara. Other articles on Keita include: 'The Mansa of Mali: the rise of Malian singer, Salif Keita' by Kwabena Fosu-Mensah, in *West Africa* (24 Aug. 1987), p. 1636-38 and 'Keita's musical homecoming' by Don Palmer, in *Down Beat* vol. 59, no. 9 (Sept. 1992), p. 11.

692 **'Bilali of Faransekila': a West African hunter and World War I hero according to a World War II veteran and hunters' singer of Mali.**
David C. Conrad. *History in Africa*, vol. 16 (1989), p. 41-70. bibliog.

Conrad recorded in October 1975, in Bamako, and here translates, annotates and analyses the 454-line song composed and sung by the late Malian hunters' singer Seydou Camara, 'Bilali of Farensekila'.

693 **Chansons d'Afrique et des Antilles.** (Songs of Africa and the West Indies.)
Paris: L'Harmattan, 1988. 134p. (Itinéraires et Contacts de Cultures, vol. 8).

This book, with a preface by Bernard Magnier, includes three brief but interesting essays on Malian music (p. 11-37): 'L'épopée mandingue et le titre d'honneur de Sunjata Keita', by Massa Makan Diabaté; 'Des hymnes à la maternité: les chants de veillées de circoncision (solisi) du Birgo', by Drissa Diakhité; and 'Salif Keita, un héritier singulier', by Catherine Mazauric.

694 **Essai sur la musique traditionnelle au Mali.** (Essay on traditional music in Mali.)
Mamadou Diallo. Paris: Agence de Coopération Culturelle et Technique, 198-[?]. 83p. map.

This booklet is well illustrated with drawings and photographs and consists of two parts. Part one (p. 9-21) considers traditional music of Mali's ethnic groups. Part two (p. 23-83) describes diverse instruments, musical scales and song lyrics.

695 **The healing drum: African wisdom teachings.**
Yaya Diallo, Mitchell Hall. Rochester, Vermont: Destiny Books, 1989. 211p. bibliog.

This collaboration by Diallo, a Malian-born (1946-) musician now residing in Montreal, and Hall, an American writer, teacher and health therapist, 'tells the story of

Yaya Diallo's life, of the culture of his tribe, the Minianka and of the sacred, healing role of music in that culture' (Preface, p. vii). Hall provides introductions to the chapters on Diallo's life, a pronounciation key and glossary (p. 201-3) and a brief bibliography (p. 205-6). Diallo's forty-minute 'The healing drum audiocassette: African ceremonial and healing music' on which he plays 'sacred and celebratory rhythms of the Minianka' on the *djémé* hand drum, the *tama* talking drum and the *balafon* is also available from Inner Traditions International, One Park Street, Rochester, Vermont 05767.

696 **Instruments de musique et genres musicaux traditionnels: symposium du 3-13 juillet 1982.** (Musical instruments and traditional musical genres: symposium from 3 to 13 July 1982.)
République du Mali. Ministère des Sports, des Arts.   Bamako: Ministère des Sports, des Arts, 1982. 134p.

Published on the occasion of the 7th Biennale Artistique et Culturelle, this volume contains chapters by each of Mali's eight Directions Régionales de la Jeunesse. Since they are not written by social science researchers or musicologists, they are aimed at the general public. For each chapter, which varies because of the different ethnic groups represented in the region, the music covered includes ritual music, working music ('musique de travail'), recreational music and the respective regional musical instruments. The Region of Mopti is the only chapter to have illustrated its text with line-drawings of their instruments.

697 **Janjon et autres chants populaires du Mali.** ('Janjon' and other popular songs of Mali.)
Massa M. Diabaté, preface by Djibril T. Niane.   Paris: Présence Africaine, 1970. 110p.

A brief Introduction (p. 15-16) precedes this descriptive commentary on eleven traditional songs, especially pertaining to Sun Jata ('Sun Jata Faasa', p. 29-36; 'Chants à la mémoire de Sun Jata', p. 37-42). 'Janjon' (p. 43-52), 'one of the most popular in Mali' (p. 43) is a victorious battle song associated with the memory of Fakoli-kun-ba; 'Keme Birama Faasa' (p. 63-68) is about the brother of Samory Touré. Winner of the Grand Prix Littéraire d'Afrique Noire in 1971.

698 **Jelimusow: the superwomen of Malian music.**
Lucy Durán.   In: *Power, marginality and African oral literature.* Edited by Graham Furniss, Liz Gunner.   Johannesburg: Witwatersrand University Press, 1995, p. 197-207. bibliog.

Post-independent Manding music has seen the rise of *jelimusow* (sing.: *jelimuso*), the female *jeliw* (sing.: *jeli*) or griottes. These women are stars in the local music scene, especially in urban areas, where they perform in traditional ceremonies such as a wedding or baptism, and can be frequently heard on the radio. The author briefly surveys the role of past and present women singers in Manding music and describes the distinction between male and female *jeliw*: women sing praise songs, men recite history or epics. Women are not permitted to speak their lyrics.

699 **Littérature et musique.** (Literature and music.)
Massa Makan Diabaté. In: *Colloque sur littérature et esthétique négro-africaines*. Abidjan: Nouvelles Editions Africaines, 1979, p. 277-89.

This essay by Diabaté demonstrates the wide net he casts when discussing the oral tradition of Mande griots. Music and oral tradition are inseparable. The spoken rhythmic texts are accompanied by the *nkoni, kora*, or *balafon*. He describes the various techniques used by griots to vary their rhythms and to make the story more interesting to the audience. He concludes with the texts of two songs, 'Sunjata Fasa' and 'Mandekora'.

700 **Mali.**
Ronnie Graham. In: *The world of African music*. Written and edited by Ronnie Graham. London: Pluto Press, 1992, p. 59-67. (Stern's Guide to Contemporary African Music, vol. 2).

This fine source describes 'music and society', 'traditional music', lists a discography of 31 titles from the 1960s to 1988, and provides brief notes and a discography for female vocalists (Fanta Damba, Fanta Sacko, Tata Bambo Kouyate, Ami Koita, Nahini Diabate, Nahawa Doumbia, Oumou Sangare, Kandia Kouyate, Sali Sidibi), male instrumentalists (Keletigui Diabate, Sidiki Diabate, Sekou Batorou Kouyate, and Toumani Diabate), and 'modern music' (Sory Bamba, Ali Farka Touré [sometimes called Ali Farka], Ambassadeurs, Rail Band, Salif Keita, Super Djata, Super Biton, National Badema, Kasse Mady, Baboucar Traoré, Boncana Maiga, and Abdoulaye Diabate). Graham's earlier *The Da Capo guide to contemporary African music* (New York: Da Capo, 1988. 315p.) introduces the country's music and provides a list of recordings of traditional music and of Sory Bamba, Monkontafe Safo, Sekou Batourou Kouyate, Ali Farka Touré, Les Ambassadeurs, Salif Keita, Ousmane Kouyate, Super Djata, Rail Band, Maravillas, Super Biton and Ama Maiga. In 'Silk voice of Mali', *West Africa*, no. 3858 (19-25 Aug. 1991), p. 1393, 'BA' describes the work of Oumou Sangare, Mali's most popular female singer. Sangare who sings of the problems of women 'torn between old country values and modern city life' sold over 200,000 copies in Mali alone of her first album 'Women'.

701 **Music in Africa: the Manding contexts.**
Roderic Knight. In: *Performance practice: ethnomusicological perspectives*. Edited by Gerard Béhague. Westport, Connecticut; London: Greenwood Press, 1984, p. 53-90. bibliog. (Contributions in Intercultural and Comparative Studies, no. 12).

This chapter focuses on the performance practice of the Manding griot and drummer, as it can be witnessed in southern Senegal, Gambia, Guinea-Bissau, Guinea, southern Mali (among the Maninka (Malinke) and the Bamana (Bambara)), and western Côte d'Ivoire. Knight analyses the role of the griot and drummer, details the instruments played (the *kora* or harp lute; the *kontingo* or *ngoni*, another stringed instrument; the *balo* or *balofon*, a xylophone; and a *ne*, a tubular iron bell), discusses the aesthetics of the music and its performance, describes the griot's learning process of apprenticeship, and summarizes the subjects covered in the content of the song texts.

702 **Musique traditionnelle de l'Afrique noire: discographie. Mali.**
(Traditional music of Black Africa: discography. Mali.)
Chantal Nourrit, Bill Pruitt. Paris: Radio-France Internationale,
Centre de Documentation, 1978. 125p. map. (Radio-thèques).
Number one of this comprehensive set of discographies of African music covers Mali
in 117 entries, with each band of the recording separately described. It includes both
commercially made and field recordings of 33⅓, 45 and 78 r.p.m. speeds. Although
many of the recordings are not dated, coverage appears to span from 1948 to 1977.
Each LP is classified into one of the following categories: traditional (popular music
with traditional instruments); traditional/griot music; modernized traditional popular
(traditional music with new words and modern instruments); modernized traditional/
griot music; contemporary music of traditional type with orchestra; and variety. In
addition to the bibliography and biographies of seven griots, there are indexes of
ethnic groups, musical instruments, singers/orchestras, places, personalities, themes,
song titles, and album titles.

703 **The new Grove dictionary of music and musicians.**
George Grove, edited by Stanley Sadie. London: Macmillan;
Washington, DC: Grove's Dictionaries of Music, 1980. 20 vols.
bibliog.
The entry under Mali (volume 11, p. 573-77) in this standard reference source
provides a brief overview and bibliography of Malian music. There are sections on
Manding and Dogon music which describe Malian musical instruments and the role of
music and dance in Malian rituals. Other volumes contain articles pertinent to Mali:
'Tuareg music' (vol. 19, p. 236-37), 'Songhay music' (vol. 17, p. 522-24), 'Fulani
music' (vol. 7, p. 23-25), 'Balo' (balofon) (vol. 2, p. 98), and 'Kora' (vol. 10,
p. 188-90). Several musical instruments are illustrated.

704 **The politics of music in Mali.**
Charles H. Cutter. *African Arts*, vol. 1, no. 3 (Spring 1968), p. 38-39,
74-77.
The author describes the important role of the griot historically and the political nature
of songs in the 1960s, when contemporary themes emphasized political individuals
and public policies. The article includes one photograph and words to several songs in
English and Bamana (Bambara). 'Just as the griots of Sundjata energized the enthusiasm of the warriors of Mandé, the musician of today must mobilize his audience
for the collective tasks of nation-building' (p. 77).

705 **Première anthologie de la musique malienne.** (First anthology of
Malian music.)
Gilbert Rouget. *The World of Music*, vol. 14, no. 1 (1972), p. 55-65.
This is a record review of the six-volume anthology produced by Mali's Ministry of
Information (Bärenreiter Musicaphon, BM 30L 2501-06). 'By virtue of its scope and
the high quality of the material it presents, this Anthology is a real discographic event,
a landmark in the history of our knowledge of African music' (p. 55). The work is in
English, French and German.

706 **Sooninka'ra gànnìnkà-n-sùugú Maàñù-n-sùugú kútúntá-n-súugù do suugu ta'nanu, ì wùtí Kàyìháydì yá – Morita'ni = Chants traditionnels du pays soninké: chants nuptiaux, de circoncision et autres recueillis à Kaédi – Mauritanie.** (Traditional songs of the Soninke country: nuptial songs, circumcision songs, and others collected at Kaedi, Mauritania.)
Ousmane Moussa Diagana. Paris: L'Harmattan, 1990. 268p. bibliog.

This anthology of traditional Soninke songs from Mauritania, Mali and Senegal contains both the Soninke (Sarakole) text and the French translation. It is divided into the following categories: 'chants nuptiaux' (wedding songs); 'chants de circoncision' (circumcision songs); 'autres chants' (other songs). The Introduction and the many footnotes to the songs help the reader put them in their appropriate context.

707 **Sweet mother: modern African music.**
Wolfgang Bender. Chicago, Illinois: University of Chicago Press, 1991. 235p. bibliog. (Chicago Studies in Ethnomusicology).

This translation by Wolfgang Freis of Bender's 1985 work *Sweet Mother: Moderne Afrikanische Musik* (Trickster Verlag) contains a chapter 'The griot style' (p. 1-41) which discusses 'Great female singers: Mali' (p. 21-31), notably Fanta Damba, Mokontafe Sako, Fanta Sacko and Bazoumana Sissoko. In addition, there are notes (p. 191-204), a bibliography (p. 205-13) and a discography (p. 215-35), which for Mali (p. 219-20) includes modern, neotraditional, traditional and Christian recordings. In *Goodtime kings: emerging African pop* (New York: Quill, 1985. 143p.), Billy Bergman describes eight contemporary musical styles in Africa, providing a short discography for each. 'Griots' (p. 94-107) includes discussion and a photograph of Salif Keita.

708 **Les tengere, instruments de musique Bozo.** (The *tengere*, a Bozo musical instrument.)
G. Dieterlen, Z. Ligers. *Objets et Mondes*, vol. 7, fasc. 3 (automne 1967), p. 185-216.

The *tengere* is a wooden musical instrument used by the Bozo fishermen who live along the Niger River. The article includes thirty line-drawings and eight photographs of *tengere*. Other older articles by noted ethnologists include: 'Notes sur les tambours-de-calebasse en Afrique occidentale' (Notes on calabash drums in Western Africa), by G. Dieterlen and Z. Ligers, in *Journal de la Société des Africanistes* (vol. 33, fasc. 2 (1963), p. 255-74); 'Notes sur un luth dogon' (Notes on a Dogon lute), by D. Zahan, in the same journal (vol. 20, fasc. 2, (1950), p. 193-207); and 'Symbolisme des tambours soudanais' (Symbolism of Sudanese drums), by Marcel Griaule, in *Mélanges d'histoire et d'esthétique musicales offerts à Paul-Marie Masson* (Paris: Richard-Masse, 1955, p. 79-86).

709 **West African harps.**
Eric Charry. *Journal of the American Musical Instrument Society*, 20 (1994), p. 5-53. map. bibliog.

This is a comparative study of the diverse harps of the West African region. The distribution map (p. 6) clearly shows Mali's harps.

710 **World music: the rough guide.**
Editors Simon Broughton, Mark Ellingham, David Muddyman,
Richard Trillo, and contributing editor Kim Burton. London: Rough
Guides, 1994. 697p.
Mali is covered on pages 241-62 of this standard music reference source. There are
sections on the Manding *jalis* (griots) of Mali, Guinea and Senegambia; the women
singers of Mali; ensembles and ballets; the *kora*; the Rail Band of Mali; and songs of
Ali Farka Touré. The discographies (p. 259, 262) contain recent releases on compact
disc.

Film

711 **Africa on film and videotape, 1960-1981: a compendium of reviews.**
David S. Wiley with Robert Cancel, Diane Pflugrad, and T. H. Elkiss
and Amie Campbell. East Lansing, Michigan: African Studies
Center, Michigan State University, 1982. 551p.
Although this publication is by now dated, it is still a useful reference source for film
and videotape reviews. It includes at least 25 documentaries on Mali although some
films with Malian content are not listed in the index under Mali (e.g., *Maninka
villages in transition*). Each film is rated from one to five stars, each is summarized
and critiqued, and the authors suggest the appropriate educational level of the
audience. It is far superior to a more up-to-date source, *Films & videos for African
studies* (University Park, Pennsylvania: Audio-Visual Services, Pennsylvania State
University, 1992), which includes only three brief unevaluated entries of interest to
those studying Mali: *Africa 2: mastering a continent; The ancient Africans; Griottes
of the Sahel.*

712 **The African tale of cinema.**
Amadou Hampaté Bâ. *Discourse*, vol. 11, no. 2 (Spring-Summer
1989), p. 99-106.
In this charming story, Bâ recounts the first time films came to his village in
Bandiagara. Because the marabouts proclaimed films to be the work of Satan, he had a
difficult time convincing his mother to accompany him to a viewing. This article was
translated from 'Le dit du cinéma africain', *Films ethnographiques sur l'Afrique noire*
(Paris: Unesco, 1967).

713 **Ciné-rituel de femmes dogon.** (Ritual cinema of Dogon women.)
Nadine Wanono. Paris: Editions du Centre National de la Recherche
Scientifique, distributed by Presses du CNRS, 1987. 138p. map.
bibliog.
The author, an apprentice film-maker of ethnographic films, describes her experience
filming and studying the daily life of Dogon women in the Bandiagara. Two of her
films which are discussed here, about making oil from *sa* (*Lannea acida*) and from

sesame seeds, are available for viewing in the Bibliothèque Publique d'Information, Musée Georges Pompidou, Paris. This book would be of interest to all students of ethnographic films.

714 **Le cinéma au Mali.** (The cinema of Mali.)
Victor Bachy. Brussels: Editions OCIC, 1982. 87p. map. bibliog. (Collection Cinémédia. Série Les Cinémas en Afrique Noire, no. 3).

This small volume, illustrated with photographs from Malian films, describes three Malian film organizations – l'OCINAM (L'Office Cinématographique National du Mali, 1962-), le SCINFOMA (Service Cinématographique du Ministère de l'Information du Mali, 1966-77) and le CNPC (Le Centre National de Production Cinématographique, 1977) – and major film-makers (Djibril Kouyaté, Alkaly Kaba, Souleymane Cissé, Séga Coulibaly, Kalifa Dienta and Issa Falaba Traoré) and their films. The bibliography (p. 79-83) includes French, Italian and Malian newspaper articles. For an English-language summary of Malian cinema by Bachy, see pages 32-35 of his *To have a history of African cinema* (Brussels: OCIC, 1987. 69p.). See also Claire Andrade-Watkins's 1989 Boston University doctoral thesis 'Francophone African cinema: French financial and technical assistance, 1961-1977' (314 leaves).

715 **Dictionnaire du cinéma africain.** (Dictionary of African cinema.)
L'Association des Trois Mondes. Paris: Karthala; Ministère de la Coopération et du Développement, 1991. 398p. (Collection Caméra des Trois Mondes, vol. 1).

The Malian directors covered on pages 187-204 are: Abdoulaye Ascofare, Moussa Camara, Camera Club du Lycée Technique de Bamako, Mahamadou Cissé, Souleymane Cissé, Mambaye Coulibaly, Sega Coulibaly, Moussa Diallo, Kalifa Dienta, Adama Drabo, Alkaly Kaba, Cheikh Hamada Keita, Drissa Kone, Assane Kouyate, Djibril Kouyate, Moussa Sidibe, Cheick Oumar Sissoko, Mamadou Souleymane Toure, Bekay Traore, and Issa Falaba Traore. For each director, a brief biography is followed by a chronological filmography, the original title, the French translation of the title, the running time, the category (e.g., documentary), the actors for feature-length films, the producers, the distributors (when known), and a brief description or summary of the film.

716 **Directory of African film-makers and films.**
Keith Shiri. Trowbridge, England: Flicks Books; Westport, Connecticut: Greenwood Press, 1992. 194p. bibliog.

Mali is here represented by Abdoulaye Ascofare, Mahamadou Cissé, Souleymane Oumar Cissé, Mambaye Coulibaly, Sega Coulibaly, Kalifa Dienta, Adama Drabo, Alkaly Kaba, Djibril Kouyate, and Cheick Oumar Sissoko. For each film-maker, a brief biography is followed by a filmography which gives the original film title, its language if it is in an African language ('Bambara' should be substituted for 'Bambana'), the French title, and the English translation.

717 **Essai sur les fondements du cinéma africain.** (Essay on the foundations of African cinema.)
Pierre Haffner. Abidjan: Nouvelles Editions Africaines, 1978. 274p. bibliog.

Mali rather than Africa is, in fact, the primary focus of this book on African cinema. Part 1 covers the ethics of the African spectator and includes an analysis of the Malian traditional theatre, the *koteba*. Part 2 discusses the aesthetics of African cinema, and uses as examples Wangrin, Sun Jata, and the *koteba*. Part 3, Documents, includes excerpts of interviews (with, for example, Malian journalists, music professors, and students) as well as several reprintings from the Malian newspaper *L'Essor* (q.v.).

718 **Five West African filmmakers on their films.**
Françoise Pfaff. *Issue: A Journal of Opinion*, vol. 20, no. 2 (Summer 1992), p. 31-37.

The author describes themes and production problems of West African cinema and the work of Safi Faye (b. 1943, Senegal), Gaston Kaboré (b. 1951, Burkina Faso), Idrissa Ouedraogo (b. 1954, Burkina Faso), Ousmane Sembène (b. 1923, Senegal) whose first film *L'Empire Sonhrai* (1963) was about Timbuktu, and Souleymane Cissé (b. 1940, Mali), whose five feature films are described. In the same issue, Sheila Petty mentions S. Cissé's *Yeelen* (Mali, 1987) and discusses Cheick Oumar Sissoko's *Finzan* (Mali, 1990) in 'Africa cinema and (re)education: using recent African feature films' (p. 26-30).

719 **Interview with Souleyman Cissé.**
Souleyman Cissé. *West Africa*, no. 3669 (7 Dec. 1987), p. 2378.

The Malian film-maker, trained at the VGIK film school in Moscow in the 1960s, discusses production and distribution issues of *Finye* ('The wind', 1982) and *Yeelen* ('Brightness', 1987) which won the Cannes Film Festival Jury Prize. Earlier he produced and directed *Baara* (1982) and *Den Muso* ('The girl', 1975). The catalogue of the Library of African Cinema (available on the Internet) describes *Yeelen* (105 minutes), *Finzan* ('A dance for the heroes', 1990, 107 minutes) and *Guimba the Tyrant* (1995, 93 minutes) by Cheick Oumar Sissoko, and *Ta Dona* ('Fire!', 1991, 100 minutes) by Adama Drabo, all in Bambara with English subtitles except for *Guimba* which is also in Fulfulde. In addition, it lists *Keita* ('The heritage of the griot', 1995, 94 minutes, in Jula and French with English subtitles) by Dani Kouyaté of Burkina Faso and *Rouch in reverse* (1995, 52 minutes, in French and English with English subtitles) by Manthia Diawara. These films are available for rental or purchase from California Newsreel, 149 Ninth Street/420, San Francisco, California 94103 (www.newsreel.org).

720 **Jean Rouch: cinéma et ethnographie.** (Jean Rouch: cinema and ethnography.)
Jean Rouch, Dominique Desanti, Jean Decoch. *African Arts*, vol. 2, no. 1 (Autumn 1968), p. 36-39, 76-80.

The interviewers spoke in April 1968 at a University of California Los Angeles colloquium with the famed film-maker, pioneer of visual anthropology, about his work. The article appears in French. See also Paul Stoller's *The cinematic griot: the ethnography of Jean Rouch* (Chicago, Illinois; London: University of Chicago Press, 1992. 247p.) which also includes a detailed filmography of Rouch from 1946 to 1990 (p. 227-33).

721 **Kadiatou Konaté.**
Jadot Sezirahiga. *Ecrans d'Afrique*, vol. 3 (1994), no. 8, p. 28-29.
Malian Konaté is one of the few African women to succeed as a film-maker. She
began as a production assistant to Souleymane Cissé, did some editing for Gaston
Kaboré, then became assistant director for Mambaye Coulibaly's *La geste de Ségou*.
Her first work, *L'enfant terrible*, is an animated folk tale. She is also working on two
documentaries, one about the education of girls in Mali, the other about women and
development. This journal, *Ecrans d'Afrique*, publishes the entire text in French and
English, and is an excellent source on Malian cinema. There are five other articles on
Malian film-makers and subjects in the six issues from 1994 and 1995, including
articles on Souleymane Cissé (vol. 3, no. 7, p. 8-11; vol. 4, no. 11, p. 44-47; vol. 4, no.
13/14, p. 36-40), Cheick Oumar Sissoko (vol. 3, no. 9/10, p. 8-13; vol. 4, no. 12,
p. 22-24), actress Abiba Diarra, from Cote d'Ivoire and Mali (vol. 4, no. 13/14,
p. 34-35), and Burkinabè film-maker Dani Kouyaté's *Keita*, the story of Soundiata
Keita (vol. 4, no. 12, p. 25-30). Another journal of interest is *Le film africain*, which
contains brief articles and interviews on Malian cinema such as 'Le cinéma au Mali'
(no. 7, July 1992, p. 6-8), 'Nijugu Guimba (Le tyran) de Cheick Oumar Sissoko
(Mali)' (no. 12, May 1993, p. 8), and 'Mohamed Soudani, directeur de la photo et
réalisateur (Mali)' (no. 13, Nov. 1993, p. 20-21). See also articles in the journal *Bingo*
on topics such as 'Souleymane Cissé: le choix du jury' (no. 457, April 1991, p. 49),
'Adama Drabo: le chouchou du public' (same issue, p. 50-51), and 'Cheick Omar
Cissoko: un goût amer' (no. 458, May 1991, p. 51).

722 **Mali.**
Roy Armes. *International Film Guide* (1991), p. 256-57.
The new generation of Mali's film-makers are all Socialist trained. This brief
overview features film-makers: Falaba Issa Traoré, Cheick Oumar Sissoko, Djibril
Kouyaté, and Souleymane Cissé, the latter 'towering above his Malian contem-
poraries' and 'a major figure in black African film-making' (p. 257).

723 **Representation of female circumcision in *Finzan*, a dance for the
heroes.**
Laura DeLuca, Shadrack Kamenya. *Research in African Literatures*,
vol. 26, no. 3 (Fall 1995), p. 83-87.
Finzan has received much attention, at least in part, because of its treatment of the
topic of female circumcision. In the film, female circumcision is portrayed as evil and
harmful to the woman's health. 'The problem with *Finzan*'s call to action is the
underlying assumption that African women are helpless victims with no agency of
their own. Related to this assumption is the ethnocentric notion that Western feminists
must come to the aid of the poor African women and that African men are in some
way more chauvinistic than Western men' (p. 86).

724 **Sub-Saharan African films and filmmakers: an annotated
bibliography = Films et cinéastes africains de la région
subsaharienne: une bibliographie commentée.**
Nancy Schmidt. London and New York: H. Zell, 1988. 401p.
In this remarkable compilation of 3,993 items, the vigorous film industry of Mali is
well documented in 133 citations, indexed not only under film-makers Souleymane

Cissé (79 citations) and Mustapha Diop (22 citations), but also under 'Mali – distribution' (3), 'Mali – film clubs' (2), 'Mali – ideology' (2), 'Mali – infrastructure' (13), 'Mali – theaters' (14) and 'Mali – themes' (1). The introduction to the volume (p. 5-22) is in both English and French. The author's 1987-92 supplement, winner of the 1996 Conover-Porter award, and published under the same title (London; New Jersey: H. Zell, 1994. 468p.) lists twelve additional citations in the subject index on Mali. The author updates this bibliography annually in the *African Literature Association Bulletin*. In her well-indexed listing of 1,690 books and articles, *Sub-Saharan African films and filmmakers: a preliminary bibliography* (Bloomington, Indiana: Indiana University, 1986. 112p.), there are fifty-three references to Mali. Earlier compilations by Helen W. Cyr, *A filmography of the Third World, 1976-1983: an annotated list of 16mm films* (Metuchen, New Jersey: Scarecrow, 1985. 275p.) and Steven Ohrn and Rebecca Riley, *Africa from real to reel: an African filmography* (Waltham, Massachusetts: African Studies Association, 1976. 144p.) list two and twenty films, respectively.

725 **Visages de femmes: *Finzan* et *Les Soleils des indépendances*.**
(Womens' faces: *Finzan* and *The suns of independence*.)
Madeleine Borgomano. In: *With open eyes: women and African cinema*. Amsterdam; Atlanta, Georgia: Rodolpi, 1997, p. 111-24. (Matatu, no. 19).

Borgomano maintains that Malian director Cheick Oumar Sissoko was inspired by Ivoirian author Ahmadou Kourouma's 1970 novel *Les soleils des indépendances*. She shows the parallels between the oppressed female protagonists of Nanyuma, in Sissoko's 1990 film *Finzan* and Salimata, in Kourouma's 1970 novel *Les soleils des indépendances*. She concludes that African cinema, much more than literature, makes us aware that while contemporary African men have made progress in modern society, they still do not want to give up the privileges due to them as males.

726 *Yeelen*: **a political fable of the Komo blacksmiths/sorcerers.**
Suzanne H. MacRae. *Research in African Literatures*, vol. 26, no. 3 (1995), p. 57-66. bibliog.

In this analysis of Souleymane Cissé's *Yeelen* ('Brightness', 1987), MacRae states that 'Cissé's social and cinematic purpose remains elusive' if not taken in the context of the *Komo* secret society of blacksmiths/sorcerers (p. 57). The film is also an indictment of the corrupt regime of President Moussa Traoré. See also Rabita Hadj-Moussa and Denise Pérusse's 'L'arbre de la connaissance: *Yeelen* de Souleymane Cissé' in *Films d'Afrique*, edited by Michel Larouche (Montreal: Guernica, 1991, p. 113-26) which covers the major themes of the movie set in the thirteenth-century Mali Empire (e.g., father–son antagonism, return to tradition, Mali's passage into modern times) and is followed by a bio-bibliography of Cissé (p. 125-26).

West Africa: the rough guide.
See item no. 78.

An archeological ethnography of blacksmiths, potters, and masons in Jenne, Mali (West Africa).
See item no. 129.

Togu na: the African Dogon: 'house of men, house of words'.
See item no. 304.

Buffoons, queens, and wooden horsemen: the Dyo and Gouan societies of the Bambara of Mali.
See item no. 357.

Nation-building in Mali: art, radio, and leadership in a pre-literate society.
See item no. 415.

Oral Literature and Folklore

Epic of Soundiata

727 **The epic of Son-Jara: a West African tradition, analytical study and translation.**
John William Johnson, text by Fa-Digi Sisòkò. Bloomington, Indiana: Indiana University, 1986. 242p. map. bibliog. (African Epic Series).

This fine study examines the 3,084-line version of the founding of the empire of Old Mali 750 years earlier, performed in 1968 in Kita by the 'renowned bard' Fa-Digi Sisòkò (father of Magan Sisòkò) and recorded by Charles S. Bird. Part one (p. 3-83) 'The study' examines the social setting, the bard (griot), characteristics of Mande epic and the African epic belt, with notes and references. Part two 'The text' (p. 91-239) has an introduction, résumé of the plot, the epic itself (p. 100-81), annotations to the text, genealogy charts and an excellent bibliography (p. 227-39).

728 **The epic of Sun-Jata II, according to Magan Sisòkò.**
John William Johnson, Magan Sisòkò. Bloomington, Indiana: Indiana University, 1979. 2 vols. bibliog. (Folklore Monograph Series, vol. 5).

In Kita, in April 1974, Johnson recorded the 3,628-line epic presented here in his English translation (p. 32-194) with descriptive notes (p. 195-265), an interview after the performance (p. 267-74) and genealogy charts (p. 275-80). Magan Sisòkò was accompanied by a guitarist while he sang for over two hours. In the introduction (p. 9-31), Johnson describes the bard, son of Fa-Digi Sisòkò, the Maninka dialect of Mande, his three assistants, the circumstances of the recording and gives a synopsis of the complex plot. A Maninka text of the epic is available from the Forum Society, 504 North Fess, Bloomington, Indiana 47401. Johnson's 1978 doctoral thesis at Indiana University was 'The epic of Sun-jata: an attempt to define the model for African epic poetry'.

729   **L'épopée du Sunjara, d'après Lasine Diabate de Kela (Mali).** (Epic of Son-Jara, according to Lansine Diabate of Kela (Mali).)
Text collected, translated and annotated by Jan Jansen, Esger Duintjer, Boubacar Tamboura.   Leiden, The Netherlands: Research School CNWS, 1995. 221p. bibliog.

This is one of the recent transcriptions of the Soundiata epic. Lansine Diabate, 'master of the word' of Kela's griots, was recorded in 1992 with two *ngoni* (lute) accompanists. The 664 lines appear in French and Manding (Mande). Helpful features include 'Succession des thèmes dans l'épopée de Sunjara' (p. 16), which serves as a sort of table of contents of the epic according to the verse number, as well as an index of people cited (p. 216-19) and an index of geographical locations cited (p. 220-21).

730   **La grande geste du Mali: des origines à la fondation de l'Empire.**
(The great epic of Mali: from its origins to the foundation of the Empire.)
Youssouf Tata Cissé, Wâ Kamissoko.   Paris: Karthala; Association Arsan, 1988-91. 2 vols. maps. bibliog.

Malian ethnologist Y. T. Cissé recorded Wâ Kamissoko's version of the classic Soundiata epic (in French and Malinke) as well as his participation in two international colloquia in Bamako in 1975 and 1976. For a discussion on Wâ Kamissoko's controversial role, i.e., his inability to stay within the bounds of the traditional griot/informant/performer, see P. F. de Moraes Farias', 'The oral traditionalist as critic and intellectual producer: an example from contemporary Mali' (p. 14-38) in *African historiography: essays in honour of Jacob Ade Ajayi,* edited by Toyin Falola (London: Longman, 1993. 244p.).

731   **The guardian of the word (Kouma Lafôlô Kouma.)**
Camara Laye.   London: Collins, 1980; New York: Vintage Books, Random House, 1984. 223p. map. (Aventura. Vintage Library of Contemporary World Literature).

This remarkable story of Sundiata, the warrior-king who founded the empire of Mali, translated and with a brief preface (p. 9-11) by James Kirkup, was told to the Guinean writer (1924-80) by Malinké griot Babu Condé from 16 March to 16 April 1963. 'Kouma Lafôlô Kouma' is Malinké for 'History of the first word' or 'The history of the great Sundiata, the son of the buffalo-panther woman and of the lion, the first Emperor of Mali' (p. 30). Laye provides introductory chapters (p. 15-34) on African oral traditions, griots, and especially on 'Babu condé: "Bélen-tigi", or traditional griot' preceding his translation of the legend of Sundiata. The book was originally published as *Le Maître de la parole: Kouma Lafôlô Kouma* (Master of the word) (Paris: Librairie Plon, 1978).

732   **Sundiata: an epic of old Mali.**
D. T. Niane.   Harlow, England: Longman Drumbeat, 1979. 96p. map. bibliog.

This popular translation by G. D. Pickett of *Soundjata, ou l'Epopée Mandingue* (Paris: Présence Africaine, 1960) contains a brief preface by Niane and helpful notes. It is an account of the founder of the ancient Mali empire, Maghan Sundiata, by the Guinean griot Mamadou Kouyaté, originally published in English in 1965, in paperback in 1979. Niane authored *Recherches sur l'Empire du Mali au Moyen âge* (Research on the Empire of Mali in the Middle Ages (Paris: Présence Africaine, 1975. 112p.) in which he examines oral traditions and the 'problem' of Soundjata (Soundiata or Sunjata). See also his *Le Soudan occidental au temps des grands empires: XI-XVIe siècles* (The Western Sudan in the time of the great empires: the 11th to the 16th centuries) (Paris: Présence Africaine, 1975. 271p.); and, with J. Suret-Canale, *Histoire de l'Afrique occidentale* (History of Western Africa) (Paris: Présence Africaine, 1961. 233p.). Robert Pageard's 'Soundiata Keita et la tradition orale' (Sundiata Keita and oral tradition), in *Présence Africaine*, vol. 36 (1961), p. 51-70, is also of interest.

733 **Sundiata: lion king of Mali.**
David Wisniewski. New York: Clarion Books, 1992. 32p. map.
The author, inspired by D. T. Niane and D. M. Kouyate's *Sundiata: an epic of old Mali* (q.v.), has added brilliant cut-paper illustrations in this marvellous children's book to tell the story of the boy who could neither speak nor walk but who became king of the thirteenth-century Mali Empire. It includes a map (p. 1) and note (p. 32) describing the story and creation of the book. Wisniewski thanks Patrick McNaughton for enhancing the book's accuracy but admits 'artistic license came into play'. Joe Lasker reviews it in the *New York Times Book Review* (8 Nov. 1992, p. 55), praising the 'fine production' and the 'fool-the-eye three-dimensionality' of the illustrations. Other literature for young people on this topic include Roland Bertol's *Sundiata: the epic of the lion king, retold* (New York: Crowell, 1970. 81p.) and R. J. Wingfield, *The story of old Ghana, Melle and Songhai* (London: Cambridge University Press, 1957. 59p.).

734 **Sunjata Epic Conference proceedings: held November 13-15, 1992, at the Institute for the Advanced Study & Research in the African Humanities at Northwestern University.**
Sunjata Epic Conference, Northwestern University, 1992. 1 vol. (unpublished).
These unpublished conference proceedings, written by several noted West African oral tradition scholars, represent important research on the Sunjata epic. The authors of the thirteen papers are: Ralph A. Austen, Stephen Belcher, Charles S. Bird, Stephen P. D. Bulman, Seydou Camara, David C. Conrad, Mamadou Diawara, Paulo F. de Moraes Farias, Thomas A. Hale, James R. McGuire, Tal Tamari, Karim Traoré, and Ivor Wilks. Also included is the 110-page transcript of the conference. The proceedings are available upon demand at the Herskovits Library of Africana at Northwestern University Library, Evanston, Illinois.

735 **A town called Dakajalan: the Sunjata tradition and the question of ancient Mali's capital.**
David C. Conrad. *Journal of African History,* vol. 35, no. 3 (1994), p. 355-77. map. bibliog.
Conrad uses evidence from Arabic texts, oral traditions, and the archaeological work of Susan and Roderick McIntosh to argue that Dakajalan, the town in which Sunjata lived as a youth and to which he returned from exile and which seems to have been protected as a sacred place for centuries, was probably one of several capitals of ancient Mali. As the empire expanded, the *mansadugu* ('king's town') may have

moved 'down the River Niger to take advantage of widening commercial opportunities and to govern an expanded population of imperial subjects' (p. 377). Niani was most probably the political capital in the sixteenth century under Mansa Mamadu. The discussion, supported by a map of 'Mande heartland' (p. 356) and marvellously detailed footnotes, extends an examination begun by John O. Hunwick's 'The mid-fourteenth century capital of Mali', *Journal of African History*, vol. 14, no. 2 (1973), p. 195-208 (see item no. 200), which primarily attempts to establish the route of Ibn Battuta's travels in 1352. See also Conrad's paper 'Searching for history in the Sunjata epic: the case of Fakoli', in *History in Africa* (vol. 19 (1992), p. 147-200), which reviews in detail the Sunjata epic's usefulness and limitations as an historical source through careful examination of the central legendary Fakoli character. The references (p. 187-200) are extensive.

Other epics

736 **Da Monzon de Ségou: épopée bambara.** (Da Monzon of Segou: Bambara epic.)
Lilyan Kesteloot with Amadou Traore, Jean-Baptiste Traore. Paris: F. Nathan, 1972. 4 vols. maps. bibliog. (Classiques du Monde) (Classiques du Monde. Littérature Africaine, nos. 13-16).

These volumes, originally published as *Littérature africaine*, vol. 1, no. 13 (64p.), no. 14 (63p.), no. 15 (80p.) and no. 16 (63p.), offer texts in French of oral traditions of Da Monzon, king of the Bambara Segou empire from about 1808 to 1827, and to a lesser extent of Ngolo Diarra (1750-87) as rendered by griots Sissoko Kabiné, Seydou Dramé, Kéfa Diabaté, Mabal Samburi, Sory Komara and Gorké [*sic*]. Each volume contains notes. The first has genealogies of the kings of Segou as collected by C. Monteil and A. Hampâté Bâ (p. 62-63). See also Kesteloot's 'The West African epics', *Présence Africaine*, vol. 58, no. 2 (1966), p. 197-202; *Le mythe et l'histoire dans la formation de l'Empire de Ségou* (Myth and history in the formation of the Empire of Segou) (Dakar: IFAN, 1980, p. 578-681); and *L'épopée bambara de Ségou* (item no. 739).

737 **La dispersion des Mandeka: d'après un récit du généalogiste Kélé-Monson Diabaté à Karaya cercle de Kita.** (The dispersion of the Mandinkas; according to a story by genealogist Kélé-Monson Diabaté at Karaya Cercle of Kita.)
Diango Cissé, Massa Makan Diabaté. Bamako: Editions Populaires, 1970. 110p. (Collection 'Hier').

This is the epic poem of the foundation of the city of Kita, as told by genealogist (and griot) Kélé-Monson Diabaté. The text is in Bambara, with French translation in verse and well as free translation.

738 **The epic of Askia Mohammed.**
Recorded, translated, edited, and annotated by Thomas A. Hale,
recounted by Nouhou Malio. Bloomington, Indiana: Indiana
University Press, 1996. 88p. bibliog. (African Epic Series).

This great Songhay epic of Mohammed I, Askia of Songhai (1443-1538), ruler of Gao
from 1493 to 1528, was performed in 1980-81 by griot Nouhou Malio and translated
by Hale into English in 1,602 lines. Hale also published this text in Songhay (Songai)
and English in his *Scribe, griot, and novelist: narrative interpreters of the Songhay
Empire* (Gainesville, Florida: University of Florida Press: Center for African Studies,
1990. 313p.), which helps place the epic in a broader context. The original title in
Songhay is: Mamar Kassaye deeda.

739 **L'epopée bambara de Ségou.** (The Bambara epic of Segou.)
Collected and translated by Lilyan Kesteloot with the collaboration of
Amadou Traoré, Jean-Baptiste Traoré. Paris: L'Harmattan, 1993.
2 vols. maps. bibliog.

The esteemed authors produced this text of the famous African epic of Segou, second
only to *Soundiata*. This is a fine French translation of the Bambara story of the
Kingdom of Segou in the eighteenth and nineteenth centuries. Six different griots were
recorded in the field between 1964 and 1971. The twelve episodes include: Da
Monzon et Bassi de Samaniana, Biton Koulibaly, Ngolo Diarra, Monzon Diarra, Da
Monzon, Bakari Dian et Bilissi, Da Monzon trahit Bakari Dian, Bakari Dian et les
Peuls de Kounari, Da Monzon et Koumba Silamagan, Da Monzon et Silamaka du
Macina, Le roi de Koré, and Kârta Tiéma et Da Monzon. Volume one (p. 125-26)
contains the family trees of the dynasties of the Segou kings, according to Charles
Monteil and Amadou Hampâté Bâ.

740 **La grande épopée d'al Hadj Omar.** (The great epic of El Hadj
Omar.)
Chiaka Diarassouba. Bamako: Editions-Imprimeries du Mali,
[between 1981 and 1985]. 73p. maps. bibliog.

This is an epic poem of El Hadj Omar Tall (Umar Tal; 1794-1864), founder of the
Tukulor Empire, one of West Africa's great leaders and subject of the songs of Malian
griots. This Muslim cleric led his people to victory against the powerful nobles of the
Senegal-Niger River region and the French colonial forces. He defeated the Bambara
kingdom of Segou in 1861. The numerous maps and genealogical tables of the
dynasties help place him in his proper historical context.

741 **The heart of the Ngoni: heroes of the African kingdom of Segu.**
Harold Courlander, with Ousmane Sako. New York: Crown, 1982.
178p. map. bibliog.

In this standard text, the authors base their narration of the kingdom of Segou upon the
tales of several griots, 'singers and keepers of history'. In weaving the tales of the
great kings, the folklore of the Bambara and Soninke (Sarakole) peoples is revealed.
The kingdom of Segou emerged in the early seventeenth century and flourished until
1892 when French and Muslim conquerors drove out the then king.

742 **L'histoire du Mandé.** (The history of the Mande.)
[Performed by] Jeli Kanku Madi Jabaté de Kéla, text collected,
translated, and annotated by Madina Ly-Tall, Seydou Camara, Bouna
Diouara. Paris: Association SCOA pour la Recherche Scientifique en
Afrique Noire, 1987. 296p. map.

'Master of the word' of Kela, Jeli Kanku Madi, recites this historic epic poem only
once every seven years for the Kamablon ceremony which marks the raising of the
roof of the sacred dwelling in Kela. The epic consists of 1,937 lines and appears in
Manding with a literal French translation on facing pages. A freely translated and
condensed French version is also included (p. 9-75).

743 **Kaïdara.**
Amadou Hampâté Bâ. Washington, DC: Three Continents Press,
1988. 159p. map. bibliog.

Bâ, the revered Malian defender of oral tradition, has written numerous books and
articles on history, oral tradition and religion. This is the first English-language
translation of *Kaïdara* and only the second of Bâ's works translated into English. It
includes the text in verse of *Kaïdara*, a traditional Fulani initiatory text about a hero in
search of profound knowledge. It also contains quite helpful chapters including an
introduction by Lilyan Kesteloot as well as a chapter, 'Kings, sages, rogues: the
historical writings of Amadou Hampâté Bâ' by Whitman and an English translation of
an interview Whitman conducted with Bâ in 1979. The three glossaries include Arabic
words and concepts, Fulani words and concepts, and proper names. The excellent
bibliography (p. 157-59) includes primary and secondary sources on Bâ. A version in
verse of *Kaïdara* also appeared in French and Fulfulde (Paris: Julliard, 1969. 183p.)
and was also published in French prose (Abidjan: Nouvelles Editions Ivoiriennes,
1994. 112p.). *Kaïdara* along with *Njeddo Dewal* are published in Bâ's *Contes
initiatiques peuls* (Peul initiation tales) (Paris: Stock, 1994. 397p.). Some of Bâ's
other important works include: *The fortunes of Wangrin* (q.v.); *Amkoullel, l'enfant
peul* (Amkoullel, Peul child) (q.v.); *Petit Bodiel et autres contes de la savane* (Little
Bodiel and other tales of the savannah) (Paris: Stock, 1994. 259p.); *L'Empire peul du
Macina* (The Peul Empire of Macina) (q.v.) and *Jésus vu par un musulman* (Jesus
viewed by a Muslim) (Paris: Stock, 1994. 125p.).

744 **Oral epics from Africa: vibrant voices from a vast continent.**
John William Johnson, Thomas A. Hale, Stephen Belcher.
Bloomington, Indiana: Indiana University Press, 1997. 331p. map.
bibliog. (African Epic Series).

This introductory anthology of excerpts specifically aimed at the English-language
reader is destined to become a classic text on oral African epics. Nineteen of the
twenty-five epics are from West Africa, and all are of interest to readers of this
bibliography. Those collected in Mali include: *Wagadu* (Soninke), *Son-Jara*
(Malinké), *Fa-Jigi* (Wasulunka), *Bamana Segu* (Bambara), *Sonsan of Kaarta*
(Bambara), *Kambili* (Wasulunka), *Sara* (Malinké), *Hambodedio and Saïgalare*
(Fulfulde), and *Silâmaka and Poullôri* (Fulfulde). The introduction, together with the
brief description of each epic, places it in its proper context. For further study,
publication details of the full text is given, when available. The work includes an
excellent bibliography (p. 303-14).

745 **Récits épiques des chasseurs bamanan du Mali.** (Epic tales from
Bambara hunters of Mali.)
Mamadu Jara, [collected and translated by] Annik Thoyer. Paris:
L'Harmattan, 1995. 255p.
There are numerous collections of epic poems about hunting from Mali. This
collection contains corrections and modifications of the first two volumes of the
author's 1978 *Chants de chasseurs du Mali* (Hunters' tales from Mali). The four
poems performed by Mamadu Jara are: 'Sirankòmi', 'Banjugu', 'Manden Mori', and
'Kanbili'. Bambara text and French translation are given on facing pages. Thoyer also
published the bilingual hunting poem *Nyakhalen la forgeronne* (Nyakhalen the
blacksmith) (Paris: A. Thoyer, 1986. 69p.). Dosseh Joseph Coulibaly published *Récit
des chasseurs du Mali: Dingo Kanbili* (Hunters' tales from Mali: Dingo Kanbili)
(Paris: Conseil International de la Langue Française, 1985. 117p.) as sung by Bala
Jinba Jakite. Myeru Baa and Mahamadu Lamini Sunbunu performed *La geste de
Fanta Maa: archétype du chasseur dans la culture des Bozo* (The epic of Fanta Maa:
the archetype of the hunter in the culture of the Bozos) (Niamey: CELHTO, 1987.
201p.) which was translated and edited by Shekh Tijaan Hayidara and also published
as *Le fils des sept femmes bozo: Fanta Maa* (The son of seven Bozo women: Fanta
Maa) (Bamako: Institut des Sciences Humaines, 1986. 81[i.e. 162]p.).

746 **Silâmaka & Poullôri: récit épique peul.** (Silâmaka & Poullôri: Fulah
epic tale.)
Told by Tinguidji, edited by Christiane Seydou. Paris: A. Colin,
1972. 227p. map. bibliog. (Classiques Africains, no. 13).
Griot Boûbacar Tinguidji recorded this traditional Fulah epic from the Empire of
Macina (end of the eighteenth to the beginning of the nineteenth century) in which the
Fulah (Peul) leaders rebel against the authority of the Bambara kingdom of Segou.
French and Fulah (Fulfulde) appear on opposite pages. Three sound discs of
Tinguidji's performance are included, as he accompanies himself on the *hoddu* or
ngoni (a lute). Seydou also published *La geste de Ham-Bodêdio, ou, Hama le Rouge*
(The epic of Ham-Bodêdio, or, Hama the Red) (same publisher, 1976. 419p.), *Contes
et fables des veillées* (Evening tales and fables) (Paris: Nubia, 1976. 300p.) which
contains 35 tales from Mali in French and Fulah, as well as *Des preux, des belles –
des larrons: contes du Mali* (Warriors, beauties – thieves: tales from Mali) (Paris:
Nubia, 1987. 95p.) which contains three Fulah tales translated into French. Gilbert
Vieillard's *Récits peuls du Macina, du Kounari, du Djilgodji et du Torodi (Mali-
Haute-Volta-Niger)* (Peul tales from from Macina, Kounari, Djilgodji and Torodi
(Mali-Upper Volta-Niger) (Niamey: Centre Culturel Franco-Nigérien, 1966. 142p.)
contains eight tales in French and Fulah.

747 **The songs of Seydou Camara. Volume one: Kambili.**
Translation by Charles S. Bird, with Mamadou Koita and Bourama
Soumaoro. Bloomington, Indiana: African Studies Center, Indiana
University, 1974. 120 leaves. (Occasional Paper in Mande Studies,
no. 1).
This 2,727-line epic Maninka song by Camara appears here in English translation. In
the introduction Bird describes: the bard Seydou Camara, born in the Wasulu region
of Mali near the Guinea border, who makes his living primarily as a harp-lute player
and singer for hunters; the hunters; the poetic form combining the praise-proverb,

narrative and song modes; and the story itself, the origins and events in the life of Kambili the great hunter. See also Bird's 'Heroic songs of the Mande hunters', in *African folklore,* edited by Richard M. Dorson (Bloomington, Indiana: Indiana University Press, 1972, p. 275-93), and (with Martha B. Kendall) his chapter 'The Mande hero: text and context' in *Explorations in African systems of thought* (Bloomington, Indiana: Indiana University Press, 1980, p. 13-26). Gerald A. Cashion's 'Hunters of the Mande: a behavioral code and worldview derived from the study of their folklore' (PhD thesis, Indiana University, 1982. 2 vols), which contains in addition two epics sung by Seydou Camara, is also of interest in this context.

748 **Stability and change: praise-poetry and narrative traditions in the epics of Mali.**
Stephen Paterson Belcher IV.   PhD thesis, Brown University, Providence, Rhode Island, 1985. 405p. (Available from University Microfilms International, Ann Arbor, Michigan, order no. 8519808).

This is an analysis of three great Malian epics: Sunjata (Malinke), Cycle of Segou (Bambara), and Silamaka and Hambodedjo (Fulfulde). It includes five appendices: 'Narrative analysis of the Sunjata', 'The songs in the Sunjata', 'Epic material in Mali', 'The Malinke and Bambara creation myths', and 'Narrative analysis of Silamaka and Poullori'.

749 **A state of intrigue: the epic of Bamana Segu according to Tayiru Banbera.**
Edited by David C. Conrad.   New York: Oxford University Press for the British Academy, 1990. 368p. maps. bibliog. (Union Académique Internationale. Fontes Historiae Africanae, Series Varia VI).

This account of people, events and customs of the eighteenth- and nineteenth-century Bambara city-state of Segu was narrated by Tayiru Banbera, a professional bard, in Segu during six sessions from 28 February to 11 March 1976. The exceptional account was transcribed and translated with the assistance of Soumaila Diakité in 1976-77 and 1983-84. In his introduction (p. 1-40), Conrad analyses and gives it historical context. The 7,942-line narration itself (p. 41-327) is made thoroughly accessible by detailed notes. Three maps of Segu and the region, chronological tables of Segu leaders (p. 336-38), a glossary (p. 339-41) and a useful bibliography (p. 343-48) complete the excellent volume which Richard Roberts praises in his review 'Bamana Segu: an annotated epic', *Journal of African History,* vol. 33, no. 1 (1992), p. 141-42.

Tales, fables and legends

750 **A l'écoute des anciens du village.** (Listening to the village elders.)
El Hadji Sadia Traoré.   Bamako: Editions Populaires, 1972. 104p. (Collection 'Hier').

The thirty-seven short tales each tell a moral lesson.

751   **African folktales in the New World.**
William Bascom.   Bloomington, Indiana; Indianapolis, Indiana:
Indiana University Press, 1992. 243p. bibliog.
In the foreword, Alan Dundes explains that the same or similar folktale is found not only in adjacent areas, but in places removed by time and place. Thus an African-American tale could have many African variants. In this publication, the tales are translated into English and grouped into related themes. The ethnic groups from Mali represented here include the Malinke, Fulani (Peul), Bambara, Bozo, Dogon and Twareg (Tuareg). A cluster of Malian tales appears under the subject 'agreement to sell mothers'.

752   **L'arbre et l'enfant; Sassa: 2 contes du Mali trilingues: français,
bambara, soninké.** (The tree and the child; 2 trilingual tales from
Mali: French, Bambara, Soninke.)
Penda Soumaré.   Paris: L'Harmattan, 1996. 79p. (Contes du Mali).
L'Harmattan has recently been publishing bilingual and trilingual Malian tales for children. Another trilingual tale by the author is: *Femme sorcière; Galadio* (Female witch; Galadio) (Paris: L'Harmattan, 1996. 57p.). Aliette Sallée and Denis Rolland authored *Téné*, available in Soninke–French or Bambara–French parallel texts (Paris: L'Harmattan, 1995. 21p.).

753   **Au coin du feu: légendes du pays bamanan.** (By the fireside: legends
from the land of the Bamana.)
Issa Baba Traoré.   Bamako: Jamana, 1989. 94p.
These tales, riddles, and legends of the Bambara are both timeless and full of atmosphere.

754   **Contes bambara: Mali et Sénégal oriental.** (Bambara tales: Mali and
Eastern Senegal.)
Texts collected and translated by Veronika Görög-Karady, Gérard
Meyer.   Paris: Conseil International de la Langue Française: EDICEF,
1985. 174p. map. bibliog. (Fleuve et Flamme. Série Bilingue).
One of several anthologies of Bambara tales collected by Meyer and/or Görög-Karady, this is a collection of twelve tales collected in Bamako in 1972 and 1973. Themes covered in the tales about people include marriage, family and polygamy. In the tales about animals, one finds a physically weak but shrewd animal playing opposite a physically strong but stupid animal. In French and Bambara on facing pages. *L'Enfant rusé, et autres contes bambara: Mali et Sénégal oriental* (The crafty child, and other Bambara tales: Mali and Eastern Senegal) (same publisher, 1984. 160p.) contains twenty-four tales translated into French, including all twelve published here. Meyer also published *Contes du pays manding: Guinée, Mali, Sénégal, Gambie* (Tales from Mande country: Guinea, Mali, Senegal, Gambia) (same publisher, 1988. 162p.), and Görög-Karady published *Contes bambara du Mali* (Bambara tales from Mali) (Paris: Publications Orientalistes de France, 1979. 119p.).

755 **Contes de Tombouctou et du Macina.** (Tales from Timbuktu and Macina.)
Albakaye Ousmane Kounta. Paris: L'Harmattan, 1987-89. 2 vols.
(Collection 'La Légende des Mondes').

These traditional tales, in verse, contain moral lessons. All the heroes, whether human, animal or plants, are diligent workers. The collection contains nine tales from the Peul of the Niger River Bend.

756 **Contes et légendes du Kourmina.** (Tales and legends of Kourmina.)
Bocar Cissé. Bamako: Jamana, 1989. 127p.

Kourmina was the most important province of the Songhay Empire ruled by the Askia dynasty. These historical tales date from the tenth to the sixteenth century and include subjects taken from the Tarikh-el-Fettach under the reign of Askia Daoud (1549-82) as well as from a tenth-century Jewish tribe called the Bâni-Israël, located in present-day Tindirma.

757 **Contes et légendes Soninké = Soninkan dongomanu do burujunu.**
(Soninke tales and legends.)
Texts collected and translated by Oudiary Makan Dantioko. Paris: Conseil International de la Langue Française: EDICEF, 1978. 180p.
bibliog. (Fleuve et Flamme).

These twelve tales from Mali, Senegal and Mauritania are about animals and people. The introduction includes a description of the Soninke region, the Soninke alphabet and transcription rules, and a one-page summary of regional variations of Soninke. The text appears in French and Soninke on opposite pages. *Contes soninké* (Soninke tales) (Paris: Présence Africaine; Agence de Coopération Culturelle et Technique, 1987. 132p.) contains twelve tales in French and Soninke as well as a few proverbs and maxims (p. 127-29).

758 **Les contes et les légendes d'Aroun: une hyène 'manding'.** (Aroun's tales and legends: a 'Manding' hyena.)
Harouna Kouyaté. Paris: Pensée Universelle, 1981. 93p.

Aroun, the author's pseudonym, weaves tales of the savannah and tropical forests in which he grew up. The animals talk to each other and to the people they meet in this story of Sister Hyena.

759 **Contes populaires du Mali.** (Popular tales from Mali.)
Mamby Sidibé, with the collaboration of Jacques Djian, illustrated by Elisabeth Moritz. Paris: Présence Africaine, 1982. 2 vols. (Collection 'Jeunesse').

These two volumes of Malian tales based on oral tradition contain fifty-two tales in 240 pages. They are aimed at young readers, aged eleven and older. The subjects range from animals, real and fantastic, to exemplary heroes and supernatural beings. Mohamed Lamine Cissé's *Contes du Mali* (Tales from Mali) (Paris: Nathan; ACCT; EDIM, 1989. 127p.) is also aimed at young readers and contains twelve tales.

760 **Légendes du Mali.** (Legends from Mali.)
Abdoulaye Amadou Sagara. Bamako: Jamana, 1990. 106p.
The four popular legends and stories included here are *La colère du Wagadou-Bida,*
Tapama Djénépo de Djenné, Bafoulabé Mali-Sadio, and *Lalla de Sansanding.* Eternal
love is the central theme.

761 **La pierre barbue et autres contes du Mali: édition bilingue**
bambara–français. (The bearded stone and other tales from Mali:
Bambara–French bilingual edition.)
Text transcribed and translated by G. Dumestre, illustrated by Caroline
Hawkins. Angers, France: Bibliothèque Municipale, 1989. 127p.
bibliog.
One of several recent collections of Malian folk literature (including tales, proverbs,
riddles and songs) in bilingual editions. The eighteen works appear in French and
Bambara, on opposite pages. This volume was published in order to aid in Mali's
literacy campaign. It includes a brief *'lexique'* which defines fifteen French terms that
are unknown in France or have a different meaning there.

762 **Soudan français: contes soudanais.** (French Soudan: Sudanese tales.)
C. Monteil, preface by M. René Basset. Paris: E. Leroux, 1905.
Reprinted, Nendeln, Liechtenstein: Kraus Reprint, 1977. 205p.
(Collection de Contes et Chansons Populaires, no. 28).
This volume includes forty-seven Islamic-influenced tales of Soninke (Sarakole),
Bambara, Khasonkhe (Khassonke) people, and an essay, 'Les traditions religieuses
musulmanes chez les Soudanais' (Moslem religious traditions of the Sudanese)
(p. 169-202).

763 **Tales and ideology: the revolt of sons in Bambara-Malinké tales.**
Veronika Görög-Karady. In: *Power, marginality and African oral*
literature. Edited by Graham Furniss, Liz Gunner. Johannesburg:
Witwatersrand University Press, 1995, p. 83-91.
Görög-Karady discusses two representative types of Bambara-Malinké father/son
tales. In the first, the domineering father confines his son in order to prevent him from
establishing sexual relations. In the second, the father requires that his sons jump over
a spear to prove that they have not had sexual relations. They are each put into a
Bambara-Malinké social context. See also Görög-Karady and Gérard Meyer's *Images*
féminines dans les contes africains: aire culturelle manding (Female images in
African tales: Mande cultural space) (Paris: Conseil International de la Langue
Française, 1988. 172p.).

764 **Veillées au Mali.** (Evenings in Mali.)
Bokar N'Diaye. Bamako: Editions Populaires, 1970. 221p.
(Collection 'Hier').
The twenty-three tales contained in this volume are French translations of popular
Malian tales passed down through Toucouleur (Tukulor) oral tradition. N'Diaye also
authored *Groupes ethniques au Mali* (q.v.) and served in Mali's cabinet until 1973.

Proverbs and riddles

765 **Devinettes bambara.** (Bambara riddles.)
Gérard Meyer, with the collaboration of Jean-Pierre Onattara, Issa
Diarra.   Paris: L'Harmattan, 1978. 68p. bibliog. (Les Dossiers
d'Afrique et Langage).

The authors characterize this collection of ninety-five Bambara riddles as
'provisional'. They come from Sikasso, Mali and Tambacunda, Senegal. Each riddle
is given in Bambara and French translation, accompanied by brief explanations for
'foreigners'.

766 **Devinettes recueillis du Mali.** (Riddles collected in Mali.)
Guissé Maliendy.   *Notes Africaines,* 112 (1966), p. 133-35.

The ninety-two riddles contained here are divided into those about people, animals,
plants, things, and moral lessons. No indication is given regarding their source or
ethnicity.

767 **Devinettes touaregues (Mali et Niger).** (Touareg riddles: Mali and
Niger.)
Mohamed Aghali Zakara.   In: *Devinettes berbères.* Under the
direction of Fernand Bentolila.   Paris: Conseil International de la
Langue Française, 1986, vol. 2, p. 215-48. (Fleuve et Flamme).

The fifty Touareg riddles, collected in Niger in 1974 and in Mali in 1984, are divided
into the following themes: body; human feelings and social relations; animal and
vegetable world; technical world; and topographical and cosmological world. For each
riddle, the original Touareg (Tuareg) text is followed by a literal French translation, a
free French translation, and any necessary explanatory notes.

768 **L'image, la langue et la pensée.** (Image, language and thought.)
Jean Cauvin.   St. Augustin, Germany: Anthropos-Institut–Haus
Völker und Kulturen, 1980. 2 vols. maps. bibliog. (Collectanea Instituti
Anthropos, nos. 23-24).

These two scholarly volumes (over 1,450 pages), based on the author's 1977 doctoral
thesis from the University of Paris-III, stem from the eight years Father Cauvin spent
among the Minianka in Karangasso, Mali. The first volume is an analysis and
classification of Minianka proverbs, including an analysis of their manner of thinking.
It also includes several excellent bibliographies: one ethnological and another
linguistic, on the Senufo-Minianka; a third on oral tradition; and a fourth on Black
African proverbs. Volume 2 is a compilation of proverbs from Karangasso, in
Minianka and French translation, including their origins, a description of how they are
used, and a French 'abstract' of the proverb, stripped of its imagery.

769 **Initiation à la culture bamanan à travers les proverbes.** (Initiation to Bamanan culture through proverbs.)
Yiritié Bagayoko. Milan, Italy: Federazione Organismi Cristiani di Servizio Internazionale Volontario, 1991. 160p. (Collana Contributi, no. 16).

The author has gathered 709 Bambara proverbs which are organized into ten chapters such as the spoken word, family, attachment to traditions and beliefs, etc. Thirty-one selected riddles appear at the close of the book. Also published in the same series: Jean Gabriel Diarra's *Proverbes bwa* (Bwa proverbs) (1991. 86p.), from the Bozo people.

770 **Proverbes et contes bambara, accompagnés d'une traduction française et précédés d'un abrégé de droit coutumier bambara et malinké.** (Bambara proverbs and tales, accompanied by a French translation and preceded by a summary of Bambara and Malinke customary law.)
Moussa Travélé. Paris: P. Geuthner, 1923. Reprinted, 1977. 240p.

This is another important work published in 1923 by the French Sudanese chief interpreter after his *Petit manuel français–bambara* (Little French–Bambara manual) and *Petit dictionnaire français–bambara et bambara–français* (q.v.). Part one covers Bambara and Malinke customary law (p. 5-34) in some detail. The remainder of the volume is written in Bambara with French translations. Part two is a collection of Bambara proverbs (p. 36-50) and riddles (p. 50-53), while part three contains a collection of tales (p. 56-236).

771 **Recueil de proverbes bambaras et malinkes.** (Collection of Bambara and Malinke proverbs.)
Mgr Molin. Issy-les-Moulineaux, France: Presses Missionnaires, 1960. 315p.

No less than 2,123 Bambara and Malinke proverbs, with their French translations, are contained within this publication written by Bishop Molin, of Garba, and collected for many years by the White Fathers. They are grouped by themes such as religion, family, society, the vicissitudes of life, etc.

Other folklore and oral traditions

772 **Chants de femmes au Mali.** (Women's songs from Mali.)
René Luneau. Paris: Luneau Ascot, 1981. 175p.

This a a study on women's songs from the Bambara village of Beleko. The women suffer during certain stages of their lives such as when they undergo excision at puberty or if they find themselves sterile. The songs are transcribed only into French.

773 **Gens de la parole: essai sur la condition et le rôle des griots dans la société malinké.** (People of the word: essay on the condition and role of griots in Malinke society.)
Sory Camara. Paris: ACCT and Karthala; Conakry: SAEC, 1992. 375p. maps. bibliog. (Collection 'Hommes et Sociétés').

The griot (*dyeli* in Bambara) has a unique, hereditary position in Malinke society: he is an entertainer, musician, genealogist, buffoon, and keeper of oral history. In this in-depth study of the griots, who are members of an inferior 'caste', Camara first analyses traditional Malinke society, then focuses on the social conditions of the griot. The griot's complex role in Malinke social and political life is the subject of the third part, which includes a number of griot texts and women's songs (p. 265-342). The superb bibliography (p. 357-70) which consists of publications nearly all in French, is divided into specific helpful topics and sub-topics. Unfortunately it was not updated from its first edition of 1976.

774 **Islam in the oral traditions of Mali: Bilali and Surakata.**
David C. Conrad. *Journal of African History,* vol. 26, no. 1 (1985), p. 33-49. bibliog.

The author establishes the Islamic origins of Bilali and Surakata (two characters found in the songs of Bambara and Mandinka bards), describes aspects of Islamic and pre-Islamic cultural influences on the bardic art, and notes their current status in Mali. Conrad's 1981 doctoral thesis at the School of Oriental and African Studies, University of London, was entitled 'The role of oral artists in the history of Mali'. See also his 'Maurice Delafosse and the pre-Sunjata *trône du Mandé*' (Mande throne) in the *Bulletin of the School of Oriental and African Studies,* vol. 46, no. 2 (1983), p. 335-37.

775 **La mémoire senufo: bois sacré, éducation et chefferie.** (Senufo memory: sacred woods, education, and chieftaincy.)
Ferdinand Ouattara Tiona. Paris: ARSAN, 1988. 175p. maps.

This collection of Senufo texts of oral tradition were collected in two departments of southern Mali, Korogo and Ferké, in 1978. The first part consists of generalities, the methodology of the study, and a linguistic notice of Senari consonants, vowels and tones. The second part contains seven Senari texts with a literal French translation. The third part is a catalogue of Senufo sacred woods mentioned in the preceding texts.

776 **Siramuri Diabate et ses enfants: une étude sur deux générations des griots Malinke.** (Siramuri Diabate and her children: a study of two generations of Malinke griots.)
Jan Jansen, translated by Cemako Kante. Utrecht, The Netherlands: ISOR; Bamako: ISH, 1991. 147p. bibliog.

The unusual perspective represented here is twofold: first, the author examines the changes between two generations of Malian griots in their performance, repertory, competencies and method of communication; second, both male and female griots were studied. Research is based on field recordings made in Bamako, Kangaba, and Kela in 1988-89. The work includes a summary in English (p. 144).

777 **West African tricksters: web of purpose, dance of delight.**
Robert D. Pelton. In: *Mythical trickster figures: contours, contexts, and criticisms.* Edited by William J. Hynes, William G. Doty. Tuscaloosa, Alabama; London: University of Alabama Press, 1993, p. 122-40.

The Ashanti of southern Ghana, the Fon of Benin, the Yoruba of Nigeria, and the Dogon of southern Mali and northern Burkina Faso are the subjects of this article on the trickster. In the mythology of the Dogon trickster, Ogo-Yurugu begins as Ogo, who rebels against Amma, the high god and his father. As punishment for trying to gain control of his own destiny, he is transformed into Yurugu, the pale fox, and forced to walk the earth on all fours. For a more complete analysis of the trickster, see Pelton's full-length monograph (especially chapter five), *The trickster in West Africa: a study of mythic irony and sacred delight* (Berkeley, California; Los Angeles, California; London: University of California Press, 1980. 312p.).

778 **Women, servitude and history: the oral historical traditions of women of servile condition in the kingdom of Jaara (Mali) from the fifteenth to the mid-nineteenth century.**
Mamadou Diawara. In: *Discourse and its disguises: the interpretation of African oral texts.* Edited by Karin Barber, P. F. De Moraes Farias. Birmingham, England: Centre of West African Studies, University of Birmingham, 1989, p. 109-37. map. bibliog.

The author examines the *tanbasire*, a corpus of Soninko (sing.: Soninke) songs sung by middle-aged and elderly female royal servants. He analyses their songs, the role of women in conveying historical traditions and the originality and value of servile women's traditions and includes a glossary of Soninke expressions (p. 130-33), a map of the kingdom of Jaara during its maximum extension in the early seventeenth century (p. 134), and extensive notes (p. 127-30). He also authored *La graine de la parole* (The seed of the word) (Stuttgart, Germany: F. Steiner, 1990. 189p.) which is a revision of his 1985 doctoral thesis at the Ecole des Hautes Etudes en Sciences Sociales, Paris: 'La dimension sociale et politique des traditions orales du Royaume de Jaara (Mali) du XVe au milieu du XIXe siècle' (The social and political dimensions of the oral traditions of the Kingdom of Jaara (Mali) from the fifteenth to the middle of the nineteenth century) (2 vols).

Sports and Leisure Activities

779 **African dolls for play and magic = Poupées africaines pour jeux et magie.**
Esther A. Dagan. Montreal, Canada: Galérie Amrad African Arts, 1990. 143p. maps. bibliog.
Dolls and figurines from thirty-five African countries and over eighty ethnic groups are represented in this presentation of dolls as playthings, items of magic, religion, and ritual. Their role and value as objects of the fertility cult in certain African societies is examined. A section on Malian dolls and figurines, with nineteen black-and-white illustrations, is included on pages 54-58.

780 **The art of West African cooking.**
Dinah Ameley Ayensu, drawings by Diane Robertson. Garden City, New York: Doubleday, 1972. 1st ed. 145p.
In this cookbook by Ghanaian Ayensu, there are fifteen recipes from Mali, ranging from chicken peanut butter soup, stewed okra (a Bambara dish), to broiled fish with finger-pepper sauce.

781 **Jeux et jouets de l'Ouest africain.** (Games and toys of West Africa.)
Charles Béart. Dakar: IFAN, 1955. 2 vols in 1 (888p.). bibliog.
(Mémoires de l'Institut Fondamental d'Afrique Noire, no. 42).
This is a broad examination of various West African toys, games, play objects and leisure pursuits: dolls, bicycles, drawing, acrobatics, playing cards, board games, water toys and games, magic, dancing, rituals and parodies, music, word games, storytelling, theatre, etc. Béart has included an extensive index of games and toys; many terms are in various African languages, including Dogon and Fula (Fulfulde), followed by the French equivalent if one exists.

782 **Match.**
Bamako: Match, [1993?]- . bimonthly.
This newspaper is devoted to Malian sports and sports personalities. A recent special issue (23 July 1997) focused on soccer and basketball. The earliest known issue is number 16 (25 Nov. 1993).

783 **Les recettes culinaires de la 'Baramousso'.** (Culinary recipes of the 'Baramousso'.)
Ami Sow. [n.p.]: [n.p.], 1994[?]. 64p.
Sixty recipes are given in this cookbook from Mali. They include hors d'oeuvres such as *n'gôyô* or African eggplant, potato croquettes, several meat or smoked fish stews, sauces made from peanuts or vegetable greens, as well as a few desserts such as banana beignets (i.e., fritters, which can also be served as an accompaniment to a meat dish), and drinks such as sorrel juice. Most of the ingredients should be available in the United Kingdom or in the United States, although occasionally some of the terms used do not appear in a French dictionary and are not otherwise explained. Ten colour illustrations are included.

784 **Salif Keita, mes quatre vérités.** (Salif Keita, my four truths.)
Igor Follot, Gérard Dreyfus. Paris: Chiron, 1977. 128p.
In this biography of the famous Malian soccer player, Keita recounts his childhood, his youth on the streets of Bamako, his break into the world of African soccer, his eventful departure for Europe, and the joys and disappointments of his career. He reveals his feelings towards his career and speaks about the future of African soccer, not to mention the great political problems that trouble the African continent. Also noteworthy is his rigorous analysis of the evolution of professional soccer at a time when the tendency is for it to fall prey to monetary forces. Keita's profound and lingering attachment to traditional African values is evident throughout the book. A list of Keita's awards and achievements is included.

785 **Scott 1998 standard postage stamp catalogue.**
Sidney, Ohio: Scott Publishing, 1997. 154th ed. 6 vols.
This annual reference tool contains numerous black-and-white illustrations of Malian stamps under the headings 'French Sudan' and 'Mali, Republic of'. Because of its comprehensiveness and the inclusion of descriptions of stamps which are not illustrated, this catalogue is essential for any philatelist, expert or novice.

786 **Standard catalog of world coins.**
Chester L. Krause, Clifford Mishler, edited by Colin R. Bruce II.
Iola, Wisconsin: Krause Publications, 1997. 1998, 24th anniversary ed. 1,792p.
This annual catalogue contains coins from 1901 to the present; in this edition, coins of Mali are illustrated in black and white under 'French West Africa' and 'Mali'. A similar recent source for Malian coins is *Collecting world coins* (Iola, Wisconsin: Krause Publications, 1995. 6th ed.).

Libraries, Archives, Museums and Research

Libraries

787 **African libraries.**
Glenn L. Sitzman.   Metuchen, New Jersey: Scarecrow Press, 1988.
486p. bibliog.
Containing much useful information about African libraries and librarianship, this work includes essays, a chronology, a nation-by-nation survey of libraries, and an extensive bibliography (about 2,700 entries). Malian libraries receive special attention on pages 207-9, where the author describes five public libraries, the National Library in Bamako, eight academic libraries and eighteen special libraries. Helen Daview includes seven entries for Mali (p. 63-64) in *Libraries in West Africa: a directory* (Oxford: Hans Zell; Munich: Saur, 1982. 170p.). A. O. Banjo's *Social science libraries in West Africa: a directory* (Lagos: Nigerian Institute of International Affairs, 1987. 63p.) provides a very brief description of Mali and mention of its largest libraries (p. 15) and the addresses of four libraries (p. 57).

788 **Mali, National Library of.**
Abdoul Aziz Diallo.   In: *Encyclopedia of library and information science*.   New York: Dekker, 1990, vol. 45, p. 246-53.
A description of the National Library of Mali, including a brief history, its operation, and its collections.

789 **The SCOLMA directory of libraries and special collections on Africa in the United Kingdom and in Europe.**
Tom French, Harry Hannam.   London and New York: H. Zell, 1993.
5th ed., revised and expanded. 355p.
This Standing Conference on Library Materials on Africa (SCOLMA) directory of European libraries identifies significant holdings of materials relevant to African

studies. The Bibliothèque Nationale in France and the Rijksuniversiteit Utrecht Bibliotheek Centrum Uithof in The Netherlands are the two institutions specifically indexed under Mali, but other Africana collections are cited as having relevant Malian materials, such as the Centre des Archives d'Outre-Mer, Aix-en-Provence, France.

790 West Africa, libraries in.
Dorothy S. Obi. In: *Encyclopedia of library and information science.* New York: Dekker, 1982, vol. 33, p. 4-18.
Although there is little specific information about Mali to be found, this is an excellent overview of libraries in West Africa as a whole. The coverage is up to 1980.

Archives

791 The A. O. F. Archives and the study of African history.
May Niles Maack. *Bulletin de l'IFAN,* vol. 42. Series B, no. 2 (1980), p. 277-98. bibliog.
Maack has arranged this substantive article about the history of the French West African archives in Dakar into the following parts: 'French African archives prior to 1911'; 'The foundation of the A.O.F. archives'; 'The archives and oral tradition'; 'The revival of interest in African history'; and, finally, 'The Archives Nationales and the Archives Culturelles'. Saliou Mbaye, Director of the Archives of Senegal, provides a history of the archives (p. 11-16), a detailed description of the major holdings of each series (p. 28-163), and directions on their use and major legislative texts (p. 166-85) in *Guide des archives de l'Afrique occidentale française* (Dakar: Archives du Sénégal, 1990. 204p. bibliog.). The volume is indexed by author and subject and includes numerous bibliographical references throughout.

792 Archival resources in Mali.
David Conrad. *History in Africa,* vol. 3 (1976), p. 175-80.
This article not only offers an outline of the 'Classification of archival material' (p. 178-80) and describes the national archives and other sources of historical data, but is also full of practical information on obtaining permits for research and photography, and on the archives' opening times. René Lamey describes 'Les Archives de la Société des Pères Blancs (Missionnaires d'Afrique)' in *History in Africa,* vol. 1 (1974), p. 161-65, in which the records of the Dioceses of Bamako, Gao, Keyes and Sikasso are to be found. Carole W. Dickerman reports 'On using the White Fathers' archives', *History in Africa,* vol. 8 (1981), p. 319-22; these are in Rome and are 'a researcher's delight – well-organized, convenient, and valuable' (p. 322).

793 **The archival system of former French West Africa.**
G. Wesley Johnson. *African Studies Bulletin,* vol. 8, no. 1 (April 1965), p. 48-58.

The author reports on his archival centre visits in French West Africa in September-October 1964. He describes the origin of the federal archives and the territorial archival system, and gives many details about the history, holdings and organization of the archival centres in Senegal, Mauritania, Mali/French Soudan (p. 52-53), Upper Volta (Burkina Faso), Niger, Dahomey (Benin), Ivory Coast (Côte d'Ivoire) and Guinea. In addition, he adds notes on research conditions in 1965, singling out Mali for the greater difficulties encountered. In *Répertoire des archives* (Catalogue of the archives) (Dakar: Services des Archives du Haut Commissariat de la République en Afrique Occidentale Française, 1954-56, 1958. various pagings), Claude Faure and Jacques Charpy provide a detailed inventory through each topical series of the materials held in the French West African archives in Dakar, Senegal. The series are: Series A, Official acts, 1817-1895 (1958. 18p.); Series B, General correspondence, 1779-1895 (1955. 70p.); Series D, Military affairs, 1763-1920 (1956. 90p.); Series E, Councils and assemblies, 1819-1920 (1958. 37p.); Series F, Foreign affairs, 1809-1921 (1955. 57p.); Series G, General politics and administration, 1782-1920 (15-G is 'Soudan', 1954. 43p.); Series H to T, Social, judicial, economic and financial affairs, 1782-1920 (1958. 213p.).

794 **CEDRAB: the Centre de Documentation et de Recherches Ahmad Baba at Timbuktu.**
John O. Hunwick. *Sudanic Africa,* vol. 3, 1992, p. 173-81.

Having been invited by Unesco, in 1976, to propose a ten-year development plan for the Centre, the author here describes the facility and its manuscript holdings at the time of a 1992 return visit.

795 **Guide to federal archives relating to Africa.**
Researched and compiled by Aloha P. South. Waltham, Massachusetts: Crossroads Press, 1977. 556p. bibliog. (The Archival and Bibliographic Series).

This catalogue of material housed in the National Archives in Washington, DC, includes both textual and non-textual materials covering the US Congress and other government agencies and committees. The separate indexes of subjects, places, and ethnic groups are excellent and permit easy access to information on Mali.

796 **Guide to non-federal archives and manuscripts in the United States relating to Africa.**
Researched and compiled by Aloha P. South. London and New York: H. Zell, 1989. 2 vols. bibliog.

Arranged by state and then city, this impressive compilation of American archival and manuscript material is a companion to the author's *Guide to federal archives relating to Africa* (q.v.). Like its predecessor, it includes both textual and non-textual materials. Volume 2 (p. 1106-9) contains a bibliography of sources. The index (vol. 2, p. 1125-50) lists entries for Bamako, Bambara, Bozo, Dogon, French Sudan, French West Africa, Mali, the Sahel, Timbuktu and other relevant names. Topics covered include artists, folksongs, photographs, the Malian Arabic manuscript microfilming project, missionaries, and railroads.

797 **The Malian National Archives at Kaluba: access and applicability.**
Stephen A. Harmon. *History in Africa,* vol. 19 (1992), p. 441-44.
bibliog.
The author describes the Malian National Archives at Kaluba, a suburb of Bamako, near the presidential palace. Only two-thirds of the archives, directed by M. Onguiba, has been classified. Harmon describes the contents of seven cartons he examined from circa 1916 to 1952, and he also gives details about the official procedures necessary for archival research.

798 **Writings on African archives.**
John McIlwaine (et al.). London; New Providence, New Jersey: Hans Zell Publishers, 1996. 279p.
Containing over 2,300 entries, this bibliography is an important inventory of various materials written about archival and manuscript collections held by African countries as well as Africa-related archives located overseas in Europe, North and South America, and Asia. A section on Mali contains 16 entries. Beginning in 1993 (Issue 62), a preliminary version of this work was published in a series of articles in *Africa Research and Documentation*, a journal which regularly contains information about African archives.

Museums

799 **Birth of a museum at Bamako, Mali.**
Alpha Ouma Konare. *Museum,* vol. 33, no. 1 (1981), p. 4-8.
Written as the first stages of building were nearing completion, this article appraises plans for Mali's National Museum. The author describes its intended role and functions, the site and the buildings, and events which prompted its creation. Some maps and photographs accompany the text.

800 **Bulletin (West African Museums Project).**
London: International African Institute, 1990- . annual.
This journal features articles and news, in both English and French, about the activities and developments of museums in West African countries. Information on Malian museums can often be found. Beginning with no. 4 (1993), this publication is issued under the Project's later name, the West African Museums Programme.

801 **The creation of regional museums in Mali.**
Moussa Konaté. In: *What museums for Africa?: heritage in the future: Benin, Ghana, Togo, 18-23 November 1991.* Paris[?]: International Council of Museums, 1992, p. 197-200.
Konaté presents a history of Mali's regional museums, the idea for which dates from a 1976 seminar in Bamako called 'Museums and Cultural Heritage'. He emphasizes the difficulties they have in common and considers some of the more important characteristics of Mali's museum policy, which also developed from the seminar.

802 **Directory of museums in Africa = Répertoire des musées en Afrique.**
Susanne Peters. Paris: ICOM; London and New York: Kegan Paul, 1990. 211p.

Three Malian museums (the Musée National, the Musée du Sahel, and the Centre de Documentation Arabe) can be found in this directory, two of which have minimal information supplied about their location, status (national, provincial, or private), hours, entry fee, collections, services, history, and publications. Two of these museums are included under the three listed for Mali in *Museums of the world* (Munich, Germany: Saur, 1992, 4th ed.), which covers the Musée Soudanais instead of the Musée du Sahel.

803 **Musée Regional de Sikasso: première exposition ouverture sur la vie quotidienne en 3è Région.** (Regional museum of Sikasso: opening of the first exhibit on daily life in the third region.)
Edited by Abdoul Aziz Diallo, Y. Coulibaly, C. O. Mara, A. Diawara.
Bamako: Division du Patrimoine Culturel and the Ford Foundation, [n.d.]. 17p.

The brief text of this small, illustrated exhibition booklet describes the history, social groups, economic activities, housing and music of the region of Sikasso, the third economic region of Mali. *Vivre au bord du désert: première exposition sur les Kel Adrar* (Life in the desert: first exhibition on the Kel Adrar) (Bamako: Ministère des Sports, des Arts et de la Culture, 1981. 56p. map) by the Musée du Sahel de Gao is a heavily illustrated catalogue on the Tamachek (Tamasheq) 'Kel Adrar', a large region north and east of Gao. The catalogue has brief descriptions of prehistoric sites, geography, flora and fauna, living conditions, dress, cultural activities, pastoralism, transportation and development in the area.

804 **The National Museum of Mali–Museum of Cultural History: collaborative textiles documentation and collection project.**
Rachel Hoffman. *Bulletin* (West African Museums Project, Dakar), (1990), no. 1, p. 9.

Describes a joint project established in 1987 between the National Museum of Mali and the Museum of Cultural History at UCLA to research and document traditional weaving in Mali, and to collect and preserve, at both museums, examples of locally produced Malian textiles.

805 **A national treasure.**
Howard Schissel. *Africa Report,* vol. 35, no. 1 (March-April 1990), p. 64-66.

The author describes the National Museum in Bamako, its educational role and the collection of 4,000 artefacts. The article includes three photographs. Claude Daniel Ardouin, director of the museum, describes the museum in *Musée National du Mali* (Bamako: Ministère des Sports, des Arts et de la Culture, [n.d.]. 55p. map).

806   **The regional museums at Gao & Sikasso, Mali.**
Moussa Konaté. In: *Museums & the community in West Africa.*
Edited by Claude Daniel Ardouin, Emmanuel Arinze. Washington,
DC: Smithsonian Institution Press; London: J. Currey, 1995, p. 116-19.
The author describes mistakes that were made while establishing the Musée du Sahel
at Gao in 1980, and how the experience led to other approaches being used to create a
regional museum at Sikasso, beginning in 1983.

807   **The relationship between local museums & the national museum.**
Baba Moussa Konate. In: *Museums & the community in West Africa.*
Edited by Claude Daniel Ardouin, Emmanuel Arinze. Washington,
DC: Smithsonian Institution Press; London: J. Currey, 1995, p. 11-17.
In low-income countries eager to establish museum institutions, the preferred method,
which is more affordable, is to form a museum network in which one well-equipped
institution is the designated technical coordinator of activities at the others. In this
chapter, the author uses Mali's experience in reorganizing and rehabilitating the
Musée National to examine the role a strong museum can play in relation to local
museums with fewer technical resources – in this case the museums at Gao and
Sikasso.

Research

808   **The African studies companion: a resource guide & directory.**
Hans M. Zell, Cecile Lomer. London; New Providence, New Jersey:
Hans Zell, 1997. 2nd rev. and expanded ed. 276p. bibliog.
This compact guide is packed with a variety of sources of information which will be
useful to anyone studying Africa or Mali, or those who are interested in Africana
publishing. The first section is an annotated bibliography of major general and current
reference sources, followed by current bibliographies and continuing sources, and a
selective listing of important African studies periodicals and magazines. It lists major
libraries outside of Africa which own substantial African studies collections, and
names publishers with African studies lists, and dealers and distributors of African
studies materials. In addition, the guide features awards and prizes in African studies
and organizations; African studies associations and societies; foundations; donor
agencies; and network organizations which support African studies research or which
are active in Africa.

809   **African studies information resources directory.**
Compiled and edited by Jean E. Meeh Gosebrink. Oxford, England:
H. Zell, 1986. 572p. bibliog.
An extensive directory of American libraries, archives, missions, and other institutions
and organizations which count material on Africa among their resources; 437 in all are
included. This reference/research tool was the winner of the African Studies

251

Association's Conover-Porter award in 1988. The index contains a small number of entries under Mali. This remains a valuable reference source, despite the fact it is now rather dated.

810   **International directory of African studies research = Répertoire international des études africaines.**
Philip Baker.   London and New York: H. Zell, 1994. 3rd fully rev. and expanded ed. 319p.

This directory of worldwide research on Africa updates *Baker's International guide to African studies research* (London: H. Zell, 1987. 2nd ed.). Twenty-six research institutions in Mali are listed; longer entries include those for the Centre Djoliba, the Direction Nationale de l'Alphabétisation Fonctionnelle et de la Linguistique Appliquée, the Division du Patrimoine Culturel, the Institut d'Ophtalmologie Tropicale de l'Afrique, the Institut Marchoux, and the Station de Recherche Agronomique de Baguinéda. The work includes indexes of ethnonyms and language names, serial publications and monograph series, and personnel.

Archives nationales du Mali: répertoire, 1855-1954. (National Archives of Mali: holdings, 1855-1954.)
See item no. 902.

Books and Publishing

811 **The African Book Publishing Record.**
Edited by Hans Zell. Munich, Germany: H. Zell & K. G. Saur,
1974- . quarterly.
Bibliographical information is provided in this journal, along with reviews of signifi-
cant new and forthcoming books from the African continent and its offshore islands.
Publications from Mali are covered, but entries are few because of the nature of
Malian publishing.

812 **The African book world & press: a directory = Répertoire du livre
et de la presse en Afrique.**
Hans M. Zell. London and New York: Hans Zell, 1989. 4th ed. 306p.
This directory attempts to provide current and accurate information on libraries,
publishers and the retail book trade, major periodicals and newspapers, government
and commercial printers, research institutions with publishing programmes, and book
industry and literary associations throughout Africa. This edition contains for Mali
(p. 96-97) basic information (address, phone number, name of director, size and
emphasis) on Mali's six main libraries, ten special libraries, four booksellers, three
publishers, two periodicals, one newspaper, one literary society and the government
printer, as well as the national news agency (p. 287).

813 **African books in print = Livres africains disponibles.**
Edited by Hans Zell. London: H. Zell, 1993. 4th ed. 2 vols.
This remarkable resource indexes some 25,000 books published by 745 publishers in
forty-five countries. Volume one (869p.) contains an introduction, keys, author index
and title index. Volume two (p. 871-1448) is a subject index in which there are nine
entries under Mali (p. 1215), one under Soninke (Sarakole), two for Tuareg, two for
Bambara and none for Dogon. Since Mali, like many other African countries, seldom
publishes a regular national bibliography, this work, and its previous three editions, is
indispensable in providing an impression of the extent of publishing in Mali and on the
continent.

814 **Bellagio Publishing Network Newsletter.**
Buffalo, New York: Comparative Education Center, State University
of New York at Buffalo, 1992- . irregular (four times a year).

This informative newsletter about publishing and book development in the Third
World contains news and reports on publishing, articles and book reviews; it also
highlights new publications.

815 **The book in francophone black Africa: a critical perspective.**
Gunter Simon. *African Book Publishing Record,* vol. 10, no. 4
(1984), p. 209-15.

An in-depth analysis of the state of the book and the book industries in francophone
African countries, including Mali.

816 **The book trade of the world. Vol. IV. Africa.**
Edited by Sigfred Taubert, Peter Weidhaas. Munich, Germany; New
York: K. G. Saur, 1984. 391p. maps. bibliog.

The brief chapter 'Mali: Republic of Mali' by Chérif Moctar Fofana (p. 187-89)
reflects the paucity of book publishing in the country but offers some sparse notes on
the trade, retail prices, sources of information, international memberships, books and
young people, publishing, retail trade and book fairs.

817 **Books in Francophone Africa.**
Jerry Prillaman. In: *Publishing and development in the Third World.*
Edited by Philip G. Altbach. London and New York: Hans Zell,
1992, p. 199-210.

This article discusses the present state of the predominantly French-language book
market in francophone Africa, and includes treatment of school textbooks, general
literature, bookstores, and selection policies and censorship. This market, which as a
whole is dysfunctional, is analysed in global terms, and French government book
programmes and the assistance they give to African publishers are described. The
author stresses that helping these publishers is the key to changing the grave problems
of the book industry, the long-term goal being to make it viable.

818 **A publication survey trip to West Africa and France.**
Julian W. Witherell. Washington, DC: Reference Dept., General
Reference and Bibliography Division, Library of Congress, 1964. 42p.

This report, which presents information gathered on a publication survey trip in
1963-64, documents the publishing activities of government agencies, research
organizations, universities, libraries, archives and museums of selected African
countries, including Mali. A number of libraries and research organizations in France
with links to African affairs were also visited as a part of this survey.

819   **A publication survey trip to West Africa, Ethiopia, France, and Portugal.**
Julian W. Witherell.   Washington, DC: Reference Dept., General Reference and Bibliography Division, Library of Congress, 1968. 61p.
This title is a complement to Julian Witherell's report of his trip to West Africa and France in 1963-64, *A publication survey trip to West Africa and France* (q.v.) and Susan Lockwood's report of her trip to West, Central, and Southern Africa in 1966, *A publication survey trip to West, Central and Southern Africa.* Like Witherell's previous report, this documents the major publishing activity in Mali at the time, and notes some improvements that had been made in the number of publications issued and the efficiency of distribution systems.

820   **Publishing and book development in Sub-Saharan Africa: an annotated bibliography.**
Hans M. Zell, Cécile Lomer.   London; New Providence, New Jersey: Hans Zell, 1995. 409p. (Hans Zell Studies on Publishing, no. 3).
With over 2,200 entries, covering approximately the period from the early 1960s to late 1995, this extensive work features material published on all aspects of the book industry, book marketing and distribution, and the retail book trade in Sub-Saharan Africa. Literature on specialist areas of book publication, such as children's books and African-language publishing, and related special topics (the African book famine, acquisition of African-published material, etc.) are also included. Annotations are provided for about 80 per cent of the entries. There are only three entries under Mali, but some more general works listed also contain information about the country. This volume supersedes Zell's *Publishing & book development in Africa: a bibliography* (Paris: Unesco, 1984. 143p. [Studies on Books and Reading, no. 15]).

821   **Publishing for sustainable literacy in Francophone West Africa.**
Diana C. Newton.   *African Book Publishing Record,* vol. 20, no. 2 (1994), p. 107-11.
Information for this paper comes from a four-month-long research project undertaken in Mali, Côte d'Ivoire, and Benin during the years 1993-94. The author describes literacy and related publishing issues in French West Africa and argues in favour of special publishing efforts related to literacy and post-literacy. Mali's official adult literacy rate of seventeen per cent is the lowest in francophone West Africa.

822   **Publishing in Francophone Africa.**
Diana C. Newton, edited by Philip G. Altbach, Edith S. Hoshino.
In: *International book publishing: an encyclopedia.*   New York: Garland Publishing, 1995, p. 373-84.
Drawn mostly from unpublished sources and reports commssioned by donors, this essay is an excellent overview of the present status of the book publishing industry in Mali and nine other francophone African countries. It also analyses factors that have operated against the growth and evolution of a profitable, autonomous publishing industry under majority African control in this region, as well as factors that favour its future development. The author also predicts future trends and challenges that will affect publishing in this part of Africa.

Mass Media

823 **Broadcasting in Africa: a continental survey of radio and television.**
Edited by Sydney W. Head. Philadelphia, Pennsylvania: Temple University Press, 1974. 453p. bibliog.

A variety of authors have contributed to this study of broadcasting in Africa, which aims to be as comprehensive as possible. An exception is the conscious decision to keep discussion of politics, which are inextricably linked to African broadcasting, more general by not including politics of individual countries or guerrilla movements. Following descriptions of national broadcasting systems throughout Africa, there are discussions of topics such as international broadcasting to African audiences, religious broadcasting, foreign aid, training, educational uses of broadcasting, commerce and broadcasting, and research. Broadcasting in Mali is treated (p. 107-24) together with other independent states which emerged from colonial French West Africa, French Equatorial Africa, and the Belgian Congo. A later study, in which the author identifies the level of development of broadcasting in Africa, problem areas, and mechanisms of control is John Bosco Tindwa's *Broadcasting in Africa* (Tampere, Finland: Tampere University, 1977. 107p.).

824 **La coopérative Jamana.** (The Jamana cooperative.)
Souleymane Drabo. In: *Ça presse au Sahel.* Paris[?]: Institut Panos-UJAO, 1991, p. 25-28.

This paper briefly describes the Malian cultural cooperative known as Jamana, and its journal of the same title, whose ambition is the promotion of culture and intellectual life in Mali. Created in 1983 by current Malian president Alpha Oumar Konaré, the cooperative produced the first independent press group in Mali six years later.

825 **ECOWAS situation of telecommunications in member states.**
Yao Kouame, Cephas Pobi. Lagos: Economic Community of West
African States, 1980. 175 leaves. maps.

This report is an inventory of existing telecommunications equipment, and of national
and regional telecommunications projects within ECOWAS member countries; Mali is
found on pages 58-62.

826 **L'état de la presse au Mali.** (State of the press in Mali.)
Souleymane Drabo. In: *L'Etat de la presse en Afrique de l'Ouest
francophone.* Panos-UJAO with the collaboration of the Ford
Foundation (et al.). [n.p.]: [n.p.], 1991[?], p. 69-88.

Following a general description of the state of the press in Mali, this chapter discusses
specific publications of the independent and government presses, their manufacture,
distribution, publicity, financing, etc., as well as radio and television.

827 **Institutional reform of telecommunications in Senegal, Mali, and
Ghana: the interplay of structural adjustment and international
policy diffusion.**
Cheikh Tidiane Gadio. PhD thesis, Ohio State University, 1995.
283 leaves. bibliog. (Available from University Microfilms
International, Ann Arbor, Michigan, order no. 9526026).

Gadio presents a study of the significant changes that occurred during institutional
reform of telecommuncations in selected countries of low telephone density: Senegal,
Mali and Ghana. Chapter six focuses specifically on the case of Mali. The conclusion
contains an interesting comparative analysis of the reform experience of the three
countries.

828 **Législations et pluralisme radiophonique en Afrique de l'Ouest.**
(Legislation and pluralism in radiobroadcasting in West Africa.)
Cheikh Tidiane Thiam, Demba Sy, with the collaboration of Renaud de
La Brosse. Paris: L'Harmattan, 1997. 143p.

The objectives of this study are to make available to the the key players in radio
broadcasting in West Africa a reference tool indicating the state of legislation in
different countries of the region, and to provide them with information allowing them
to advance and improve proposed legislation in their countries. In this guise, a certain
number of proposals for modifications of legislation already in force are put forward,
especially as concerns the regulation of communication and information in West
Africa.

829 **Liberté pour les radios africaines: actes du Colloque de Bamako
sur 'Le Pluralisme Radiophonique en Afrique de l'Ouest' =
Freedom for African radios: proceedings of the Bamako
Symposium on 'Radio Pluralism in West Africa'.**
Paris: L'Harmattan, 1994. 220p.

Following in the footsteps of the French-speaking African press, the radio stations of
West Africa are developing and gaining their political, economic and financial

independence with the gradual liberalization of the airwaves. This set of papers is from a 1993 symposium, by which time there were some twelve independent radio stations in Mali. The authors recognize and assess the progress of this liberalization and suggest measures that will be likely to promote and strengthen free expression on radio in the West African region. Some papers are in French, some in English; one that is specifically about Mali is entitled 'L'émergence des radios privées au Mali' by Sidiki Konaté.

830 **Mass media in West Africa: a bibliographic essay.**
Barbara S. Monfils. In: *Mass communication, culture, and society in West Africa.* Edited by Frank Okwu Ugboajah. Munich, Germany; New York: H. Zell, 1985, p. 285-308.

The subject of this bibliographical essay, consisting of four main sections, is mass media in West Africa. The first section is a bibliography of bibliographies, the second focuses on general media studies, the third concerns print media, and the fourth broadcast media.

831 **The press in Africa: communications past and present.**
Rosalynde Ainslie. London: Gollancz, 1966. 256p. bibliog.

Also including general chapters on radio and television broadcasting, this publication is a general work on the press in Africa. The study devotes a chapter to the press in Sub-Saharan francophone Africa, 'L'Afrique Noire' (p. 130-41), in which the history of the major newspapers of the colonial and the immediate post-colonial period is traced, including those of Mali.

832 **Presse francophone d'Afrique: vers le pluralisme: actes du Colloque Panos/UJAO, Unesco-Paris, les 24 et 25 janvier 1991.**
Institut Panos, Union des Journalistes de l'Afrique de l'Ouest. (The francophone press in Africa: toward pluralism: acts of the Colloquium Panos/UJAO.)
Paris: L'Harmattan, 1991. 278p.

These papers from a 1991 conference on pluralism in the West African press include some items about Mali and/or by Malians: 'La presse d'état dans un contexte concurrentiel' by Souleymane Drabo; 'Le défi de la liberalisation de l'audiovisuel en Afrique' by Cheikh Fofana; 'Genèse et développement d'une entreprise' by Alpha Oumar Konaré; and 'Accès aux sources d'information pour un journal indépendant' by Cheibane Coulibaly.

833 **Radio pluralism in West Africa: a survey conducted by the Panos Institute, Paris, and l'Union des Journalistes d'Afrique de l'Ouest (West Africa Journalists' Association).**
Panos Institute, Union des Journalistes de l'Afrique de l'Ouest. Paris: L'Harmattan, 1993. 3 vols.

This survey is a compilation of information gathered by African journalists and researchers as part of a project on pluralism in West African radio broadcasting, undertaken by the Panos Institute in Paris. It covers members of the Economic Community of West African States (except Liberia). Survey data on Mali are presented in a chapter in volume three and include information about the political, legal and institutional framework of the country; state, private, and other radio stations; radio station budgets, resources, equipment, programming, etc.

834   **Reporters sans frontières 1996 report: freedom of the press throughout the world.**
      Reporters Sans Frontières.   London: John Libbey, 1996. 381p.
This detailed annual report, available in both English and French, documents as accurately as possible worldwide attacks on press freedom. The section on Mali indicates that political figures have demonstrated a commitment to freedom of information, but a number of incidents cited clearly suggest that both journalists and the public must remain ready to push in order to retain that freedom.

Nation-building in Mali: art, radio, and leadership in a pre-literate society.
See item no. 415.

An evaluation of educational radio programmes for primary school teachers in Mali.
See item no. 594.

Statistics

835 **African Statistical Yearbook, 1992/93. Volume 1, Part 2, West Africa.**

United Nations. Economic Commission for Africa. Addis Ababa: Economic Commission for Africa, United Nations. 1 vol. (various pagings).

For each of sixteen West African countries, statistical tables cover population, national accounts (i.e., gross domestic product), agriculture, forestry, fishing, industry, transport and communications, foreign trade, prices, finance and social statistics. Mali's data span the years from 1984 to 1993 (pages 2-16-1 to 2-16-17). The 1990/91 edition of this title spans the years 1982 to 1991.

836 **Annuaire Statistique du Mali.** (Statistical Annual of Mali.)

Bamako: Direction Nationale de la Statistique et de l'Informatique, 1961-94. annual.

This basic annual source of statistical data on Mali includes more detailed and definitive tables than those published in the *Flash des Informations Statistiques* (q.v.). The introductory text, which contains brief geographical and historical sketches, is followed by a calendar of annual events. The statistical tables and graphs follow, and cover climatology and hydrography, population, health, education, employment, economic resources (agriculture, animal breeding, water and forestry), industry, vehicle registration, air and water traffic, tourism, public finances, and prices. As of 1995, this publication seems to have merged with the *Flash des Informations Statistiques*. For annual statistics of the regions of Mali, see the *Annuaire Statistique* for each of the regions: Gao, Kayes, Mopti, and Segou.

837 **Bulletin Mensuel de Statistique.** (Monthly Statistical Bulletin.)
Bamako: Direction Nationale de la Statistique et de l'Informatique,
1977- . bi-monthly.

This official publication lists monthly data although it is issued bi-monthly (i.e., for two-month periods). It gives statistical information on demography, transport, production, prices and public finance. It continues the *Bulletin Mensuel de Statistique: Statistique et Economie.*

838 **Compendium of Social Statistics and Indicators, 1988.**
New York: United Nations, irregular. 685p. (Social Statistics and
Indicators. Series K).

Prepared by the UN 'in close collaboration' with the ILO, FAO, Unesco and WHO, this important statistical source covers in 35 subject tables the social and economic conditions and changes in 178 countries. The UN also publishes *Compendium of human settlements statistics* (New York: United Nations Publications, 1995. 5th issue. 519p.) which covers, in 30 tables, housing and population statistics for 243 countries and 338 cities (including Bamako, Mopti, Sikasso, Ségou) and is based on a 1992 questionnaire sent to national statistics offices.

839 **Etat civil du Mali: données brutes.** (Civil state of Mali: raw data.)
Direction Nationale de la Statistique et de l'Informatique, Centre
d'Etudes et de Recherches sur la Population pour le Développement.
Bamako: Centre d'Etudes et de Recherche sur la Population pour le
Développement, INSAH, CILSS; Direction Nationale de la Statistique
et de l'Informatique du Mali, 1991. 741p.

This publication contains national statistics on births, marriages and deaths under two series: administrative and demographic.

840 **Flash des Informations Statistiques: FIS.** (Flash of Statistical
Information: FIS.)
Bamako: Direction Nationale de la Statistique et de l'Informatique,
1989- . annual.

This official annual publication is an excellent source of recent statistics on population, education (including regional details on schools, classes, and their staff), climatology and hydrography, vehicle registration, air traffic, economics, prices, and public finances. It also includes a detailed chronology of the year's events which serves more as a calendar of official events than as a summary of important political events (e.g., the 1995 chronology does not mention the Tuareg civil war). At its inception, it was designed to supplement the *Annuaire Statistique du Mali* (q.v.) by publishing the data in a more timely fashion, sometimes necessitating the use of 'provisional estimates' (Preface, 1989), but since 1995 seems to have taken its place.

841 **The new book of world rankings.**
George Thomas Kurian, James Marti.   New York: Facts on File,
1991. 3rd ed. updated by James Marti. 324p. bibliog.

Two hundred and seven countries are ranked in 230 statistical tables which cover a
wide range of subjects such as vital statistics, population, politics, foreign aid, military
power, economy, agriculture, industry, housing, health, and crime. At US$5 per
capita, Mali ranks in the bottom ten worldwide in public educational expenditures
(130th out of 138 ranked), 48th (of 129) in area of irrigated land at 340,000 hectares,
and 28th (of 111) in foreign economic aid at US$41.50 per capita. Mali appears in
many but not all of the tables. The source for each table is given.

842 **World handbook of political and social indicators.**
Charles Lewis Taylor, David A. Jodice.   New Haven, Connecticut:
Yale University Press, 1983. 3rd ed. 2 vols.

This publication, which is by now dated, includes statistics of economic and political
variables for 138 countries. Volume 1 is entitled 'Cross-national attributes and rate of
change' and volume 2 is entitled 'Political protest and government change'. The
authors have continued their work, not in print but in computer datafiles, published in
the mid-1980s by the Inter-University Consortium for Political and Social Research
(Ann Arbor, Michigan).

Mali, a handbook of historical statistics.
See item no. 175.

Africa, Mali: selected statistical data by sex.
See item no. 245.

Perspectives de population par cercle/arrondissement, 1993-1997.
(Population perspectives by circle/ward, 1993-97.)
See item no. 248.

Analyse du recensement. (Analysis of the census.)
See item no. 261.

Enquête démographique au Mali, 1960-1961. (Demographic study of Mali,
1960-61.)
See item no. 262.

Enquête démographique de 1985: résultat préliminaire. (Demographic
study of 1985: preliminary results.)
See item no. 263.

**Recensement général de la population et de l'habitat (1er au 14 avril
1987): principaux résultats d'analyse.** (General census of the population
and habitat (1-14 April 1987): principal results of analysis.)
See item no. 265.

Agroclimatology of West Africa: Mali.
See item no. 555.

Encyclopaedias, Directories and Yearbooks

843 **100 great Africans.**
Alan Rake.   Metuchen, New Jersey: Scarecrow Press, 1994. 431p. maps.

Complemented by maps illustrating the rise and fall of empires, the adventures of great explorers, conquests of kings and campaigns against colonialism, this reference tool is an attempt to select and profile the one hundred greatest Africans of all time. A chapter entitled 'Golden kings' includes four rulers from the Mali and Songhai (Songhay) empires; some other figures associated with the area of present-day Mali are also found, such as Al-Haj Omar (Umar Tal) and Samory Touré. Rake's *Who's who in Africa: leaders for the 1990s* (Metuchen, New Jersey; London: Scarecrow Press, 1992. 448p.), which is limited to the most prominent African political figures of recent times, includes profiles of three Malians.

844 **Africa.**
Sean Moroney.   New York and Oxford: Facts on File, 1989.
rev. and updated ed. 2 vols. (Handbooks to the Modern World).

Volume one contains 'Mali' (p. 326-36) with a useful description of geography, government, economy, education, mass media and biographical sketches of five people, and is complemented by Alan Rake's compilation of 'Comparative statistics' (p. 626-65). Volume two covers political, economic and social affairs; information about Mali is easily accessed through the index. John Stewart's compilation *African states and rulers: an encyclopedia of native, colonial and independent states and rulers past and present* (Jefferson, North Carolina; London: McFarland & Co., 1989. 395p.) includes among its 10,500 names 'French West Africa' (p. 110-11), and 'Mali Autonomous Federation', 'Mali Empire', 'Mali Federation', 'Mali kingdom', and 'Mali Republic' (p. 170-71). There is a brief but useful bibliography (p. 303-5) and a lengthy 'Index of rulers' (p. 307-95).

845 **Africa Contemporary Record.**
London: Africa Research Ltd, 1969- . annual.

Colin Legum edited the first twenty volumes of this valuable annual survey tracing
political and economic developments for every African country and compiling
important documents which serve as a record of contemporary African history (e.g.,
updated text of constitutions, resolutions of regional and international organizations,
statistics, etc.). Malian topics include 'Traoré grows stronger despite severe economic
setback', vol. 16 (1983-84), p. B484-92; 'A start with economic and political
liberalization', vol. 20 (1987-88), p. B79-89; and 'Resistance to multiparty
democracy', vol. 22 (1989-90), p. B75-87. It has been described by reviewers as 'the
single most important reference work in the field'.

846 **Africa South of the Sahara.**
London: Europa, 1971- . annual.

This might well be one of the first resources one should consult to learn about Mali. In
the 1997 edition (26th ed. 1,111p.), Mali (p. 603-19) is described by experts R. J.
Harrison Church, who wrote 'Physical and social geography', Pierre Englebert who
wrote 'Recent history' and Edith Hodgkinson who authored 'Economy'. Following
these essays are a 'Statistical survey', based on data from the Direction de la
Statistique et de l'Informatique, Ministère des Finances et du Commerce, Koulouba,
Bamako; a 'Directory' of important officials and ministries, publications, financial
institutions, development organizations, major companies and transport; and a
succinct bibliography. For a more introductory survey about Mali, a sister publication
is also available, the *Europa World Year Book*.

847 **An African biographical dictionary.**
Norbert C. Brockman.   Santa Barbara, California: ABC-CLIO, 1994.
440p. bibliog.

This useful reference work offers sketches of 549 prominent political leaders, cultural
figures, scientists, and religious personalities from Sub-Saharan Africa. Most are
African, though some non-Africans are included by virture of their impact on the
continent. People from all periods of history can be found, but emphasis is given to
those from the post-colonial contemporary period. Entries are listed alphabetically by
name and conclude by noting the existence of any autobiography and principal
biographies as well as representative works for young adults. There is a general index
in which Mali, French Soudan, Mali Empire, Mali Federation, and Songhay Empire
are all found. An index of entries by nation (17 names are listed under Mali) and field
of significance are also included.

848 **The Cambridge encyclopedia of Africa.**
General editors, Roland Oliver, Michael Crowder.   Cambridge,
England; New York: Cambridge University Press, 1981. 492p. maps.
bibliog.

Numerous references to Mali and Malian-related topics appear in this marvellous
resource, including, for example, Roger G. Thomas's 'The Western and Central
Sudan' (p. 130-35), J. D. Hargreaves's 'French expansion: tropical Africa' (p. 161-62)
and Michael Crowder's 'French black Africa' (p. 179-81). There are also brief
references to Al-Hajj Umar (Umar Tal), Seku Ahmadu (Cheikou Amadou), Macina,
Jenne, Timbuktu, the Bambara and the Dogon.

849 **Dictionary of African historical biography.**
Mark R. Lipschutz, R. Kent Rasmussen. Berkeley, California; Los
Angeles: University of California Press, 1986. 2nd expanded and
updated ed. 328p. maps. bibliog.

The second edition of this useful work includes biographical information on important
individuals up to 1980 in its 'Supplement of post-1960 political leaders' (p. 258-90).
Among those relevant to Malian history are: Abdallah ibn Yasin (d. 1059), Abu Bakr
ibn 'Umar (d. 1087), Sundjata (Soundiata) Keita (Mari-Djata, c. 1210-c. 1260),
Sumanguru Kante (d.c. 1234), Ibn Battuta (1332-82), Ibn Khaldun (1332-82), al-
'Umari ibn Fadl 'Allah (1301-49), 'Umar ibn Sa'id Tall (Umar Tal, c. 1794-1864),
Ahmadu ibn 'Umar Tall (Amadou Tall, c. 1833-98), Ahmad al-Bakka'i (fl. 1846-64),
Ba Lobbo (fl. 1860-64), Ahmadu Tijani (Tijani Tall, d.c. 1887), and Moussa Traoré
(1936-). Editor-in-Chief Ralph Uwechue's *Makers of African history: profiles in
history* (London: Africa Journal Limited, 1981. 591p. maps. bibliog.) provides
biographical sketches of at least five people from Mali: Modibo Keita (one of the
longest entries in the volume); Mamadou Konaté; T. G. Kouyaté; F. D. Sissoko; and
Yoro Diakité.

850 **Dictionnaire des femmes célèbres du Mali: des temps mythico-
légendaires au 26 mars 1991.** (Dictionary of famous Malian women:
from mythical-legendary times to 26 March 1991.)
Adam Ba Konaré. Bamako: Editions Jamana, 1993. 520p. bibliog.

This useful reference tool, created largely using information gathered orally and by
questionnaire, is divided into three parts. Following a large section entitled 'Le rôle et
l'image de la femme dans l'histoire du Mali' is an extensive list (338 in total) of
Malian women from Arab times to 26 March 1991. Names of mythical and legendary
figures, martyrs, mothers, wives, queens, princesses, political figures, artists, pioneers
and others are accompanied by many fictional or biographical details. A third part
consists of several appendices which list women victims of the events associated with
the coup of March 1991, holders of Malian orders and decorations, women's
associations, etc. Some maps and interesting photos richly complement the text and a
name index is included.

851 **Directory of African Experts = Répertoire d'Experts Africains.**
Addis Ababa: PADIS; TCDC-Africa, 1983- . irregular.

Essentially a compilation of personal data about African specialists, scientists and
social scientists from a wide variety of fields, the main part of this directory is
arranged alphabetically by name. A subject index by field of specialization is
included, as well as an index by nationality; seventy-nine names are listed for Mali.

852 **Directory of African technology institutions.**
J. C. Woillet, M. Allal. Geneva: International Labour Office, 1985.
2 vols.

This is one of the better science or technology directories dating from the 1980s. For
Mali (vol. 2, p. 37-74), sixteen institutions are included, and cover energy,
construction, implements, and processing. *Survey of major science and technology
resources in Africa* (Dakar: African Regional Centre for Technology, 1986. 358p.), a
publication in French, lists fifteen institutions and seventy-six researchers (briefly)

from Mali (p. 118-26). In *Recherche scientifique et développement, 1980* (Scientific research and development, 1980) (Paris: Agence de Coopération Culturelle et Technique, 1980. 2 vols), there are eighteen institutions listed under Mali in volume 1 and a number of researchers are found in volume 2, which unfortunately lacks a geographical index; it is therefore difficult to locate the Mali-related entries. The most recent publication, *Profiles of African scientific institutions, 1992* (Nairobi: African Academy of Sciences, 1992. 282p.) lists only five institutions for Mali (p. 144-48).

853 **L'Encyclopédie coloniale et maritime.** (The colonial and maritime encyclopaedia.)

Edited by Eugène Guernier. Paris: Encyclopédie coloniale et maritime, 1944-51. 7 vols in 10. maps. bibliog.

The territory which became several francophone countries, including Mali, is presented in a comprehensive and integrated manner. Two volumes are devoted to West Africa; volume one (390p. 178 photographs, 34 maps and plans, 34 figures, 8 plates) covers history and geography (including prehistory, ethnic groups, population, religion, language, flora and fauna, geology and meteorology); political and administrative structures (organization, budget, justice, education, indigenous medicine, the Pasteur Institutes); and the economy (labour problems, credit institutions, agriculture, irrigation, herding and forestry). Volume two (400p. 244 photographs, 24 maps and plans, 17 figures and 8 plates) continues discussion of the economy (agriculture, textiles, coffee and cacao, tobacco, citrus, mines, industry, fishing, commerce, chambers of commerce and banks); infrastructure (roads, railroads, ports and wharfs, cities and urbanism, electrification, post and telecommunications, civil aeronautics and modernization plans); tourism and hunting; and, finally, fine arts (artisans, musicians, literature). Among the numerous contributors to this important work were Antoine Demougeot, Governor of the Colonies, Marcel Griaule, Raymond Mauny and Théodore Monod.

854 **New African Yearbook.**

London and New York: IC Magazines Ltd, 1988- . irregular.

This publication provides a succinct overview of fifty-two African countries and about thirty African organizations. Claude Jacquemot's chapter 'Mali' (p. 217-22) in the 1993-94 edition (edited by Linda Van Buren, consulting editor Alan Rake. 9th ed. 436p.) describes political history and current events up to 1992 and includes economic data for the early 1990s.

855 **Profiles of African scientists.**

African Academy of Sciences. Nairobi: African Academy of Sciences, 1991. 2nd rev. and expanded ed. 661p.

In this directory of African scientists, Mali is represented on pages 238-41 with: Lassana Keita (physics), Sylla Malick Ladji (forestry management), Abderhamane Sotbar (physics), and Yeya Tiemoko Toure (animal biology). For each scientist, his speciality, academic and employment records, research interests, major achievements, and address are given.

856 **Répertoire d'unités d'information au Mali.** (Information directory for Mali.)
RESADOC Mali. Bamako, Mali: Centre de Coordination du RESADOC/Mali, Institut d'Economie Rurale, Division Documentation Information, 1988. 2nd ed. 82p. (Document RESADOC/Mali, no. 7).

This useful directory lists in alphabetical order seventy-five organizations, offices, societies, ministries or institutes (from Archives Nationales to the Union Nationale des Travailleurs du Mali) in Bamako. Information on the unit's statutory or organizational authority, services, library or document collections and special characteristics is included when known. There are both subject and organization indexes. RESADOC is the Réseau Sahelien d'Information et de Documentation Scientifique et Technique (Sahelian Network of Information and Scientific and Technical Documentation).

857 **West African Annual.**
Ikeja, Nigeria: John West Publications, 1962- . irregular.

In the twelfth edition (1982. 496p.) of this useful handbook there is a general survey of West Africa (p. 1-64) followed by chapters on eighteen countries. Information on Mali (p. 268-81) covers geography, political history, general information, an economic survey, and trade and business data. In the eleventh (1981) and tenth (1975) editions, chapters on Mali include similar topical information.

858 **Worldmark encyclopedia of the nations.**
Detroit, Michigan: Gale Research Inc., 1995. 8th ed. 5 vols.

This work is a useful guide to the United Nations system (vol. 1) and the geographical, historical, political, social and economic status of all nations of Africa, the Americas, Asia and Oceania, and Europe (vols 2-5, respectively) and their international relationships. Mali is covered (p. 253-62) in fifty subject headings including migration, transport, history, animal husbandry, agriculture, mining, balance of payments, economic and social development, famous Malians, libraries and museums; a brief bibliography of eleven references is included. The *African international organization directory* and *African participation in other international organizations 1984/85*, edited by the Union of International Associations (Munich, Germany; New York; London: K. G. Saur, 1984. 604p.) lists organizations to which Mali belongs and treaties to which it is a signatory (p. 181, 383-89).

Historical dictionary of Mali.
See item no. 7.

Encyclopedia of world cultures. Volume IX, Africa and the Middle East.
See item no. 277.

The peoples of Africa: an ethnohistorical dictionary.
See item no. 289.

The AED African Financial Directory.
See item no. 495.

Dictionnaire des oeuvres littéraires africaines de langue française. (Dictionary of African literary works in the French language.) *See* item no. 615.

Dictionnaire des oeuvres littéraires négro-africaines de langue française des origines à 1978. (Dictionary of Black African literary works in the French language from the earliest times to 1978.) *See* item no. 616.

L'art africain contemporain: guide = Contemporary African art: guide. *See* item no. 645.

The world encyclopedia of contemporary theatre. Volume 3, Africa. *See* item no. 687.

The new Grove dictionary of music and musicians. *See* item no. 703.

World music: the rough guide. *See* item no. 710.

Dictionnaire du cinéma africain. (Dictionary of African cinema.) *See* item no. 715.

Directory of African film-makers and films. *See* item no. 716.

The SCOLMA directory of libraries and special collections on Africa in the United Kingdom and in Europe. *See* item no. 789.

Directory of museums in Africa = Répertoire des musées en Afrique. *See* item no. 802.

The African studies companion: a resource guide & directory. *See* item no. 808.

African studies information resources directory. *See* item no. 809.

International directory of African studies research = Répertoire international des études africaines. *See* item no. 810.

The African book world & press: a directory = Répertoire du livre et de la presse en Afrique. *See* item no. 812.

Newspapers and Periodicals

Newspapers

859 **Aurore.** (Dawn.)
   Bamako: Aurore, 1990- . weekly.
In 1991, publisher Sadou A. Yattara and editor-in-chief Chouaïdou Traoré founded this political newspaper, which began with an eight-page issue for 22 February-8 March 1990; circulation is about 20,000.

860 **Les Echos.** (News Items.)
   Bamako: Les Echos, 1990- . bi-weekly.
Each issue of this eight-page newspaper has editorials, news of Mali, a crossword puzzle and political cartoons. It appears weekly or bi-weekly with frequent special issues, has a circulation of about 25,000, and bills itself as a weekly or daily edition of *Jamana* (see item no. 870). Founded by current Malian president Alpha O. Konaré, it was a vehicle for pressuring General Moussa Traoré and his government to introduce reforms during the 1990-91 pro-democracy movement.

861 **L'Essor.** (Progress.)
   Bamako: UDPM, 1949- . daily.
This eight-page government newspaper, 'La voix du peuple, Organe de l'Union Démocratique du Peuple Malien (UDPM)' covers local and international news, general political and economic issues and developments, trips made by government officials, introduces new members of government and contains speeches. From 1953 to 1968, it was the official publication of the Union Soudanaise-RDA; from 1968 to 1979, it was published by the Comité Militaire de Libération Nationale; since 1979, by the UDPM. Mali's Minister of Information and Telecommunications, S. Drabo, was editor-in-chief in October 1991; circulation was about 40,000. Prior to the collapse of the former Soviet Union and the Communist regimes of Eastern Europe, news articles and feature stories exhibited a distinct Marxist slant.

862 **Kibaru.** (News)
Bamako: Agence Malienne de Presse et de Publicité, 1972- . monthly.
This Bambara newspaper appeared first in March 1972 in Bamako. It is now published in Bambara and three other languages, and has a circulation of about 5,000. It is the first periodical for rural areas.

863 **Le Soudan Français.** (French Sudan.)
Bamako: Soudan Français, 1949-58. weekly.
According to Helen Kitchen's *The press in Africa* (Washington, DC: Ruth Sloan, 1956, p. 90) 'this was the only significant newspaper in French Sudan'. This pre-independence weekly carried social, political and economic news items, had a circulation of about 1,000 and was edited by Felix Roggero, a French civil servant. Publication was suspended from 17 November 1955 to 12 October 1956.

Periodicals

864 **AFP Sahara.**
Paris: Agence France-Presse, 1984-91. bi-weekly.
Each issue of this 'Bulletin quotidien d'informations' (daily information bulletin) compiled news items filed by the Agence France-Presse (AFP) on general issues and on the countries of Tunisia, Algeria, Morocco, Mauritania, Mali, Niger, Chad and Libya. It continued *Sahara*, published from 1957 to 1983.

865 **Africa Confidential.**
London: Miramoor Publications, 1967- . bi-weekly.
Known as *Africa* from 1960 to 1966, this publication is an excellent source of current information about important and lesser events in Mali.

866 **Africa Report.**
New York: African-American Institute, 1956-95. bi-monthly.
Africa Report, 'America's leading magazine on Africa', continues *Africa Special Report: Bulletin of the Institute of African-American Relations*, which began with vol. 1, no. 1 (5 July 1956). Each issue has a theme, but also provides broad, balanced coverage for the continent. In addition to articles on current issues, and an 'update' section reporting briefly on several countries, one strength of the magazine is its interviews with heads of state and prominent officials throughout Africa. Major stories on Mali appear occasionally and lesser news more regularly in the 'update' section.

867   **Bulletin de l'Institut Français d'Afrique Noire.** (Bulletin of the
       French Institute of Black Africa.)
       Dakar: University of Dakar, L'Institut Français d'Afrique Noire,
       1939- . irregular.

This publication is an important source of often lengthy professional articles on topics ranging from geography and ethnography to botany and zoology. Since 1954 it has been divided into Series A, natural sciences, and Series B, human sciences. Vol. 46, nos. 1-2 (1984-85), Series B, contains an index (p. 29-114) for 1960-78, in which at least twenty-six articles are on Malian topics. In that issue there appears Pascal Baba F. Couloubaly's 'L'Enfance bambara: approche psycho-culturelle de trois phases précirconcisionnelles en pays bambara (Republique du Mali)' (Bambara childhood: a psycho-cultural approach to the three precircumcision phases in Bambara country, Mali).

868   **Cahiers d'Etudes Africaines.** (African Studies Notebooks.)
       Paris: Editions de l'Ecole des Hautes Etudes en Sciences Sociales,
       1961- . quarterly.

This important general academic journal is considered to be one of the best about the region. It covers history, the social sciences, and literature. Some articles are in English, but the majority are in French usually accompanied by English summaries.

869   **Etudes Maliennes.**
       Bamako: Institut des Sciences Humaines du Mali, 1969- . quarterly,
       annual.

This journal, published by the Institut des Sciences Humaines of the Ministère des Sports, des Arts et de la Culture, publishes articles on history, society, linguistics, archaeology, health and the sciences. Examples of articles include: 'Les Populations nomades du nord du Mali et le dromadaire', by M. Ag Erless, no. 42 (1990), p. 3-18, and Klena Sanogo's 'Tradition orale et archéologie' (p. 19-25); 'Une circoncision Malinké' by Etienne Gerard in no. 1-4 (1980), p. 26-37, and S. W. Toure's 'Problèmes de lexicographie appliquée: le cas du dictionnaire mondingue bamanan' (p. 38-58). A. C. Heringa and M. Raimbault authored 'Prospections archéologiques dans la zone de la Boucle du Baoulé (Mali)' in no. 38 (1986), p. 2-109, with numerous maps and photographs and with a fold-out map of 'Sites archéologiques Boucle du Baoulé' (scale 13 mm to 10 km).

870   **Jamana.**
       Bamako: Jamana, 1984- . bi-monthly.

This independent quarterly review, now published bi-monthly, was founded and edited by Alpha Oumar Konaré. It has articles on history, education, events in the villages and cities and numerous other topics as well as special theme issues. The special issue in May 1985 was 'Femmes Maliennes: émancipation ou alienation?' (64p.); an undated issue, probably from 1985, was 'La télévision malienne' (112p.). Issue no. 1 appeared in October-December 1984.

871 **Jeune Afrique.** (Young Africa.)
Paris: Groupe JA, 1955- . weekly.

Those who read French will find this weekly magazine carries most important Malian news items. Coverage of politics and the economy is especially good. Publication was monthly between 1955 and 1960.

872 **Journal Officiel de la République du Mali.** (Official Journal of the Republic of Mali.)
Koulouba, Mali: Secrétariat Général du Gouvernement, etc., 1960- . monthly.

This official journal of Mali publishes official proclamations and announcements, ordnances and statutes. It continues a long succession of name changes: *Journal Officiel de la Fédération du Mali*, April 1959 to August 1960; *Journal Officiel de la République Soudanaise*, October 1958 to April 1959; *Journal Officiel du Soudan Français*, February 1921 to September 1958; and *Journal Officiel du Haut Sénégal et Niger*, August 1906 to February 1921.

873 **Pop Sahel.**
Bamako: Centre d'Etudes et de Recherches sur la Population pour le Développement, 1986- . irregular.

This periodical features articles on issues related to population, development, and social conditions in Sahelian countries, such as urbanization, migration, education, women's fertility and employment, and women and family in development.

874 **Sunjata.**
Bamako: Agence Malienne de Presse et de Publicité, 1978- . monthly.

This illustrated news monthly has varied articles on the nation, society, culture, sports, and occasionally on politics, health, population and world news; circulation is about 3,000.

875 **West Africa.**
London: West Africa, 1917- . weekly.

This oldest and most respected weekly news magazine contains a wide range of political, economic, social and cultural information. Articles on current events in Mali appear with some frequency. Regular articles also appear on regional organizations such as ECOWAS and the Organization of African Unity (OAU). An annual index is available.

Bulletin de l'Association des Naturalistes du Mali. (Bulletin of the Association of Malian Naturalists.)
See item no. 102.

Mandenkan.
See item no. 345.

Revue de Médecines et Pharmacopées Africaines. (Review of African Medicine and Pharmacology.)
See item no. 407.

African economic and financial data.
See item no. 496.

Baarakèla.
See item no. 547.

Contact.
See item no. 589.

African Arts.
See item no. 643.

Match.
See item no. 782.

Bulletin (West African Museums Project).
See item no. 800.

The African Book Publishing Record.
See item no. 811.

Bellagio Publishing Network Newsletter.
See item no. 814.

La coopérative Jamana. (The Jamana cooperative.)
See item no. 824.

Africa South of the Sahara.
See item no. 846.

New African Yearbook.
See item no. 854.

West African Annual.
See item no. 857.

Africa Index to Continental Periodical Literature.
See item no. 877.

Africa South of the Sahara: Index to Periodical Literature, 1900-[ ].
See item no. 878.

Current Contents Africa.
See item no. 884.

Periodicals from Africa: a bibliography and union list of periodicals published in Africa.
See item no. 890.

Recently Published Articles.
See item no. 891.

Bibliographies

General

876 **Africa Bibliography.**
Compiled by Christopher H. Allen, with assistance from A. M. Berrett,
in association with the International African Institute. Edinburgh:
Edinburgh University Press, 1984- . annual.

Before 1991 this bibliography was compiled by Hector Blackhurst and published by
Manchester University Press. It appears as a separate number of *Africa*, contains
books, chapters from books by single authors, essays in edited volumes, and periodical
articles about the entire African continent and associated islands, all published in the
previous year. Principally, subject areas covered are the social sciences, environmental sciences, and the humanities and arts; a selection of items from the medical,
physical, and biological sciences is also included, and government publications and
literary works are excluded. Arrangement is by region and country, with a preliminary
section for the entire continent; within each section entries are arranged by subject.
This is a good source for material in English.

877 **Africa Index to Continental Periodical Literature.**
Oxford, England: H. Zell Publishers for the Africa Bibliographic
Centre, 1976-81. annual. 6 vols.

The Index covers selected scholarly and semi-scholarly journals published but not
necessarily printed within the African continent, excluding South Africa. The articles
are grouped in thirty-one subject categories and indexed by author and subject, and in
some numbers, by geography. No. 2, edited by C. Darch and O. C. Mascarenhas
(1978; covering 1977. 53p.) has five articles on Mali; no. 3 (1980; covering 1978.
191p.) has eight on Mali. Another invaluable on-going publication is *Africa South of
the Sahara: Index to Periodical Literature* (q.v.).

878 **Africa South of the Sahara: Index to Periodical Literature, 1900-[ ].**
Boston: G. K. Hall; Washington, DC: Library of Congress, 1971-85.
4 vols. 3 supplements.

The aim of this work is to provide citations to the contents of journals not covered in standard guides to periodical literature. The main work, published by Hall in 1971, covers 1900-70; the first supplement, covering 1971-72, was published in 1973 and indexes 960 serials; the second supplement, covering 1973-76, was issued in 1982. The last supplement, the first to be published by the Library of Congress, appeared in 1985 and covers 1977. Cards are not reproduced, as in all other parts of this title; instead, it has a newly adopted six-part subject division (anthropology, languages and the arts; education, health and social conditions; geography, history and religion; economic development; politics and government; and international relations). The *Cumulative Bibliography of African Studies* (q.v.) and its successors, together with this work, which has been suspended, are essential for preliminary access to the periodical literature on Mali.

879 **American and Canadian doctoral dissertations and master's theses on Africa, 1974-1987.**
Compiled by Joseph J. Lauer, Alfred Kagan, Gregory V. Larkin.
Atlanta, Georgia: Crossroads Press for the African Studies Association, 1989. 377p.

This invaluable unannotated listing of 6,414 doctoral theses and 2,123 master's theses for the fourteen-year period is organized by geographical area and by country. It lists at least thirty-eight doctoral theses for Mali. This volume continues the compilation by Michael Sims and A. Kagan, *American & Canadian doctoral dissertations & master's theses on Africa, 1886-1974* (Waltham, Massachusetts: African Studies Association, 1976. 365p.) which lists eleven theses for Mali (p. 165). Works in both volumes are accessed by author and subject. Supplements in the *ASA News* by J. Lauer continue the 1989 work.

880 **Bibliographie de l'Afrique Sud-Saharienne, Sciences Humaines et Sociales.** (Bibliography of Sub-Saharan Africa: Humanities and Social Sciences.)
Tervuren, Belgium: Musée Royal de l'Afrique Centrale, 1978- .
annual.

The title of this bibliography is somewhat misleading, as it lists journals and collective works which primarily deal with Central Africa, especially the ex-Belgian possessions. It does, however, include materials about Mali and is well indexed. Starting with the volume issued in 1986, covering 1981-83 publications, only journal articles are listed. The title of this annual varies: it was first published as *Bibliographie Ethnographique du Congo Belge et des Régions Avoisinantes* in 1925; it later became *Bibliographie Ethnographique de l'Afrique Sud-Saharienne*, and was most recently known as *Bibliographie de l'Afrique Sud-Saharienne, Sciences Humaines et Sociales*.

881 **Bibliographies for African Studies, 1987-1993.**
   Yvette Scheven.   London and New York: Hans Zell Publishers, 1994.
   176p.

A continuation of Scheven's *Bibliographies for African Studies, 1970-1986* (London
and New York: H. Zell, 1988. 615p.) This previous volume was the winner of the
Conover-Porter Award, presented by the African Studies Association for the best
Africana reference tool, in 1990. Like its predecessor, the current work is a well-
organized, annotated bibliography of bibliographies primarily in the social sciences
and humanities; it lists approximately 900 new bibliographies, arranged by Library of
Congress subject headings. It also cumulates titles published in the annual lists of new
Africana reference works appearing in *The African Book Publishing Record* (q.v.)
from 1986 through to 1993. Titles included are books, essays, articles, indexes,
filmographies, guides to archives and manuscripts, or parts of edited volumes; all
African countries and the Indian Ocean islands are covered. This work is intended
primarily for those working in English and French, although bibliographies published
in other major European languages and Afrikaans are included. Few other
bibliographies of African bibliographies have been published. See also Theodore
Besterman's *A world bibliography of African bibliographies*, revised by J. D. Pearson
(Totowa, New Jersey: Rowman & Littlefield, 1975); in that work, books only are
included and the period up until the end of 1973 is covered. The earliest work of
substance is the outdated *A bibliography of African bibliographies covering territories
south of the Sahara* (Cape Town: South African Public Library, 1961. 4th ed. 79p.
[Grey bibliographies, no. 7]), which covers the period through to 1960.

882 **Cumulative Bibliography of African Studies.**
   Boston: G. K. Hall, 1973. 5 vols.

A cumulative index listing all the titles of books and articles published in the
bibliographical section of *Africa*, a quarterly journal, from 1929 to 1970, and in the
International African Bibliography from 1971 to 1972. Entries are in catalogue-card
format, and are arranged by author (2 vols) or broad topic (3 vols) within countries or
geographical areas. References for Mali appear in vol. 2, p. 318-29. It is continued by
the *International African Bibliography* (q.v.).

883 **Current Bibliography on African Affairs.**
   Edited by Paula Boesch.   Farmingdale, New York: Baywood
   Publishing, 1962-67. New series, 1968- . quarterly.

A broad, annotated bibliography of African and international sources, including
books, periodical articles and documents. Its greatest coverage is on contemporary
political and social concerns, as well as materials appearing in non-scholarly journals
that tend to escape notice in other serial Africana bibliographies. Frequently
containing items on Mali, this is an excellent source for more works in English.

884 **Current Contents Africa.**
   Oxford, England: H. Zell, 1975- . four times a year (irregular).

This useful publication, consisting of facsimile reproductions of the contents pages of
Africanist serials, includes standard academic journals, some important, irregularly
published titles with limited distribution, and the news magazines *Jeune Afrique* (q.v.)
and *West Africa* (q.v.). Non-Africanist serials are included if they contain papers on
African studies. Over 120 titles covering a wide range of subjects are featured. The

State Library of Frankfurt published this title from 1975 to 1978.

885 **Guide to research and reference works on Sub-Saharan Africa.**
Compiled by Helen F. Conover, Peter Duignan, with the assistance of
Evelyn Boyce, Liselotte Hofmann, Karen Fung. Stanford, California:
Hoover Institution Press, Stanford University, 1971 [or 1972]. 1,102p.

Prepared especially with the student and librarian in mind, this valuable bibliography
contains a total of 3,127 entries, most with excellent annotations. It is divided into
four parts. Part I contains sections on centres, institutions and records of research;
libraries and archives in Europe, America and Africa; and publishers and book
dealers. Part II covers various forms of bibliographies for Africa in general as well as
acquisitions lists, official publications, atlases and maps, dissertations and lists of
serials. Literature in Part III is arranged by subject, and Part IV groups titles about the
regions and countries of Africa under the former colonial powers. A useful 58-page
index completes the volume. The author compiled another bibliography with L. H.
Gann that provides similar coverage, *Colonialism in Africa 1870-1960. Volume 5.
A bibliographical guide to colonialism in Sub-Saharan Africa* (Cambridge, England:
Cambridge University Press, 1973. 552p.).

886 **Index Africanus.**
Joseph O. Asamani. Stanford, California: Hoover Institution Press,
1975. 659p.

This work lists citations for articles in Western languages found in over 200 Africana
serials, 20 *Festschriften*, and nearly 60 conference proceedings. All were published
between 1885 and 1965. Arrangement is primarily by geographical area, then by
subject, with the total number of citations being approximately 23,000; those for Mali
number exactly 200.

887 **International African Bibliography: Current Books, Articles and
Papers in African Studies.**
London: Mansell for the School of Oriental and African Studies,
1973- . quarterly.

Compiled at the SOAS, this bibliography lists works on Africa, current at the time,
and in the general subject areas of the social sciences. Each issue is arranged
thematically under Africa first, then by individual country; the number of references
on Mali varies. In 1981 Mansell published a five-year cumulation for 1973-78 (of 368
pages and with almost 20,000 references). Previous to 1973 this work existed in
various forms back to 1929 and was issued by the International African Institute in its
journal *Africa*.

888 **Joint Acquisitions List of Africana.**
Evanston, Illinois: Northwestern University, Melville J. Herskovits
Library of African Studies, 1962-96. bi-monthly.

This is not a true bibliography, but an accessions list; therefore, no journal articles are
included. All entries have been published within the past five years, and frequently
include titles on Mali. It recently ceased publication.

889 **List of French doctoral dissertations on Africa, 1884-1961.**
Marion Dinstel, Mary Darrah Herrick. Boston, Massachusetts:
G. K. Hall, 1966. 336p.

Following a brief preface (p. iii), by Mary Darrah Herrick, are the photoduplications of 2,923 numbered catalogue cards largely from the *Catalogue des thèses de doctorat soutenues devant les universités françaises* (Paris: Ministère de l'Education Nationale. Direction des Bibliothèques de France) and *French doctoral theses. Sciences, 1951-53* (New York: French Cultural Service of New York, Dec. 1955). Arranged by country and region, from 1885-86 to 1960 are listings for Mali, particularly emphasizing geology, health and medicine, and ethnology. The earliest work included is Noel-Joseph-Dominique Duclot's 'Contribution à la géographie mèdicale: Haut-Sénégal et Haut Niger' (Bordeaux, 1886. 111p.). Herrick notes that microfilm copies can usually be obtained from the Centre National de la Recherche Scientifique, Service de Documentation, 16 Rue Pierre-Curie, Paris 5. The compiler was librarian at the African Documents Center, African Studies Program, Boston University Library, Boston, Massachusetts.

890 **Periodicals from Africa: a bibliography and union list of periodicals published in Africa.**
Compiled by Carole Travis, Miriam Alman, edited by Carole Travis.
Boston, Massachusetts: G. K. Hall, 1977. 619p.

Among the 24,000 entries listing all periodicals published in Africa up to the end of 1973, there are at least seventy-three publications cited for Mali (p. 168-70). The first supplement to this work, compiled and edited by D. Blake and C. Travis (Boston, Massachusetts: G. K. Hall, 1984. 217p.), adds another 7,000 titles published from 1974 to August 1979 (Mali is on p. 71).

891 **Recently Published Articles.**
Washington, DC: American Historical Association, 1976-90.
tri-annual.

Initially published as an informal column in the *American Historical Review*, this valuable serial bibliography has unfortunately ceased publication. Every available issue of the work is divided into almost twenty geographical areas, each prepared by a specialist in that area. Africa is thoroughly covered and articles on Mali, many of which are in English, are easily located, as the section on Africa is further divided by country. One drawback to this tool is its lack of indexes, but its coverage is broad.

892 **Répertoire des Thèses Africanistes Françaises.** (List of French Africanist theses.)
Paris: CARDAN, 1977- . annual.

Lists theses on Africa, including theses about Mali, completed at universities in France.

893 **Sources d'information sur l'Afrique noire francophone et Madagascar: institutions, répertoires, bibliographies.** (Sources of information on francophone black Africa and Madagascar: institutions, lists, bibliographies.)
Laurence Porgès. Paris: Ministère de la Coopération, 1988. 389p.
(Collection Analyse des Sources d'Information).

This useful guide, which strives to provide all present and former information sources available, is an excellent source of both general and specialized bibliographies on Mali. Also listed is information on scientific, research and technical institutions, universities, archives, libraries, and learned societies. Author and institution indexes are included.

894 **Theses on Africa, 1976-1988, accepted by universities in the United Kingdom and Ireland.**
Edited by Helen C. Price, Colin Hewson, David Blake. London: Mansell, published for the Standing Conference on Library Materials on Africa (SCOLMA), 1993. 338p.

This impressive compilation continues SCOLMA's *Theses on Africa accepted by universities in the United Kingdom and Ireland* (Cambridge, England: W. Heffer, 1964. 74p.), which covers the period 1920-62, and *Theses on Africa, 1963-1975, accepted by universities in the United Kingdom and Ireland* (London: Mansell, 1978. 123p.), compiled by John McIlwaine. The first title includes no theses specifically on Mali or the French Sudan; the second contains only four, but this latest volume, which lists 3,654 items to the 3,497 of its two predecessors combined, lists 12 theses on Mali from all levels of higher education.

895 **U.S. Imprints on Sub-Saharan Africa.**
Washington, DC: Library of Congress, 1986- . annual.

This title lists monographs published or distributed in the United States and catalogued by the Library of Congress during the current and previous two years. An excellent source for contemporary materials on Mali in English.

896 **United Kingdom Publications and Theses on Africa.**
Cambridge, England: Heffer, 1963- . irregular.

Arranged by sections: Africa in general; regions; and individual countries, each of which is subdivided by subject, this title lists books, journal articles and theses.

897 **The United States and Sub-Saharan Africa: guide to U.S. official documents and government-sponsored publications, 1976-1980.**
Julian W. Witherell. Washington, DC: Library of Congress, 1984. 721p.

This title updates Witherell's previous work, *The United States and Africa: guide to U.S. official documents and government-sponsored publications on Africa, 1785-1975* (Washington, DC: Library of Congress, 1978. 949p.). Containing 100 entries on Mali, this first volume was the winner of the Conover-Porter award in 1980. The current volume, like the first, is limited to unclassified documents. It is based on the holdings of the Library of Congress and other Washington, DC-area collections, and on selected titles found in other American libraries. Entries are grouped by region and are further subdivided by country and subject; 96 entries on Mali are included.

Regional

898 **Bibliographie de l'Afrique occidentale française.** (Bibliography of French West Africa.)
Edmond Antoine Joucla, Bernard Maupoil. Paris: Société d'Editions Géographiques, Maritimes et Coloniales, 1937. 704p.

A standard source for works issued prior to 1937, containing 9,543 entries. Entries for Mali can easily be located in a section of the index under 'Soudan, Haut Sénégal-Niger, Haute Volta' (p. 695-704).

899 **French colonial Africa: a guide to official sources.**
Gloria Westfall. New York: Hans Zell, 1992. 226p.

Containing informative commentary and annotations, this work is a valuable aid for researchers wishing to exploit the wealth of information that can be found in official documents on political, social, economic and cultural conditions in the former French colonies of West Africa. Organized by type of resource, the first chapter discusses basic reference tools on the region, and lists sources that will foster the familiarity with the organization of the French colonial administration and its officials that is necessary for utilizing and understanding official records. The second chapter presents information about sources held by French and African archives; the third, official publications issued by the central administration in Paris; and the fourth, semi-official publications by colonial societies (most notably the Comité de l'Afrique Française and the Union Coloniale), congresses, international expositions, and colonial administrators. Completing the volume is a bibliography listing some of the most important published records of colonial governments, and a useful index. Christopher Gray reviews the work favourably in *African Studies Review*, vol. 37, no. 2 (Sept. 1994), p. 186-87.

900 **French-speaking West Africa: a guide to official publications.**
Compiled by Julian W. Witherell. Washington, DC: Library of Congress, Reference Department, General Reference and Bibliography Division, 1967. 201p. bibliog.

This is an excellent bibliography that lists, as comprehensively as possible, official government publications of French-speaking West Africa. Following a brief historical note, there are formal citations for 2,431 items, most of which are held by the Library of Congress and other American libraries. Including works from the mid-19th century through to the immediate post-independence period, it contains specific entries about Mali in the following sections: Mali (Federation) 1959-60 (33 entries); Mali (Republic) (153 entries); some references in 'French West Africa, 1895-1959' and in 'France: publications on French-speaking West Africa' would also be of interest.

There is a combined listing of maps of French West Africa and Mali, and publications on botany, fish, nutrition, demography, censuses, cities and towns, budgets, commerce, constitutions, forests, ethnic groups, geology, health, history, labour, laws, the Niger River, rural development, soils, statistics, stock raising and zoology.

901 **Handbook to the Arabic writings of West Africa & the Sahara.**
John O. Hunwick.   Cairo: [n.p.], 1979- . 3 vols.

A preliminary version of a proposed work of the same title, this bibliography of Arabic manuscripts lists sources found in various published works such as bibliographies, biographical works, and catalogues of manuscript collections. Visits by the compiler to important collections of Arabic manuscripts, including some in Timbuktu, have supplemented this information. Entries are arranged alphabetically by author, and consist at minimum of a numbered list of known works, including alternative titles if they exist, and their dates of composition. Authors' names and titles of works are given in both Arabic script and transliteration. Volume one, divided into three parts, covers West Africa.

Mali

902 **Archives nationales du Mali: répertoire, 1855-1954.** (National
Archives of Mali: holdings, 1855-1954.)
Moussa Niakaté.   Bamako: République du Mali, Ministère de
l'Enseignement Supérieur, Secondaire et de la Recherche Scientifique,
Direction Nationale des Enseignements Supérieurs et de la Recherche
Scientifique, Institut des Sciences Humaines du Mali, 1974. 194 leaves.

This compendium is divided into twenty-four subject areas from official acts to meteorology and including censuses, administration, elections, taxes, cultures, external relations, the police, health, the post, railways and navigation. For each category, Niakaté lists the archival holdings. See also his articles in *Etudes maliennes*: 'Les archives nationales du Mali et leur possibilités dans le cadre de la recherche' (The National Archives of Mali and their possibilities in research), no. 5 (April 1973), p. 69-83; and 'Répertoire des Archives Nationales du Mali' (Holdings of the National Archives of Mali), no. 23 (1977), p. 1-51.

903 **Bibliographie des ouvrages relatifs à la Sénégambie et au Soudan
occidental.** (Bibliography of works relating to the Senegambia and
Western Sudan.)
F.-J. Clozel.   Paris: C. Delagrave, 1891. 60p.

First published in the *Revue de géographie* in 1890 and 1891, this bibliography was compiled by a former governor of the territory. It contains 1,155 references to literature on the French Sudan and Senegambia. Some titles are in English, but most are in French or German.

904 **Bibliographie générale du Mali; (anciens, Soudan français et Haut-Senégal-Niger).** (General bibliography of Mali (formerly the French Sudan and Upper Senegal-Niger.)
Paule Brasseur.   Dakar: Institut Francais d'Afrique Noire, 1964. 461p. map. (Catalogues et Documents, no. 16).

This essential compilation of 4,902 numbered, sometimes briefly annotated sources, stops at 1960 and contains relevant items from E. Joucla's 1937 *Bibliographie de l'Afrique occidentale française* (q.v.). Brasseur presents items in six broad categories: sources; le Soudan; physical milieu; human milieu; [mise en valeur]; and biographies. These are further subdivided into numerous topics including maps, bibliographies, the Niger Valley, geology, fossils, hydrology, climate, botany, medicinal plants, zoology, physical anthropology, demography, medicine, ethnic groups, social organization, religion, languages, education, arts and literature, prehistory, archaeology, exploration, history, administration, cities, pastoralism, agriculture, transport, and economy. The volume has an informative introduction (p. 11-18), a thorough index (p. 417-610), and a fold-out map (scale 1:5,000,000).

905 **Bibliographie générale du Mali, 1961-1970.** (General bibliography of Mali, 1961-70.)
Paule Brasseur.   Dakar: Nouvelles Editions Africaines, Université de Dakar, Institut Fondamental d'Afrique Noire, 1976. 284p. (Catalogues et Documents, no. XVI-2).

This important source continues Brasseur's 1964 work (see item no. 904). It contains an introduction (p. 11-13) and 7,941 items, some with minimal annotations, grouped into seven parts, the first five of which are subdivided into numerous useful categories: sources; Mali; physical milieu; human milieu; institutions; development; and biographies. This volume, together with its predecessor, are essential for anyone conducting scholarly research on Mali. The compilation by Brasseur and Jean-François Maurel, *Les sources bibliographiques de l'Afrique de l'ouest et de l'Afrique equatoriale d'expression française* (Dakar: Bibliothèque de l'Université de Dakar, 1970. 88p.) is a useful descriptive list of unnumbered sources in French, English and German divided by subjects and by fifteen countries and areas. Those for Mali appear on pages 61-63.

906 **Index des documents microfichés au Mali.** (Index to documents microfilmed in Mali.)
Assefa Mekonnen.   Addis Ababa: Centre International Pour l'Elevage en Afrique, 1991. 238p.

Mr Assefa, for the Documentation Centre of the International Livestock Centre for Africa, compiled, in August-September 1990, a list of 1,337 documents from four research stations in Bamako and Sotuba. Among the seventy categories are agriculture, economy, ecology, climate, population studies, conservation and numerous topics on livestock. J. M. Kenworthy reviews the work briefly in *African Book Publishing Record*, vol. 19, no. 1 (1993), p. 18.

907 **Inventaire de la Bibliothèque 'umarienne de Ségou: (conservée à la Bibliothèque nationale, Paris).** (Inventory of the Umarian library of Segu, preserved in the Bibliothèque Nationale, Paris.)
Noureddine Ghali, Sidi Mohamed Mahibou, Louis Brenner. Paris: Editions du Centre National de la Recherche Scientifique, 1985. 417p. (Documents, Etudes et Répertoires) (Fontes Historiae Africanae. Subsidia Bibliographica, no. 2).

Scholars of the period will forever be indebted to the compilers of the 518 varied, mostly nineteenth-century works listed here from the library of Umar Tal (1794?-1864).

908 **Mali: a bibliographical introduction.**
Charles H. Cutter. *African Studies Bulletin*, vol. 9, no. 3 (Dec. 1966), p. 74-88.

This excellent bibliography, easily the most informative guide in English until Imperato's *Historical dictionary of Mali* (q.v.), is an attempt to introduce the reader to some of the best and most important works concerning Mali, while at the same time stressing materials that have appeared in English or since the publication of the Brasseur work (q.v., p. 74). The discursive essay presents historical studies and then material under the following headings: 'Peoples'; 'The colonial administration'; 'The politics of independence'; and 'The economics of independence'.

909 **Mali, bibliographie commentée.** (Mali, annotated bibliography.)
Bamako: REMADOC, CDHD; Paris: IBISCUS, 1995. 213p. (Réseaux Documentaires pour le Développement).

This annotated bibliography, covering the political, social, economic, and cultural life of Mali, consists of 868 titles in French published between 1985 and 1995, a short period particularly rich in Malian literary and scientific contributions. Documents and studies are listed under topics such as agriculture, commerce, culture, demography, finance, macroeconomics, health, sociology, transport, and others. Titles of 112 audio-cassettes and 27 video-casettes relating to the traditional pharmacopoeia complete the volume. It also includes a chronology of landmark dates in Malian history, and author, geographical and keyword indexes.

910 **Répertoire des travaux scolaires et universitaires de maliens au Mali (1960-1980).** (List of scholarly and academic works by Malians in Mali, 1960-80.)
Bibliothèque Nationale (Mali). Bamako: Bibliothèque Nationale, 1984-87. 3 vols.

This bibliography lists reports and theses undertaken by Malians at Malian technical and professional schools, *facultés*, colleges and research institutes from 1960 to 1980. Each volume is arranged by institution, and citations are listed by subject under each school. Author indexes are included.

Bibliographie archéologique du Mali: 1900-1981. (Archaeological bibliography of Mali: 1900-81.)
See item no. 131.

Bibliographie générale du monde peul. (General bibliography of the Peul world.)
See item no. 269.

Bibliographie analytique des langues parlées en Afrique subsaharienne, 1970-1980. (Analytical bibliography of the languages spoken in Sub-Saharan Africa, 1970-80.)
See item no. 308.

Mande languages and linguistics.
See item no. 344.

The Ghana–Guinea–Mali Union: a bibliographic essay.
See item no. 454.

Material on Soviet relations with West Africa: problems involved and a specimen bibliography, with special reference to Mali.
See item no. 464.

Women and development in Mali: an annotated bibliography.
See item no. 490.

Bibliographie sur les systèmes de production: Burkina Faso, Mali, Niger. (Bibliography on production systems: Burkina Faso, Mali, Niger.)
See item no. 516.

Bibliographie commentée des écrivains contemporains. (Annotated bibliography of contemporary writers.)
See item no. 609.

The Arts of Africa: an annotated bibliography.
See item no. 646.

Sub-Saharan African films and filmmakers: an annotated bibliography = Films et cinéastes africains de la région subsaharienne: une bibliographie commentée.
See item no. 724.

Guide to federal archives relating to Africa.
See item no. 795.

Guide to non-federal archives and manuscripts in the United States relating to Africa.
See item no. 796.

Writings on African archives.
See item no. 798.

The African Book Publishing Record.
See item no. 811.

Publishing and book development in Sub-Saharan Africa: an annotated bibliography.
See item no. 820.

Mass media in West Africa: a bibliographic essay.
See item no. 830.

Indexes

There follow three separate indexes: authors (personal and corporate); titles; and subjects. Title entries are italicized and refer either to the main titles, or to many of the other works cited in the annotations. The numbers refer to bibliographical entry rather than page numbers. Individual index entries are arranged in alphabetical sequence.

Index of Authors

A

Abel-Smith, B. 392
Abercrombie, Thomas J. 32
Abitbol, Michel 238, 241, 243
Adediran, Biodun 368
Adeleke, Tunde 284
Aebi, Ernst 58
African Academy of Sciences 855
Agence de Coopération Culturelle et Technique 582, 633
Agnely, Suzanne 2
Aherne, Tavy D. 664
Ahmed, Manzoor 601
Ainslie, Rosalynde 831
Aisiku, J. U. 592
Ajala, Adekunle 456
Ajayi, J. F. Ade 170, 173, 176
Albaret, Lucette 663
Alexandre, Pierre 5
Aliou, Mohamadou 337
Allal, M. 852
Allan, J. A. 576
Allen, Christopher H. 876
Allen, Philip M. 55
Alman, Miriam 890
Alojaly, Ghoubeïd 354
Alston, A. H. G. 108

Amado, Léopoldo Victor T. 624
Amselle, Jean-Loup 287, 358
Andah, B. Wai 166, 170
Andrade-Watkins, Claire 714
Andriamirado, Sennen 60
Anquetil, Jacques 653
Ardouin, Claude Daniel 805-806
Aremu, David A. 147
Arhin, K. 170
Arinze, Emmanuel 806
Armbruster, Barbara 661
Armes, Roy 722
Arnoldi, Mary Jo 350, 681
Asamani, Joseph O. 886
Ascofaré, Abdoulaye 617
Ashe, Jeffrey 494
Asher, Michael 58
Assefa Mekonnen 906
Association des Naturalistes du Mali 102
Association SCOA 91
Aubréville, André 110
Aubriot, Bernard 97
Autra, Ray 90
Ayensu, Dinah Ameley 780
Ayensu, Edward S. 116
Azuonye, Chukwuma 284

B

Bâ, Amadou Hampaté 172, 187, 220, 378, 616, 620, 631, 712, 743
Bachy, Victor 714
Badian, Seydou 616, 631, 639
Bagayoko, Adama 676
Bagayoko, Mamadou 598
Bagayoko, Yiritié 769
Baier, S. 170
Bailleul, Charles 317, 350
Baker, Philip 810
Ballarini, Roberto 165
Ballo, Amadou 566
Bamako. Direction Régionale de la Jeunesse, des Sports, des Arts et de la Culture 614
Bane, Mamadou Chérif 586
Banga, P. 154
Banjo, A. O. 787
Bannerman, David Armitage 101
Barber, Karin 778
Barker, G. 576
Barnard, G. W. 573
Barraud, Jean 2
Barros, Philip de 132
Barrows, David Prescott 25

Barry, Abdoul Wahab 501
Barth, Hans Karl 83
Barth, Heinrich 44
Bascom, William 751
Baselitz, Georg 658
Bass, Thomas 56
Bassot, J. P. 87
Bathily, Abdoulaye 341
Batran, A. 170
Battestini, S. M. 639
Bazin, Hippolyte 323, 351
Bazin, Jean 217
Bazin-Tardieu, Danielle 380
Béart, Charles 781
Beaudoin, Gérard 276
Bedaux, Rogier M. A. 145, 154, 159-160
Beek, Walter E. A. van 286, 367
Béhague, Gerard 701
Belcher, Stephen Paterson 744, 748
Bell, Mrs. Arthur (Nancy) 29
Bell, Nawal Morcos 182
Bender, Wolfgang 707
Bennett, Valerie Plave 434
Benoist, Edmond 212
Benoist, Joseph-Roger de 10, 361
Bergman, Billy 707
Bernardi, Bernardo 162
Bernus, Edmond 305
Bernus, S. 135
Berrett, A. M. 876
Berthe, Abou Lamine 572
Bertol, Roland 733
Bertrand, J. M. 86
Bertrand, Monique 582
Beuchelt, Eno 11
Beusekom, Monica M. van 470
Bibliothèque Nationale (Mali) 910
Bierma, M. 154
Bingen, R. James 514, 528, 534
Binger, Louis Gustave 28
Bird, Charles 313, 316, 321, 747
Blair, Dorothy S. 607

Blake, David 894
Blakely, Thomas D. 367
Blanc-Vernet, L. 89
Blanck, Jean Pierre 85
Blondé, Jacques 312
Blum, Charlotte 197
Blumenthal, Susan 55
Bluzet, R. 236
Boahen, A. Adu 180
Bocquier, Philippe 255
Bodin, Claudette 253
Boesch, Paula 883
Bolibaugh, Jerry B. 588
Bolland, Rita 133, 160
Bonnafous, Alain 546
Bonnardel, Régine 92
Bonnier, Gaëtan 236
Boone, Sylvia Ardyn 79
Boorman, John 124
Booth, A. H. 114
Borgomano, Madeleine 725
Bornstein, Ronald 455
Boser-Sarivaxévanis, Renée 160
Botti, M. 598
Bouche, Denise 234
Boudet, G. 104
Boughton, Duncan 515
Boulnois, Jean 190
Bourdier, Jean-Paul 669
Bourdin, Jean-François 308
Bourgeois, Jean-Louis 672
Bovill, E. W. 34, 504
Boyer, Allison 438
Boyle, T. Coraghessan 33
Branch, Bill 105
Brasseur, Gérard 94, 670
Brasseur, Paule 904-905
Brassié, Raymond 64
Breedveld, J. O. 330
Brenner, Louis 208, 213, 243, 378, 439, 907
Brent, Michael 143, 151
Brett-Smith, Sarah C. 652, 659
Brévié, J. 370
Brinkerhoff, Derek W. 574
Brockman, Norbert C. 847
Brooks, George E. 219
Broughton, Simon 710
Brown, Robert 31

Brown, W. A. 210
Brownlie, Ian 450
Bruce, Colin R. 786
Bruijn, Mirjam de 267, 292
Bundy, Carol 629
Bureyma, Nyaalibuuli 331
Burkill, H. M. 122

C

Caillié, René 47
Calame-Griaule, Geneviève 307, 325
Calvocoressi, D. 152
Camara, Seydou 742, 747
Camara, Sory 773
Campbell, Amie 711
Camps, Gabriel 161
Cancel, Robert 711
Canon, L. 88
Cansdale, G. S. 120
Canut, Cécile 310
Capot-Rey, Robert 88
Caprile, Jean Pierre 308
Carde, Martonne M. 92
Carelli, M. D. 598
Carney, Diana 528
Caron, Edmond 27
Carpenter, Allan 12
Cashion, Barbara 391
Cashion, Gerald 13
Caughman, Susan 490, 492-493
Cauvin, Jean 768
Cazes, Marie-Hélène 275
Cekan, Jindra Monique 478
Celles, J. C. 156
Centre de Littérature Evangélique 347
Centre Régional de Documentation pour la Traduction Orale 327
Cervenka, Zdenek 541
Chafer, Tony 463
Chailley, Marcel 30
Chambre de Commerce, d'Agriculture et d'Industrie de Bamako 836
Charpy, Jacques 793

Charry, Eric 709
Chasin, Barbara H. 577
Chemin, M. C. 88
Chéron, Georges 319
Chevrier, Jacques 2, 624
Chu, Daniel 192, 205
Church, R. J. Harrison 80, 581
Cissé, Bocar 756
Cissé, Diango 737
Cissé, Ibrahima 254
Cissé, Mohamed Lamine 759
Cissé, Souleyman 719
Cissé, Youssouf 657, 730
Cissé, Youssouf Tata 273
Cissoko, Sékéné Mody 170, 242, 616
Cissoko, Siriman 616
Clarke, Peter B. 377
Clair, André 205
Claudot-Hawad, Hélène 178
Clément, Etienne 150
Close, Angela 152
Clozel, F.-J. 6, 903
Club du Sahel 561
Cohen, William B. 419
Cole, Roy 518
Coleman, James S. 414
Collectif 630
Colleyn, Jean-Paul 359
Collion, Marie-Hélène 530
Comité de Coordination des Actions des ONG au Mali 563
Commelin, D. 156
Condé, Maryse 637
Connah, Graham 166
Conover, Helen Field 885
Conover, Ted 77
Conrad, David C. 182, 209, 303, 692, 735, 749, 774, 792
Coombs, Philip H. 601
Coquery-Vidrovitch, C. 206
Coronel, Patricia Crane 163
Costins, R. A. 625
Coulibaly, Dosseh Joseph 745

Coulibaly, Mahamadou Somé 635
Coulibaly, Salif 396
Coulibaly, Y. 803
Coulon, Virginia 629
Couloubaly, Pascal Baba F. 296
Coulter, Jonathan 498
Courlander, Harold 741
Creese, A. 392
Creevey, Lucy E. 540
Critchley, Will 568
Crowder, Michael 173, 224, 848
Crowther, Geoff 77
Crum, David Leith 497
Cuoq, Joseph 203
Curry, Peter J. 113
Cutter, Charles H. 415, 704, 908
Cyr, Helen W. 724

D

D'Aluisio, Faith 388
D'Ans, André Marcel 310
Dagan, Esther A. 649, 683, 690, 779
Daget, Jacques 118, 149, 187, 338
Dahl, Gudrun 119
Dalby, David 309
Dalziel, J. M. 108, 122
Damase, Jacques 655
Dantioko, Oudiary Makan 757
Darkowska-Nidzgorska, Olenka 685
Dave, R. H. 598
David, N. 152
David, Rosalind 469
Davidson, Basil 196, 672
Davies, Susanna 512
Daview, Helen 787
De Wolf, Paul P. 329
Decock, Jean 682
Decraene, Philippe 22
Degoulet, A. 555
Delafosse, Louise 6
Delafosse, Maurice 6, 211, 321

DeLancey, Mark W. 454
Delavignette, Robert Louis 413
Delibrias, G. 156
Del Marmol, Gérard 66
DeLuca, Laura 723
Dembelé, Edmond 528
Dembele, Kassim 635
Dembélé, M. 140, 153
Dembele, Nagognimé Urbain 612
Dembélé, Niama Nango 520
Dembele, Sidiky 616
DeMott, Barbara 286, 649
Derrick, Jonathan 578
Dettwyler, Katherine A. 391, 393, 398
Dettwyler, Steven P. 536
Devisse, Jean 52, 170
Diabaté, Kélé-Monson 737
Diabate, Lansine 729
Diabaté, Massa M. 612-613, 616, 627, 697, 699, 737
Diaby, Moussa 318
Diaby, Sékou Mamadou Chérif 448
Diagana, Ousmane Moussa 706
Diagana, Yacouba 328
Diagram Group 290
Diakite, Almadane 253
Diakite, Noumou 115
Diakité, Soumaïla 603
Diakité, Yoro 616
Diallo, A. 532
Diallo, Abdoul Aziz 788, 803
Diallo, Djibril 71
Diallo, Mamadou 613, 694
Diallo Pesg, Mamadou 251
Diallo, Yaya 695
Diarassouba, Chiaka 740
Diarra, D. Y. Pierre 371
Diarra, Issa 765
Diarra, Jean Gabriel 769
Diarra, Mandé Alpha 612
Diarra, Marthe Doka 491

Diarra, Minabe 587
Diarra, Nyamaton 659
Diarra, Pobanou Hugues 87
Diarrah, Cheick Oumar 421, 426, 435, 480
Diawara, A. 803
Diawara, Gaoussou 606, 680
Diawara, Georges 527
Diawara, Mamadou 616, 778
Dickerman, Carole W. 792
Dieterlen, Germaine 362, 373, 648, 708
Dijk, Han van 267, 292
Dinstel, Marion 889
Dioné, Josué 526
Diop, Majhemout 381
Diop, Mamadou 602
Diouara, Bouna 742
Djata, Sundiata A. 185
Djian, Jacques 759
Dochard, Surgeon 46
Dolo, Jean 580
Domian, Sergio 667
Domschke, Eliane 261
Donohoe, Joseph I. 332
Doty, William G. 777
Doumbi-Fakoly 635
Doumbia, Mamadou 51
Drabo, Souleymane 824, 826
Dreyfus, Gérard 784
Drisdelle, Rhéal 16
Du Bois, Victor D. 542
Du Pouget, Françoise 600
Dubois, Félix 42
Dubresson, Alain 582
Duignan, Peter 413, 885
Duintjer, Esger 729
Dulucq, Sophie 583
Dumestre, Gérard 310, 315, 322, 761
Dumett, R. E. 191
Dumont, Bernard 588
Dunn, Ross E. 32
Dupuis-Yakouba, A. 244, 346
Durán, Lucy 698
Durand, Jean René 109
Durou, Jean-Marc 305
Dwyer, David J. 181, 332

E

Echenberg, Myron J. 223, 229
Edwards, Ted 54
Eerenbeemt, Marie-Louise van den 400
El Fasi, M. 170
Elgood, John H. 101
Elkiss, T. H. 711
Elleh, Nnamdi 666
Ellis, William S. 554
Else, David 53, 77
Ensemble of the Republic of Mali 674
Evrard, Jacqueline 141, 163
Eyraud, Arlette 52
Ezenwe, Uka 459
Ezra, Kate 650-651

F

Fafunwa, A. Babs 592
Fage, J. D. 167, 170, 173, 176, 195
Fagerbery, Sonja 181
Faidherbe, Louis León César 333
Falgayrettes-Leveau, Christiane 150
Falloux, François 560
Falola, Toyin 368, 730
Farias, Paulo F. de Moraes 142, 730
Faure, Claude 793
Faure, Hugues 88
Fernandez de la Pradilla, César 116
Fidler, Peter, 476
Field, Ralph Ted 123
Filipovich, Jean 223
Fischer, Rudolf 193
Fisher, Allan George Barnard 209
Fisher, Humphrey 169, 197, 203, 209, 215
Fishman, Claudia 398
Flam, Jack D. 660
Flight, Colin 152
Fokkens, H. 154
Foley, Gerald 573

Follot, Igor 784
Foltz, William J. 457
Fosu-Mensah, Kwabena 691
Fottorino, Eric 71
France. Ambassade à Bamako 19
France. Ministère des Relations Extérieures. Section Géographique 96
France. Service de la Statistique Générale 266
Frank, Barbara E. 303
Franke, Richard W. 577
Freeman-Grenville, G. S. P. 176
French, Tom 789
Frey, Henri Nicolàs 222
Freyssinet, Philippe 87
Furniss, Graham 698, 763

G

Gadio, Cheikh Tidiane 827
Gage, James D. 574
Gallais, Jean 81, 178
Gallay, Alain 135, 157
Gallieni, Joseph Simon 49, 225
Ganga, Raymond C. 209
Gann, L. H. 413
Gardi, Bernhard 226
Gardner, Brian 237
Garrard, Timothy F. 134, 660
Gaudio, Attilio 174
Gaussen, Jean 164
Gaussen, Michel 161, 164
Gayet, M. 156
Gendron, Jean-Denis 314
Gerster, George 554
Ghali, Noureddine 213, 907
Gibb, H. A. R. 32
Gibbal, Jean-Marie 365
Girier, Christian 349
Glantz, Michael H. 571
Gledhill, D. 121
Glen, Simon 66
Goetz, Anne Marie 486

Goldscheider, Calvin 258
Goldwater, Mike 562
Gologo, Mamadou 626
Gomez, Michael A. 240
Görög-Karady, Veronika
754, 763
Gorse, J. E. 560
Gosebrink, Jean E. Meeh
809
Goyer, Doreen S. 261
Graham, Ronnie 700
Grandidier, G. 225
Grant, A. Paige 561
Grant, C. H. B. 101
Grant, William 489
Gray, Clive S. 404
Gray, John 688
Gray, William 46
Green, Kathryn L. 195,
199
Grevoz, Daniel 178
Griaule, Marcel 124, 286,
360, 373, 708
Griffeth, Robert 510
Grosskreutz, Béatrice 631
Grosz-Ngaté, Maria Luise
268
Groupe de Recherche des
Coutumes Dogon 271
Grove, George 703
Grundy, Kenneth W. 427
Grunne, Bernard de 144,
150, 162-163
Güdel, Christoph 20
Guernier, Eugène 853
Guerrier, Eric 360
Guez, Nicole 645
Guibbert, Jean-Jacques
584
Guindo, Boubacar 601
Gunner, Liz 698, 763
Gutkind, Peter C. W. 549

H

Hacquard, Augustin 346
Hadj-Moussa, Rabita 726
Haffner, Pierre 717
Haïdara, Youssouf
Mohamed 341
Hale, Thomas A. 738, 744
Hall, Leland 41

Hall, Mark W. 15
Hall, Mitchell 695
Hanel, Petr 489
Hannam, Harry 789
Hanson, John 181
Happold, D. C. D. 114
Hargreaves, John D. 219,
227-228
Harmon, Stephen 364, 797
Harris, Gordon 464
Harrison, Christopher
227-228
Harrow, Kenneth W. 619
Hayidara, Shekh Tijaan
745
Haywood, A. H. W. 40
Haywood, Mark 557
Hazard, John N. 428, 444,
447
Head, Sydney W. 823
Henige, David 206, 215
Henry de Frahan, Bruno
515
Hepper, R. N. 108, 122
Herbert, Eugenia 134
Heringa, A. C. 149
Herrick, Mary Darrah 889
Hewson, Colin 894
Higson, F. G. 80
Hijkoop, Jan 568
Hill, Allan G. 400
Hiskett, M. 167, 181, 377
Hodgkin, Thomas 414
Hoffman, Rachel 804
Holas, B. 297
Holden, Michael 118
Holsinger, D. C. 169
Homberger, Lorenz 651
Honegger, M. 135
Hopkins, A. G. 473
Hopkins, J. F. P. 169
Hopkins, Nicholas S. 430
Hornemann, Friedrich 34
Horowitz, Michael M.
533
Hosken, Fran P. 399
Houdas, Octave Victor
211-212
Hough, J. R. 595
Houlet, Gilbert 51
Hourst, Lieutenant 29
Hubert, Bernard 578
Hudgens, Jim 78

Hudson, Peter 76
Hué, Pascal 590
Huet, Jean-Christophe
673
Hugon, Philippe 551
Huizinga, John 154
Huizinga, Marijke 342
Human Relations Area
Files, Inc 281
Hunwick, John O. 134,
190-191, 200, 208-209,
735, 794, 901
Hutchinson, J. 108, 122
Hutchison, John P. 313,
341
Huysecom, Eric 127-128,
135, 153
Hymans, Jacques Louis
227
Hynes, William J. 777

I

Ibn Batuta 32
Ibn Khaldūn 194
Idowu, Paxton 460
Ifeka, Caroline 179
Imperato, Eleanor M. 71,
175
Imperato, Pascal James 7,
17, 71, 159, 163, 175,
211-212, 236, 243, 357,
390, 409, 431, 625, 908
Inskeep, R. R. 140
Insoll, Timothy 127, 139
Institut d'Urbanisme de
Paris 582
Institut des Sciences
Humaines (Mali) 869
Institut Géographique
National (France) 93
Interafrican Committee for
Hydraulic Studies 575
International African
Institute 876, 882, 887
International Court of
Justice 449
International Institute for
Adult Literacy Methods
604
International Livestock
Centre for Africa 557

International Service for
National Agricultural
Research 539
Iroko, Felix 190
Issébéré, Hamadoun
Ibrahima 611
Izard, M. 170

J

Jabaté de Kéla, Jeli Kanku
Madi 742
Jackson, James Grey 24
Jacobberger, P. A. 578
Jago, N. D. 531
Jagu-Roche, Jacqueline 61
Jah, Omar 216
Jahn, Janheinz 641
Jansen, Jan 729, 776
Jara, Mamadu 745
Jay, Salim 250
Jeng, Mamadu 331
Jenkins, Mark 73
Jespers, Philippe 654
Jobs and Skills
Programme for Africa
548
Jodice, David A. 842
Joffre, Joseph-Jacques-
Césaire 35
Johnson, G. Wesley 793
Johnson, Harry G. 485
Johnson, John William
727-728, 744
Johnson, Marion 186
Johnson, Segun 451
Jonckers, Danielle 299
Jones, William I. 424, 484
Jouannet, Francis 311
Joubert, Jean-Louis 624
Joucla, Edmond Antoine
898

K

Kaba, Alkaly 616, 628
Kaba, Lasiné 201
Kaba, Mamadou 177
Kagan, Alfred 879
Kahn, E. J. 21
Kalu, Kalu Ndukwe 461

Kamenya, Shadrack 723
Kamian, Bakari 22
Kane, Moustapha 181
Kanoute, Moussa 638, 679
Kante, Cemako 776
Kanté, Mamadou 313, 316
Kanya-Forstner, A. S.
223-224
Kassogué, Armand 580
Kastenholz, Raimund 344
Kâti, Mahmoûd Kâti ben
El-Hâdj El-Motaouakkel
211
Kawada, Junzo 270
Kaya, Bocary 568
Keay, R. W. J. 108, 122
Keita, Abdoulaye 257
Kéita, Aoua 412
Keïta, Cheickh
Mahamadou Cherif 613,
634
Keita, Fallo Baba 663·
Keita, Mamadou 342
Keita, Modibo S. 453, 608
Kerjean, Alain 62
Kerkhof, Paul 573
Kervran, Marcel 326, 348
Kesteloot, Lilyan 736, 739
Ki-Zerbo, J. 170
Kitchen, Helen 863
Klein, Martin A. 387
Knight, Roderic 701
Koch, Klaus-Friedrich 71
Koenig, Dolores 260, 533,
538
Kom, Ambroise 616
Konaké, Sory 616, 622
Konare, Alhassen 118
Konaré, Alpha Oumar
131, 171, 233, 799
Konaré Ba, Adam 171,
850
Konate, Baba Moussa 807
Konate, M. 555
Konaté, Mamadou 395,
635
Konaté, Moussa 612, 801,
806
Konaté, Yacouba 524
Koné, Bacari 525
Koné, Mamadou 647
Konipo, M. 338
Koslow, Philip 198

Kouame, Yao 825
Kounta, Albakaye
Ousmane 636, 755
Kouroupas, Maria
Papageorge 150
Kouyate, Damou 253
Kouyaté, Harouna 758
Krause, Chester L. 786
Krings, Thomas 68
Kun, Nicolas de 86
Kuntz, Patricia S. 13
Kurian, George 599, 841
Kurtz, Donn M. 458
Kwamena-Poh, M. 176

L

L'Association des Trois
Mondes 715
La Brosse, Renaud de 828
La Duke, Betty 665
Labatut, Roger 337
Labonne, Michel 408
Labouret, Henri 339
Ladipo, R. O. 452
Lafon, Michel 308
Lagarde, Michel 335
Laing, Alexander Gordon
34
Lamine, Male 605
Lamy, René 792
Lange, Dierk 190
Langewiesche, William 77
LaPointe, Mark 12
Larkin, Gregory V. 879
Larouche, Michel 726
Last, Murray 169
Laude, Jean 642
Lauer, Joseph J. 879
LaViolette, Adria Jean
129
Law, Robin 218
Laye, Camara 731
Le Berre, Michel 107
Le Houérou, H. N. 564
Le Moal, G. 94
Lebeuf, Annie M. D. 130
Lebrun, J.-P. 104
Legvold, Robert 464-465
Leiris, Michel 283
Leisinger, Klaus M. 539
Leloup, Hélène 658

292

Lems-Dworkin, Carol 686, 688
Lent, Peter van 613
Lenz, Oskar 43
Leo, Africanus 31
Leveau, Michel 150
Lévêque, C. 109
Levinson, David 277
Levtzion, Nehemia 167, 169, 183, 209
Lewis, I. M. 191
Lewis, John Van Dusen 519
Lewis, Sydney A. 482
Ligers, Ziedonis 149, 302, 708
Lipschutz, Mark R. 849
Lloyd, Christopher 38
Lockwood, Susan 819
Lomer, Cecile 808, 820
Lovejoy, Paul E. 204, 206, 209, 218
Luery, Andrea 499
Lugard, Flora Louisa Shaw, Lady 214
Lundy, John K. 145
Luneau, René 272, 772
Ly, Fakoney 601
Ly, Ibrahima 640
Ly-Tall, Madina 170, 742

M

M'Bodj, Djibi 337
Maack, May Niles 791
Maas, Pierre 82, 226, 668
McCaskie, T. C. 206, 215
McConnell, Grant D. 314
McDougall, E. Ann 206
McFarlane, Catherine 386
McGuire, James Reed 627
McIlwaine, John 798
McIntosh, Roderick 81, 127, 134-135, 137-138, 140-141, 143-144, 147, 150-153, 166
McIntosh, Susan Keech 127, 134, 136-138, 140-141, 147, 150-153, 166, 202
McKissack, Fredrick 205
McKissack, Patricia 205

McLain, Rebecca J. 574
McMellan, Donna M. 394
McNaughton, Patrick R. 150, 656, 662
MacRae, Suzanne H. 726
Mackworth-Praed, C. W. 101
Magasa, Amidu 230
Mage, Eugène 50
Maghili, Muhammad ibn 'Abd al-Karim 208
Mahibou, Sidi Mohamed 213, 216, 907
Maiga, Ismaïl 343
Maïga, Mohamed Bagna 341
Maïga, Youssouf Billo 341
Mainguet, M. 88
Malgras, Denis 406
Mali 18
Mali. Bureau Central de Recensement 261, 265
Mali. Commissariat au Tourisme 98
Mali. Direction de la Planification 246
Mali. Direction Nationale de l'Alphabétisation Fonctionnelle et de la Linguistique Appliquée 320, 334, 336, 341, 353
Mali. Direction Nationale de l'Urbanisme et de la Construction 585
Mali. Direction Nationale de la Géologie et des Mines 87
Mali. Direction Nationale de la Statistique et de l'Informatique 248, 263, 836-837, 839-840
Mali. Direction Nationale des Eaux et Forêts 569
Mali. Division du Patrimoine Culturel 155
Mali. Ministère des Sports, des Arts 696
Mali. Ministère du Plan et le l'Economie Rurale 487
Mali. Service de la Statistique 262

Maliendy, Guissé 766
Malio, Nouhou 738
Malzy, P. 106
Mamadi, Kaba 689
Mango, Cecily 15
Mann, Charles C. 382
Mann, Kristin 441
Mann, Michael 309
Manning, Patrick 228
Mara, Adama 659
Mara, C. O. 803
Marcoux, R. 582
Marnham, Patrick 383
Marriner, John 69
Marti, James 841
Martin, Guy 462, 488
Marty, Paul 363
Maugham, Robin 70
Mauny, Raymond 158
Maupoil, Bernard 898
May, Jacques Meyer 394
Maydell, H.-J. von 121
Mayor, A. 135
Mazur, Robert E. 258
Mbaye, Saliou 791
Meillassoux, Claude 200, 217, 341, 385
Méloux, J. 87
Melville J. Herskovits Library of African Studies 888
Melville, K. E. M. 66
Méniaud, Jacques 231-232
Menzel, Peter 382, 388
Mercier, P. 94
Merryfield, Mary 23
Meunier, Dominique 206
Meyer, Gérard 754, 763, 765
Meyer, Laure 660
Michel-Jones, Françoise 295
Middleton, John 277
Mikell, Gwendolyn 260
Mills, Dorothy 37
Miner, Horace 63
Minta, Ousmane 597
Mishler, Clifford 786
Mohammed I, Askia of Songhai 208
Moisset, Jean 596
Mokhtar, G. 170
Molin, Monseigneur 771

Mommersteeg, Geert 82, 226, 668
Mondot-Bernard, Jacqueline M. 408
Monfils, Barbara S. 830
Monimart, Marie 491
Monnier, Yves 90
Monod, Théodore 305
Monteil, Charles 189, 282, 762
Monteil, P.-L. 26
Morel, Gérard J. 101
Morel, P. C. 112
Morgan, Ted 39
Morgan, W. B. 80
Morgenthau, Ruth S. 414, 417
Moroney, Sean 844
Morton, J. K. 125
Moss, Joyce 289
Moss, Rowland Percy 581
Mozaffar, Shaheen 437
Mukendi, Aleki 560
Musée Royal de l'Afrique Centrale 880

N

N'Diayé, Bokar 279, 764
N'diaye Thiam, Mariam 493
Naylor, Kim 8, 57
Ndukwe, Pat I. 284
Neff, June 402
Neres, Philip 219
Netherlands. Directorate General International Cooperation. Operations Review Unit 474
Newbury, Catharine 439
Newton, Alex 77
Newton, Diana C. 821-822
Newton, Robert C. 355
Ngyrie, Emmanuel 578
Niakaté, Moussa 902
Niane, D. T. 170, 732
Nicolson, Sharon E. 88
Nielsen, M. S. 111
Nivomé de Jaime, Jean Gilbert 27

Noblet, Richard 52
Nolan, Brian 392
Nordmann, Almut 641
Norris, H. T. 184
Notre Librairie 623
Nourrit, Chantal 702
Nsouli, Saleh M. 467
Nwanunobi, C. O. 284

O

O'Brien, Donal B. Cruise 195
O'Toole, Thomas 8, 12
Obi, Dorothy S. 790
Obichere, Boniface I. 603
Oboli, H. O. N. 80
Office du Niger 567
Ohler, F. M. J. 579
Ohrn, Steven 724
Ojo-Ade, Femi 228
Ojo, Oyediran 558
Okpoko, A. 166
Oliver-Bever, Bep 116
Oliver, Roland 167, 848
Olivier de Sardan, Jean-Pierre 301
Oloruntimehin, B. O. 207
Olorode, Omotoye 111
Onattara, Jean-Pierre 765
Opération Lecture Publique 609
Organization of African Unity 99
Osborn, Donald W. 327, 332
O'Toole, Thomas 8
Otreppe, Albert d' 66
Ottenberg, Simon 683
Ouallet, Anne 582
Ouane, A. 598
Ouane, Adama 352
Ouane, Ibrahima Mamadou 616
Ouattara Tiona, Ferdinand 775
Ouologuem, Yambo 610, 616
Oxfam UK & Ireland 16
Oyhus, Arne Olav 556

P

Pageard, Robert 732
Painter, Thomas M. 533
Palmer, Don 691
Panos Institute 832-833
Pâques, Viviana 130
Park, Mungo 33, 45, 76
Pasachoff, Jay M. 57
Paulme, Denise 288
Peaslee, Amos J. 446
Pélissier, P. 94
Pelos, Carollee 672
Pelton, Robert D. 777
Perera, D. A. 598
Perinbam, B. Marie 278, 369, 510
Pern, Stephen 285
Perry, A. E. 80
Person, Alain 140
Péruse, Denise 726
Peters, Susanne 802
Petit-Maire, N. 89, 156
Petty, Sheila 718
Pfaff, Françoise 718
Pfeffermann, Guy 553
Pflugrad, Diane 711
Philippi, Thomas 543
Pichard, E. 401
Pick, Hella 15
Pierre Matisse Gallery 655
Pius Ngandu Nkashama 615
Pobi, Cephas 825
Pollet, Eric 300, 537
Poncet, Yveline 91
Ponsioen, Tom 580
Porch, Douglas 168
Porgès, Laurence 893
Porquet, Jean-Luc 250
Pory, John 31
Posnansky, Merrick 134, 152
Prasse, Karl-G. 306, 354, 420
Preston, George Nelson 163
Price, Helen C. 894
Priest, Cecil D. 41
Prillaman, Jerry 817
Pringle, Robert M. 115
Prost, André 340, 348
Pruitt, Bill 702

Prussin, Labelle 671
Pugh, J. C. 80

Q

Qasim ibn Sulayman 241
Queffélec, Ambroise 311
Quensière, Jacques 117
Quiminal, Catherine 252

R

Raffenel, Anne 36
Raimbault, Michel 146,
  149, 153, 156
Rake, Alan 75, 843
Randall, Sara 293, 400
Rasilly, Bernard de 324
Rasmussen, R. Kent 849
Rassam, Amal 277
Ravenhill, Philip L. 131,
  150
Rawson, David P. 433
Redden, Kenneth Robert
  445
Reed, William 118
Rémy, Mylène 61
Renaudeau, Michel 274
Rennell, James 45
Reporters Sans Frontières
  834
RESADOC Mali 856
Réseau de Recherche sur
  la Résistance à la
  Sécheresse. Comité de
  Coordination
  Documentaire 516
Réseau Malien de
  Documentation 609
Richard-Molard, J. 94
Richard, Patricia 578
Richmond, Edmun B.
  588
Riley, Rebecca 724
Riser, J. 156
Riser, Jean 89
Ritter, Hans 67
Roberts, Richard L. 218,
  389, 441, 503, 507, 511
Robertshaw, Peter 132
Robin, Nelly 249

Robinson, David 181, 195,
  213, 227, 376
Roch, Jean 578
Rolland, Denis 752
Rondeau, Chantal 384
Rosberg, Carl G. 414
Rosevear, D. R. 100, 103
Rouch, Jean 375
Rouget, Gilbert 705
Roussin, Michel 648
Rowland, Jacky 420
Royal Academy of Arts
  150
Royal Tropical Institute
  523
Rubin, Don 687
Rubin, William 658
Rugh, Michael A. 466
Russell, Karen 482

S

Saad, Elias N. 238
Sabatier, Peggy R. 593
'Sadī, 'Abd al-Raḥmān ibn
  'Abd Allāh 212
Sadie, Stanley 703
Sagara, Abdoulaye
  Amadou 760
Saint-Martin, Yves-Jean
  188
Sako, Ousmane 741
Saliba, M. 598
Sallée, Aliette 752
Salvioni, Giovanna 675
Sanankoua, M. 338
Sangaré, Luc 374
Sanneh, Lamine 372
Sanogho, Nampaa N. 565
Sanogo, Kléna 153
Sarr, Mamadou 251
Sauvain-Dugerdil,
  Claudine 157
Savonnet, G. 94
Sawadogo, Patrice 264
Sayer, J. A. 113, 559
Sayers, A. R. 532
Schatzberg, Michael G.
  422
Scheven, Yvette 881
Schijns, Wolf 668
Schild, Ulla 641

Schissel, Howard 805
Schmidt, Nancy 724
Schmidt, Peter R. 143
Schmitt, Karin 539
Schunk, Thomas 661
Scott, Earl P. 201
Seabrook, William 244
Seddon, David 537
Seddon, Grace 537
Segal, Aaron 55
Selby, Bettina 59
Sellin, Eric 610
Semaine du Théâtre
  Africain 684
Sembène Ousmane 621
Senghor, Léopold Sédar
  458
Serafini, Phil 513
Serle, William 101
Serra, Richard 658
Seydou, Christiane 269,
  746
Sezirahiga, Jadot 721
Shah, Tahir 71
Shapiro, Daniel 150
Shaw, C. T. 170
Shaw, T. 166
Shinnie, Peter L. 135
Shiri, Keith 716
Sidibe, Cheick O. 591,
  603
Sidibé, Mamby 759
Sidibe, Moussa 594
Sidibé, Samuel 143, 150
Sidiyene, Ehya Ag 112,
  354
Sikainga, Ahmad Alawad
  181
Silla, Eric 403
Simon, Gunter 815
Sims, Michael 879
Sinclair, P. 166
Singer, Ronald 145
Singh, Shamsher 509
Sironto, Leon 141
Sisòkò, Fa-Digi 727
Sisòkò, Magan 728
Sissoko, Fily Dabo 616,
  632
Sissoko, Sada 677
Sitzman, Glenn L. 787
Siva Kumar, M. V. K.
  555

Skinner, Elliott Percival 192, 205
Skinner, J. 579
Skolle, John 65
Slane, William MacGuckin, baron de 194
Slobin, Kathleen O. 397
Smith, Andrew B. 148, 161
Smith, Lawrence D. 506
Smith, Susan E. 88
Smith, Zeric Kay 436, 439
Snyder, Francis G. 416, 425, 429
Snyder, John 386
Snyder, Sarah 386
Soares, Benjamin F. 376
Soleillet, Paul 50
Soumaré, Penda 752
South, Aloha 795-796
Sow, Ami 783
Spawls, Stephen 105
Spini, Sandro 304
Spini, Tito 304
Spitz, Georges 22, 535
Spriggs, Karyl T. 445
Stanley, Janet L. 646
Stanton, Cynthia 395
State University of New York at Buffalo. Comparative Education Center 814
Steeds, D. R. 560
Steentoft, Margaret 111
Stewart, C. C. 184, 210, 216
Stewart, John 844
Stieber, Michael T. 235
Stockman, Anita 3
Stoller, Paul 298, 720
Stoneham, Doreen 163
Stotz, D. F. 561
Strassmann, Beverly Ilse 294
Stride, G. T. 179
Sudrie, Olivier 551
Suret-Canale, J. 549, 552, 732
Sutton, J. E. G. 147, 152
Swartz, B. K. 191
Sy, Boubacar Sada 513
Sy, Demba 828

Sy, Mamadou 51
Szumowski, G. 149

T

Tahari, A. 481
Tal, Umar 216
Talbot, M. R. 88
Tamboura, Boubacar 729
Tangara, Mahamadou 521
Taubert, Sigfred 816
Tauxier, Louis 280
Tawanda, Michael 259
Taylor, Charles Lewis 842
Thiam, Cheikh Tidiane 828
Thom, Derrick J. 522
Thomas, Benjamin E. 545
Thompson, J. Malcom 379
Thomson, Anne Margaret 506
Thomson, Dennis L. 367
Thomson, James T. 529
Thoyer, Annik 116, 745
Tidy, M. 176
Timbo, Adama 23
Tindwa, John Bosco 823
Tinguidji, Boûbacar 746
Togola, Téréba 126, 150
Topouzis, Daphne 691
Tosh, J. 176
Toulmin, Camilla 517
Toure, Ahmadou 592
Touré, Kanté Dandara 398
Traoré, Abdoul 635
Traore, Amadou 736, 739
Traoré, Baba 395
Traoré, El Hadj Sadia 750
Traoré, Falaba Issa 618
Traoré, H. 87
Traoré, Issa Baba 97, 753
Traore, Jean-Baptiste 736, 739
Traoré, Madjoun 635
Traore, Sadio 255
Traoré, Seydou 616
Travélé, Moussa 351, 770
Travis, Carole 890
Trench, Richard 58
Triaud, Jean-Louis 216, 376

Trillo, Richard 78
Trimingham, J. Spencer 377
Trinh, T. Minh-Ha 669
Troupe, Quincy 691
Turbat, Vincent 392
Turrittin, Jane 410, 432, 483, 596
Twose, Nigel 562
Tyson, Remer 72

U

Uchendu, Victor C. 603
Udo, Reuben K. 80
Ugboajah, Frank Okwu 830
Unesco Institute for Education 598
Union des Journalistes de l'Afrique de l'Ouest 832-833
United Nations 838
United Nations Development Programme 263, 496
United Nations Economic Commission for Africa 544, 835
United Nations Fund for Population Activities 247
United Nations. Industrial Development Organization. Regional and Country Studies Branch 479
United States. Agency for International Development 15
United States. Agency for International Development. Office of Development Information and Utilization 245
United States. Central Intelligence Agency 95
United States. Dept. of State 3, 14
United States. Office of Geography 84

University of Wisconsin Land Tenure Center 573
Urvoy, Y. 291
Uwechue, Ralph 849

V

Vaes, Bénédicte 66
Van der Poel, Piet 568
Van der Waals, J. D. 140
Vengroff, Richard 440
Vernet, Joël 178
Vialard, Dominique 256
Vieillard, Gilbert 746
Villien-Rossi, Marie-Louise 4
Villiers, André 120
Virmani, S. M. 555

W

Wâ Kamissoko 730
Wagenaar, K. T. 532

Waller, R. 176
Wanono, Nadine 274, 713
Ward, Jennifer Claudette 221
Warms, Richard L. 500, 502
Warshall, Peter 569
Watts, Daud Malik 239
Webster, Leila 476
Weidhaas, Peter 816
Welcomme, Robin 554
Welch, Galbraith 48
Wells, John C. 522
Werewere Liking 678
Westfall, Gloria 899
Wiley, David S. 711
Willett, F. 152
Williams, A. Olufemi 401
Williams, M. A. J. 88
Willis, John Ralph 195, 209, 366
Wilson, George 289
Wingfield, R. J. 733
Winter, Christopher 82
Winter, Grace 300

Winter, Michael 293
Wisniewski, David 733
Witherell, Julian W. 818-819, 897, 900
Woillet, J. C. 852
Wolpin, Miles D. 423
World Bank 496
Wright, J. B. 86
Wright, William 150

Z

Zahan, Dominique 356, 644, 708
Zakara, Mohamed Aghali 767
Zell, Hans 629, 808, 811-813, 820
Zoghby, Samir M. 505
Zolberg, Aristide R. 411, 418, 485
Zolberg, Vera L. 602
Zoubko, Galina 329
Zubko, G. V. 331
Zulu, Justin B. 467

297

Index of Titles

A

The A.I.D. economic policy reform program in Mali 466

A l'écoute des anciens du village 750

A l'écoute des enfants 630

The A.O.F. Archives and the study of African history 791

Abubakari II: théâtre 606

Access to credit for poor women 494

An account of Timbuctoo and Housa, territories in the interior of Africa 24

ACROAMA's dancers of Mali 674

Adaptable livelihoods 512

Adjustment programs in Africa 467

Adrar Bous and Karkarichinkat 148, 161

The adventures of Ibn Battuta 32

The AED African Financial Directory 495

Aethiopia, vestiges de gloire 144

Affaire du différend frontalier 449

AFP Sahara 864

Africa 844, 865, 887

Africa Bibliography 876

Africa Confidential 865

Africa contemporary record 845

Africa from real to reel: an African filmography 724

Africa from the nineteenth century until the 1880s 170

Africa from the seventh to the eleventh century 170

Africa from the twelfth to the sixteenth century 170

Africa Guide 468

Africa Index to Continental Periodical Literature 877

Africa: a Lonely Planet shoestring guide 77

Africa, Mali: selected statistical data by sex 245

Africa: North and West 99

Africa on file 1

Africa on film and videotape, 1960-1981 711

Africa Report 866

Africa Research and Documentation 798

Africa Review 468

Africa's Sahel: the stricken land 554

Africa South of the Sahara 846

Africa South of the Sahara: Index to Periodical Literature, 1900- 877-878

Africa Special Report 866

Africa, the art of a continent 150

Africa through the eyes of women artists 665

African art of the Dogon 642

African Arts 643

An African biographical dictionary 847

The African Book Publishing Record 811, 881

The African book world & press 812

African books in print 813

African boundaries 450

African civilizations: precolonial cities and states 166

African dolls for play and magic 779

African economic and financial data 496

African feminism 260

African folk medicine 390

African folklore 747

African folktales in the New World 751

African historiography 730

African history in maps 176

African history on file 1

African international organization directory 858

African labor history 549

African libraries 787

African literature in French 607

African military labour and the building of the Office du Niger installations, 1925-1950 223

African music 688

African Statistical Yearbook, 1992/93 835

African music: a bibliographical guide 688

African participation in other international organizations 1984/85 858

The African past 196

African socialism 427

African states and rulers: an encyclopedia 844

The African studies
  companion 808
African studies
  information resources
  directory 809
The African tale of cinema
  712
Afrique de l'Ouest:
  introduction géologique
  86
L'Afrique du Sahel 2
Afrique, ma boussole 606
Afrique Nord et Ouest 99
L'Afrique occidentale
  française de 1944 à
  1960 10
Afrique occidentale
  française. Togo 51
After the Jihad 181
The age of Mansa Musa of
  Mali 182
Agribusiness and public
  sector collaboration in
  agricultural technology
  development and use in
  Mali 513
Agricultural development
  policy and grassroots
  democracy in Mali
  514
Agricultural research
  impact assessment
  515
Agroclimatology of West
  Africa: Mali 555
Agroforestry in Africa
  573
Ahmad Baba and the
  Moroccan invasion of
  the Sudan (1591) 191
AIDS: an African
  perspective 401
L'aigle et l'épervier 613
'Al Hajj 'Umar b. Sa'id
  al-Futi al Turi 366
Al-Maghili's replies to the
  questions of Askia al-
  Hajj Muhammad 208
Amélioration des pays
  arides du Mali 556
Aménagements en
  quartiers spontanés
  africains 582

American and Canadian
  doctoral dissertations
  and master's theses on
  Africa, 1974-1987 879
American Historical
  Review 891
Amkoullel, l'enfant peul
  220, 743
An ka bamanankan kalan,
  introductory Bambara
  313, 316
Analyse du recensement
  261
An analysis of educational
  reforms in Mali 586
Une ancienne industrie
  malienne 149
Ancient civilizations of
  Africa 170
Ancient Ghana and Mali
  183
Ancient pottery from Mali
  144
Ancient sculpture of the
  Inland Niger Delta and
  its influence on Dogon
  art 162
Ancient treasures in terra
  cotta of Mali and Ghana
  163
Les angoisses d'un monde
  296
Annuaire Statistique du
  Mali 836, 840
Anthologie de chants
  mandingues 689
Anthropological research
  in Mali 154
Anthropology and rural
  development in West
  Africa 533
Antilopes du soleil 644
Aoua Kéita and the
  nascent women's
  movement in the French
  Soudan 410
Apartheid: poèmes 638
Aperçu de la situation
  ethno-linguistique du
  Mali 587
Un appel de nuit 612
The Arab conquest of the
  Western Sahara 184

L'arbre et l'enfant;
  Sassa 752
Arbres et arbustes
  guérisseurs des savanes
  maliennes 406
Archaeological
  investigations of Iron
  Age sites in the Mema
  region, Mali (West
  Africa) 126
Archaeological
  reconnaissance in the
  region of Timbuktu,
  Mali 127
Archaeology in West
  Africa 152
The archaeology of
  Africa: foods, metals
  and towns 166
Die archäologische
  Forschung in Westafrika
  128
An archeological
  ethnography of
  blacksmiths, potters,
  and masons in Jenne,
  Mali (West Africa)
  129
Archéologie africaine et
  sciences de la nature
  appliquées à
  l'archéologie 146
Archéologie malienne
  130
Archéologie
  ouest-africaine 141
L'archer bassari 608
Archers, musketeers, and
  mosquitoes, the
  Moroccan invasion of
  the Sudan and the
  Songhay resistance
  (1591-1612) 201
Architecture 666
The architecture of Djenne
  671
Architecture soudanaise
  667
Archival resources in Mali
  792
The archival system of
  former French West
  Africa 793

300

Les archives de la Société
  des Pères Blancs
  (Missionnaires
  d'Afrique) 792
Archives nationales du
  Mali 902
Arid ways 267
The Arma of Timbuktu
  243
Arrondissement, 1993-
  1997 248
L'art africain
  contemporain 645
An art historical approach
  to the terracotta figures
  of the Inland Niger
  Delta 150
Art of the Dogon 651
The art of metal in Africa
  660
The art of West African
  cooking 780
The artfulness of M'Fa
  Jigi 659
Les arts des métaux en
  Afrique noire 660
The Arts of Africa 646
ASA News 879
Un atelier de burins à
  Lagreich, Oued Tilemsi
  (République du Mali)
  161
Les ateliers prehistoriques
  de Manianbugu
  (Bamako, Mali) 153
Atlas des cercles de
  l'Afrique Occidentale
  Française 92
Atlas des migrations
  ouest-africaines vers
  l'Europe, 1985-1993
  249
Atlas du Mali 90
Atlas historique de la
  boucle du Niger 91
Atlas international de la
  vitalité linguistique 314
The atlas of Africa 92
An atlas of African history
  176
Au coeur de l'ethnie 358
Au coin du feu 753
Au Mali et au Niger 52

L'aube des béliers 606
Aurore 859

B

Baarakèla 547
The background and
  possible historical
  significance of a letter
  and manuscript of 1798
  concerning Timbuktu
  235
Background notes: Mali 3
Backpacker's Africa 53
Baker's International
  guide to African studies
  research 810
Bamako, capitale du Mali 4
Bamako et ses environs 93
Bamako, recensement
  1958, enquête
  démographique 1960-61
  262
The Bamana blacksmiths:
  a study of sculptors and
  their art 662
The Bamana empire by the
  Niger 185
The Bamana women
  drummers 690
The Bambara 356
Le Bambara du Mali 315
Bambara–English,
  English–Bambara
  student lexicon 316
The Bambara–French
  relationship 221
Bambara men and women
  and the reproduction of
  social life in Sana
  Province, Mali 268
Bambara sculpture from
  the Western Sudan 650
The ban on Mali's
  antiquities 150
Banamba and the salt
  trade of the western
  Sudan 206
The Banamba slave
  exodus of 1905 and the
  decline of slavery in the
  Western Sudan 218

Basic education in the
  Sahel countries 598
The bats of West Africa
  100
Beat King Salif Keita 691
Bellagio Publishing
  Network Newsletter 814
Berbers and blacks 25
Beyond reaction and
  denunciation 150
Beyond the last oasis 54
Bibliographie analytique
  des langues parlées en
  Afrique subsaharienne,
  1970-1980 308
Bibliographie
  archéologique du Mali
  131
Bibliographie commentée
  des écrivains
  contemporains 609,
  623
Bibliographie de l'Afrique
  occidentale française
  898, 904
Bibliographie de l'Afrique
  Sud-Saharienne,
  Sciences Humaines et
  Sociales 880
Bibliographie des
  ouvrages relatifs à la
  Sénégambie et au
  Soudan occidental 903
Bibliographie fulfulde 344
Bibliographie générale du
  Mali 904
Bibliographie générale du
  Mali, 1961-1970 905
Bibliographie générale du
  monde peul 269
Bibliographie mandingue
  344
Bibliographie sur les
  systèmes de production
  516
Bibliographies for African
  Studies, 1987-1993 881
A bibliography of African
  bibliographies covering
  territories south of the
  Sahara 881
'Bilali of Faransekila'
  692

301

A *biogeographical consideration of colonization of the lower Tilemsi Valley in the second millennium B.C.* 148, 161
The birds of tropical West Africa 101
Birds of the West African town and garden 101
The birds of West and Equatorial Africa 101
Birds of West Central and Western Africa 101
Birth of a museum at Bamako, Mali 799
Bogolan et arts graphiques du Mali 663
The book in francophone black Africa 815
The book trade of the world 816
Books in Francophone Africa 817
Boucle du Niger: approches multidisciplinaires 270
Le boucher de Kouta 612-613, 627
La boucle du Niger (Mali) 85
Bound to violence 610
Les bouts de bois de Dieu 621
Les boutures du soleil 611
Breastfeeding, weaning, and other infant feeding practices in Mali and their effects on growth and development 391
Bright continent 55
Bring beauty back to Mali 150
Broadcasting in Africa 823
Buffoons, queens, and wooden horsemen 357
Bulletin de l'Association des Naturalistes du Mali 102
Bulletin de l'Institut Français d'Afrique Noire 867

Bulletin Mensuel de Statistique 837
Bulletin (West African Museums Project) 800
Burkina-Mali war 451

C

Ça presse au Sahel 824
Cahiers d'Etudes Africaines 868
The Caliphate of Hambullahi 210
The Cambridge encyclopedia of Africa 848
The Cambridge history of Africa 167
Camel caravans of the Saharan salt trade 206
Campagne dans le haut Sénégal et dans le Haut Niger, 1885-1886 222
Camping with the Prince 56
Caravans of the old Sahara 504
The carnivores of West Africa 103
Cartes ethno-démographiques de l'Afrique occidentale 94
Case concerning the frontier dispute 449
The case of Faama Mademba Sy and the ambiguities of legal jurisdiction in early colonial French Soudan 441
A case of fundamentalism in West Africa 358
Catalogue des plantes vasculaires du Mali 104
Cattle, women, and wells 517
CEDRAB: the Centre de Documentation et de Recherches Ahmad Baba at Timbuktu 794
La célébration de la levée du deuil 271

101 Maliens nous manquent 250
A certificate geography of West Africa 80
Challenges of regional economic cooperation among the ECOWAS states 461
Changes in drought-coping strategies in the Segu Region of Mali 518
Changes in land use and vegetation in the ILCA/Mali Sudano-Sahelian project zone 557
Changing paradigms, goals & methods in the archaeology of francophone West Africa 132
Changing places?: women, resource management and migration in the Sahel 469
Chansons d'Afrique et des Antilles 693
Chants de chasseurs du Mali 745
Chants de femmes au Mali 772
Chants traditionnels du pays soninké 706
Le chat et les souris 612
Les chemins de la noce 272
Les chemins de Nya 359
Chiefs and clerics 195
'The chronicle of the succession' 213
Chronique d'une journée de répression 612
Ciné-rituel de femmes dogon 713
Le cinéma au Mali 714
The cinematic griot: the ethnography of Jean Rouch 720
Une cité soudanaise: Djénné 282
Cities of the Pondo 82

Cities without citadels
166
Les clandestins 250
The climates of West
Africa 558
Clothing from burial caves
in Mali, 11th–18th
century 133
Le coiffeur de Kouta 613
Coiffures traditionnelles et
modernes au Mali 647
Collecting world coins
786
Colloque sur littérature
et esthétique
négro-africaines 699
Colonial conscripts 223
Colonial policy and the
family life of black
troops in French West
Africa 379
Colonial rural
development 470
Colonialism in Africa
1870-1960. A
bibliographical guide
885
Colonialism in Africa
1870-1960, vol. 2.
The history and politics
of colonialism,
1914-1960 413
Comme une piqûre de
guêpe 613
Commentaries on a
creative encounter 613
Commerce and community
500
Le commerce du sel de
Taoudeni 206
Comparative advantage,
trade flows and
prospects for regional
agricultural market
integration in West
Africa 501
A comparative survey of
seven adult functional
literacy programs in
Sub-Saharan Africa 588
Compendium of human
settlements statistics
838

Compendium of Social
Statistics and
Indicators, 1988 838
Complex societies of West
Africa 134
A comprehensive
geography of West
Africa 80
Concepts et conceptions
songhay-zarma 301
Concours de la meilleure
nouvelle en langue
française 614
Conflict management in
the West African
sub-region 452
La confrérie des chasseurs
Malinké et Bambara
273
Connaissance de la
République de Mali 22
The conquest of the
Sahara 168
The conquest of the
Western Sahara 224
Conservation of large
mammals in the
Republic of Mali 559
Constitutions of nations
446
Contact 589
Contemporary African art
645
Contes bambara 754
Contes de l'Afrique noire
628
Contes de Tombouctou et
du Macina 755
Contes du Mali 759
Contes du pays manding
754
Contes et fables des
veillées 746
Contes et légendes du
Kourmina 756
Contes et légendes
Soninké 757
Les contes et les légendes
d'Aroun 758
Contes initiatiques peuls
743
Contes populaires du Mali
759

Contes soninké 757
Continuity and change in
Franco-African
relations 462
Continuity and change in
patterns of trade in
southern Mali 502
Conversations with
Ogotemmêli 286, 360
La coopérative Jamana
824
Copper in the Iron Age
134
Corbeille de paroles 636
Corpus of early Arabic
sources for West African
history 169
Cost recovery in public
health services in
Sub-Saharan Africa
392
Country development
strategy statement
FY1985: Mali 15
Country Profile:
Côte d'Ivoire, Mali
471
Country Report 471-472
The coup and after 422
Cours pratique de
bambara 317
The course of Islam in
Africa 377
Coutumiers juridiques de
l'Afrique occidentale
française 442
Creating political order
411
Creation of a local growth
standard based on
well-nourished Malian
children 391
The creation of regional
museums in Mali 801
Cumulative Bibliography
of African Studies 878,
882
Current Bibliography on
African Affairs 883
Current Contents Africa
884
Current directions in West
African prehistory 166

Current research and
recent radiocarbon
dates from northern
Africa, III 152

D

The Da Capo guide to
contemporary African
music 700
Da Monzon de Ségou:
épopée bambara 736
Daɲɛgafe kɛrɛnkɛrɛnnen
318
Les danseurs africains:
l'Ensemble National du
Mali 674
Dancing skeletons 393
The dangerous snakes of
Africa 105
Danze dogon e bambara
675
Decline of the Mali
Empire 170
De Koulikoro à
Tombouctou à bord du
'Mage', 1889-1890
27
De Saint-Louis à Tripoli
par le lac Tchad 26
De Saint-Louis au port de
Tombouktou 27
Le défi démocratique au
Mali 435
Dege: l'héritage dogon
658
Le Delta intérieur du
Niger 81
Democracy and civic
community in Mali
436
Democratic transition and
electoral systems in
Africa 437
Dependency and
conservative militarism
in Mali 423
Des arbres et des arbustes
spontanés de l'Adrar
des Iforas (Mali) 112
Descendants and crops
519

Desertification control and
renewable resource
management in the
Sahelian and Sudanian
zones of West Africa
560
Desertification in the
Sahelian and Sudanian
zones of West Africa
560
Des preux, des belles – des
larrons 746
Deux campagnes au
Soudan Français 225
The development of
urbanism in West Africa
138
Devinettes bambara
765
Devinettes recueillis du
Mali 766
Devinettes touaregues
(Mali et Niger) 767
Le dialecte senoufo du
Minianka 319
Dialectes manding du
Mali 320
The dialects of Mandekan
321
Dictionary of African
historical biography
849
Dictionnaire
bambara–français
322
Dictionnaire
bambara–français,
précédé d'un abrégé de
grammaire bambara
323, 351
Dictionnaire
boomu–français 324
Dictionnaire des femmes
célèbres du Mali 850
Dictionnaire des oeuvres
littéraires africaines de
langue française 615
Dictionnaire des oeuvres
littéraires
négro-africaines de
langue française des
origines à 1978 616
Dictionnaire dogon 325

Dictionnaire
dogon–français donno
so 326
Dictionnaire du cinéma
africain 715
Dictionnaire élémentaire
fulfulde–français–Englis
h 327
Dictionnaire
peul–français 329
Dictionnaire peul
(fula)–russe–français
331
Dieu d'eau: entretiens
avec Ogotemmêli 360
Dilettantism and plunder
140, 151
La dimension sociale et
politique des traditions
orales 778
Directory of African
experts 851
Directory of African film-
makers and films 716
Directory of African
technology institutions
852
Directory of museums in
Africa 802
Discourse and its
disguises: the
interpretation of African
oral texts 778
Discovery guide to West
Africa 57
La dispersion des
Mandeka 737
Divine gestures and
earthly gods 144
Djenné-jeno – cité sans
citadelle 138
Djenné 668
Djenné, il y a cent ans 226
Djenné, sur le Nil-des-
Noires 5
Djenné-jeno – cité sans
citadelle 138
Dogon 284
Les Dogon 274, 648
Dogon art at the Musée
Dapper 150
Les Dogon de Boni 275
Dogon masks 284, 649

Les Dogons du Mali 276
Domestiquer le rêve 617
Downfall of a dictator
  431
Draft environmental
  report on Mali 561
Drawn from African
  dwellings 669
Drums, the heartbeat of
  Africa 690
Du Niger au Golfe de
  Guinée par le pays de
  Kong et le Mossi 28
Duel dans les falaises
  618
Dynamiques linguistiques
  au Mali 310

E

Early Arabic sources and
  the Almoravid conquest
  of Ghana 169
The early city in West
  Africa 137-138
Les Echos 860
The ecology of
  malnutrition in the
  French-speaking
  countries of West Africa
  and Madagascar 394
Economic analysis of
  traders' response to
  cereals market reforms
  in Mali 520
The economic foundations
  of an Islamic theocracy
  186
An economic history of
  West Africa 473
Economic nationalism in
  old and new states
  485
Economics of the coup
  424
ECOWAS and the
  economic integration of
  West Africa 459
ECOWAS situation of
  telecommunications in
  member states 825
Education 590

Education and
  development of
  non-formal education
  in urban areas as a
  national development
  strategy for Mali 598
Education & politics in
  tropical Africa 603
Education and society
  591, 603
Education for rural
  development 601
Education in Africa:
  a comparative study 592
Education in Mali 592
Education, the state and
  class conflict: a study of
  three education policies
  in Mali 603
Educational development
  in Guinea, Mali,
  Senegal and Ivory Coast
  588
Eglise et pouvoir colonial
  au Soudan français 10,
  361
Eléments de grammaire du
  soninke 328
Elite education in French
  West Africa 593
The emergence of a grain
  market in Bamako,
  1883-1908 503
L'Empire de Gao 190
L'Empire peul du Macina
  187, 743
L'empire toucouleur,
  1848-1897 188
L'empire toucouleur et la
  France 188
Les empires du Mali 189
Emploi, potentialités et
  priorités au Mali 548
Encyclopedia of Islam 182
Encyclopedia of world
  cultures 277
L'Encyclopédie coloniale
  et maritime 853
L'enfant rusé 754
English–Fula dictionary
  329
Enquête démographique
  au Mali, 1960-1961 262

Enquête démographique
  de 1985 263
Enquête démographique et
  de santé au Mali, 1987
  395
Enquête démographique et
  de santé, Mali
  1995-1996 396
Enseignement du Soninké
  349
The epic of Askia
  Mohammed 738
The epic of Son-Jara 727
The epic of Sun-Jata II,
  according to Magan
  Sisòkò 728
L'epopée bambara de
  Ségou 736, 739
L'épopée du Sunjara 729
An era ends in Mali 425
Essai de méthode pratique
  pour l'étude de la
  langue songoï 244, 346
Essai sur la cosmogonie
  des Dogon 360
Essai sur la musique
  traditionnelle au Mali
  694
Essai sur la religion
  bambara 362
Essai sur les fondements
  du cinéma africain 717
An essay on the religion of
  the Bambara 362
L'Essor 177, 717, 861
Les établissements
  humains au Mali 670
Etat civil du Mali 839
L'Etat de droit 443
L'état de la presse au Mali
  826
L'Etat de la presse en
  Afrique de l'Ouest
  francophone 826
Ethnoarchéologie
  africaine 135
Ethnologie et langage 307
Etude des pluies
  journalières de
  fréquence rare au Mali
  555
Etudes Maliennes 869
Etudes soudanaises 187

Etudes sur l'Islam et les
tribus du Soudan 363
Europa World Year Book
846
An evaluation of
educational radio
programmes for primary
school teachers in Mali
594
Evaluation of Netherlands
aid to India, Mali and
Tanzania 474
Excavation and survey in
and near Djenné, Mali
137
Excavations at
Jenné-Jeno,
Hambarketolo, and
Kaniana (Inland Niger
Delta, Mali) 136
An exemplary transition
438
The expansion of Islam
among the Bambara
under French rule,
1890-1940 364
Experiences in
appropriate technology
493
An exploration near
Agades and Timbuktu
57
Explorations in African
systems of thought 747

F

Le fabuleux empire du
Mali 205
Faces of Islam in African
literature 619
Family identity and the
state in the Bamako
Kafu, c.1800-c.1900 278
Family mediation of
health care in an
African community 397
Family social structure,
farm operation
characteristics and the
adoption of new
technologies for

sustainable farming
systems in Mali 521
Famines et epidémies à
Tombouctou et dans la
Boucle du Niger du xvie
au xviiie siècle 242
Fanfannyégèné I 128
Farming systems in the
Niger Inland Delta,
Mali 522
La faune avienne du Mali
(Bassin du Niger) 106
Faune du Sahara 107
A feasibility study for the
preparation of
educational
administrators in the
Republic of Mali 601
Femme d'Afrique 412
Femme sorcière 752
Femmes du Mali 380
The ferns and fern-allies
of west tropical Africa
108
La fête du bilɛ chez les
Dogon du Kamma 271
A field guide to the birds
of West Africa 101
Field research in Macina
for vitamin A
communications 398
The fight against the
plundering of Malian
cultural heritage and
illicit exportation 143
Fighting the famine 562
Figure sculptures of the
Bamana of Mali 650
Figures equestres du delta
intérieur du Niger 144
A filmography of the
Third World, 1976-1983
724
Films d'Afrique 726
Films ethnographiques sur
l'Afrique noire 712
Un fils d'El Hadj Omar
188
Les fils des sept femmes
bozo 745
Finding West Africa's
oldest city 137
Fishing in the Pondo 82

Five West African
filmmakers on their films
718
Flash des Informations
Statistiques 836, 840
Flora of west tropical
Africa 108, 122
Flore et faune aquatiques
de l'Afrique
sahelo-soudanienne
109
Flore forestière
soudano-guinéenne 110
Flowering plants in West
Africa 111
Les flux migratoires à
Bamako 251
Food strategies in four
African countries 523
Forbidden sands 58
Foreign Economic Trends
and Their Implications
for the United States
475
The foreign policy of Mali
453
Forestry policy reform in
Mali 574
Forgotten tells of Mali
138
Form and meaning in
Fulfulde 330
The fortunes of Wangrin
620, 743
Fouilles de l'abri sous
roche de
Kourounkorokale 149
Frail dream of Timbuktu
59
Le Français hors de
France 312
France and Islam in West
Africa, 1860-1960 227
La France et les villes
d'Afrique francophone
583
Francophone African
cinema 714
Francophone Sub-Saharan
Africa 228
Freedom and authority in
French West Africa 413
French African policy 463

French attitudes and policies towards Islam in West Africa, 1900-1940 227

French colonial Africa: a guide to official sources 899

French enterprise in Africa 29

French-speaking West Africa 219

French-speaking West Africa: a guide to official publications 900

The French West African railway workers' strike, 1947-1948 549

'From demons to democrats' 439

From French West Africa to the Mali Federation 457

From Mande to Songhay 190

Frontier disputes and problems of legitimation 210

Fula–russko–frantsuzskii slovar' 331

Fulani 284

A Fulfulde (Maasina)–English–French lexicon 327, 332

Functional literacy in Mali 588

Functional literacy pilot projects 604

Les funerailles et le yimu-kɔmɔ chez les Dogon du Kamma 271

Fusion of the worlds 298

G

Gallieni 225

Gao and the Almoravids 191

Gao and the Almoravids revisited 191

Gao before 1500 134

Gao, des origines à 1591 190

General history of Africa 170

Génies du fleuve 365

Genii of the River Niger 365

Gens d'ici, gens d'ailleurs 252

Gens de la parole 773

Géochimie et minéralogie des latérites du Sud-Mali 87

Geology and mineral resources of West Africa 86

La geste de Fanta Maa 745

La geste de Ham-Bodêdio 746

La gestion des ressources naturelles au Mali 563

Ghana Empire 183

The Ghana–Guinea–Mali Union 454

A glorious age in Africa 192, 205

God's bits of wood 621

Gold aus Mali 661

Gold, Salz und Sklaven 193

The golden trade of the Moors 504

The good collector and the premise of mutual respect among nations 150

Goodtime kings: emerging African pop 707

Governance and the transition to democracy 440

La graine de la parole 778

Grammaire de la phrase bambara 334

Grammaire et vocabulaire de la langue poul à l'usage des voyageurs dans le Soudan 333

Le grand destin de Soundjata 622

La grande épopée d'al Hadj Omar 740

La grande geste du Mali 730

Grandes dates du Mali 171

Les grandes missions françaises en Afrique occidentale 30

The grazing land ecosystems of the African Sahel 564

Groupes ethniques au Mali 279, 764

The guardian of the word (Kouma Lafôlô Kouma) 731

Guérisseurs et magiciens du Sahel 365

Guide de Bamako 61

Guide de tourisme au Soudan Français 51

Guide de transcription et de lecture du bambara 334

Guide des archives de l'Afrique occidentale française 791

Le guide du Mali 51

Guide du Sahara 66

Guide du tourisme au Soudan français 51

Guide du tourisme en Afrique Occidentale Française 51

Guide pour la détermination des arbres et des arbustes dans les savanes ouest-africaines 112

Guide pour la lutte contre les feux de brousse 565

Guide to federal archives relating to Africa 795-796

Guide to non-federal archives and manuscripts in the United States relating to Africa 796

Guide to research and reference works on Sub-Saharan Africa 885

Guide touristique de Bamako 98

H

L'habitat des familles sahéliennes en Ile de France 253
Hamdallahi, capitale de l'empire peul du Massina, Mali 135
The handbook of national population censuses 261
Handbook to the Arabic writings of West Africa & the Sahara 901
Hatumere 671
Haut-Sénégal-Niger 6
The healing drum 695
The heart of the Ngoni 741
Heroic riders and divine horses 144
Higher education and social change: promising experiments in developing countries 588
Histoire de l'Afrique occidentale 732
Histoire des Bambara 280
Histoire des Berbères et des dynasties musulmanes de l'Afrique septentrionale 194
Histoire des classes sociales dans l'Afrique de l'ouest 381
L'histoire du Mandé 742
Histoire du Sahel occidental malien des origines à nos jours 172
Historical atlas of Africa 176
Historical dictionary of Mali 7, 211-212, 236, 243, 625, 908
The history and description of Africa 31
History, design, and craft in West Africa strip-woven cloths 133
A history of African archaeology 132
A history of Islam in West Africa 377

History of West Africa 173
The holy war of Umar Tal 195
Les hommes du bakchich 628
Hommes du Sahel 81
The Hosken report 399
Household income and agricultural strategies in the peri-urban zone of Bamako, Mali 524
A human ideal in African art 650
Human Relations Area Files 281
Hunters of the Mande 747
Hydrologie du Niger (Mali) à l'Holocène ancien 156

I

Ibn Battúta: travels in Asia and Africa 32
The ideology of slavery in Africa 218
Ideology, slavery, and social formation 218
The Ijil salt industry 206
L'image, la langue et la pensée 768
Images féminines dans les contes africains 763
The impact of direct taxation and government price policies on agricultural production in a developing African country 525
The impact of the Western Sudanic empires on the trans-Saharan trade 505
Implementing in law post-Keita Mali's retreat from scientific socialism 444
Impossible journey 58
In the path of Allah 366
In sorcery's shadow 298
Index Africanus 886

Index des documents microfichés au Mali 906
Inefficiency in education 595
Infant and child mortality in rural Mali 400
L'infection par le virus de l'immunodéficience humaine (VIH) au Mali 401
Influence du barrage de Sélingué dans la cuvette du Niger 566
Influences de l'arabe sur la langue bambara 335
The informal sector and microfinance institutions in West Africa 476
Informing food security policy in Mali 526
Initial perspectives on prehistoric subsistence in the Inland Niger Delta (Mali) 137
Initiation à la culture bamanan à travers les proverbes 769
Initiation à la linguistique africaine par les langues du Mali 336
The Inland Niger Delta before the empire of Mali 138
The innocent sorcerer 367
Institutional reform of telecommunications in Senegal, Mali, and Ghana 827
Instruments de musique et genres musicaux traditionnels 696
Integrated literacy in Mali 596
Intégration des variables démographiques dans les plans et les programmes de développement de la République du Mali 246
International African Bibliography 882, 887
International atlas of language vitality 314

International book
publishing: an
encyclopedia 822
International Conference
of Donors for the
Economic Recovery and
Development of the
Republic of Mali 477
International directory of
African studies research
810
Interview with Souleyman
Cissé 719
Introduction to the
flowering plants of West
Africa 111
The inundation zone of the
Niger as an environment
for Palaearctic migrants
113
Inventaire de la
Bibliothèque
'umarienne de Ségou
213, 907
Inventaire des études
linguistiques sur les
pays d'Afrique noire
d'expression française
352
Inventaire des
particularités lexicales
du français au Mali
311
Inventory of Population
Projects in Developing
Countries Around the
World 247
Irrigation and the Soninke
people 527
Irrigation du delta central
nigérien 567
Islam and Christianity in
West Africa 368
Islam and politics on the
Senegal 195
Islam, archaeology and
history 139
Islam in the Banamba
region of the eastern
Beledugu, c 1800 to
c. 1900 369
Islam in the oral traditions
of Mali 774

Islam in tropical Africa
191
The Islamic regime of
Fuuta Tooro 181
Islamisme contre
'naturisme' au Soudan
français 370
L'itinéraire d'Ibn Battuta
de Walata à Mali 200

J

Jam tan: initiation à la
langue peule 337
Jama Jigi 676
Jamana 860, 870
Janjon et autres chants
populaires du Mali 613,
697
Jean Rouch: cinéma et
ethnographie 720
Jelimusow: the
superwomen of Malian
music 698
Jenne and its regional
roots 147
Jenné-jeno: an ancient
African city 138
Jésus vu par un musulman
743
Jeune Afrique 871, 884
Jeux et jouets de l'Ouest
africain 781
Joint Acquisitions List of
Africana 888
Journal d'un voyage à
Temboctou et à Djenné
47
The journal of a mission to
the interior of Africa, in
the year 1805 33
Journal Officiel de la
République du Mali 872
Just say shame 143

K

Kadiatou Konaté 721
Kaïdara 743
Kala Jata 613
Les Khassonké 282

Kibaru 862
Kolokèlen 676
Le kòtèba et l'évolution du
théâtre moderne au
Mali 677
Kulturwandel bei den
Bambara von Ségou 11
Die Kunst der Dogon 651

L

Land-locked countries of
Africa 541
Language map of Africa
and the adjacent islands
309
Language policy and
literacy development
597
La langue bozo 338
La langue des Peuls ou
Foulbé 339
La langue mandingue et
ses dialectes 321
La langue secrète des
Dogons de Sanga 283
La langue sonay et ses
dialectes 340
Langues et métiers
modernes ou modernisés
au Mali 310
Large mammals of West
Africa 114
The last Sahelian
elephants 115
Law in colonial Africa 441
A leaf in the wind 76
Learning strategies for
post-literacy and
continuing education in
Mali, Niger, Senegal
and Upper Volta 598
The legal system of Mali
445
Légendes du Mali 760
Législations et pluralisme
radiophonique en
Afrique de l'Ouest 828
Let's visit Mali 8
Lexique bambara–français
322, 341
Lexique bore–français 324

Lexique touareg–français 354

Lexique médical 342

Liberalisation of agricultural markets 506

Liberalising trade 460

Liberté pour les radios africaines 829

Libraries in West Africa: a directory 787

Le lieutenant de Kouta 613

Life before the drought 201

List of French doctoral dissertations on Africa, 1884-1961 889

Listening to one's clients 478

Littérature africaine: histoire et grands thèmes 624

Littérature et musique 699

Littérature malienne 609, 623

Littératures africaines et histoire 613

Littératures francophones d'Afrique de l'Ouest 624

Long distance trade and production 507

Looking after our land 568

Looting the antiquities of Mali 140

The lost cities of Africa 196

Love for three oranges, or, the askiya's dilemma 197

Une lutte de longue haleine 568

M

Makers of African history 849

The making of Bamana sculpture 652

Mali 9-13, 95-96, 174, 414, 446, 479, 599, 653, 700, 722

Mali: 1995 post report 14

Mali: a bibliographical introduction 908

Mali, a country profile 15

Mali, a handbook of historical statistics 175

Mali: a prospect of peace? 16

Mali: a search for direction 17

Mali and the second Mandingo expansion 170

Mali and Senegal and the Dakar–Niger railroad 542

Mali and the U.M.O.A. 497

Le Mali 22

Le Mali aujourd'hui 60

Mali: autour du lac Débo 178

Mali, bibliographie commentée 909

Mali, bilan d'une gestion désastreuse 480

Mali biological diversity assessment 569

Le Mali, carrefour des civilisations 18

Mali, Côte d'Ivoire, Sénégal 61

Mali: a country profile 15

Mali, crossroads of Africa 198

Le Mali de Modibo Keïta 426

Mali, dissolution of the Provisional Consultative Committee of the National Union of Malian Workers 550

Mali: éducation et développement au Mali 600

Mali: educational options in a poor country 601

Mali: eine geographische Landeskunde 83

Mali: guide d'information, décembre 1992 19

Mali, ils ont assassiné l'espoir 612

Mali – in pictures 8

Mali: langues nationales, nouvelle donnée 343

Mali, National Library of 788

Mali, Niger 52

Mali: official standard names approved by the United States Board on Geographic Names 84

Mali: people topple Traoré 432

Mali – potential and problems 20

Mali, recent economic developments 481

Mali's socialism and the Soviet legal model 447

Mali: soldiers as politicians 433

Mali: the prospects of 'Planned Socialism' 427

Mali – Tukulor 224

Mali, women in private enterprise 482

Mali-sud: d'un aménagement anti-érosif des champs à la gestion de l'espace rural 568

Malian antiquities and contemporary desire 150

The Malian experience in financing the cereals trade 498

The Malian National Archives at Kaluba 797

The Malian union of cotton and food crop producers 528

Malinke 284

The Mande blacksmiths 662

'Mande Kaba', the capital of Mali 199

Mande languages and linguistics 344

Mandenkan 345

Manuel de la langue songay parlée de Tombouctou à Say dans la boucle du Niger 244, 346
Marionnettes du Mali 678
Marxian socialism in Africa 428
Masked dancers of West Africa 285
Le masque et la parole 654
Masques dogons 286
Mass communication, culture, and society in West Africa 830
Mass media in West Africa 830
Massa Makan Diabaté: un griot mandingue à la rencontre de l'écriture 613
Match 782
Material on Soviet relations with West Africa 464
Material world 382, 388
Maternal income-generation activities and child nutrition 402
Maurice Delafosse 6
Médecine Traditionnelle et Pharmacopée 407
Medicinal plants in tropical West Africa 116
Medicinal plants of West Africa 116
Medieval textiles from the Tellem caves in central Mali, West Africa 160
Mélanges d'histoire et d'esthétique musicales 708
Mélanges maliens 287
La mémoire senufo 775
Men, women, and market trade in rural Mali, West Africa 483
Methodology and African prehistory 170
The mid-fourteenth century capital of Mali 200

Middle Niger terracottas before the Symplegades Gateway 141
Migration & espace rural 251
Les migrations agricoles au Mali 254
Migrations et urbanisation en Afrique de l'ouest (MUAO) 255
Les migrations militaires en Afrique occidentale française 229
Military government in Mali 434
The mineral resources of Africa 86
La mission catholique auprès des Bwa avant et après l'indépendance du Mali, 1888-1988 371
Mission d'exploration du Haut-Niger 225
Missions to the Niger 34
Modern legal systems cyclopedia 445
Moktar Cissé 625
Mon coeur est un volcan 626
Mopti: tradition in the present 584
La mort de Chaka 639
Mourir pour vivre 628
The Muqaddimah 194
Musée National du Mali 805
Musée Regional de Sikasso 803
Museums & the community in West Africa 806-807
Museums of the world 802
Music in Africa 701
Musique traditionnelle de l'Afrique noire 702
Les musulmans en Afrique 203
My march to Timbuctoo 35
Le mythe et l'histoire dans la formation de l'Empire de Ségou 736

Mythical trickster figures 777

N

Nakunte Diarra 664
Narrating the Mande 627
Nation-building in Mali 415
National goals, social mobility and personal aspirations 602
National governments, local governments, pasture governance and management in Mali 529
The National Museum of Mali–Museum of Cultural History 804
A national treasure 805
Nègres, qu'avez-vous fait? 628
New African yearbook 854
The new atlas of African history 176
The new Bambara grammar 347
The new book of world rankings 841
The new Grove dictionary of music and musicians 703
New light on Islamic Africa 203
New Oxford University policy on TL authentication services 140
New radiocarbon dates for northern and western Africa 152
A new reader's guide to African literature 629
New skills for rural women 492
A new survey of radiocarbon and thermoluminescence dates for West Africa 152

The Niger explored 34
The 1981 season at
 Jenne-jeno 137
The nineteenth-century
 Islamic revolutions in
 West Africa 170
The nineteenth-century
 jihads in West Africa
 167
Noces sacrées 639
Nomads of the Sahel 383
North-West Africa: from
 the Maghrib to the
 fringes of the forest 167
Notes d'archéologie sur
 Gao 158
Notes on slavery in the
 Songhay Empire 209
Notes sur le théâtre total
 679
Notre beau Niger 42
Nouveau voyage dans le
 pays des nègres 36
Nouvelles d'hier . . . et
 d'aujourdhu. 177
Nouvelles d'ici 630
Nyakhalen la forgeronne
 745

O

Objets-signes d'Afrique
 654
L'occupation de
 Tombouctou 236
Of slaves, and souls of
 men 209
Old Africa rediscovered
 196
The oldest extant writing
 of West Africa 142
L'ombre du passé 618
On African socialism 458
On building a partnership
 in Mali between farmers
 and researchers 530
100 great Africans 843
One-party government in
 Mali 416
On the cultural context of
 terracotta statuettes
 from Mali 141

On using the White
 Fathers' archives 792
An optimal zone: the West
 African savanna 166
Op zoek naar mens en
 materiële cultuur 154
L'or, est-il l'une des
 futures sources de
 richesses pour le Mali?
 87
Oral epics from Africa 744
The Organisation of
 Senegal River States
 455
Organisation sociale des
 Dogon 288
Organisation
 socio-économique des
 Minyanka du Mali 299
The origins of clericalism
 in West African Islam
 372
Oui, mon commandant 220
An outline geography of
 West Africa 80

P

The pale fox 286, 362, 373
Pama Sinatoa 665
Pan-Africanism 456
Panorama critique du
 théâtre malien dans son
 évolution 606, 680
Papa-commandant a jeté
 un grand filet devant
 nous 230
Un parler dogon, le donno
 so 348
Parlons soninké 349
Paroles de nouvel an 374
Paroles pour un continent
 640
Passeport touristiquė,
 République du Mali 64
Les passereaux du Mali
 106
Pays du Sahel 178
Les paysannes du Mali
 384
La pêche dans le delta
 central du Niger 117

The pen, the sword, and
 the crown 201
People are not the same
 403
Peoples and empires of
 West Africa 179
The peoples and kingdoms
 of the Niger Bend and
 the Volta basin from the
 12th to the 16th century
 170
Peoples of the world 289
Peoples of West Africa
 290
Pérégrinations
 sahéliennes 256
The performance of
 soldiers as governors
 433
Performance practice:
 ethnomusicological
 perspectives 701
Periodicals from Africa
 890
Le personnage de l'ancien
 dans le roman
 sénégalais et malien de
 l'époque coloniale 631
Perspectives de population
 par cercle 248
Perspectives
 démographiques du
 Mali 248
Pesticides on millet in
 Mali 531
Petit atlas ethno-
 démographique du
 Soudan entre Sénégal et
 Tchad 291
Petit Bodiel et autres
 contes de la savane
 743
Petit dictionnaire
 bambara–français,
 français–bambara 350
Petit dictionnaire
 français–bambara et
 bambara–français 351,
 770
Le petit frère d'Amkoullel
 220
Petit manuel français –
 bambara 351, 770

Petites et moyennes villes
d'Afrique noire 582
Peuls et Mandingues 292
Phonologie du tamasheq
341
La pierre barbue et autres
contes du Mali 761
The pillage of
archeological sites in
Mali 150
Les pionniers du Soudan,
avant, avec et après
Archinard 231
La piste interdite de
Tombouctou 62
Plan minéral de la
République du Mali 87
Plan national de lutte
contre la desertification
et l'avancée du désert,
1985-2000 570
Plan quinquennal de
développement
économique et social,
1987-1991 487
Planning and economic
policy 484
Plantes médicinales contre
les hepatites 116
Plantes médicinales du
Mali 116
Playing with time 350,
681
Plight of ancient Jenne
151
Plundering Africa's past
143
Poèmes de l'Afrique noire
632
Poèmes d'ici 630
Les poissons du delta
central du Niger 118
Les poissons du Niger
supérieur 118
Political and educational
reform in French-
speaking West Africa
603
Political integration in
Africa 458
Political parties and
national integration in
tropical Africa 414

Political parties in
French-speaking West
Africa 417
Political revival in Mali
418
The political thought of
Modibo Keita 429
Political transitions in
Africa 439
The political use of
economic planning in
Mali 485
The politics of integrating
gender to state
development processes
486
The politics of music in
Mali 704
The politics of natural
disaster 571
Politique forestière
nationale 574
Politiques d'emploi,
politiques commerciales
et financières 551
Les politiques
d'intégration des
systèmes économiques et
scolaires dans les pays
africains 596
Pop Sahel 873
La poterie ancienne du
Mali 144
La poterie en pays
Sarakolé (Mali, Afrique
occidentale) 157
The pottery from Mali
(10th-14th century A.D.)
165
Pottery variation in
present-day Dogon
compounds (Mali) 145
Poupées africaines pour
jeux et magie 779
Pour une plus grande
efficacité de l'inventaire
des sites archéologiques
du Mali 146
Power, marginality and
Africa oral literature
698, 763
Power, prosperity and
social inequality in

Songhay (1464-1591)
201
Pré-théâtre et rituel 682
Prehistoric investigations
in the region of Jenne,
Mali 147
The prehistory of West
Africa 170
Preliminary
reconnaissance and
survey at Gao 127
Preliminary report of
excavations at
Karkarichinkat Nord
and Karkarichinkat Sud,
Tilemsi Valley, Republic
of Mali, Spring, 1972
148
Preliminary report on
excavations at
Hamdallahi, Inland
Niger Delta of Mali 127
Première anthologie de la
musique malienne 705
Preserving the landscape
of imagination:
children's literature 355
The press in Africa 831,
863
Presse francophone
d'Afrique 832
Primary health care in
Africa 404
The primitive city of
Timbuctoo 63
La problématique de
l'émigration des
Soninkés de Kayes, Mali
257
Production and
reproduction of warrior
states 218
Productivity of
transhumant Fulani
cattle in the Inner Niger
Delta of Mali 532
Profil d'environnement
Mali-Sud 572
Profiles of African
scientific institutions,
1992 852
Profiles of African
scientists 855

Projet Bois de Villages, Burkina Faso and Mali 573
Prospection archéologique aux Alentours de Dia, Mali 127
Prospections archéologiques dans la zone de la Boucle du Baoulé (Mali) 149
Protecting Mali's cultural heritage 150
Proverbes bwa 769
Proverbes et contes bambara 770
Public health problems in 14 French-speaking countries in Africa and Madagascar 405
A publication survey trip to West Africa and France 818
A publication survey trip to West, Central and Southern Africa 819
A publication survey trip to West Africa, Ethiopia, France, and Portugal 819
Publishing and book development in Sub-Saharan Africa 820
Publishing for sustainable literacy in Francophone West Africa 821
Publishing in Francophone Africa 822
The pulse theory . . . specialization in the Inland Niger Delta 134
Puppet theatre in the Segou Region in Mali 681

Q

Quarterly Economic Review 472
Quel usage des plantes médicinales au Mali aujourd'hui? 406

Quelques donnés sociolinguistiques sur le Mali 352
The quest for Timbuctoo 237

R

Radio pluralism in West Africa 833
The rape of Mali 151
Rapport sur l'évaluation, l'ajustement et l'analyse des données du recensement de la population de décembre 1976 264
Rapport sur le plan quinquennal de développement économique et social de la République de Mali, 1961-1965 487
Reading the contemporary African city 584
Recensement de la population non autochtone 266
Recensement général de la population et de l'habitat (1er au 14 avril 1987) 265
Recent archaeological research and dates from West Africa 152
Recently Published Articles 891
Les recettes culinaires de la 'Baramousso' 783
Recherche scientifique et développement, 1980 852
Recherches archéologiques au Mali 153
Recherches ethno-archéologiques sur la poterie des Dogon (Mali) 154
Recherches sur l'Empire du Mali au Moyen âge 732

Récit des chasseurs du Mali 745
Récits épiques des chasseurs bamanan du Mali 745
Récits peuls du Macina 746
Recommendations for a new Malian forest code 574
Reconnaissances archéologiques le long du moyen-Niger 153
A reconsideration of Wangara/Palolus, Island of Gold 202
Recueil de littérature manding 633
Recueil de proverbes bambaras et malinkes 771
Recueil des sources arabes concernant l'Afrique occidentale du VIIIe au XVIe siècle 203
Recurrent costs in the health sector 392
Red gold: copper arts of Africa 660
Rediscovering the Tellem of Mali 154
Regard Touareg 178
La Région de Tombouctou 236
The regional museums at Gao & Sikasso, Mali 806
Règles d'orthographe des langues nationales 353
Regulatory reform in transport 546
Relations of production: Marxist approaches to economic anthropology 537
The relationship between local museums & the national museum 807
Religion and state in the Songhay Empire, 1464-1591 191
La religion et la magie Songhay 375

314

Religion et pratiques de puissance 299
Religion in Africa 367
Religious élite of Timbuktu 238
The reluctant spouse and the illegitimate slave 293
Le renard pâle 373
Répertoire d'unités d'information au Mali 856
Répertoire des archives 793
Répertoire des Thèses Africanistes Françaises 892
Répertoire des travaux scolaires et universitaires de maliens au Mali 910
Répertoire général des sites historiques et archéologiques du Mali 155
Reporters sans frontières 1996 report 834
Representation of female circumcision in Finzan, a dance for the heroes 723
The reproductive ecology of the Dogon of Mali 294
The Republic of Mali 64, 604
République du Mali 96-97
République du Mali, précipitations journalières de l'origine des stations à 1965 575
Research for rural development 533
Resolved: to act for Africa's historical and cultural patrimony 151
Retour aux Dogon 295
Revue de Médecines et Pharmacopées Africaines 407
Revue des Douanes du Mali 508

Rite et société à travers le Bafili 296
The road to Timbuctoo 65
The road to Timbuktu 21, 37
The rodents of West Africa 103
Les rois de Gao-Sané et les Almoravides 190
The role of oral artists in the history of Mali 774
The role of the state in food production and rural development 534
The role of the Wangara in the economic transformation of the Central Sudan in the fifteenth and sixteenth centuries 204
Le roman et l'évolution sociale au Mali 634
Romans, Byzantines and the trans-Saharan gold trade 134
The royal kingdoms of Ghana, Mali, and Songhay 205
Rulers of empire 419
Rural migration in developing nations 258
Rural out-migration and labor allocation in Mali 258

S

La saga des fous 612
Sahara 864
The Sahara and the Nile 88
The Sahara, ecological change and early economic history 576
Le Sahara français 88
Sahara handbook 66
The Sahara in the nineteenth century 170
The Sahara in northern Mali 156

Le Sahara malien à l'Holocène 156
Sahara ou Sahel?: quaternaire récent du bassin de Taoudenni (Mali) 89
Sahara: prehistory and history of the Sahara 153
The Sahara reconsidered 206
Sahel, Land der Nomaden 67
Sahel! Sanglante sécheresse 612
Sahel: Senegal, Mauretanien, Mali, Niger 68
A Sahel transportation survey 543
Sailing to Timbuctoo 69
Les saisons 612
Salif Keita, mes quatre vérités 784
Salt of the desert sun 206
Salts of the western Sahara 206
Le sang des masques 639
Les sanglots du Songhoy 635
Sanglots et dédains 636
Sanhaje scholars of Timbuctoo 184
Sansanding: les irrigations du Niger 535
Le Sarnyéré dogon 157
Satisfaction of food requirements in Mali to 2000 A.D. 408
La savane rouge 632
Schéma directeur d'aménagement et d'urbanisme de Bamako et environs 585
The SCOLMA directory of libraries and special collections on Africa in the United Kingdom and in Europe 789
Scott 1998 standard postage stamp catalogue 785

315

Scribe, griot, and novelist: narrative interpreters of the Songhay Empire 738

Sculpture of the Tellem and the Dogon 655

The search for the Niger 38

Seasons of sand 58

Secret sculptures of Komo 656

The secrets of ancient Jenne 137

Seeds of famine 577

The Ségou experience: landmarks to guide concerted action 561

Ségou: la ville au bord du fleuve 178

Segu: a novel 637

The Segu Tukulor Empire 207

Selective bibliography on the famines and the drought in the Sahel 578

Séminaire National sur le Dromadaire, 2-9 décembre 1985, Gao 119

Senoufo migrants in Bamako 536

Les Sénoufo (y compris les Minianka) 297

Sensuous scholarship 298

Les serpents de l'ouest africain 120

Seydou Badian: écrivain malien 639

Seydou Keita 657

Shari'a in Songhay 208

A short geography of West Africa 80

Sikasso, ou, l'histoire dramatique d'un royaume noir au XIXe siècle 232

Sikasso Tata 233

Silâmaka & Poullôri 746

Siramuri Diabate et ses enfants 776

La situation du français au Mali 312

Slavery & Abolition 209

Slavery and Islamization in Africa 209

Slavery and Muslim society in Africa 209

Slavery in Bambara society 209

Slavery in pre-colonial Africa 217

Slaves and slavery in Muslim Africa 209

The slaves of Timbuktu 70

Small mammals of West Africa 114

The social dynamics of rural population retention 259

Social history of Timbuktu 238

The social organisation of agricultural labour among the Soninke (Dyahunu, Mali) 537

Social science libraries in West Africa 787

Social stratification and labor allocation in peanut farming in the rural Malian household 538

Socialism and social change in rural Mali 430

Socialism, economic development and planning in Mali 488

La société minyanka du Mali 299

Une société rurale bambara à travers des chants de femmes 296

La société senufo du sud Mali (1870-1950) 384

La société Soninké (Dyahunu, Mali) 300

Sociétés d'initiation bambara 356

Les sociétés Songhay-Zarma, Niger-Mali 301

Some reflections of a comparative nature on first millenium A.D. complex societies in West Africa 134

Some thermoluminescence datings of terracottas from the Inland Delta of the Niger (Mali) 163

Songhay 284

The Songhay from the 12th to the 16th century 170

Songs of lonely river 638

The songs of Seydou Camara 747

Soninkan dongomanu do burujunu 757

Soninke 284

Sooninka'ra gànnìnkà-n-sùugú 706

Sorcerers 726

Les Sorko (Bozo), maîtres du Niger 302

Le Soudan Français 22, 863

Soudan français: contes soudanais 762

Le Soudan occidental au temps des grands empires 732

Soudan: population en 1951 par canton et groupe ethnique 266

Les sources bibliographiques de l'Afrique de l'ouest 905

Sources d'information sur l'Afrique noire francophone et Madagascar 893

Source materials for the career and the jihad of al-Hajj 'Umar al-Futi 217

Sous l'orage 639

Southern Saharan scholarship and the bilād al-sūdān 210

Soviet policy in West Africa 464-465

Spectacular vernacular 672

The spirit's dance in Africa 683

The spirit's image: the African masking tradition 649

The spiritual economy of
Nioro du Sahel 376
Stability and change 748
Standard catalog of world
coins 786
A state of intrigue 749
States and people of the
Niger Bend and the
Volta 170
Statuaire Dogon 658
Les statuettes en terre
cuite du Mali 163
Status and identity in West
Africa 303
Stay alive in the desert 66
The story of old Ghana,
Melle and Songai 733
Stratégies communicatives
au Mali 310
Stratégies de résolution du
conflit du choix
vocationnel en contexte
malien 602
Strike movements as part
of the anticolonial
struggle in French West
Africa 552
The strong brown god 39
Studies in religious
fundamentalism 358
A study of the business
climate in Mali 489
A study of the causes and
effects of pupils'
dropout in the
fundamental school
level in Mali 605
Study on the co-ordination
of transport and
communications 544
Sub-Saharan African films
and filmmakers 724
Sub-Saharan agriculture
509
Sundiata: an epic of old
Mali 732
Sundiata: the epic of the
lion king, retold 733
Sundiata: lion king of
Mali 733
Sunjata 177, 874
Sunjata Epic Conference
proceedings 734

Survey of major science
and technology
resources in Africa 852
A survey of recent results
in the radiocarbon
chronology of northern
and western Africa 152
A survey of recent results
in the radiocarbon
chronology of western
and northern Africa
152
Survival in the Sahel 539
Survol de l'archéologie
malienne 131
Sweet mother 707

T

Tableau géographique de
l'Ouest africain au
Moyen Age, d'après les
sources écrites, la
tradition et
l'archéologie 158
Tableaux morphologiques
354
Tales and ideology 763
Tambours d'eau 365
Tarikh el-fettach 211
Tarikh es-Soudan 212
Taxonomy of West African
flowering plants 111
Teaching about
Francophone Africa 23
Tellem: een bijdrage tot de
geschiedenis van de
Republiek Mali 159
Tellem, reconnaissance
archéologique d'une
culture de l'ouest
africain au moyen âge
154, 160
Tellem textiles 160
Le temps des marabouts
376
Ten years of
archaeological research
in the Sahara 161
Téné 752
Les tengere, instruments
de musique Bozo 708

Terra d'Africa, terra
d'archeologia 162
Terracotta statuettes from
Mali 141
La terre et le pain 606
Terres australes 638
Terres cuites anciennes de
l'ouest africain 163
A text for another time 208
Textes et documents
relatifs à l'histoire de
l'Afrique 32
Les textes fondamentaux
de la IIIe République du
Mali 448
Textes forestiers 574
Théâtre africain, théâtres
africains? 684
Théâtre populaire de
marionnettes en Afrique
sud-saharienne 685
A thesaurus of African
languages 309
Theses on Africa,
1976-1988 894
Through Timbuctu and
across the great Sahara
40
Le Tilemsi préhistorique et
ses abords 164
Timbouctou: voyage au
Maroc, au Sahara et au
Soudan 43
Timbuctoo 41
Timbuctoo the mysterious
42
Timbuctoo, the myth and
reality 71
Timbuktu 72, 239
Timbuktu, Reise durch
Marokko, die Sahara
und den Sudan 43
Timbuktu under imperial
Songhay 240
To Timbuktu 73
Togu na: the African
Dogon 304
To have a history of
African cinema 714
Toiles d'araignées 640
Tombouctou 74
Tombouctou au milieu du
xviiie siècle 241

Tombouctou et l'empire
Songhay 242
Tombouctou et les Arma
243
Tombouctou: un défi au
Sahara 178
Tondiadarou: spectacular
evidence of a West
African protohistoric
civilization 140
Topics in West African
history 180
Tortues et crocodiles de
l'Afrique noire
française 120
Touaregs: un peuple du
désert 305
Tourist passport, Republic
of Mali 64
Toward regional
development 461
Towards better woodland
management in the
Sahelian Mali 579
A town called Dakajalan
735
Trade and politics at early
Jenne-jeno 134
Trade and politics on the
Senegal and Upper
Niger, 1854-1900
510
Trade and trade routes in
West Africa 170
Trade routes of Algeria
and the Sahara 545
Trade unions and politics
in French West Africa
during the Fourth
Republic 553
Traditional and modern
hairstyles of Mali 647
Traditional soil and water
conservation on the
Dogon Plateau, Mali
580
Transafrique: description
de routes 66
Transafrique: toute
l'Afrique en voiture 66
Transformations in slavery
209
The traveler's Africa 55

Traveller's guide to West
Africa 75
Travels and discoveries in
North and Central
Africa 44
Travels in the interior
districts of Africa 45
Travels in Western Africa,
in the years 1818, 19,
20, and 21 46
Travels into the interior of
Africa 45, 76
Travels through central
Africa to Timbuctoo and
across the great desert,
to Morocco, performed
in the years 1824-1828
47
Trees and shrubs of the
Sahel 121
The trickster in West
Africa: a study of mythic
irony 777
A tropical dependency 214
Trucking in Sub-Saharan
Africa 546
The Tuareg rebellion 420
The Tuaregs: the blue
people 306, 420
Two against the Sahara 58
Two rivers: travels in West
Africa on the trail of
Mungo Park 76
Two worlds of cotton 511

U

U.S. efforts to protect
cultural property 150
U.S. Imprints on
Sub-Saharan Africa 895
Umar's jihad 195
Umarian jihad 181
United Kingdom
Publications and Theses
on Africa 896
The United States and
Sub-Saharan Africa:
guide to U.S. official
documents and
government-sponsored
publications 897

L'univers littéraire de
Massa Makan Diabaté
613
The unveiling of
Timbuctoo 48
Urbanization of an
African community 385
The useful plants of west
tropical Africa 108, 122

V

The vanquished voice 215
Variation, culture and
evolution in African
populations 145
Varieties of African
resistance to the French
conquest of the Western
Sudan, 1850-1900 510
Vasellame del Mali
(X°–XIV° Sec. d.C.)
165
Veillées au Mali 764
Vers la Troisième
République du Mali 421
La viande et la graine:
mythologie dogon 356
Videos of African and
African-related
performance 686
La vie au continent noir
42
Vie et enseignement de
Tierno Bokar 378
The view from Awdaghust
206
A view from Unesco 150
A view inside the illicit
trade in African
antiquities 143
Les villages de liberté en
Afrique noire française
234
Villages perchés des
Dogon du Mali 673
La ville à guichets fermés?
582
Ville de Bamako, carte
touriste 98
Visages de femmes 725
A vision in Mali 123

318

Vivre au bord du désert: première exposition sur les Kel Adrar 803
Voilà ce qui est arrivé 216
Voyage à Ségou, 1878-1879 50
Voyage au Soudan français (Haut-Niger et pays de Ségou) 49
Voyage au Soudan occidental (1863-1866) 50
Voyage d'Ibn Batouta 32
Voyage dans le Soudan 32

W

Walanda 628
War and servitude in Segou 217
Warriors, merchants, and slaves 218
Water music 33
West Africa 80, 875, 884
West Africa: environment and policies 581
West Africa, a Lonely Planet travel survival kit 77
West Africa: a study of the environment and of man's use of it 581
West Africa and Islam 377
West Africa before the seventh century 170
West Africa, libraries in 790
West Africa: the former French states 219
West Africa: the rough guide 78
West African Annual 857
West African butterflies and moths 124
West African culture dynamics 191
West African economic and social history 206, 215
West African freshwater fish 118
West African harps 709
West African international atlas 99
West African lilies and orchids 125
West African prehistory 166
West African resistance 224
West African snakes 120
West African Sufi 378
West African travels 79
West African trees 121
West African tricksters 777
The western Maghrib and Sudan 167
What museums for Africa?: heritage in the future 801
Where camels are better than cars 386
The White Monk of Timbuctoo 244
Who's who in Africa: leaders for the 1990s 843
Who's who in African literature 641
A wind in Africa 409
With open eyes: women and African cinema 725
Women and development in Mali 490
Women and slavery in Africa 387
Women and sustained development in the Sahel 491
Women at work in Mali 492
Women farmers in Africa 540
Women finding suitable assistance 493
Women in slavery in the Western Sudan 387
Women in the material world 388
Women's economic activities and credit opportunities in the Opération Haute Vallée (OHV) zone, Mali 499
Women's roles in settlement and resettlement in Mali 260
Women's work and women's property 389
Women, servitude and history 778
Words and the Dogon world 307
The workers of African trade 206
The World Bank Atlas 496
A world bibliography of African bibliographies 881
World Development Report 496
World Education Encyclopedia 599
The world encyclopedia of contemporary theatre 687
World handbook of political and social indicators 842
The world of African music 700
World music 710
World travel map, Africa North-West 99
Worldmark encyclopedia of the nations 858
Writing and publishing in national languages today 355
Writings on African archives 798

Y

Yeelen: a political fable of the Komo blacksmiths 726

Index of Subjects

A

Administration 413, 419
African literature
  bibliographies 811
African studies 808-810
  bibliographies 876,
    880-883, 887
  directories 789
  periodicals 868
Agricultural ecology
  539
Agricultural innovations
  580
Agricultural systems 522
  bibliographies 516
Agriculture 13, 254, 260,
  402, 408, 470, 501,
  503, 506, 509,
  513-515, 517-521,
  524-530, 533-538,
  540, 555, 562
Agroforestry 572
AIDS 401
Alphabets 336, 341
Animism 370
Anthropology 281
Antiquities 130, 133,
  135-136, 139-142,
  144-145, 150-151,
  153, 155, 157,
  159-160, 162-165,
  557
Appropriate technology
  493
Arabic language 335
Arabic literature 623
Arabs 184
Archaeology 126-130,
  132-138, 140-141,
  143-158, 160-161,
  163-164, 166
  bibliographies 131
Archinard, Louis 231
Architecture 667-670,
  672-673
  Islamic 671

Archives 791-794, 797, 809
  bibliographies 795-796,
    798, 902
Archives Nationales du
  Mali 797, 902
Archives of the AOF 791
Arid regions 267
Arid regions agriculture
  556
Armed forces 433
Art 159, 653
  bibliographies 646
  directories 645
  Dogon 304, 642,
    648-649, 651
  Minianka 654
  periodicals 643
  see also Sculpture,
    Masks, etc.
Art and religion 644
Artisans 129, 303
Arts 415
Atlases 90-92, 99, 291

B

Bâ, Amadou Hampaté 220
Bamako 4, 93, 98
Bambara language 310,
  313, 315, 317, 323,
  334, 347, 350
  Arabic influence 335
  dictionaries 316, 318,
    322-323, 342, 351
Bambara people 185, 221,
  268, 272-273, 278,
  280, 293, 296,
  356-357, 362, 364,
  390, 517, 519, 644,
  652, 656, 659, 675,
  677, 681, 741, 754,
  770, 772
Bandiagara caves 160
Banks and banking 476
  directories 495
Bats 100

Berber people 194
Bibliographies 7, 885-886,
  888, 893, 895, 898,
  901, 903-905,
  907-909
  African literature 811
  African studies 876,
    880-883, 887
  agricultural systems 516
  archaeology 131
  archives 795-796, 798,
    902
  art 646
  book trade 820
  books and reading 820
  droughts 577
  economic conditions
    600
  education 600
  ethnology 269
  famines 578
  films 724
  government
    publications 897,
    899-900
  international relations
    454, 464
  languages 308, 344
  literature 609
  mass media 830
  microforms 906
  music 688
  periodicals 878, 884,
    890-891
  publishers and
    publishing 820
  theses 879, 889, 892,
    894, 896, 910
  women in development
    490
Bibliothèque Nationale
  (France) 907
Bibliothèque Nationale
  (Mali) 788
Biography see
  Dictionaries
    (biography)

Biological diversity
    conservation 569
Birds 101, 106, 113
Birth control 247
Blacksmiths 659, 662, 726
Bobo people 371
Bogolanfini 663-665
Bomu dialect
    dictionaries 324
Bonnier, Tite Pierre Marie
    Adolphe Eugène 236
Book trade 815-819, 822
    bibliographies 820
    periodicals 814
Books and reading 815
    bibliographies 820
Botany 104, 108, 111, 122
Boundaries 449, 451-452
    encyclopaedias 450
Bozo language 338
Bozo people 82, 302
Butterflies 124

C

Caillié, René 30, 48, 62
Camels 119
Carnivores 103
Catholic Church 361, 371,
    374
Cattle 517, 532
Censuses 261-266
Ceramics 135
Cerno Bokar 378
Christianity 368
Chronologies 7, 171, 250,
    909
Church and state 361
Church history 374
Cissé, Souleyman 719
City planning 582-585
Climate 558, 576
Commercial policy 551
Conservation 559,
    568-569, 572, 579
Constitution 446, 448
Cookbooks 780, 783
Cooperative societies
    492-493
Cosmology, Dogon 360,
    373
Costume 657

Cotton 511, 513
Creation 373
Crops and climate 518,
    555
Cross-cultural studies 382,
    388
Cults 359, 365, 375
Customs (trade) 508

D

Dance 674-675, 683
Deforestation 579
Desertification 554, 560,
    570
Diarra, Nakunte 664
Diarra, Nyamaton 659
Dictionaries 7, 845
    Bambara language 316,
        318, 322-323, 342,
        350-351
    biography 843, 847, 849
    Bomu dialect 324
    Dogon language
        325-326
    ethnology 289
    films 715
    Fulfulde language 327,
        329, 331-332, 339
    history 849
    literature 615-616
    music 703, 710
    national languages 341
    theatre 687
    women 850
Diplomatic service 14, 19
Directories 846
    African studies 789,
        808-810
    archives 809
    art 645
    banks and banking 495
    book trade 812
    films 716
    financial institutions
        495
    information services
        856
    libraries 789, 809, 812
    museums 802
    newspapers 812
    periodicals 812

publishers and
    publishing 812
scientists 851, 855
specialists 851
technology 852
Disaster relief 15, 570
Divination 659
Djenne 5, 226, 668
Djenné-jeno 137-138, 147
Dogon language 348
    dictionaries 325-326
Dogon people 159, 256,
    271, 274-276, 283-
    286, 288, 294-295,
    304, 307, 325, 360,
    367, 373, 384, 648,
    673, 675, 730, 777
Dolls 779
Droughts 518, 571
    bibliographies 578
Drums 690
Dualism 295
Dupuis-Yakouba, A. 244
Dwellings 304, 670, 673

E

Ecology 56, 112, 560-561,
    564, 571, 576-577
Economic assistance 466,
    474, 477
Economic conditions 21,
    218, 418, 424, 428,
    467-468, 471-473,
    475, 477-479, 481,
    489, 502, 512, 517,
    525, 539, 541, 548,
    551
    bibliographies 600
    periodicals 496
    women 388
Economic development
    382, 477, 488
Economic indicators 841
Economic integration
    455-456, 459-461,
    497, 501
Economic policy 246, 427,
    467, 470, 477, 480,
    485, 487-488, 548
    women 482
Economic relations 475

Economic stabilization 467
Economics
  prehistoric 576
  statistics 835
ECOWAS (Economic
  Community of West
  African States)
  459-461
Education 586, 590, 592,
  595, 599, 601, 603
  bibliographies 600
  continuing 598
  periodicals 589
  primary 591, 594, 605
  secondary 593, 602
Elections 438, 440
Elephants 115
Employment 402
Encyclopaedias 848, 858
  boundaries 450
  ethnology 277
  French colonies 853
  international relations
    450
Environment 267, 568, 580
Environmental policy 569,
  572
Epic poetry 693, 734-735,
  741, 744, 748
  Bambara 736, 739, 745,
    749
  Malinke 727-733
  Manding 737, 742, 747
  Peul 743, 746
  Songhay 738
  Tukulor 740
Ethnic relations 292
Ethnology 81, 262, 270,
  279, 284, 290-291,
  293, 298, 670, 675
  Bambara 268, 272-273,
    278, 280, 296, 681
  bibliographies 269
  Bozo 302
  dictionaries 289
  Dogon 271, 274-276,
    283, 285-286, 288,
    294-295, 304, 307
  encyclopaedias 277
  films 713
  Khassonke 282
  Malinke 273, 303
  Manding 278, 287, 292

Minianka 299
Peul 267, 292
Sarakole 300, 349
Senufo 297, 775
Songhay 298, 301
Tuareg 305-306
videos 686
Zarma 301
Exploration 24-40, 42-50

F

Family 379, 382, 397, 521
Famines 383, 478, 562,
  571, 577
  bibliographies 578
Fanfannyégèné I Site 128
Farmers 514, 517, 519,
  530, 536, 540
  social conditions 384
Fauna 107, 109
Female circumcision 399,
  723
Fertility 293-294, 393
Films 359, 618, 686,
  711-714, 717-723,
  725-726
  bibliographies 724
  catalogues 715-716
  directories 716
Finance 494, 498-499
  periodicals 496
Financial institutions
  directories 495
Fire prevention 565
Fish 118
Fishing 117
Flora 104, 108-111, 122,
  406
  medicinal 116
Folk literature 732-733,
  743, 778
  Bambara 697, 736, 739,
    745, 761
  Malinke 727-728, 731
  Manding 742, 747
Folklore 751, 756
  Bambara 741, 753-754
  Dogon 730
  performance 681
  Sarakole 741
  videos 686

Food policy 523
Food supply 469, 512,
  526
Forest management 579
Forestry projects 573
Forests 574
France
  immigration 250,
    252-253
Freedom From Hunger
  Campaign 494
French colonies
  encyclopaedias 853
French language 312
  dictionaries 311
Fulfulde language 330,
  333, 337, 339, 740
  dictionaries 327, 329,
    331-332

G

Games 781
Gazetteers 84
Gazettes 872
Geography 80-84, 97, 554,
  581
Geology 85-89
Geomancy 296
Ghana Empire 192, 205
Gold 661
Gold ores 87
Grain trade 520
Griaule, Marcel 274,
  675
Griots 698-699, 701, 704,
  773, 776

H

Hair ornamentation 647
Hairdressing 647
Hamaliyah 376
Handbooks 844-845
Handicrafts 653
Harps 709
Health 398
  children 393
  infants 391
Health services 404
Health surveys 395-396

History 7, 41-42, 63, 91, 139, 167-180, 206, 235-244, 281, 473
  dictionaries 849
  French colonial 220-234, 379, 413, 419, 510-511
  periodicals 870
  pre-colonial 181-205, 207-219, 504-505, 507, 510
Households 259, 524
Housing 669

I

Illegal aliens
  France 250
Imperato, Pascal James 409
Income 524
Industries 479
Infibulation 399
Informal sector 476
Information services
  directories 856
Initiation societies 273, 356, 656, 743
Inscriptions 142
International Institute for Educational Planning Library (Paris) 600
International Monetary Fund 467
International relations 434, 453, 462-463, 465
  bibliographies 454, 464
  encyclopaedias 450
  Mali Federation 457-458
  regional 449, 451-452, 455-456
Irrigation 470, 527, 535, 567
Islam 139, 201, 358, 363-364, 366, 368-370, 372, 376-377, 619, 762, 774
Islam and politics 227, 510

Islam in literature 619
Islamic law 208
Island of Gold 202

J

Jaara Kingdom 778
Jamana 824
Journalists and journalism 834

K

Kéita, Aoua 410, 412
Keita, Modibo 422-426, 428-429, 453
Keita, Salif 691, 784
Keita, Seydou 657
Khassonke people 282
Konaré, Alpha Oumar 438
Kotéba 676-677, 717

L

Labour 230, 537-538, 548, 552-553
Land settlement 260
Land use 557
Languages 309-310, 336, 343, 352, 587, 597
  bibliographies 308
  national 314, 334, 353, 355
  orthography 353
Laudatory poetry 748
Law 441, 443-445, 447, 573
  Bambara 770
  constitutional 448
  customary 442
  electoral 448
Legends 753, 756, 760
Leprosy 403
Libraries 787-788, 790, 809, 818-819
  directories 789
Lilies 125
Literacy 587-588, 596-597, 604, 821

Literature 613, 621, 623-624, 630, 633
  analysis 607, 615, 619, 627, 629, 631, 634
  bibliographies 609
  bio-bibliographies 615, 629, 641
  dictionaries 615-616
  fiction 608, 610, 612, 614, 618, 620, 625, 635, 637, 639-640
  plays 606, 622, 628
  poetry 611, 617, 626, 632, 636, 638
Loans 467

M

Madanī, Amad al-Kabīr 181, 907
Maize 515
Mali Empire 183, 189, 192, 200, 205, 730, 742
  plays 622
Mali Federation 457-458
Mali (general) 1-3, 6, 10-11, 13-23, 174, 178
  juvenile literature 8-9, 12
Mali Rural Health Project 404
Malians in France 250, 252-253
Malinké people 273, 303, 730, 773, 776
Malnutrition 394
Mammals 103, 114
Man, prehistoric 88, 136
Mande languages 320-321, 345
  bibliographies 344
Manding people 278, 284, 287, 292, 662, 689, 737, 742
Manpower policy 548, 551
Maps 1, 7, 93-99, 309, 557, 567
Markets 506
Marriage 268, 293

Masks
  Bamana 644
  Dogon 286, 649
  Minianka 654
Mass media 415, 826, 831
  bibliographies 830
Medical anthropology
  275
Medical assistance 409
Medical care 397
Medicinal plants 406
Medicine
  dictionaries 342
Menstruation 294
Mental illness 676
Merchants 500
Metalwork 660
Meteorology, agricultural
  555
Migration 229, 257-258,
  469, 536
Migration, external 249,
  255
Migration, internal 251,
  254, 256, 259
Millet 531
Mineral resources 86-87
Minianka language 319
Minianka people 299, 359,
  384, 654, 768
Missions 361, 371
Mohammed I, Askia of
  Songhai 738
Monetary policy 551
Mortality 400
Moths 124
Mud cloth see Bogolanfini
Musée du Sahel 806
Museums 799-801,
  803-807
  directories 802
Music 78, 691, 693-694,
  696, 698-702, 704-
  705, 707
  bibliographies 688
  dictionaries 703, 710
Music and health 695
Musical instruments 694,
  696, 701, 708
  dictionaries 703
Muslims 195, 209, 363,
  378
  politics 227

N

National Archives (US)
  795
National language
  dictionaries 341
National Museum of Mali
  799, 804-805, 807
National Union of Malian
  Workers 547, 550
Natural history 102
Natural resources 561,
  563, 569
Newspapers 859-863
  sports 782
Niger River 28-29, 34,
  38-39, 45, 57, 73, 365
Niger River Basin 85
Niger River dam 566
Niger River Delta 81-82,
  270
Nomads 67, 383
Numismatics 786
Nutrition 398, 408, 523
  children 402
  infants 391, 393

O

Office du Niger 470
Opération Haute Vallée
  (Mali) 499
Opération Riz-Ségou 534
Oral literature 698, 774
Oral tradition 699, 737,
  744, 775-776
Orchids 125

P

Pan-Africanism 456
Park, Mungo 76
Performing arts 679
  videos 686
Periodicals 824, 846, 854,
  857, 864-867,
  869-871, 874-875
  African studies 868
  art 643
  bibliographies 878, 884,
  890-891

book trade 814
  economic conditions
  496
  education 589
  finance 496
  history 870
  indexes 877
  museums 800
  pharmacology 407
  politics 872
  population 873
  publishers and
  publishing 811, 814
  trade unions 547
  traditional medicine 407
Peul Empire 186-187, 216
Peul people 267, 284, 292,
  339
  bibliographies 269
Pharmacology
  periodicals 407
Philately 785
Philosophy 295
Photography 657
Physical anthropology 275
Plant diseases and pests
  531
Policy 484
Political indicators 842
Political parties 414, 417,
  440
Politics 185, 227,
  410-412, 414-418,
  420-427, 429,
  431-440, 443-444,
  446-448, 456-458,
  480, 484-485, 488,
  497, 529, 553, 704
  periodicals 872
Population 247, 262, 264,
  400
  periodicals 873
  statistics 245, 248, 261,
  263, 265-266, 839
Population policy 246
Pottery 141, 144-145, 157,
  165
Precipitation 574
Prehistory 126, 134,
  136-137, 147-148,
  156, 166
Press 310, 824, 826,
  831-832, 834

Prospecting 87
Proverbs
    Bambara 769-771
    Bwa 769
    Manding 771
    Minianka 768
Public health 392, 405
Publishers and publishing
    813, 817-819,
    821-822
    bibliographies 820
    periodicals 811, 814
Puppets 678, 681, 685

R

Radio broadcasting 415,
    594, 823, 828-829,
    833
Railroads 542, 549, 621
Rangelands 564
Reclamation of land 556
Religion 365, 370
    Bambara 356-357, 362,
    364
    Bobo 371
    Dogon 360, 367
    Minianka 359
    Songhay 375
Rice 534
Riddles 766
    Bambara 765
    Tuareg 767
Rouch, Jean 686, 720
Ruma people 243
Rural conditions 519, 525,
    534, 570
Rural development 257,
    470, 533-534
Rural development
    projects 556
Rural families 259
Rural–urban migration
    259

S

Sahara 54, 58, 66
Sahel 68, 539
Sarakole people 284, 300,
    349, 741, 757

emigration 250, 252,
    257
Scientists
    directories 851, 855
Sculpture 163
    Bambara 357, 644, 650,
    652, 656
    Dogon 655, 658
    Manding 662
    Tellem 655
Secret societies 357, 644,
    659
Segou Kingdom 736, 739,
    741
Senari language 775
Senufo people 297, 384,
    536, 775
Sex customs 399
Shrubs 112, 121
Slavery 70, 209, 217, 234,
    387
Snakes 105, 120
Soccer players 784
Social classes 381
Social conditions 178,
    379, 381-382, 385-
    386, 430, 517
    farmers 538
    peasants 384
    women 380, 384, 387-
    389
Social indicators 841-842
    statistics 838
Social policy 487
Socialism 427-428, 430,
    447, 488
Sociology 281
Soil erosion 568
Soil management 556
Songhay Empire 192-193,
    201, 205, 208, 242
Songhay language 340,
    346
Songhay people 284, 298,
    301, 375, 582, 738
Songs 693, 773, 778
    Bambara 772
    hunting 273, 692, 697,
    745, 747
    Manding 689
    Sarakole 706
Soninke language 328,
    349

Soundiata 622, 697,
    727-735
Specialists
    directories 851
Spirit possession 359
Sports 784
    newspapers 782
Squatter quarters 582
Statistics 175, 262, 555,
    836, 840-841
    periodicals 835, 837
Strikes and lockouts 549,
    552
Students
    politics 439
Sufism 376

T

Tal, Umar 195, 366, 740,
    907
Tales 273, 741, 750-752,
    756-759, 761-764
    Bambara 753-754, 770
    Peul 746, 755
Tamasheq language 354
Tamasheq people 293
Taysīr al-fattāh 215
Taxation 525
Teaching guides 23
Technical assistance 533
Technology 513, 515, 521,
    528
    directories 852
Telecommunications 544,
    825, 827
Television broadcasting
    823
Tellem people 154,
    159-160
Textiles 511, 664-665, 804
    Manding 663
    Marka 389
    Tellem 133, 160
Theatre 674, 676-682,
    684-685
    dictionaries 687
Tijaniyah members 378
Timbuktu 24-25, 27, 35,
    37, 41-43, 48, 59,
    62-63, 65, 69-71,
    73-74, 235-244

Toucouleur Empire 181, 207, 216, 510
Toucouleur people 188, 211
Tourism 174
Toys 781
Trade 206, 209, 468, 483, 498, 500-511, 545
Trade unions 549-550, 553
  periodicals 547
Traditional medicine 102, 390
  periodicals 407
Transport 541, 543-544
Traoré, Amadou 438
Traoré, Moussa 422, 431-434
Travel 39, 54, 56, 58-59, 62, 64-65, 67, 69-74, 76, 409
Travel guides 51-53, 55, 57, 60-61, 66, 68, 75, 77-79, 174
Trees 112, 121, 123
Trickster 777
Trucking 546

Tse tse flies 112
Tuareg people 29, 67, 168, 305-306, 420
Tyi Wara 644

U

Union soudanaise R.D.A. 416-417

V

Videos 686, 711
Voluntary associations 385

W

Water resources development 585
West African Monetary Union 497
Wildlife conservation 569

Women 260, 379, 402, 483, 492-494, 499, 540, 698, 725, 778
  dictionaries 850
  Dogon 713
  economic conditions 388
  economic policy 482
  folklore 772
  politics 410, 412
  social conditions 380, 384, 387-389
Women in development 469, 482, 486, 490-491
Wood-carving 652
World Bank 476
Wunderman, Lester 642

Y

Yearbooks 854, 857

Z

Zarma people 301

327

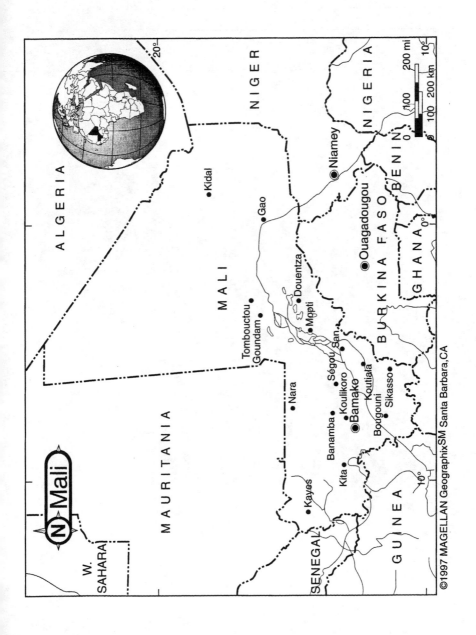

©1997 MAGELLAN GeographixSM Santa Barbara,CA

ALSO FROM CLIO PRESS

INTERNATIONAL ORGANIZATIONS SERIES

Each volume in the International Organizations Series is either devoted to one specific organization, or to a number of different organizations operating in a particular region, or engaged in a specific field of activity. The scope of the series is wide-ranging and includes intergovernmental organizations, international non-governmental organizations, and national bodies dealing with international issues. The series is aimed mainly at the English-speaker and each volume provides a selective, annotated, critical bibliography of the organization, or organizations, concerned. The bibliographies cover books, articles, pamphlets, directories, databases and theses and, wherever possible, attention is focused on material about the organizations rather than on the organizations' own publications. Notwithstanding this, the most important official publications, and guides to those publications, will be included. The views expressed in individual volumes, however, are not necessarily those of the publishers.

VOLUMES IN THE SERIES

1 *European Communities*, John Paxton

2 *Arab Regional Organizations*, Frank A. Clements

3 *Comecon: The Rise and Fall of an International Socialist Organization*, Jenny Brine

4 *International Monetary Fund*, Anne C. M. Salda

5 *The Commonwealth*, Patricia M. Larby and Harry Hannam

6 *The French Secret Services*, Martyn Cornick and Peter Morris

7 *Organization of African Unity*, Gordon Harris

8 *North Atlantic Treaty Organization*, Phil Williams

9 *World Bank*, Anne C. M. Salda

10 *United Nations System*, Joseph P. Baratta

11 *Organization of American States*, David Sheinin

12 *The British Secret Services*, Philip H. J. Davies

13 *The Israeli Secret Services*, Frank A. Clements